D0999414

"*Burke Files has done a thorough job in presenting and analyzing due diligence issues essential to be considered by professionals committed to excellence.*"
Richard D. Heideman, Esq. Senior Counsel,
Heideman Nudelman & Kalik, P.C.
Washington, DC

"*Files brings a fresh, critical and frequently amusing perspective to the well plowed topic of financial due diligence, and the results are terrific. This book should be required reading for all well intentioned lawyers, accountants, bankers, investment advisors, regulators and other professionals who practice in the international financial sector and can perform a crucial gate keeping function.*"
F. R. Jenkins, Esq., Meridian 361
International Law Group, PLLC, Inner Temple
London

"*This is it, this is what is missing in the world of due diligence. A well written guide to the thought process and not another book of mindless check lists.*"
Juan A. Benavides, FBINA, CPP, CPO, DVSA
Retired Chief of State Police
Nuevo Leon, Monterrey City, Mexico
Principal of IPACITEFO International
Training for Police and Security.
Monterrey City, Mexico

"*Any CFO who does not read and head these lessons will make errors that could have been foreseen and miss a good read.*"
Thomas E Ferneau, III Esq. CFO
Tarsus Trust Company
Charlestown, Nevis

"*As a security consultant advising global corporations, investment institutions and governments on various aspects of their business, I am required from time to time to carry out due diligence procedures on behalf of my clients. The complexity of the international financial environment today and the increasing vulnerability of companies in our networked age to well-organized fraud make this is challenging task even for the well-prepared professional.*"

In answer to this pressing problem, Burke Files has produced a concise yet comprehensive guide to the techniques, best practices and timesaving tools that help to combat and overcome the wily fraudsters inhabiting our financial environment. With this book as part of your personal armory, you are equipped to steer a confident path through the due diligence processes required in M&A planning, business partnerships, supplier agreements, key employee hires and many other forms of corporate activity.

Most important of all, this book is a great read. In an area of endeavor not generally known for its entertaining nature, the author's light and humorous touch keeps the pages turning nicely, and the colorful characters we encounter throughout the book alternately appall and intrigue us by their single-minded devotion to defrauding their partners, customers and the authorities.

Bravo Mr. Files - this book will remain a permanent feature of my library for many years to come!"

Jules Trocchi, Senior Consultant,
Electronics & Security Practice, Frost & Sullivan
London

"A refreshingly comprehensive guide explaining the process of financial due diligence. Well written and presented in succinct yet humorous fashion, this book allows readers to go above and beyond the overly simplistic check-box approach that so many have unfortunately been lulled into reliance upon. This should be requisite reading by various business and risk managers, investigators and various gatekeepers associated with or serving those in the financial community, as well as anyone who has interest in this subject matter."

Shaun M. Hassett, CAMS
The LUBRINCO Group
Algonquin, IL

Due Diligence

For The Financial Professional

L. Burke Files

Aegis Journal, LLC
POB 27314
Tempe, AZ 85285
Tel (877) 4243 – Fax (877) 438-2603

e-mail: Publisher@AegisJournal.com

Sales are available at: www.AegisJournal.com, Amazon and at Quality Book Stores. Special discounts are available on quantity purchases. Please contact by e-mail for details. For classroom use, please inquire about the availability of additional support materials.

Orders for bookstores, please contact by e-mail

Editor: John Conway

Cover design: Zoe Lowney

Aegis Journal, LLC, the title "Aegis Journal", the Aegis Journal logo, and "Due Diligence for the Financial Professional" are all the property of the Aegis Journal, LLC.

To book speaking engagements please contact Mr. Files through Aegis Journal, LLC.

Library of Congress Cataloging-in-Publication Data:

Files, L. Burke
Due Diligence for the Financial Professional

Library of Congress Control Number: 2010912845

Printed in the United States of America

1 3 5 7 9 8 6 4 2

ISBN 978-0-9823723-3-3

Introduction

"Liberation is freedom from ignorance."

Unknown

The purpose of this book is to help the financial professional avoid ever being misled again.

Financial professionals are challenged by the need for due diligence, not because it is a requirement but because it is not a stocked item. It is a process not a thing. Stale, regimented, check-box information is not due diligence. What's needed is relevant information gathered in a timely manner. This is key. Properly executed, a due diligence process provides tools for informed choice and eliminates fact noise.

So Why Buy This Book...

This is not a book of mind-numbing irrelevant checklists, nor is it scribbled by an academic. This book will show you how to filter information and discern the noise from the substance of due diligence.

It does not waste time or pages telling you what you already know about AML, SOX, risk management or how to read a balance sheet. No, this book goes into the guts of the idea – due diligence or, as I like to say, Do Diligence.

So then, what's different about this book from the many others like it? It is penned by someone who has run and or overseen thousands of investigative cases from the mundane to the outrageous, involving thousands of dollars to hundreds of millions of dollars in many countries. It is penned by someone who has done due diligence and mopped up when it has not been done. It's about wiping the lipstick off the pigs!

Like any thought experiment, which is the format of this book, the presentation leaves out many complicating details in an attempt to tease out something interesting about core issues.

How To Use This Book

The book is set up with stand-alone chapters. You can read from beginning to end or read the chapters you choose. Don't lean on the questionnaires and lists without reading the corresponding chapters that precede them. This way you will know questionnaires and lists are not mindless forms to be followed, an end destination – rather they are a road map for journeys.

If you are to read a few chapters only, please include Heuristics, Art and Due Diligence, and the Frontiers of Fraud. These take you out of routine thinking and challenge you to think laterally about due diligence and fraud.

By the way, I get it – due diligence as practiced by many is so exciting you would rather water the moss garden. On the other hand if you were putting down $1,000,000 of your money on the outcome of the Super Bowl, you would know the entire personal and professional histories of every player and you could follow key players up to the hour of the bet to see who is working out and who is out on the town. Now that's fun. Or if you are investing other people's money, are you just going to the mean, median and mode of the Vegas and street bookies, weighing the numbers by a quant formula? It is the difference between doing your own work and relying on a ratings agency. After over 25 years in finance and 19 as an international investigator, I have seen some of the worst and best in finance. My attempt is to offer to you my experiences and encapsulate 14 more years of experience of my own and my firm's operations conducted on six continents.

This book is about change. It is about a change in the social contract that says a little fraud is OK. It is my wish that with the tools in this book you can help change the paradigm and thus the social contract.

This book is not a "how to" on due diligence and fraud. Rather, the book's purpose is to give the reader no refuge but to think about the due diligence process and how fraud attempts to circumvent the process. May we all do well as we do good.

L. Burke Files – August 2010

Table Of Contents

Chapter 4   Background Investigations............................. 69

Preamble

"In order to preserve your self-respect, it is sometimes necessary to lie and cheat."

Robert Byrne

Conter's Law - "A fool and his money are soon popular."

Edward N. Conter, Esq.

Why Are You Doing Due Diligence?

Due diligence, in a nutshell, is the process of separating fact from fiction, for the purpose of legal compliance and the evaluation of risk. It's that simple, that broad, and that complex. This book goes through several topics that many people never associate with due diligence. The diversity is intentional as it is a recognition of the inescapable inability to accurately quantify risk, and/or to know where it will originate in all its forms. Good due diligence cannot be measured by the number of reams in the file folder, or by the number of authorities consulted. And while thorough due diligence cannot be measured by the pound, bad due diligence usually can.

Evaluating risk means not only understanding what can go wrong, it includes understanding how it can go wrong, how badly it can go wrong, how to recover from it, and what other options will be available to you. To understand risk you must understand the likely probability of an event, your liability, managing the risk and your ability to mitigate losses.

A sum of money invested in a real estate project is a lot different from the same sum invested in an oil well. In the event of failure, you can foreclose on real estate, mitigating your losses and reducing your risk – while failure of an oil well is likely to be a complete loss. A failed million dollar investment that returns as receivables on 100 automobiles is a lot harder to recover than the same investment that returns as a nearly completed home. In either case, understanding the process of asset recovery is an important part of understanding risk. Asset Recovery is an investment's post failure return.

In the process of separating fact from fiction, it is important to understand the number of methods unscrupulous people use to make fiction look like fact. It would take me about an hour to create a business identity, complete with a Web page and a toll-free number. Recognizing fiction is a big part of the due diligence process, and while no book can do justice to this topic, I enrich my contribution to the discussion with real life examples woven into this text.

Risk is presented by regulations, contracts, methods, economic change, political change and a myriad of other factors. People are always at risk. There are not only the risks of fraud or incompetence; there are also the risks of lifestyle and proclivities. An employee who crashes a company vehicle while drunk, who assaults or simply harasses a customer or co-worker, presents real liability – and risk.

Very little of what constitutes effective due diligence is intuitive or scripted. We have regulations and checklists, but these should always be viewed as the framework to ask the right questions and as minimum standards. While we attempt to understand risk, over the past decade the line between risk management and regulatory compliance has been blurred to the point where, in many organizations, it is impossible to determine if they are not one and the same. Let's start by understanding that mere compliance is far too low of a standard for risk management or due diligence.

Due Diligence Is Much too Serious of a Matter to Be Entrusted to Your Risk Management Team!

I wish to discuss due diligence mischief. Twenty years ago, due diligence on many public offerings consisted of a $1,000 due diligence report, an all-hands meeting, and assurances that everyone belonged to the right clubs. The club was an important vetting component, because it allowed everyone to meet colleagues on common turf and discuss issues while playing golf or squash.

To manage a public offering today, you will have a 50-page SOX checklist, and regulators that may even follow you to family functions. (SOX is a common acronym for the Sarbanes-Oxley Act, aka Sarbox.) I receive so many seminar mailers promising insights into due diligence and money laundering that I could use them as fuel to stave off a Maine winter. For the most part, the checklists they offer are shallow, and the literature is myopic. Due diligence has evolved from dysfunctional incest toward an assault on common sense. This is not progress.

For more than 25 years my work has taken me into finance, investment banking, international due diligence, and fraud recovery. I have been there, done that, and have the extensions in my passport to prove it. Get ready because I have some strong opinions from experience.

Following is the first paragraph of an editorial in *The Economist* on December 18th, 2008, titled "Dumb Money and Dull Diligence."

> *"WRITING about one of the great swindles of the 1930s, J.K. Galbraith pointed to three traits of any financial community that he believed put it at risk of fraud. There was the tendency, he wrote in 1961, to confuse good manners and good tailoring with integrity and intelligence. There was the sometimes 'disastrous interdependence' between the honest man and the crook. And there was the 'dangerous cliché that in the financial world everything depends on confidence. One could better argue the importance of unremitting suspicion.'"*

This article went on to discuss the Bernie Madoff scandal, which became apparent almost 50 years after Galbraith made his observations. And remember, in 1961 Galbraith was referring to swindles that took place 30 years before he made his dire warning. His warning was the importance of unremitting suspicion. If you have money at risk, always assume the worst and take everything you are told with a grain of salt.

The old model provided a well-regulated market, decent information from reasonable sources, and plenty of laws to hold people accountable. It failed by not holding people accountable. Only the largest and most egregious cases of financial fraud were prosecuted, because law enforcement, prosecutors and judges did not (and still do not, collectively) understand finance. Almost every person in the process, unless a finance major, relies upon their brief and informal exposure to finance, a complicated topic. Thus, as a victim, you face the sum total of all their fears and ignorance when trying to seek justice. By many professionals involved in the law, this is summed up as, "I'm sorry, this is a civil matter."

While our knowledge has improved, it's certainly not good. In a financial IQ test developed by the Business Literacy Institute and Alliant International University, more than 300 U.S. managers were asked 21 questions. Here's an example –

> A company has more cash today when:
>
> A) Customers pay their bills sooner.
> B) Accounts receivable increases.
> C) Profit increases.
> D) Retained earnings are increased.

Just over 25 percent of the managers got the answer correct. Statistically, this is identical to a random guess (the answer is A).

The investment bankers have had their own shortcomings:

> *"Cid Kedah possesses 40 years in the investment banking and securities industry. He has been a director with the parent company for 16 years."*

This is taken from a prospectus prepared by a major family of mutual funds, and represents the entire biography for one of the principals. It contains no useful information. When I contacted the fund, its representatives refused to even acknowledge that Cid was a director. Truly stunning. Yet this fund had an investment grade rating from all of the ratings agencies. The fund, of course, paid to get those ratings – and wasn't much interested in speaking to a truly independent investigator. In truth, my call wasn't that innocent. I was attempting to find out if Cid was the same person who had defrauded a client of mine two years earlier in a prime banknote scheme. Having no success on the phone, I sent an express package containing my evidence to the chairman of the board. I never received a response from the chairman, and exactly one-week later Cid resigned, for "personal reasons." I learned of this through an 8-K filing.

During litigation we learned that Cid had embellished his résumé, and had been in litigation for more than two years over the banknote schemes while serving as a director in a public company. We recovered funds from several parties who were found liable and/or negligent in the assistance they provided Cid. This case exposed several serious flaws for public companies:

> 1) Inadequate disclosure.
> 2) Cheap and cheerful background checks that, in the end, were neither.
> 3) The rating agencies did the complex stuff very well but missed again and again in some very basic, yet key areas.

Enron and WorldCom, the poster children for dot-com to dot-bomb, brought us the SOX regulations. Bernie Madoff, R. Allen Stanford (Sir Stanford in Antigua), and banks too big to fail are the genesis for a new wave of regulation. All of these failures and flaws were predictable if investors had studied the management in these companies or the markets they served. I was one of many who warned clients to stay away from Madoff and Stanford, as well as from banks investing in real estate and subprime mortgages. I was far from alone. FBI officials were even testifying before Congress telling lawmakers of the massive looming defaults from real-estate fraud. Still, look what happened. All of the information was available to anyone who chose to look. Our opinion-shapers, the popular media, did not look at what information was available, and thus were not exposed to the predictive value of that information. After the frauds and losses were evident – the pundits expressed surprise, and scrambled to construct a plausible narrative to explain it. Popular media are now demanding that something be done about these frauds and losses. The unspoken undercurrent of what they are requesting is to save the ignorant and lazy from their choices. What the pundocracy forget is that these were well-regulated investment-grade securities.

We are, as I write this, in another round of regulatory hysteria. We've seen this before, and I have no doubt my observations and comments will survive well into the future. It starts with the media reaching a fevered pitch, and is followed with legislators clutching their analysts and lining them up in lock step. Next, collectively, the media and legislators begin parading and pillorying company executives in a harsh and inaccurate "make-wrong" exercise. The unfortunate part is that in the end, the public is wooed by the jargon of the intelligentsia (facts are unimportant). The government and the regulators will pass yet another piece of restrictive and intrusive legislation. At this point, with new laws and regulations in place, they have done, to their satisfaction, something. Then they assure us that everything will be all right for evermore.

Not only is this the wrong outcome, making legitimate business more difficult, it misses the point. The point is all of these frauds were, and still are, illegal. Their only success has been to handicap legitimate business. The end result of these types of exercises is simple – in time, if we apply sufficient scrutiny, regulation and blame – we will kill innovation and domesticate risk. Bad times make bad law.

These reactions stem from a failure to hold people responsible for their actions. We must remove the presumption that investing is riskless, or that all risks are, or can be, known. Our failure to do this has resulted in mind-numbing proposals. What are frequently seen as new failures are frequently the unintended consequences of old regulations. We are in some very difficult times, indeed.

The practice of due diligence has evolved into SOX checklists, anti-money laundering policy, and procedure manuals. Best practice awards are given to the weightiest presentations (by the pound), and third-party vendors are predominantly selling "perfect solutions" for enterprise risk management that will seriously impede your ability to conduct business.

Back to Our Roots

I think about investment decisions and business practices as if I were investing money for my mother or her company. Managers and employees must be given local autonomy to do what needs to be done, and be provided with a rich feedback mechanism. Should people fail, they need to be held both accountable and responsible. Any losses from fraud or theft must impact the profitability of that division, that manager and subsequently their compensation. A company that collectivizes losses from fraud and theft incentivizes irresponsible risk-taking. What is needed today is a less rigid, less quantified, more qualified, and thoughtful approach to due diligence. We need what our moms used, a more holistic approach.

Chapter 1

Heuristics and Biases

"It is only about things that do not interest one that one can give really unbiased opinions, which is no doubt the reason why an unbiased opinion is always valueless."

Oscar Wilde

Heuristics are cognitive strategies people use to simplify assessments or judgments of probability. We use heuristics to filter information from noise so that we can make quick perceptions and decisions. Also known as intuitive inferences, this process of abstraction is used when we lack sufficient unbiased information to assimilate or judge the probability of all possible outcomes – so we generalize.

While useful, heuristics can often lead to systematic errors when applied, because they rely on information that is subject to many **biases** as it is sampled and categorized.

These inferences or filters we use, and the preconceived notions we have, are biases. The problem with biases is that if left unchecked – or more importantly, if we are unaware of them and their potential impact – the errors they produce are often systemic and large.

As an example, an employer might use the heuristic "long hair on a man shows him to be a failure" while making hiring decisions. The employer has a bias against long hair. An honest evaluation of a person's ability is prevented because of a bias or filter. Albert Einstein's hair probably did not interfere with his ability to reason or perform, but an employer with this bias would have excluded him.

There Are Five General Categories of Heuristics:

> Judgment
> Representative

Availability
Adjustment and anchoring, and
Risk and loss aversion

Judgment

Judgmental heuristics are principles or methods by which one makes assessments or judgments of probability simpler. For example, judging a person based upon their style of dress, or judging an investment based upon the beauty of a brochure. In both cases we fail to look at the substance of what is offered and make a choice based upon what has penetrated our filters.

Representative

An event is judged to be probable because it is deemed to represent all of the essential features of the parent population. We use an event heuristic when we choose grapes. All large grapes are sweet, and small ones are sour.

Availability

We judge the frequency of objects and events based upon the availability or recollection of objects and events in our mind – all of which is distorted by the process of perception. These are very powerful and personal distortions. War is perceived to be a major cause of death, when in actuality you are five times more likely to take your own life as to die in a war. (war 0.3 percent, suicide 1.53 percent).[1] Even more dangerous are auto accidents at 2.09 percent. The leading causes of death are heart disease at 29.34 percent and infections at 19.12 percent.[2] We are willing to get in a car and drive, but not to exercise and eat smart. Why? Our recall is from the news of accidents and wars – not of suicides and heart attacks. We come to conclusions based upon the availability of events we can recollect or from reports in the media – not from a dispassionate analysis.

---

1 Rates are from the World Health Organization (WHO) for 2005
2 Ibid

Adjustment and Anchoring

Conservatism is suggested when adjusting our beliefs or methods in light of new information. For example, acting on the idea that a well-established belief should be discarded only when you have solid evidence against it – or the belief that a reliable method should be changed only when it meets significant failure. People anchor to an original value or perception, and are resistant to change even with the input of new information that suggests change. People have a bias toward an initial value or proposition.

Risk and Loss Aversion

Many people are averse to taking risks. They tend to question a $10 bet on a coin toss where the winner gets $20 – even though it is a fair game. While most people avoid risk, they clearly show that they would rather take a risk than suffer a loss. Equivalent problems will frequently get different responses depending on whether the problem is framed in terms of losses or gains. Captain Rob has 500 men and needs to retreat, if he goes through the valley he has a 50 percent chance of losing 200 men, and if he crosses the river he will lose 100 to hypothermia. Which path should the captain choose? While statistically equal, most people will choose the odds rather than the certainty. The odds can swing both ways – and we decide based upon our belief that we may be able to manage probability. We create our own psychological probability to replace true odds. People will psychologically value a lottery ticket higher because they choose the numbers or because it is in their pocket.

Biases: A Sampling

The biases produced by our uses of heuristics come under a number of different categories. Decision-making biases, probability and belief, social biases and memory errors are the main categories. The collection of specific biases I have been able to identify is well over 100. As financial professionals, the ones that get us in trouble are generally decision-making and probability biases.

Biases I have seen produce real problems are:

Authority bias. Altering your perception based upon the opinion of an authority figure, boss or an expert.

Availability cascade. A self-reinforcing process in which a collective belief gains credibility through repetition.

Confirmation bias. Interpreting data in a manner that best confirms what you already believe.

Conservative bias. Ignoring the impact of new information and evidence.

Disregard of regression toward the mean. A bias by which one expects the tendency of excessive performance to continue.

Exposure effect. Expressing an undue aversion to something merely because you are familiar with it.

Eloquence and manners. A bias that makes people believe that just because someone is eloquent and well-manned that they know what they are talking about. This bias also applies to people who appear well dressed.

Groupthink or bandwagon bias. Where you ignore data and continue or choose to do something because everybody else is doing it.

Halo effect. A bias that allows you to let one positive trait – such as fame or prior success in another discipline – to spill over in areas requiring a more dispassionate assessment.

Illusion of control. A bias that lets you think you can control the outcome of events when you really have no control whatsoever.

Ostrich bias. Ignoring obviously negative information.

Professional bias. Looking at the world through the lens of your own profession, and ignoring a broader approach. System justification. A tendency to defend and bolster the status quo.

Zero-risk bias. A focus on reducing relatively insignificant risks as opposed to reducing overall risk.

I could go over examples of each of these, but most readers should be able to provide examples from their own experience. Awareness that we are all susceptible to these biases does not make us immune.

A Thought Experiment

You have flipped a coin nine times. Each of the tosses resulted in the outcome of heads. What are the odds of it coming up heads on the tenth flip? The answer is 50-50, assuming it's a fair coin. Just because a coin has a head on it does not give it any memory of past outcomes.

Rephrased. You have flipped a coin nine times. Each of the tosses resulted in the outcome of heads. You are now required to make a wager on the next outcome of the coin toss. Do you wager on heads or tails? Answer: We wager on tails. We know the coin has no memory, but…

I have my own biases, and I have exercised them – sometimes quite openly. I was the director of corporate finance of a small investment-banking firm in Phoenix, Arizona, during the 1980s. I had very little interest in land deals. There were actually more land deals in Arizona during the 1980s than there was land. I did like short-term leverage transactions, however, which were tied to the development of land. My favorites were construction loans on buildings, with takeout loans in place. My bias was brutal. I would not listen to a single proposal pitched to me by anyone wearing double knit slacks, a kiana shirt, or sporting gold chains. Come to think of it, I still don't. Double knits and kiana, now a fashion *faux pas*, used to be the slick thing to wear. Examples for the curious can be found in the Museum of Unfortunate Fashion Choices.

How did we develop these propensities to make illogical decisions? It's in our genes, (not the double knit kind.) The selection pressure of evolution is the source of most biases. We learned when we hear a leaf crunch under a bush that there may be an animal threatening us. Thus, when we unexpectedly hear the leaves, our senses are heightened and we run. To deal with our environment, we have evolved to use limited information to make the best decision, not to make the best possible or optimal decision.

The more we understand false beliefs and biases, the more likely we are to be receptive to the information we need to make unbiased decisions.

This chapter is hardly a chapter and verse on heuristics and biases. It is but a mere teaser of the knowledge that we do make choices, very quick choices based upon a number of know biases. The knowledge and awareness of this very human condition will at least get you to think about how not to make these thought and choice errors.

For more information about heuristics and biases, look to the many publications by Amos Tversky and Daniel Kahneman. While others have come since, their work is the first and still the clearest. Another bias of mine? Exposure effect and confirmation bias.

Awareness – Exercises to Demonstrate Heuristics And Biases

Exercise 1 (Answers at the end)

A small town is served by two hospitals. In the larger hospital about 45 babies are born each day, and in the smaller hospital about 15 babies are born each day. As we know, the chance a baby will be a boy or a girl is about a 50-50 chance. But we also know that variation occurs. For a period of one year each hospital recorded the days when more than 60 percent of the babies born were boys. Which hospital do you think recorded more days?

> Large hospital
> Small hospital
> About the same

Exercise 2

We have all tossed coins and we know that heads and tails will occur with about the same frequency, but in different patterns. Which of the following patterns do you think is most likely to occur?

> H-T-H-T-T-H
> H-H-H-T-T-T
> H-H-H-H-T-H

Misconceptions and Statistics

Misconceptions about the meaning and application of statistical data is not limited to the uneducated population, it affects supposedly sophisticated consumers of information as well. A study done by Tversky and Kahneman showed that even researchers possessed a lingering belief in what can only be called the law of small numbers. Researchers tend to believe that even small samples are highly representative of the populations from which they are drawn.

There is a belief known as the gambler's fallacy, illustrated by a roulette wheel that comes up red seven times in a row, and the belief that black is somehow due. The belief is that chance is somehow self-correcting. A follow-up problem exists when a fallacy is used to make a prediction that subsequently comes true. The person making the prediction now has the unwarranted confidence produced by a welcomed outcome. In our minds we tend to believe that all predicted outcomes that match real outcomes represent skill, even when we are aware of the factors that limit the accuracy of our predictions (such as chance).

We have a group of biases we put under the title of availability. This is demonstrated when people assess the frequency of a class or probability of an event by the ease with which an instance or occurrence can be brought to mind. They are:

Biases due to the retrieval of instances. The dangers of a shooting taking place in a school is an example of an extreme danger that can be brought to mind simply because we can retrieve stories of such events in our minds from newscasts. Most of us can probably name a school and even some of the perpetrators.

Biases due to the effectiveness of a search set. These biases manifest themselves when we are offered a comprehensive set of data that has undergone a selection pressure, such as memory, restricted sample sizes or restricted times.

Bias of imaginability. This begins when we evaluate a peril based upon what we can imagine. Imagining all of the ways a business could fail should keep all of us at home.

Illusory correlation. A bias brought on when a person perceives a correlation that doesn't exist. All people with green eyes are great people, and all people with narrow-set eyes and ponytails are shifty. Interestingly, I actually met one person with green eyes who wasn't nice. There is generally no basis for these correlations, yet people who make illusory correlations are extremely resistant to changing their opinions, even when confronted with evidence.

In short, humans are very bad at subjective assessment of probabilities, especially of infrequent events and events unknown to them.

Answers:
1: Smaller hospital, because it has a smaller sample size and thus is more prone to deviations from the mean.
2: Over a sufficient sample size, no difference, coins lack both memory and the desire for symmetry.

Chapter 2

Art and Financial Due Diligence

"Painting: The art of protecting flat surfaces from the weather and exposing them to the critic."

Ambrose Bierce, *The Devil's Dictionary*

This chapter is about you, the financial professional, being pulled away from what you know to what you think you're familiar with. I am trying to get you to look at a new market and absorb different perspectives from this exercise. The hope is that you will be able to use these perspectives, seen in a novel setting, when you return to your industry.

What Is Art?

If we are going to discuss art and due diligence, we need to craft a working definition of what is art. While many philosophers and sociologists have attempted to define and differentiate art from other less-serious works, this definition you're about to enjoy is mine. If I'm going to jump in, I might as well jump into the deep end.

First, let me rid the topic of a distraction. Art and antiquities are not the same. The terms are often used as if they are interchangeable. Typically, an antiquity is an artistic artifact (not necessarily art). An antiquity, as the name suggests, is an artifact that is old. To differentiate between what is merely old and what is an antiquity, most experts use the period from the dawn of civilization to the end of the Dark Ages as the origin of an antiquity. Experts may use different time frames for different civilizations to provide more "civilization-specific" precision. I particularly like the definition proffered by Francis Bacon "Antiquities are history defaced, or some remnants of history which have casually escaped the shipwreck of time." Antiquities can be art, but more often are aesthetically pleasing relics.

I have been interested in art for as long as I can remember. I like the aesthetics of some items, and I simply like the stories connected to other items. When I began to work on art forgery cases, I was hooked. The notion that, given two nearly identical objects, one was considered art and the other a worthless forgery, grasped my interest.

Leo Tolstoy published an essay in 1896, translated into English in 1899, titled *What is Art*. His essay worked to differentiate art from objects that were simply aesthetically pleasing. As any Russian writer was required in his day, he wrote volumes on his topic. In a condensed interpretation of his opinions, I could say Tolstoy thought art (as opposed to an aesthetically pleasing object) had to draw the creator and the observer into a relationship. To Tolstoy, art is part of the human condition, it is quite simply something humans are compelled to do. That means a true work of art could not help but draw the observer into a multi-layered exchange with the creator – the observer being able to experience the communication and emotion expressed by the creator.

Thus, art is a language, a language of images and signals that develop meaning and cross the boundaries of time – that is as long as the observer knows the language. No communication occurs if the viewer does not speak the language – the signals and images are mute. Thus it is also a culture specific language.

Art as a language was brought into clear focus while I was viewing a contemporary Chinese work. While aesthetically pleasing, it left me with nothing more. The painting was a large canvas with many children all in the same stiff erect pose, in Mao suits that were painted red. The children looked like dolls, and were floating down a river from a rural setting at the top left to an industrial setting at the bottom right. I asked the dealer in Beijing the meaning of the painting, and from his reply the concept of art being a language that one must speak began to crystallize. Mao had a little red book that shaped a nation into a rural collective existence. The word for red in Chinese is similar to the word for south and the word for fire. The painting depicted all of Mao's people on collective farms leaving the rural north and coming south, supposedly on the Pearl River, to the furnaces and the factories in Guangzhou. Once some clues were revealed to me about the symbols and images in that painting, the "object d' art" began to speak to me.

Art is a language of symbols and images that draw the creator and the observer together. This is the primary task of art. There are consumers of art who approach art with a different purpose. These consumers expect something else from a work of art, a re-tasking of the language of art's purpose if you will. In our modern society the great majority view art from this altered state. It is impossible to convince people who are in this state that art has an all together different primary task. What we see is a very interesting "social contract" that re-tasks art to fulfill these other expectations. There are many people eager to fulfill the expectations of people in this state, and they are fiercely bound together by a very interesting social contract.

A social contract, by it broadest definition, is an agreement by which people of a given group or nation maintain order. Common to a social contract is the concept of a "sovereign will" to which all members of the social contract are bound. So why would people subjugate themselves, have their tastes and opinions governed by a social contract, and eschew free will? They do so because subjugation is in their best interest. If you're unfamiliar with the concept and application of social contracts, and how powerfully they shape our world, wear shorts and sandals to your next job interview.

The induction into these social contracts that re-task art begins when people come together, under the will of a sovereign, to which they transfer their powers of adjudication and retribution. Having done this they become subject to the will of the sovereigns. This is not a democratic social contract, as proffered by John Locke, it is a sovereign oligarchy ruled by the art critics and dealers. As in any oligarchy, the critics and dealers are interested in themselves first and the members (followers) second.

The social contracts re-tasking art are:

- Art is desirable and provides social status to the owner of original works.

- Critics and dealers are the sovereigns, and the more acclaim★ they give an artist or a work the greater the status it conveys to the owner.

★ *Acclaim is bestowed sovereignly by words of praise, estimates of value, price at auction, the name of the gallery that displays an art piece, and what museums wish to display an art piece.*

Violation of these laws means immediate ostracization from the society, physical as well as in reputation. The sovereigns are the single monopoly of adjudication and enforcement in this society.

Money is a medium of exchange that is recognized by all within a community – whether it's puka shells, cocoa beans, tea, paper money or gold. Whatever the medium of exchange, it works because the social contract identifies the chosen medium as the acceptable store of value.

Art, by the social contracts described above and within the definition of money, has been re-tasked as a currency. Art is a currency of social status and a store of value – a value that is governed by the sovereign critics and dealers.

Art "experts" are the judiciary of the sovereigns. They are merely inner guards that deal with the murky issues of provenance and authenticity under guidelines set by the sovereigns. The experts rely upon the sovereigns for acceptance and recognition of their work just as much as the artists and owners of artwork. Experts are not juxtaposed to the sovereigns, they are one of the sovereign's tools.

This is not an indictment of art, whether in its pure form or as re-tasked by social contract. I am not trying to change the art market or the rules by which it is governed. This description is only to serve as an accelerated primer on the social contracts that govern attribution, provenance, the market, the opinions, whims and the price of art. It is about becoming cognizant of the market environment influencing the assumptions used for art in the financial statement.

Why are we so drawn to swirls of paint or daubs of clay?

Whose Art Is It? – Provenance

Provenance is from the French root "provenir" or "to come from" as in origins or sources.

Where did it come from? Who has owned it? How did they get it? What happened to it? When did these things occur and why are you entering into this transaction? It is all about the history, the good title to the object d' art, and the object's authenticity.

The three biggest problems for title of art are: theft, looting (or spoilating) and attribution. Here we will look at theft, looting and spoilating. Spoilated art is taken without sufficient payment – usually in some transaction under duress.

The difference between theft and looting or spoilating, is who did it. If it is done by a man in black, wearing a balaclava, in the dark of night, that is theft. If it is done by a government or its agent, it is looting or spoilating. Many conquerors, as part of their conquest, would bring back works of art and artisans from conquered territories. It was loot, to the victor go the spoils of war.

Amir Timur of Samarkand, as he conquered central Asia in the late 1300s, laid waste to his enemies and brought back to Samarkand not only works of art, but the artisans themselves to help create and glorify his empire.

Napoleon had Baron Dominique-Vivant Denon as his scout, shopping for art treasures as Napoleon conquered Europe. He accompanied Napoleon on military campaigns in Austria, Poland and Spain to oversee "collecting" activities and traveled to Italy to relocate and safeguard the treasures.

We are aware of the Nazi thirst for art. The scope of their "collecting" activities as they rampaged Europe remains unequalled. Francis H. Taylor estimates that the value of art looted by Nazi Germany was $2 billion to $2.5 billion in 1945 dollars – somewhere near $30 billion in 2008 dollars.

As Stalin re-conquered lost territories and overran German positions, his Trophy Brigades looted the treasures first taken by the Nazis, and took many items they had missed. This loot was estimated at $1.25 billion in 1945, or about $14 billion in 2008 dollars. In 2005 Anatoly Vilkov, a deputy chief of the agency overseeing cultural heritage in Russia, said Russia still held about 250,000 works of art and more than 1 million books Stalin had taken from Germany.

Americans were not immune to the temptation. American GIs also took a few looting tours during the war and occupation, and personally accumulated looted art.

All of these activities affect the title to the work of art. Art looted or spoilated in these fashions may be subject to legitimate claims by prior owners. The defense that some statute of limitations has expired or that you are a good-faith purchaser will not hold up unless these cobwebs of historical clouds (legacy issues) on title are dealt with openly and notoriously.

Stolen Works of Art

Art is stolen for many reasons. These include proving that a gallery lacks proper security, to fulfill an order for a particular item desired by an underworld figure, and theft by or for an obsessed collector. The reasons for a theft don't matter when it comes down to issues of title and clouds on title. Stolen is stolen. A clear history of title, or at least an absence of other claims, is very important.

Oddly enough, the theft of a work of art is a path to publicity for the work of art, the artist, and the museum and or galley from which it was stolen. There have been accusations that several works of art were stolen and then recovered (after a short absence) as a means to gain publicity for an artist or museum. Art theft has also been used as a quick way to get rid of a forgery, so the insurance company pays for the casualty as opposed to the duped owner suffering humiliation and loss.

An emerging problem is criminal organizations that use art as a means of payment or collateral for payment. An item of art used in a criminal enterprise may also be subject to criminal forfeiture proceedings. If sold before the authorities find it, there remains a significant cloud on the title as the proceeds of a crime. Even after a good-faith buyer has purchased a work of art, it could be clawed back by law enforcement. At the minimum, you will have a legal bill.

It is currently alleged that stolen, looted or smuggled art is in the collections of many major galleries in Europe, the U.S. and Asia. Many stolen and looted art objects have been sold by major dealers. The fact that a work or art is owned or was owned by a major gallery, or was sold by a major dealer, is no guarantee of clear title. It may be better than a private transaction – but it is not a guarantee.

Is It Genuine?

"The immature artist imitates, the mature artist steals."

Lionel Trilling

Forgers are much more interesting and devious than even art critics, dealers and their experts, surely better dinner companions. This is precisely because the former group will go to the ends of the earth to fool the latter – and so frequently succeed. The forger only needs to uncover the critic's deepest desires and make them real. Once a critic has told the world what he wants to find, the forger only needs to make the critic's dream come true.

A Gallery of ~~Forgers~~ Opportunists

Elmyr de Hory (1906 - 1976) claimed to have forged more than 1,000 pieces and sold them to reputable art galleries all over the world. De Hory was the subject of a movie by Orson Welles, *F for Fake,* and a biography by another accomplished forger, Clifford Irving. His subjects included Picasso, Matisse, and Modigliani. De Hory has become so famous as a forger that his forgeries have a robust market. In recent times, the market of known de Hory forgeries has been so good that there are now forgers forging de Hory forgeries.

Eric Hebborn (1934 - 1996) claimed to have sold many studies and drawings of old masters through Bond Street galleries and Christie's sales rooms. He would visit old libraries to get the raw materials, appropriating date-appropriate paper from old books. Hebborn created studies using time appropriate materials and styles, and would deliver them to "experts" – allowing them to daub on the acclaim by authenticating the drawings.

Guy Hain was a French art forger who produced a number of fake bronze sculptures. He made several bronzes from the original art models that were more than 75 years old at the time. Because these new/old bronzes were cast from original molds, art experts could not distinguish the forgeries from the originals.

Shaun Greenhalgh (1961 -) was an accomplished forger. He worked in various mediums – from watercolors to sculpture, including antiquities and castings. Greenhalgh was the artist behind what was called "the garden shed gang," which included many members of the family that fronted for him and sold the works.

John Drewe (1948 -) was a physics teacher who convinced John Myatt to create forgeries for him. Drewe then aged the forgeries (using the time-honored vacuum cleaner dust method), and counterfeited certificates of authenticity and invoices to create a false provenance.

Alceo Dossena (1878 - 1937) was an accomplished creator of sculpture. Dossena's work was sold by a dealer, Alfredo Fasoli, and represented as works created by Pisano, Martini and Donatello. When Dossena saw his own works misrepresented in collections, he found that his dealer was making a fortune on his work. He sued and won – but ultimately died broke.

Zhang Daqian (1899 - 1983) was a highly regarded 20th century Chinese artist and an accomplished forger.

Eduardo de Valfierno was an Argentine con man extraordinaire. He commissioned Yves Chaudron to make several copies of the Mona Lisa. He then stole the original painting in a highly public theft, and contracted sales for his copies – giving several buyers the impression they were buying the original Mona Lisa. The provenance that that they had the news story that the original was missing.

Yves Chaudron's claim to fame is that he was the forger of the several Mona Lisas that were sold by Eduardo de Valfierno to waiting customers after the original was stolen.

William Blundell (1947 –) created works of art for a gallery owner in Sydney, Australia, that was owned by Germaine M.F.T. Curvers. Hundreds of works were produced as "innuendoes" of the original, and sold by the dealer as originals. Blundell claimed that he would put clues in his paintings to show that they were not original, and that he had not signed them. His later "innuendoes" lacked these distinctions.

Giovanni Bastianini (1830 – 1868) produced works in the style of Donatello, Verrocchio, Fiesole and other Italian masters. Bastianini's works were commission by and sold through the art dealer Giovanni Freppa. Most of the forgeries were sold to recognized museums. Both were eventually exposed, not by experts, but by a jealous art dealer.

Earl M. Washington (1962 –) produced a number of woodcuts forging works in the style of M.C. Escher and Eric Gill, as well as others. His works were handled by his stripper girlfriend, cum art dealer, Stacy Ortiz. Many works were sold on eBay and it is estimated that he sold as many as 60,000 prints.

Kenneth Walton (1967 –) was a computer programmer, working as an attorney, when he began selling forged artwork on eBay. Walton was unmasked when a forgery that was a bit too interesting sold on eBay for more than $130,000. The headlines drew attention and serial frauds were unveiled. He lost his license to practice law, paid $75,000 in restitution, was sentenced to probation and wrote a tell-all book. We're waiting for the movie, but would a movie of a forger be a bad cover of the original…?

Otto Wacker (1898 – 1970), after failing at other professions, became an art dealer in 1925. Wacker commissioned a number of Van Gogh paintings, probably from his brother Leonhard. He told great tales about the provenance of the paintings, which included secreting the paintings across the Swiss border so they could not be taken by the

Russians. When he went to trial, the battle was between the experts – who could not agree on whether they were genuine. It was not until the 1970s that it was noticed that the paintings were not even on French canvas.

Tony Tetro (1950 -) had a career that lasted more than 30 years – and he forged them all: Chagall, Rembrandt, Dali and others. His works have been displayed in galleries all over the world. He was one of the most productive forgers, along with Eric Hebborn, of the 20th century. He is currently out of jail and producing copies for exclusive clients.

David Stein (1935 - 1999) was a forger who did not *copy* paintings, but like de Hory created *in the style of*, Picasso, Matisse, Braque, Klee, Miro, Cocteau and others. In 1967 when one of his paintings was found hanging in a gallery, he was arrested. In the subsequent prosecution the art dealers refused to cooperate. It may have had something to do with their credentials and experience being questioned in the process.

Jean-Pierre Schecroun, a forger of some skill, is reputed to be able to make a Picasso in three minutes. Arrested for forgery in 1962, he claimed that his purpose was to expose the credulity of the art dealers. He had learned that while his own works did not sell well, those of a known artist sold quite well.

Ely Sakhai (1952 -) was busted in 2000 when both Christie's and Sotheby's were selling the same painting, Gauguin's *Vase de Fleurs*, and both were selling them as originals. According to FBI records, he had a quite complex scheme. Sakhai, as an art dealer, would buy lesser impressionist and post-impressionist paintings and have them copied by the Chinese immigrant painters he had stashed above his gallery in Manhattan. He would sell the copies with a certificate of authenticity to buyers in Asia, knowing that they would not pay for a second expert opinion on a minor work.

Lothar Malskat (1913 - 1988) was a German art restorer who re-painted and restored frescoes of the Cathedral in Marienkirche – and also forged a number of paintings by Chagall and Toulouse-Lautrec.

John Myatt (1945 -) initially painted "genuine fakes" through an advertisement in *Private Eye* magazine, but went to the other side when a customer of his approached him. Myatt's client John Drewe told him that he had sold a number of Myatt fakes as real. Myatt estimated that he painted more than 200 such paintings of which 60 have been identified. Paintings were sold though Christie's, Phillips and Sotheby's in New York and Paris.

Hans van Meegeren (1889 - 1947) was one of the more skilled and gifted forgers who focused on Vermeer. Van Meegeren started forging paintings to expose the cupidity of critics, and kept doing it for the money. Van Meegeren was outed after World War II when he was accused of dealing with the enemy by helping to sell art to the Nazis. He had to either confess that he was a forger, or face the death penalty. Van Meegeren was a gifted forger who made his own paints, just as they did in Vermeer's day, and plowed through art critics' reports to produce works of art that fit exactly what the art critics and experts were looking for. He was an expert in painting, just as he was in creating his paints.

Geert Jansen (1943 -) forged thousands of works by Appel, Cocteau, Dufy and others. He was caught once by the Dutch police, and again by the French police, attempting to sell works at auction houses using forged certificates of authenticity.

If you'd like to do further research on the topic, research the forgeries of Giovanni Bastianini, Michel de Buy, Christian Goller, Wolfgang Helbig, Francesco Marinetti and Brigido Lara.

In 1934, *Time* magazine declared that of the 2,000 known Corot paintings – 10,000 were in the U.S. This, forgery, is not a new problem.

This short list of biographies represents a few of the art forgers that have been uncovered! The most devastating biographies are yet to be written, since these forgers have yet to be uncovered. This list is not meant to be exhaustive, but simply illustrative of a behavior that has plagued the art world for centuries. Forgers have a high opinion of themselves, they are frustrated people with excellent skills that weren't able to break into the art market on their own. They use their talents to fool and embarrass those who judge, market and sell artwork. They fool the sovereigns. Whatever their primary motivation, their belief that they play some obscure role to expose the reality of the art market provides good cover for them. The art market is highly subjective and inefficient, governed as much by attitude as it is by science – and is rife with imposters and fools. It's difficult to believe that forgers create and sell with the singular goal of exposing this world – because they could accomplish this with one painting. They don't stop – they follow the money. These people are criminals, and mirror the criminal thought pattern as it has been described in several excellent publications by Dr. Stanton Samenow.

A work with a famous name attached has a spell cast over it. But, the moment someone tells us it is a forgery – we can immediately see its shortcomings: bad anatomy, shallow palettes, poor lighting and perspective. However, if again declared authentic in some exercise of re-attribution, it is once again beautiful. It's fascinating to see a painting that was once declared a fake change hands, be given re-attribution, and go up in price. This has occurred with some very significant works of art, including Vermeer's.

It's not easy. Art forgery is difficult, and making a convincing forgery is even harder. The master forger Eric Hebborn has written two books, an autobiography of his deeds and convictions, *Drawn to Trouble*, and *The Art Forger's Handbook* in which he goes into specific detail on how to make convincing, time-appropriate forgeries. One interesting problem is contemporary fakes – fakes made at roughly the same time as the original – so the paint, materials, aging markers and other telltale marks are all roughly appropriate. Eighteenth century paintings were particularly susceptible because they were copied in mass to fulfill the demand at the time. Landscapes and still-life paintings seem to have been the most copied.

Some of the techniques forgers use to get proper attribution are stunning. Some would go through auction house libraries and remove pictures of authentic works, replacing them with pictures of the forged work. Others would either alter or create auction house records that would confirm their fake to be real. They do this by altering auction records to confirm their "certificate of authenticity" or by completely creating a history of a painting and sneaking it into the auction house records and libraries. The forgers will alter the resource material which the auction houses rely on for correct information.

Forging a painting is work, no less work than forging the resource material or certificate of authenticity. All of this is important if you are going to cast the spell and make the sale.

Today, the level of science for detecting forgeries is so high that it is getting more difficult to make a forgery that will avoid detection. That is not to say that the forgers haven't tried, and been successful – but this is the rare and skilled forger. Don't take too much comfort in the fact that we are much more skilled at detecting forgeries, as it would assume that the object d' art in question has actually been submitted for testing.

"Everything that deceives may be said to enchant."

Plato

"A critic is a bundle of biases held loosely together by a sense of taste."

Whitney Balliet

Art Dealers and Critics – the Sovereigns

Any fool can make a painting, but it takes a wise man to be able to sell it. Art is not art until it is sold – until then it's a storage problem.

The art world is a small village bound together by pragmatic concerns to not undermine its collective credibility. It is a key to the social contracts that govern art. As for cooperation among art dealers, it isn't going to happen. Fragile relationships, fierce rivalries, suspicion and secrecy are surely behavioral traits that make cooperation unlikely. BADA (British Art Dealers Association) members, who manage the British art market from the top down, squeeze out competition by snobbery – as they alone are the experts (sovereigns). Dishonest or shrewd, it is merely a reference point on a continuum of behavior in an elastic market selling goods with no intrinsic value. Therefore, truth be known, an honest dealer is an art dealer who has never been caught.

The critic is a bon vivant about the community, a gadfly with good descriptive or narrative skills. Ideally, critics should be able to speak the many different languages of art. Again, ideally. They draft articles and summaries and opinions that drive the market for works of art. A kind word by a critic, and a gallery may do a show for an artist. A coarse word of rebuke by an artist to a critic, and the critic can do irreparable damage, by never again saying a thing about the artist, and privately warning dealers that the work is no longer desirable. The work of a critic is not to make his audience believe him, but to agree with him. Once dealers agree with the critic, what more can be done? The sovereigns have aligned and adjudicated.

So, I Am Investing in Art?

According to many dealers, when a catalogue numbers pictures for minor paintings there are usually a number of paintings whose authorship can only be guessed at, and in these cases the method of guessing has been know to be as follows. A number of authors (sovereigns) gather together each having a copy of Emmanuel Benezit's *Dictionnaire critique et documentaire des Peintres, Sculpteurs, Dessinateurs et Graveurs* (Dictionary of Paintings, Sculptures, Drawers and Engravers). They close their eyes, open their volumes at random and point to a name. Names are compared, and the most likely one is adopted. As useless as this process is in choosing a master, it may be useful in giving attribution to a fake, where no particular artist has been imitated.

Not that price is a problem, but one of the best ways to give credibility to a fake is to put the fake in an auctioneer's catalogue. At the auction, bid it up and buy it back. Now the painting is "bought in," so to speak. Now you have a fake with provenance, and the auction house exercise has established a market price. So much for arm's length transactions and transparency of the marketplace.

Deciphering the code you will see in art catalogues:

Full name of artist – believed to be genuine.
First initial and last name – have some reservations.
Last name – dubious.

Art is sold with explicit disclosures and caveats, without guarantees as to history of authorship, value and other representations. Yet the dealer will encourage you, verbally, about these very things. Try doing that with a securities offering and see what happens.

In defense of the auction houses, it is almost impossible to certify every item. An auction house may handle 100-200 works of art per employee. What some auction houses do offer is a refund when an item is found to be something other than represented, or forged. But this guarantee is, like all guarantees, limited in time and scope. In reality, it may take years to determine if an item has been faked – well after any guarantee has expired.

Holding art is a storage problem. First, you have the fees to have the art delivered to your desired location. The location most likely will need to be temperature and humidity controlled, as well as insured and secured. The cost of holding art is not insignificant.

In the end, even the sale has unique issues. Art is taxed differently. It is not taxed as a capital gain, but rather as ordinary income. In the U.S., (as of this week) the tax rate on gains is 28 percent, this is on top of any sales tax in the state of sale. In France, you have a 15 percent VAT tax, but only 5.5 percent for the first time the work of art is sold. These costs are in addition to any sales fees required by the auction house.

The Art Market

As I write this, Russian art is the rage. Once appreciated only by a few, it has gained recognition as more Russian money chases a limited number of pieces. It is currently so hot that several pieces appear to have entered the market that in actuality were older un-attributed Dutch paintings retouched and given a Russian painter's signature. While several of these have been found in catalogues and pulled from sale, when the auction house is queried as to the authenticity of the paintings, their response has generally been, "The jury is still out." OK, so who empanelled a jury, and where are they? No, really.

Chinese art seems to be hot, but it is not as widely appreciate outside of China – remember the language. Tribal and primitive art and antiquities are moving up. But that is today, tomorrow it will be different.

Beware of art that is the antithesis of style, items that are bland, casual or lack color. They usually have a poor resale value.

Some investors expect the prices of modern contemporary art to fall, primarily as a response to economics. Their belief is founded on the assumption that art is in the hands of millionaires who will need to sell because of cash flow problems. In truth, there are only several hundred parties in the world that are willing to spend five to tens of millions on a work of art. If their tastes change, and they are changing, what they collected yesterday will be disposed of for what they like today. By the time this is published, the information on tastes will be old and stale – tastes in art are just that. Further, "taste" is desirable – so long as it is tax deductible. The market for art is illiquid, irregular and dominated by a few players. It is also very opaque with economically unreliable price data.

Fernwood Art Investments was one of the more recent experts that failed to monetize art and the art market for investors. Fernwood, like so many funds before and those that have followed, used a detailed financial model to analyze the market, discern trends, and synthesize future trends. To date, all of the models I have seen used make base assumptions that render them useless for art. The market analysis tools and predictive models all have an underlying assumption that the market is liquid, the items being exchanged are uniform, the market has minimal transaction costs, the cost of holding the investment is minimal, and the transactions are transparent. This may come as a shock to those fiscal gurus, but art is not uniform – it is unique. It is this uniqueness that gives it its value. The market is illiquid, transaction costs are very high, there is a cost to holding art, and the transactions are anything but transparent.

There was a great story in *Forbes*, the December 24, 2007 issue, showing a family run business that is the essential market maker, if you will, of Picassos, Modiglianis and others. The owners have a gallery in London and New York, with a large warehouse in Switzerland. The business is so big that it absorbs the liquidations of these paintings in hard times, and doles them out in good times. Their transactions are few, but very large and almost always very private. By virtue of its size and positioning, the business controls the market, the artists and genera the owners choose.

Transactions are suspect. A transaction I was made aware of had a beautiful bit of financial engineering behind it. An estate of considerable size had five paintings by a known artist. The owners wanted to sell these paintings to an art museum for $4 million. The dealer handling the transaction suggested a better way. His plan was to sell *one* painting to the museum for $4 million, and then – being so pleased with what the museum had done with the painting, to donate the other paintings – now with an established market value of $4 million each. This affects both parties to the transaction. The estate gets the $4 million it wanted, and deductions from a $16 million donation. The museum gets a new market price for this artist, substantially raising the value of its current collection (for trade or sale), and the donation of $16 million worth of art. This publicity – and the exhibition to follow – increases attendance.

The art market is anything but a free market. Thus, all of the financial gurus' models fail – immediately and spectacularly.

Last Thoughts

The art sovereigns are congenial manipulators of history and taste. The market is the only critic that matters, and the market is engineered. Being an art dealer and a gentleman are mutually exclusive. Thus, buy and collect art for real reasons – because it is beautiful, and it speaks to you.

Now, as a mental thought experiment, see where you can substitute the names of the players in the art market with the names of players in corporate finance. It's too easy.

Chapter 3

Intellectual Property and Critical Information (IPCI)

The Forgotten Asset

"Man was born to be rich, or grow rich by use of his faculties, by the union of thought with nature. Property is an intellectual production. The game requires coolness, right reasoning, promptness, and patience in the players. Cultivated labor drives out brute labor."

Ralph Waldo Emerson

In this chapter I want to offer a broad outline of Intellectual Property and Critical Information (IPCI), why the two concepts are so closely related, and some of our experiences in dealing with these types of property. This is an attempt to raise awareness about how important IPCI is in the modern enterprise.

Nothing in history has been more counterfeited than ideas. The most coveted property is always a competitor's knowledge and technology. Most of us understand this. Yet, in the modern world there are enormous losses due to the casual dissemination of IPCI by the stewards of that information. These are risks that must be understood and managed, which I hope to make clear in the following text.

Economic activity is fueled by various inputs and insights that are constantly changing and rapidly evolving. We are currently in the era of the Intangible Economy. This is the Intangible Age.

Path to the Intangible Economy

- The Industrial Age - began in Britain in the 18th and 19th centuries.
- The Information Age – took hold roughly from the 1980s to 1992.

- Knowledge Economy - started in 1992 and continued to 2002.
- Intangible Economy - By most accounts, the Intangible Economy started in 2002.

In the Intangible Economy, there are four primary factors of production that are driving economic activity. Heading the list is the category that contains intangible, knowledge assets.

1. Knowledge Assets - what people know and put into use.
2. Collaboration Assets - who people interact with to create value.
3. Engagement Assets - the energy and commitment of people.
4. Time Quality - how quickly value is created.

IPCI is an inclusive term we use to describe all sorts of intangible assets -- patents, trademarks, copyrights, trade secrets, and anything you do not want your competitors to know. In this text, while I frequently use IPCI as an inclusive term, as the text progresses I will attempt to disambiguate IPCI, identify discrete types of assets, and explore why they are different. Before we head there, I want to offer a quick overview summarizing the scope of the problem and the associated risks.

The Problem

According to the U.S. Government,[3] competitive intelligence, economic espionage, and intellectual theft costs American business $300 billion a year — and the amount is climbing. The estimated average per incident cost for a manufacturer is $50 million, with non-manufacturing victims getting off relatively easy at only $500,000.[4]

---

3 2002 Annual Report to Congress on Foreign Economic Collection and Industrial Espionage.
4 Trends in Proprietary Information Loss, American Society for Indus-trialSecurity (ASIS) with consultation from PricewaterhouseCoopers, 1999

The problem is global. *The Korea Times*[5] noted that half of South Korea's high-tech companies have suffered from leaks of proprietary information. Denmark's Economic Weekly Newsletter[6] says the number of industrial espionage attacks on Danish businesses is exploding. Other countries report similar findings.

> IPCI losses costs U.S. companies $300 billion per year.
> This loss represents approximately 2.25 percent of U.S. GDP.
> This translates into about 7,500,000 U.S. jobs needlessly lost every year.

There are a number of factors behind this epidemic:

- Although it is estimated that intangible assets represent 70 percent[7] of a modern company's value, many firms have never inventoried their Intellectual Property. They are unaware of its disposition. Further, they have never considered the economic implications of information loss, or recognized IPCI as possessing a primary economic value. They do not know what needs to be protected.

- More corporations are investing in competitive intelligence (CI) programs, making them active threats to IPCI.

- The end of the Cold War saw a shift from military to economic intelligence gathering, more than 90 percent of which involves legal Competitive Intelligence techniques.

Although information loss has become an invisible and out-of-control cost, few managers show interest in taking the steps necessary to protect their assets. The American Management Association an offer for an article on this subject, and they replied stating that the subject was of no interest to their members. The lack of concern

---

5   Korea Times, 19 June 2006. "Half of Top Tech Firms Suffer Leaks" Cho Jin-seo.

6   Børsen Online

7   IP Central Weblog, 4 June 2004.

isn't surprising. Schools of business, law and criminal justice almost never teach the dangers of IPCI loss, and even less on how to protect IPCI. Professionals in these areas have had virtually no exposure to counterintelligence measures. The FBI made a post-Cold War commitment to fighting economic espionage, but law enforcement's focus on solving crimes, as opposed to preventing them, combined with post-9/11 pressures, ended the agency's role as a significant preventive force. We are on our own.

Managers face another problem: Although they may be unaware of the dangers of competitive intelligence, theft and economic espionage — the Securities and Exchange Commission (SEC) is not. It has stated[8] that among the changes to internal controls sought by the Sarbanes-Oxley Act and related commission rules is "improving the ability of companies to track the costs and impact of economic espionage and theft of intellectual property."

Unfortunately, intellectual property has become the elephant in the boardroom. If developed in-house, it has no book value, and the Public Company Accounting Oversight Board (PCAOB) has offered no guidance on how to disclose a lack of internal controls, IPCI losses, or how to treat the accounting of losses on financial statements.

A loss between $500,000 and $50 million may seem unimportant as a percentage of revenue for a multibillion dollar company, but the SEC has been clear that mere percentage is not the driving consideration in disclosure. Shareholders can now legitimately expect that appropriate internal controls and disclosure be in place, which recognize the threat of competitive intelligence and economic espionage.

What Is Intellectual Property?

Intellectual Property (IP) is any *intangible* asset that can be expressed by knowledge. We note here that a *tangible* asset is something that has form, a creation date, and whose location can be described. A tangible asset can be created using intangible assets. While this

---

8   Letter from SEC Deputy Director Shelley Parratt, dated 5 August 2004

brief description is accurate, it also describes Critical Information – so let's try a more specific definition.

Intellectual Property is a legal concept that includes patents, copyrights, trademarks, service marks and related rights. Under Intellectual Property law, the holder of one of these abstract "properties" has certain exclusive rights to the creative work, commercial symbol, or the invention which is covered by it.[9] These "rights" are specific to the jurisdiction where the property is registered, or covered by international treaties that recognize registration in third-country jurisdictions. If some legal authority does not recognize your rights, you do not have Intellectual Property. This will pose a problem if your property lands in unprotected territory.

Economic attributes that qualify as IP.

> 1. Its description should be specific and recognizable.
> 2. It has a legal existence and protection.
> 3. It can be owned and transferred.
> 4. There should be tangible evidence of its existence.
> 5. It has a specific date or event defining its creation.
> 6. It can be destroyed at a specific date or event.

Economic attributes that do not qualify as IP.

Market share	High profitability
Lack of regulation	A protected position
Monopoly position	Market potential
Breadth of appeal	Mystique
Heritage	Competitive edge
Life cycle status	Uniqueness
Discount prices	Liquidity
Ownership control (or lack of)	

What Is Critical Information?

Critical Information (CI) is specific information about your intentions, capabilities and activities vitally needed by your

---

9 WIPO

adversaries to plan and act effectively against your interests. More specifically, it will allow your competitors to plot your failure, cause you harm, or frustrate your objectives and goals.

If this was not specific enough, it's information your competitors want from your company to assist them in destroying your company.

> *It was only a few years ago that a company dedicated to the design and manufacture of application-specific integrated circuits (ASIC) was hit by a rash of phone calls from a recruiter to its employees. A short investigation led to a security guard as the source of the information leak. The security guard had faxed the entire employee directory to a number outside the company. The security guard was convinced, over the phone, that he was speaking to a vice president of the company who needed the information. Officers of the company are, of course, listed in company literature as well as all of the public filings of the company. The company's representatives acted quickly, and with the help of an investigator (us) traced the fax number to an e-fax service. That information led to an e-mail address. The e-mail led to a public library access point and a private home. Within nine days we were on the caller's doorstep introducing ourselves and producing the evidence that led us to him. He fully admitted to making the call, receiving the fax, and selling the leads to recruiters in the semiconductor industry.*

If you are involved in an IPCI-based company, what could cause more damage than allowing a competitor to interview and recruit your work force? There was no reason a security guard should have had access to this type of critical information, or all of the equipment necessary to print, copy, fax or send the information. Both the company and the security guard learned a lesson. Thankfully, as losses go, the cost was d minimis.

Why Is IPCI So Important?

The modern economy is IPCI. Knowledge assets, both protected and unprotected, are what drive the modern economy.

The courts are responsible for interpreting and enforcing patent and copyright laws, and, like all law, the laws surrounding IP are evolving. There are, essentially, two camps trying to influence IP law. One extreme position is held by those who believe we should abandon all laws that protect intellectual property, and on the other extreme are those who believe we should expand them to include almost any idea that is new and useful.

One famous legal decision emerged from the *State Street Bank and Trust Company v. Signature Financial Group Inc.* case in 1998. This decision granted a patent to a process that "produces a useful, concrete and tangible result." This test was much broader than earlier tests for patentability, and gave rise to the "process patent." This broad expansion was challenged, and in 2008 the *In re Bilski* decision abandoned the test used in *State Street*. As a result of the *Bilski* decision, process patents, or business method patents are more circumspect. According to the majority opinion "the machine-or-transformation test would create uncertainty as to the patentability of software, advances diagnostic medicine techniques, and inventions based on linear programming, data compression, and the manipulation of digital signals", but "the Court today is not commenting on the patentability of any particular invention, let alone holding that any of the above-mentioned technologies from the Information Age should or should not receive patent protection", and "this Court by no means desires to preclude the Federal Curcuit's development of other limiting criteria that further the Patent Act's purposes and are not inconsistent with its text." This decision, in essence, transformed thousands of patents from the protected status of IP to the unprotected status of CI.

jdsupra.com

Within a period of 10 years we saw both an expansion and contraction of the courts' interpretation of what is patent eligible. Expect the legal definition separating IP and CI to always be a little blurred at the margins, and expect the cost of defending a patent claim to go up if you're not on solid ground.

Most people who have studied the issues agree that the patent process facilitates new innovation, accelerates the introduction of new ideas to the marketplace, and is good for the economy. It's interesting that every argument against IP protection is based on the assumption that all of the innovations currently protected would have appeared in the public domain even if they were not protected.

Patents are simply a method to efficiently apply emerging knowledge. It's important to understand that patents simply give a legal standing to what would, in the absence of IP protection, be Critical Information. To look at Intellectual Property outside the context of Critical Information is close to irrational. Though all IP begins as CI, some Critical Information can never rise to the level of Intellectual Property, from a strategic standpoint it's important to look at both protected and unprotected information – IPCI.

IPCI Drives Innovation

What motivates people to work 100-plus hours a week for no pay? It's the brass ring afforded by IP laws. Expecting this protection, it's extremely important to distinguish IP from CI. Critical Information is defined as proprietary information that is not eligible for protection by the government. All IP was CI prior to gaining legal recognition. The abandonment of IP protection simply turns all IP into CI. Understanding this paradigm, the use of IP protection is a matter of choice. If you seek protection for CI, IP laws are best used to your advantage when your business plan is to license the IP. If your plan is to use the IP, and the knowledge you're protecting is not revealed in the product you sell, the protection you gain may be less valuable than losses from the information you disclose.
Assuming we can agree that businessmen are not by nature altruistic, I offer the following poser.

> *Let's assume that I've discovered the holy grail of inventions – a perpetual motion machine. Free energy. This discovery has the potential to raise the living standard of every person in the world. If I can protect it, I'll be very rich – assuming that I can produce a marginal benefit to the consumer. As protected property, my discovery will be shared and applied in millions of applications. If I cannot protect it, the best way for me to monetize my discovery is to treat it as CI. I will then begin looking for energy intensive industries and use my knowledge to gain a competitive advantage. I will probably*

go into the business of selling electricity, manufacturing aluminum and transforming other materials. I will hire an army of security personnel to protect my secrets, and I might make a fortune applying it in a limited number of applications. I'll be able to earn market rate for energy that costs me very little to produce – and the benefits of these efficiencies will all accrue to me. Because these applications require a lot of capital, and I cannot disclose my discovery – unless I'm very rich – it will probably take years for the world to realize the benefits of my work. The efficiencies my discovery offers will likely dribble into the market, but the benefits of these efficiencies will all accrue to me.

Here's the dilemma. Is the world better off if I disclose and protect my critical information for a limited period of time, making it IP – or better off if I secure the information and use it for my own gain indefinitely? I would argue, as the inventor, that IP is the better choice – because my discovery will be more widely applied immediately. IP protection will provide me, in a short time, the equivalent of a lifetime's earnings from CI. It will do this by adding efficiency in all markets where licensing my invention is cheaper than alternatives. My IP will eventually be owned in the public domain. CI that is not allowed to rise to the level of IP will always remain CI.

Perpetual energy is, obviously, an extreme example. In reality, I don't need to discover perpetual motion. A discovery that produced a 5 to 10 percent increased output from electrical generators or internal combustion engines would present me with the same dilemma. In the absence of IP protection, a discovery that produced a 2 to 3 percent improved efficiency in a jet turbine would lead me to compete in worldwide transport of goods instead of disclosing my discovery to all people who use and produce jet turbines.

What motivates people to work 100-plus hours a week for no pay? It's the brass ring afforded by IP laws. Is this an incentive we want to abandon? If so, there will be no more IP – only the costs of containing CI, and the perpetual benefit to the entities holding that information.

In the following discussions of Intellectual Property and Critical

Information we use the term IPCI – which does not mean that the two terms are interchangeable, simply that they are inseparably related.

How IPCI Interacts with Markets

A critical aspect in the legal protection of IP is that for a period of time it turns intangible assets into exclusive property rights. During this period, these property rights enable your company to exploit the intangible assets to their maximum potential. IP protection makes intangible assets "a bit more tangible" by turning them into valuable exclusive assets that can be traded in the marketplace, and offer the owner a competitive edge over others in an industry.

If the ideas, designs and brands of your company are not legally protected by IP rights, then they may be freely used by any other enterprise without limitation. However, when IP is protected, their rights represent concrete value for your enterprise. These are property rights that cannot be commercialized or used without your authorization. Investors, stock market brokers and financial advisors are becoming increasingly aware of this reality, and have begun to change the way they value and protect IPCI assets.

Enterprises worldwide are increasingly acknowledging the value of their IPCI assets, and, on occasion, include them in their balance sheets. Many enterprises undertake regular technology and IPCI audits, and often these audits reveal that IPCI assets are worth more than physical assets. This is almost always the case for companies operating in knowledge–intensive and highly innovative sectors, or companies with a well-known brand name.

Intellectual capital is recognized as the most important asset of many of the world's largest and most powerful companies; it is the foundation for the market dominance and continuing profitability of leading corporations. Control of IPCI is often the key objective in mergers and acquisitions. Knowledgeable companies are increasingly using licensing routes to transfer their intangible assets to jurisdictions that allow free application of their IPCI, and who have better (more efficient, at least) property rights laws. Questions to be answered in an IPCI audit should include:

- What is the intellectual capital used in the business?
- What is the value of intellectual capital (and hence, level of risk)?
- Who owns it (can I sue or be sued)?
- How can it be better exploited (e.g., licensing of technology)?
- At what level do I need to insure the intellectual capital risk?

An information-based economy needs metrics that measure how efficient a company is at converting the costs of information management into profit. Paul A. Strassmann, professor of information sciences at George Mason University, has devised a simple ratio that he calls Information Productivity. It is simply the ratio of the economic value-added (EVA) to the total cost of information management. EVA is an established way of expressing the added value the company generates after paying a reasonable rate of interest to its shareholders. To express this as an equation:

Information Productivity = Economic Value Added /
Cost of Information Management

EVA is a well-understood and accepted accounting value. In order to make meaningful comparisons between companies, it's important to use a value for the costs of information management that is in the public domain and not subject to dispute.

How to Value IPCI

Based upon cost, market or income – every IPCI asset can be valued. In this process, we will evaluate IPCI assets by considering three discrete properties – legal entitlement, legacy brand (know-how in the case of patents) and exploitation. How we proceed may be directed by our purpose in attaching a value to the IPCI. In a case of licensing or sale, the buyer's analysis is likely to be different than the seller's. The following list contains many of the reasons why you would want to value IPCI.

Sale	License	Balance Sheet
Damages	Transfer	Retire
Insurance claim	Remainder value	Donation
Contribution to a J.V.	Cost of compromise	What to protect
Relief from royalty	Obsolescence	Choice of purpose
Acquisition of underused IP		

The Valuation of Intangibles

There are many theories, equations and rule-of-thumb guidelines that can be used to value something. When analyzed, all of them generally represent some permutation of methods that fall into three broad and general categories – cost, income and market.

> A) Costs
> Value based upon the cost of the development or purchase.
> B) Income
> Value based upon projected cash flows for a sale, license or J.V.
> C) Market Conditions
> Value based upon market-based methods either as a buyer or a seller.

Cost. Here we are estimating the cost to replace the functionality of the IPCI. Since we are looking at valuing the process for replacement we have to factor in that we now have more knowledge, we can work with more up-to-date information, eliminate some of the cost inefficiencies, and avoid the costs of previously failed attempts.

FMV = Cost of Reproduction/Replacement - Depreciation - Obsolescence

Income. Here we focus on what the IPCI can bring the company as a proprietary asset, or as a licensed asset. You are seeking to calculate the present value of the future economic benefit. Traditional models assume that this income lasts forever – the discount cash flow model.

$$FMV = \sum_{t=0}^{N} \frac{FV_t}{(1+i)^t}$$

FMV is the discounted value of the future cash flows, FV at any time period in years (t) summed over all time periods.

Market Conditions. The value of the sale of comparable property, done at an arm's length, in an active public fully disclosed market, done nearly contemporaneously to the valuation.

Which Method to Use

Cost, income and market represent valuations, techniques or methods. Which method is the best, or most proper to use, is rarely clear. Whichever method you choose, you should prepare a narrative with some detail explaining your reason for your choice, and why you believe that method most accurately reflects the value of the property.
When discussing licensing or Intellectual Property, one often hears the terms "valuation" and "evaluation" used. Many times it appears as though these terms are interchangeable, and indeed they may be depending upon how the speaker is using the terms.

The terms are related, but are by no means identical. Generally speaking, evaluation in the world of licensing is defined as the process of measuring certain attributes of a license, or potential license, against specific benchmarks, targets or rules-of-thumb. Many different examples of the attributes and metrics associated with these procedures are discussed below. Valuation, on the other hand, is defined as the calculation of the value of a specific asset, be it a patent, trademark or license. Value can certainly be considered one of the targets under which a license is to be evaluated, and may indeed be one of the most important — but it is not the only metric used.

There are many good books devoted to the valuation of Intellectual Property. If you are going to be valuing IPCI, I suggest you read a few of them to acquaint yourself with the varied approaches and methods. Most authors are detail oriented, and provide excellent examples showing how, when and why to use certain equations; as well as theories detailing why these equations work. What you will not find is much discussion about how these valuation models fail. To sensitize you to risk, and the failure of valuation models, I will concentrate on points where they commonly fail.

Here are some ways that IPCI valuations fail. A failure to:

> - State the date of the valuation and the date prepared.
> - Define the purpose of the valuation.
> - Define the standard of value (e.g. fair market).
> - Conduct a site visit.
> - Include assumptions and limiting conditions.
> - Include company background.
> - Include the industry in which the company participates.
> - State the market in which the company competes.
> - Adequately protect "exclusive" assets for both tangible or intellectual property.
> - State economic environment in which the company competes.
> - State legal environments in which the company operates.
> - Prepare a comparative financial analysis with industry performance.
> - Examine and discuss all common valuation methods
> - Adequately define "earnings".
> - Disclose assumptions and source of cash flow projections.
> - Define formulas (e.g., CAPM, WACC, APT, Fama-French).
> - Apply the proper discount/capitalization rate to "earnings" as defined.
> - Adequately discuss and analyze guideline companies selected.
> - Discuss empirical data sources for premiums and discounts applied.
> - Reconcile values indicated by each valuation method examined.

- Select one value.
- Disclose sources of information contained in the report.
- Check if registration fees have been kept current.
- Include exclusivity of use test.
- Properly identify how IPCI is protected by contacts.
- Address the presence or lack of an OPSEC program.
- Address discounts and premiums such as:
    - Control and acquisition premium;
    - Discount for lack of control;
    - Discounts for illiquidity and lack of marketability;
    - Transfer restrictions;
    - Risk issues such as regulatory;
    - Litigation;
    - Rapidity of market change; and
    - IPCI compromised by unauthorized disclosure.

The process of valuation is not only to identify the IPCI, but value the IPCI in light of all of its strengths and weaknesses with full disclosure.

IPCI Does Not Show Up on Traditional Financial Statements

For accounting purposes, IP is booked at the full cost of prosecuting the IP with the appropriate licensing bodies. A trademark may only be carried on the books for a few hundred dollars, a patent for a few thousand. So what would the market value of Oreo™ or the patent on a laser be worth? Not much — for book value.

The value of IPCI is reflected in the difference between the market value of a company and its book value. This difference, when the market value exceeds the book value, is most often referred to as "goodwill." If a company whose book value is stated at $100,000 is acquired for $20,000,000, the $19,900,000 difference in value is the value of the goodwill. This is often described as the discounted present value of the company. This is the value of the cash flow stream that may be produced by the IPCI, over a given period of time, with a stated discount rate.

The arms-length value of IPCI does not always appear in the books of a company that is creating IPCI – but it will show up on the books of a company that has purchased the IPCI, as it has established the value during the purchase.

There is no other accounting entry for the listing of, or valuation, of IPCI. The financial statements are silent – even in light of the fact that, on average, more than 75 percent of the value of a modern public company is found in its intangible assets – its IPCI.

How Is IPCI Lost

The consequences of an IPCI theft are not the actual loss of the asset. Being that the assets are intangible, you don't possess them, you control them. What is lost in IPCI theft is the exclusive use of the asset.

> *Once IPCI's use,*
> *becomes diffuse,*
> *it is of little use.*

IPCI's theft, or compromise, is an event that creates instant obsolescence.

> *Being asked to speak at an industry function is an honor as well as a career boost, so when John had the chance to finally address a conference he had previously only attended, he was delighted. The honorarium allowed him to take his wife, and reimbursement of travel expenses put a smile on his employer's face. That smile might have done a one-eighty had the company CEO known that a chief competitor, the event's secret sponsor, made it all possible. The head of the competitor's company also had a smile on his face: His firm, aggressive practitioners of competitive intelligence, had structured the entire conference to manipulate rivals to willingly – if unwittingly – reveal competitive information.*

The first source of information loss is employees. Some employees may be nefarious, some may be reckless, but the vast majority are simply unaware. Let's begin with the assumption that awareness is the issue. Has there ever been a training class for your employees, specifically telling them what you consider to be IPCI and informing them that disclosure of this information is not allowed? We also need to consider the workplace. How many employees are extreme commuters, people who travel 90 minutes or more? The number is about 4 million workers in the U.S. and they, unlike their peers who live closer to work, will attempt to use their commute time to work to be productive. How many employees are frequent travelers? Who is looking over their shoulders as they type on buses, trains or airplanes? I certainly do. While most of it is boring, I occasionally see some interesting things. Another 4 million employees work at home, at least part of the time. American industry has about 6 percent of the work force outside of a "secure" company location, creating 8 million ports of potential IPCI loss. Your computers do not have be stolen from your company, employees leave laptops on train station benches, in airports and on airplanes. If this exposure isn't bad enough, consider that employees are working at libraries, coffee shops, parks and hotels; as information storage and wireless connections increase daily. By the way, how many thumbnail drives has your organization lost?

How far can lost IPCI travel? A manufacturer of specialized lotions had a unique line of soothing lotions it developed using a series of proprietary formulas.[10] This information, including the marketing, design and product launch plans were stolen by a chemist in the company's lab. He did this the old-fashioned way – he memorized them. At home he wrote them down and e-mailed them to a similar firm in Europe. The firm in Europe was marketing a competitive line of creams and lotions within three weeks.

When IPCI is stolen, the thieves are not changing ownership of the IPCI; they are simply using it – much like borrowing a rake from a neighbor. Using a borrowed rake does not deprive the owner of the rake's utility – there is no user's license with the rake – there is no loss of value by the rightful owner. Even if the design is protected, rake manufacturers are not going to sue the borrowers claiming illegal use of the rake. If the design of the rake is copied, and "knockoff "copies are offered for sale, then an infringement may have

---

10   All lotions are soothing, if not, they are called liniments

occurred. Now you have the opportunity to retain counsel and prove an infringement occurred.

The loss of IPCI is losing the *right of exclusive use*. The owner of the IPCI has the exclusive right to designate who can make economic use of the asset.

Losses from Theft and Espionage

Why do people steal IPCI? Willie Sutton, when asked why he robbed banks answered, "Because that's where the money is!" Increasingly, IPCI is where the money is. As businesspeople we have to recognize that the theft of IPCI is a real crime, because law enforcement does not. The estimated chances of getting caught committing an IP crime are 1 in 250,000. The numerical equivalent of losing 18 consecutive passes on a craps table! Of those caught, very few are charged and convicted – of those convicted only one-third face jail time – and of those facing jail, 90 percent of sentences are under one year. IPCI theft pays. The law has not created any significant disincentives for the theft of IPCI. It is up to the owners to be vigilant, organized and ruthless in defense of their IPCI.

In some circles it's called economic espionage. Professional spies are targeting your business for your IPCI. If you don't think your business is a target, think again. According to a survey by *Fortune Magazine* several years ago, 75 percent of Fortune 500 companies had a Competitive Intelligence Department, the other 25 percent did not respond. There is an association called Society for Competitive Intelligence Professionals (SCIP) that holds seminars on how to get information legally (www.scip.org). Starting to get the picture? Let me fill in some of the details. The governments of France, China, Russia and even Israel are interested in using their intelligence capabilities to steal proprietary information and technology that furthers their commercial and military interests. I don't single these countries out because these are the only ones – they are simply the most elegant and successful in their efforts.

Impairments To IPCI's Value

At this point we have covered some basic information on the valuation of IPCI. From here we need to look at impairments to IDCI's value not yet mentioned, and not a part of traditional thinking. That is, the valuation of the IPCI when the IPCI is no longer exclusive to the owner.

As we discussed, Intellectual Property does not exist unless it is covered by a legal registration or declaration. Thus, if your property lands in a country where it is not covered – it is not protected. If you copyright a book in the U.S. but it is not registered in Russia or China, then it is not protected in Russia or China. If you patent an item in the U.S. and the E.U. but decide not to patent it in China, it's tough cookies (a legal term of art). For any future claim of infringement in China, patents outside China do not bind businesses in China, and an enterprising rival may even find your patent online and file your patent in China claiming it to be their own.

Intangible assets present special complications in valuation. In the biotech industry, a new start-up, with little or no assets save a single patented idea, may only be worth the value of that patent. But without an established customer base and sales records, the value of that patent must be *arbitrarily* assigned. IPCI valuations can be assigned using a number of different methods and by incorporating risk factors, including:

> The cost of the patent.
> The cost of developing a product around the patent.
> Estimated licensing revenue and royalties.
> The risk of a patent battle.
> The extent to which the patent will block competitors.

It is estimated that U.S. biotech firms typically assign about 60 percent of their total value to IP, as their real costs to reach the patent stage is disproportionately high. However, analysts believe that since many patents are actually useless, these companies are overvaluing their IP and may be contributing to misconceptions of their value. You only need to watch penny stocks to realize the risk of placing too much value on an unproven patent. Many biotech start-ups are here today and gone tomorrow; following IPOs based on highly valued IPCI and sales predictions, that failure to deliver.

Other impairments may be a patent ring fence put up by a competitor to prevent you from using your patent, or similar patents being filed in order to lessen the value of a competing patent.

Valuation Impairment

Valuation impairment has become more important with the recent issuance of Statement of Financial Accounting Standards 142, *Goodwill and Other Intangible Assets.* This statement changed the accounting treatment of certain intangibles during acquisitions. Instead of the more-or-less blanket treatment of acquired intangibles that featured a stated amortization period, *many of these assets will now be carried on the balance sheet at cost, and subjected to an annual impairment test.* The annual impairment tests are usually conducted under SAS 81 and or 101 guidelines.

Impairment tests are a step in the right direction toward sane valuations for public companies. It's a good start – but as is apparent in many recent failures, valuation rests heavily upon a foundation of assumptions. Weighing the balance in public demand for disclosure and corporate needs for privacy will determine how we continue. Improper valuation of privately held businesses and intangibles is an everyday occurrence, often seen as a scandal in public companies. It's often hard to tell if the people at the center of a valuation scandal are calculating liars, or if they have simply deceived themselves and taken the market along for the ride.

The following are risks that must be considered in an impairment test:

Technology Diffused – or, there are competing patents.

Some technologies are "me too" ideas that, while protected, are protecting different areas of a broad field that has been plowed many times.

Next Best Thing Technology - pricing pressures

The IP was, or is, being superseded by another

technology. Just look at what happened to photography in the last 10 years. A good film camera was usually good for 10 years – today a large segment of the population doesn't know what photographic film is.

Technology Lockup – restricted within a country's borders.

The U.S. and other countries have restrictions on the export of technology. Further, the mere exportation of technology ownership may trigger a tax event.

Precipitation upon Transfer

The development of technology and companies often have long histories. Not everyone is party to agreements signed by past management teams or are aware of all of the assets, liabilities or restrictions. So, some events are precipitated upon a transfer – such as a bonus, acceleration of a contract for royalties, or a violation of regulatory decrees.

Blocking Patents or IP

Some technologies are purchased and sold not because of their economic value, but because the purchase blocks a competitor from a market. They may also be sold because two companies are in litigation, realize they may not have full protection, and think the purchase of a third party's patent will improve their case.

Not Foreign Protected

If it's not patented in the U.S., it is not protected in the U.S. If it's not patented in China, it is not protected in China.

Manufactured Documents

> Often, when people sell a business, they will manufacture financial statements, licenses, documents and even IP opinions!

Demand Curves – short or long

> The demand cycle for products varies. For example, the demand cycle for a new memory device may be a couple of years, while the demand cycle for a recognized trade name may be 30 years or more.

Infringement

> A great number of trademarks and service marks are infringed upon. The value of a mark is compromised by infringement. If the owner of the mark does not mount what is recognized as a vigorous defense, the value may be lost.

License Drift

> A licensee is given the right to use the technology in one area, but the application drifts into areas not covered by the license. This can compromise the value of future licensing opportunities, and can subject the drifter to damages.

OPSEC – Lack of

> Operations Security (OPSEC) is a process whereby the owner of IPCI defines what information is important, what competitors want, and devises a method to secure the information and track stolen IPCI. Lack of OPSEC in an IPCI-based company should be an automatic haircut in value.

M&A Malaise and Panic

The uncertainty generated during mergers and acquisitions causes a great deal of angst in those affected. People are anticipating an upset in their lives (for some any change is an upset) and behave poorly. They may look for work at a competing company, they may sell IP, or in their panicked state may inadvertently disclose IPCI. I have seen situations where one company thought another was an excellent purchase, only to find out that two-thirds of the employees were gone within a year, along with the tradecraft that made the IPCI work.

Laundered IPCI

IPCI that belongs to another company has been laundered and vended into the company in question. The telltale sign is that there are no documents surrounding the origin of the IPCI – it just materializes in the company in question.

Family Owned Business

These businesses are often a cult of personality, and when the central figure is gone the rest of the gang leaves as well. Family run businesses usually have a much lower cost structure since all family members work hard during the day to be able to face one another in their private lives. That loyalty will rarely survive a sale.

IPCI Infringement Insurance

IPCI paired with infringement insurance is more valuable than IPCI that lacks infringement insurance. Further, if the company lacked the financial ability to defend the IPCI the business has impaired future claims against infringement.

Review all items under Valuation Failures as well.

Value Enhancement	Value Impairment
OPSEC program.	No OPSEC program.
CI program to monitor competitors both for innovation anf for use of the company's IPCI.	No inventory of both IP and CI.
Employment aggreement clearly identifies IPCI and protects it.	Employment agreement fails to address disclosure IPCI.
Vendor aggreements clearly identify and protect IPCI.	Vendor agreements fail to address disclosure IPCI.
IPCI tracking program and to look for IPCI loss "tells".	Lack of information security.
IPCI loss ID and reward program.	No programming for identification of IPCI as it is created.
Employment training on importance of IPCI.	Not tracking competing technologies.

Impairment Has a "Tell"

- A competing company is producing goods identical to yours.
- You find that your market share is shrinking.
- Other companies can suddenly match your price points.
- A sudden, and knowledgeable, market pressure on prices.

Protecting IPCI – Who's Job Is This?

The job of protecting IPCI is a function of the treasury. The hallmark of the treasury's function is to reduce uncertainty through order. Uncertainty kills finance just as effectively as fraud or over-regulation. According to James A. Kaitz, president of the Association for Financial Professionals (AFP), "Treasurers are the custodians of value of the modern company." Today's treasury is no longer just a support division, but is also looked at as a profit center.

Managers might assume that their companies are protected by security and IT departments, corporate counsel and other outside consultants – but these groups are focused on protecting information on company property from outsiders and reducing crimes of opportunity. Intellectual losses, on the other hand, are most often the result of trusted people acting off company property, whether it is information published by corporate mandate, employees betraying an employer, or talking too freely in an open forum.

Contracts

Employment - The employment contract is the first line of defense. In the employment agreement the employee needs to acknowledge that all IPCI developed by the employee belongs to the company. Unfortunately, that seems to be the extent of IPCI protection contained in 90 percent of employment agreements. The employment agreement should clearly identify what the company believes to be its Intellectual Property, its Critical Information, and specific acts prohibited both on and off the job site. Prohibited acts should include casually discussing company plans, manufacturing processes, margins, and even things as trivial as the travel plans of any other employee. Language should also be included addressing employment obligations and liabilities. If you are permitted, consider setting specific damages for each prohibited post-employment act of disclosure or use. If you are serious about protecting your IPCI, it's wise to set a serious tone in the employment agreement.

Supplier / Vendor – Suppliers and vendors may know, or guess, formulations or processes based upon key items or ingredients that you order. For the supplier-vendor relationship to work properly with your business, you are often required to disclose IPCI so the supplier/vendor can complete their task. This IPCI and other information they may become aware of needs to be clearly identified as secret. Suppliers and vendors must be forewarned of the forbidden disclosure in the same format prepared for your employees.

Landlords – There is almost always some disclosure to a landlord, prior to and during the term of a lease. If you are a tenant of a building owned by others, the landlord will always retain some access to the property — this can present a problem with the security of IPCI. If you choose to limit the landlord's access to the building, it must be agreed to in the rental agreement. Some rental contracts, most commonly for retail space, agree to a percentage of sales as part of the rent. Your sales figures are private, and it must be understood that the landlord cannot disclose those figures to third parties.

> *Why would a landlord choose to disclosure a tenant's sales figures? One client of ours who had a presence in shopping malls unexpectedly received a tender offer from a competitor. The sales figures the competitor had were exact, down to the penny. Since only the owner knew the exact numbers, he was flummoxed by his competitor gaining access to the information. The competitor's path to the information was brilliantly simple. He had shopped for retail space in all of the malls where our client had a presence, and requested other stores' sales figures as a part of his due diligence.*

Professionals, such as accountants, attorneys and consultants, have access to information almost any company would consider sensitive. While attorneys and accountants are, as a general rule, very good about respecting their clients' privacy — disclosures do occur. Your engagement agreements with professionals should clearly state, just as in the employment agreements, what information is considered proprietary. Even professionals should be advised that without prior written permission they are not to make disclosures to any third party, even in the course of providing their services to you.

Domicile - The domicile of an IPCI dispute is important. In some states it will take years just to get into court. Many states lack the knowledge infrastructure to deal with abstract disputes. Some countries actually cater to IPCI, such as the Netherlands and Malaysia, where Intellectual Property Courts are set up so matters can be litigated and resolved in as little as six weeks by legal professionals who deal with nothing but Intellectual Property. The location for the dispute is very important.

Insurance - To my knowledge, insurance can be purchased to defend your IPCI rights in court (litigation insurance), but *not* for the economic damages that are the consequence of the loss of IPCI from regular line suppliers. This may be an argument for a more creative captive insurance opportunity – but damages do not appear, at this time, to be a mainline coverage policy option.

OPSEC is the most effective tool one can use to protect their IPCI. OPSEC is the identification, valuation and protection of Intellectual Property and Critical Information from competitive intelligence, economic espionage, casual dissemination and theft.

> OPSEC is a management function.
> OPSEC is *threat-based* (not rule-based).
> OPSEC is a *process.*
> OPSEC crosses divisions and disciplines.
> OPSEC allows us to reduce vulnerabilities to – and therefore derived risk from – competitive intelligence, economic espionage, and theft of information.

Companies must protect their IPCI, and the logical model for this internal control is OPSEC.[11] This is the accepted U.S. Government standard process for identifying, valuing and protecting information that would give adversaries an advantage. It serves the very same purpose in the private sector -- it identifies, values and protects your IPCI.

OPSEC asks and addresses the answers to five critical questions:

- Who wants your information, and what are they willing to do to get it?
- What information do they want, versus what is important to you?

---

11 OPSEC is promulgated on the federal level by the Interagency OP-SEC Support Staff. The OPSEC Professionals Society is the independent professional association that provides certification of practitioners.

- What vulnerabilities would allow competitors to get information?
- What happens if they do get the information?
- What can you do to prevent this from happening?

OPSEC is conceptually simple and initially looks like traditional risk management, but there is a critical difference. OPSEC is a threat-based iterative management process that crosses divisions and disciplines, not a rule-based system relegated to one department. When properly approached by an experienced practitioner, OPSEC is very cost-effective to implement and maintain, and provides a high return on investment from reduction of losses and decreased liability costs.

OPSEC is a process whereby the owner of IPCI designates what is important, what competitors may want, and devises methods to secure and limit access to the information. Further, there are enhancements to OPSEC that can often track stolen IPCI when it leaves an enterprise all the way to its destination.

Lack of OPSEC in a company based upon IPCI should produce an automatic haircut in value to the IPCI. The problem is very clear – the company cannot know if the economic advantage proffered by an item of IPCI is exclusive or not. To put it another way, you are buying a cargo container of silver bars transported under the utmost levels of security – do you open it to see if the silver bars are inside? Of course you do, but you do not have that option with IPCI – it is not tangible – so you must rely upon the methods used to protect the property, and the only acceptable method is OPSEC. One of the problems is the definition of theft. Competitors aren't changing ownership of a thing or an idea – they're simply making use of it. What is lost with IPCI is the right of exclusive use. The rightful owner has lost the right to designate who can make use of their property.

Accounting of IPCI – This responsibility lies within the province of the treasurer's office as well as the corporate secretary. IPCI has a book value (the investment made into the creation) and a market value, which can be the discounted present value of a future stream of cash flows to the companies that control the exclusivity of its use. If you lose the exclusivity of use, you lose the value of the IPCI – book and market value. Most acquisitions made of companies are companies that possess significant "goodwill" value. Goodwill is the value of the company over and above its book value. The loss of the IPCI means an immediate write-down of all goodwill associated with the lost information. Immediately.

Taggants / Tracers

Sometimes, despite our best efforts to secure IPCI, information is disclosed by accident, mis-disclosure or theft. Seeing that what you have lost is an intangible, how do you trace the path of the missing information? It can seem a bit like looking for a fairy by tracking the fairy's footprints — and you can only see them with a magnifying glass on warm days, and only if the fairy decided to walk instead of fly.

If the IPCI has been transferred into a physical form, several things can be done to make removal from the company known, and to assist in tracing the destination of the items. Taggants can be added to items that allow a tracer to positively identify the source of the item. Taggants can be radio-frequency identification (RFID) chips, microscopic chips, or even DNA added to solution. There are procedural ways to mark documents, covert ways to mark them, and other proven methods. If the IPCI is in electronic form, there are key phrases to insert, and code that can alert the rightful owner if these electronic documents end up on an unauthorized computer or network. Any IPCI anti-theft program should have substantial rewards for the identification of IPCI leaks and thefts. I am choosing to limit the discussion and disclosure of available methods of tracking to prevent a short cut for a casual thief.

In an earlier example I mentioned the loss of a manufacturer's employee list. Let me summarize one strategy to help secure this type of data. There are several services that will lease phone numbers in any area code you want, and some only charge $3 a month per line. These numbers can then be forwarded to any other line, and will be charged a small fee per minute when used. I would create several fictitious employees, with at least one in every key department. Then I would create a profile for each employee, along with one of these fictitious home phone numbers, and insert them into the master employee list. I would forward all of the leased numbers to one secure cell phone, and have someone in either management or security carry it at all times. These numbers should never be contacted — and if they are, you have an opportunity to engage the person on the other end. If you use toll-free numbers, you will be able to capture the caller's phone number even if it has been blocked. This is an example of using fictitious information or disinformation as a taggent in a data set. The use of fictitious data can be used creatively to secure many different types of data sets.

Recovery after Theft

Recovering a stolen intangible is like trying to un-ring a bell. What can be done to defend IP is generally limited to two schools of thought. The first defense is to confront the thief and attempt to limit further use or disclosure. There are procedural measures to limit further disclosure in addition to contractual agreements that provide for more or less immediate injunctive relief and stated damages. The stated damages should represent an amount sizable enough to act as a significant deterrent to disclosure. All a plaintiff has to prove is that the release occurred, no damage calculations are needed, since the value of a breach is predetermined by agreement.

The second defense is a very public process involving law enforcement and civil litigation, or both. In my experience, unless you have a large loss, law enforcement is not much help – officers are not trained to handle IPCI crimes. As for civil remedies, they are best used as a strategic and tactical tool to name and shame the violator. Expect that a recovery, if any, will be hard won, and the calculation of damages submitted by your expert and their expert will be miles apart.

We prefer not to be limited to two schools of thought, and find a third approach to be most interesting. You can "encourage" (begrudge?) the thief to become a licensed user of the technology. The bell cannot be un-rung, and the knowledge cannot be erased from the thief's memory, in which case we believe the best strategy is to declare a position of strength and negotiate a licensing agreement. This approach minimizes expenditures associated with an adversarial approach, and harvests an economic benefit. Licensing agreements have the added benefit of aligning the interests of the adversaries to control further release of information.

Consequences Of Failure

Since most people pay little attention to the topic, it may come as a surprise that corporate officers face liability on three fronts.[12]

1. Being technically noncompliant with the Sarbanes-Oxley Act can involve both civil and criminal liability, even if auditing firms do not understand the issues involved or compliance strategies.

2. If a loss is prosecuted under the Economic Espionage Act of 1996, the perpetrator of a crime could make a compelling case that the lack of internal controls, as required by Sarbanes-Oxley, was a failure to take "reasonable measures to keep such information secret." The information would therefore not be a trade secret (as defined under the Economic Espionage Act and the model Uniform Trade Secrets Act[13]) – making prosecution impossible.

3. Shareholders may undertake shareholder negligent action lawsuits[14] asserting that managers should have known there was a high-probability threat that should have been addressed, or asserting an abandonment of trade secret status. If the managers were non-compliant with Sarbanes-Oxley, the directors

---

12   White paper "Sarbanes-Oxley POSE Compliance," for 2006 Arizona Bar Association Convention, Phoenix, Arizona.

13   Both 18 USC 90 (Economic Espionage Act of 1996) and the model Uniform Trade Secrets Act require reasonable precautions be taken to protect a trade secret. Counsel with whom we have spoken feel that this must now include a government-recognized program to protect information from competitive intelligence, economic espionage and theft.

14   LUBRINCO has been approached by class action attorneys about this issue, and most IP attorneys with whom we have spoken believe that such lawsuits are on the horizon.

and officers' insurance underwriter could claim[15] intentional indifference on the part of management and refuse to cover the defense expenses, potentially making them personal liabilities.

Although new legislation did not specifically mandate anything new on the requirement to value IP, it did impose greater responsibility on management – and significant punishment for failure. Investors and regulators are paying a lot more attention to IP in financials, evidenced by the Financial Accounting Standards Board's (FASB) recent statements on business combinations, goodwill and intangible assets. Recognizing the impact IP has on company value, rule makers continue to strive for improved IP valuation in financial statements. A primary tool is the move away from a rules-based approach to a principles-based approach, which requires more professional judgment and less follow-the-dots accounting.

Adding Teeth to IP Valuation.

Companies spend considerable time and money trying to value intangible assets and intellectual property. These efforts are necessary for buying and selling entities, for litigation support, and for accurate financial reporting and disclosures. Managers need to recognize any transactions that may impact these assets, establish a process to value them, and implement an adequate control system to prevent unwanted dissemination. They must find the relationship between the company's intangible assets and the company's performance. Even though Sarbanes-Oxley did not change the valuation rules, it did add teeth (ensuring that executives prioritize the valuation process when IP assets impact the company's value). Recent FASB Statements 141 and 142 require companies to perform an intangible assets search when they buy other companies. These statements establish categories for IP assets, including marketing-related (e.g., trademarks), contract-based (licenses), artistic (photos) and technology-based (patents) assets. Only when the acquisition price exceeds the value of tangible assets are these identified intangible assets recognized as goodwill.

Noncompliance can result in serious legal problems from violations of:

---

15 Based on private conversations with carriers.

FACTA (Fair and Accurate Credit Transactions Act). New law requiring anyone retaining consumer information for business purposes to destroy the information before discarding it.

GLBA (The Gramm-Leach-Bliley Act). Requires United States banking and financial institutions to describe how they will protect the confidentiality and security of consumer information.

HIPAA (Health Insurance Portability and Accountability Act). Requires health care providers and hospitals to protect patients' privacy and ensure the security of patient/client data. This process is known as HIPAA compliance.

One problem with compliance, especially in class-action litigation, is that you not only have to be compliant, you must also appear to be compliant. Financial losses are not just regulatory impositions; losses include having to prove yourself in front of a court and convince them that you have been, and continue to be, compliant. This is in addition to any economic harm the company may face operationally from a loss of IPCI.

The Real Economics

Industries in developed nations have responded to the theft of IPCI by innovating faster than they leak. If this were a leaking boat, the equivalent would be to develop faster and faster pumps as opposed to plugging the leaks. Unless both problems are addressed, in time the leaks will flow faster than newer pumps can be developed and deployed. Result, ship sinks.

I have yet to mention piracy, or as information patriots call it "liberated knowledge."

The different between IPCI theft and piracy is very specific. A theft occurs before an item, product or design is even released. Piracy comes after a product or design is released. If we're unfamiliar with when a release occurred, they appear to be the same act. A team of researchers from AT&T and the University of Pennsylvania found that more than 75 percent of the top 50 movies uploaded to the Internet during 2002 and 2003 were leaked by industry insiders. These insiders abused their access to the assets of their companies, stole copies of the movies, and uploaded them to the Internet before the release date. Can those who download a pre-release movie be charged with possession of stolen goods? Prosecutors are heading in that direction.

Does piracy fuel innovation? This question has to be viewed in context of the quality of innovation, and whose ox is being gored. Innovation becomes more important to a business model if piracy is inevitable, but innovation is hard to force. In businesses that are forced to rapidly upgrade and develop new features, economics will bring pressure to release products that are not fully tested. Think of all of the computer programs that are released with quality as an afterthought. (Quality is a "field installable option," often called a "service pack.") Haste lowers the quality of innovation, products and services. While piracy will make a company more fragile, it will affect start-ups and small companies very differently than large and established enterprises. For a business to weather IPCI theft it needs to have capital, good investigators and skilled lawyers. Companies without these resources can rarely survive.

Chapter 4

Background Investigations

"The men the American public admire most extravagantly are the most daring liars; the men they detest most violently are those who try to tell them the truth."

H.L. Mencken

Business leaders have known for centuries that employees are their most valuable assets. When businesses refer to "human capital" they are by their own words and definitions valuing the process of selection, hiring and training as one of the most critical processes in which an enterprise can engage. Knowing this, we could guess that the information used to hire, train and retain an employee should be made based upon verified facts.

The problem facing the employer is straightforward. The labor pool is debased with felons, murderers, rapists, and con artists, according to professional estimates that say 2 percent to 3 percent of the world's populations are psychopathic – capable of almost any crime. Unfortunately, most employers opt to deal with troubled employees by cleaning up the mess left in their wake instead of changing their hiring practices. This is the logical equivalent of using a mop as the primary defense against a leak. (Hint: Turn the faucet off first).

The goal of this chapter is to provide some of the tools and knowledge you need in order to assess, establish, and maintain a professional and effective methodology of conducting background checks for your company. Both pre-hire and post-hire background checks will be discussed in detail. This process will be highlighted and emphasized with stories about what has happened when background checks were ignored, were cheap and cheerful, as well as when background checks circumvented potential harm. The exposure you face as an employer will be evident. The case studies at the end are real, not hypothetical.

To put a perspective to the real risk companies face, consider that average employee theft is about $2,000, average employee embezzlement stands at about $430,000. Losses from employee theft range from between $20 billion to $90 billion. On top of those numbers is an additional $280 billion in losses from theft of intellectual property and critical information. Such acts destroy businesses, it's proven. Theft and embezzlement account for almost 50 percent of small-business failures.

Such numbers alone should validate the role of risk managers. These experts are faced with a dilemma when they expend funds on background checks – if a problem is found, the savings to the enterprise will never be known. On the other hand, if they find nothing, many people feel the expense was a waste of funds. A quick look at the cost of background checks will put this "expense of risk" into perspective. In an unscientific survey we found the following costs on background checks for various job functions:

Tenant screening / before renting an apartment	$ 35
Pre-licensing background check for medical doctors	12
Pre-licensing background check for teachers	13
Pre-employment screening for truck drivers	100
Pre-employment for a senior executive	500 to 1,500
Pre-IPO due diligence on executives and directors	3,000 to 8,000

In calculating risk we can't work out the savings from what hasn't happened, we can only address our perception of risk and how exposed we are to that risk. For example, many people will ask, "Do we value teachers less than truck drivers?" The correct question is "Where do we *perceive* the risks to be greater – among teachers or truck drivers?" That is the answer reflected in the table above. The price points for background checks into tenants, teachers, doctors and truckers, in my experience, reflect insufficient effort or skill of the background screeners. These "background checks are nothing more than an automated search of public records. That's it. You pay for what you get. Cheap screening means weak screening – aka "cheap and cheerful, of which it never is either." As this chapter will show, there is a high price to pay for incomplete or faulty background checks.

Inquiry into the past life and dealings of people is the single most important task in due diligence work. When personal background investigations and checks are used properly, you will begin to see their value on Day One.

Required Standard of Care

Standard of care is the degree of diligence and thoroughness you need to prosecute your background screening. It's essential to understand that standard of care is relative to the amount of damage the employee can cause to your firm or a third party. The level of scrutiny required when investigating a prospective candidate's background is in direct proportion to the responsibilities of the position, the level of contact that person has with the public, and, the amount of harm or damage that person can cause in their professional capacity. An employer's duty to investigate depends upon the particular responsibilities and trust placed in an employee. That duty is different in specific fields, such as child care, elder care, apartment supervision, security guard, and someone who handles the assets of a trust. An employer's investigation should be both proportional and specific to the function the employee is being hired to perform. The level of scrutiny is in direct proportion to the amount of damage that the prospective employee can cause.

There is no single comprehensive checklist of exactly what an employer should do before making a hiring decision. It's important to understand that all jobs and functions do not require the same level of scrutiny.

The first step in conducting a background check is to speak to the candidate's former employers and schools. It's important that when seeking information you understand that former employers have both practical and legal motivations to exercise extreme caution when deciding what information to disclose about their former employees. Likewise, as an employer, you should also be cautious about what information you're seeking on prospective employees, and what information you disclose regarding current or past employees.

Employers who are too specific or offer too many factual statements or opinions regarding former employees run the risk of being accused of defamation, blacklisting and intentional interference with a potential contract relationship. On the other hand, employers who disclose too little information about a past employee may be liable for intentional misrepresentation to a prospective employer if information that should have been disclosed is withheld.

Unfortunately, the official policy of most employers is to disclose as little information as possible. This could definitely impede a prospective employer's duty to investigate the background of applicants. From the perspective of an employer looking at hiring a new employee, investigating the background of applicants is necessary – not only to vet qualified candidates, but because failure to do so might expose the employer to legal liability under the theory of negligent hiring. Failure to perform a background check may also expose the employer to significant damage from occupational fraud, abuse and theft. Hence, in order to avoid liability and potential damages, the employer must conduct a reasonable background check.

A way around some this has been for us to ask a former employer if the person being investigated would be eligible for rehire. If yes, we ask the former employer to say so, if they are not eligible for rehire, we let them know they can remain silent and we will understand. Not an elegant solution, but one that has worked to bridge their fear and your need for information.

For example, one specific area of employee background investigation involves employees who will operate commercial vehicles. In this instance, the duty to investigate has been imposed by and codified in federal law. The employer/investigator must obtain answers to a number of questions, including:

1. The name and address of the common carrier.
2. The applicant's name, address, date of birth and Social Security number.
3. The addresses at which the applicant has resided for the preceding three years.

4. The date on which the application is submitted.
5. The issuing state, number and expiration date of each unexpired license the applicant holds.
6. The nature and extent of the applicant's experience in operating commercial vehicles.
7. A list of all motor vehicle accidents in which the applicant has been involved in the preceding three years.
8. A list of all violations of motor vehicle laws during the preceding three years.
9. A statement setting forth the facts and circumstances of any denial, revocation or suspension of any licenses.
10. A list including the names and addresses of all employers during the preceding three years.
11. The signature of the applicant.

The hiring employer is required to check all of the information provided, and the employee candidate is required to have a physical examination stating that the person is medically fit to operate a commercial vehicle. For any position that requires some form of licensing or credentials, it is proper to determine what is required for the certification and what "standard of care" is used in conducting a background check.

For employees who are not entrusted with the custody and security of either people or property, and have little or no direct contact with the public, the employer's duty may be satisfied by a less-extensive background investigation. This may include an attempt to check with prior employers, a possible review of public records and nothing more.

In any of these cases, if an employer becomes aware of information which may present risk to a third party, before or after hiring, the employer may then have the duty to take action and either further investigate or terminate the relationship.

The duty that exists in a negligent hiring case is owed to those with whom it is foreseeable that the employee will interact. Failure to exercise this duty may expose the employer to substantial liability. There is a full range of case law that documents both compensatory and punitive damage claims in negligent hiring cases.

In one particular case, Tallahassee Furniture Co. Inc. v. Harrison, a driver for the furniture company entered Mary Harrison's home, raped and stabbed her. The furniture company had not conducted an employment background or criminal record check. The level of trust the employer was placing in this employee was unsupervised access to its client's homes. Most reasonable people would conclude that this level of responsibility should be met with a high level of scrutiny. In this case, a background check would have revealed a long history of psychiatric treatment and drug abuse.

Insurance company litigators have tried to assert the legal theory that since the populace is so aware of people doing bad things, and so much information is readily available on the Internet for little or no cost, that failure to conduct a background check on a prospective employee is no longer negligence – but tantamount to an intentional act. Thus, failure to perform a background check should subject the employer to liability for intentional acts as opposed to negligence. Why would an insurance company assert that the insured acted intentionally? Because most insurance policies do not cover liability caused by intentional acts, only those caused by negligent acts.

There are statutory requirements that can make the process of background investigations increasingly difficult for the employer. For example, in California it is considered a misdemeanor to conduct a criminal investigation on someone as a condition of hiring. However, there are certain employers who have exclusions to this law – such as schools. Consider a case in 1998 in which a convicted rapist and child molester was released on probation from a California correctional facility. The convict was steered by his probation officer to a janitorial service that often hired convicted felons, though not knowingly. In this particular instance, the felon was hired by a janitorial service that had a contract with a public school. The janitor was not hired by the school, but by a contractor that worked for the school. The janitor covered up a swastika tattoo on his forehead with makeup, and went to work at a middle school in California. Within seven days of his assignment, he had assaulted and killed an 11-year-old girl. There is no easy answer for such cases.

The employer must make several subjective decisions before determining the scope of a background check, essentially rating potential employees by the functions they will perform and determining the potential liability connected to those functions. Following are the minimum considerations for any employee:

      a.   Exposure to the public.
      b.   Ability to cause harm to the public.
      c.   Potential of damage or harm that the employee could directly cause to the employer (as opposed to indirect).

Using the three categories and the scale None, Possibly, Maybe, Likely and Definitely – an employer can estimate the potential risk exposure for each position within the organization. If *any* of those positions are rated as Likely or Definitely, a thorough background check should be considered. If all three categories rate Possibly or higher, it could be argued that a combination of potential risk requires a thorough background check.

Public companies in the United Kingdom and the United States are required to disclose risk elements – both in the type of business that they operate and the environment in which they operate. Corporate governance and control are a part of opportunity management, but the marketplace is beginning to understand that risk management is as important as opportunity management. Public companies have been required to develop an "embedded" internal control system that monitors, on a risk-analyzed basis, all disclosed risks. These threats may include environmental, ethical, social and employment. Simply stated, key business risks always correlate to key business issues. Requirements for this type of risk management and reporting simply acknowledge that businesses ought to be held responsible for risks that go beyond simple finance. Without commenting on mandatory requirements, we should all understand the elusive nature of risk, and spend more time assessing our exposure. Developing a plan simply makes good business sense.

Consider employment cases in the U.S. Jury awards have risen from $150,000 per case in 1991, to $500,000 in 1997 to more than $1.3 million in 2008. Can you afford to hire someone who is litigious and likely to shape an environment that creates a liability for you? Statistics show that employers are 600 percent more likely to be sued for wrongful termination than for refusing an unfit employee in the first place. The time to stem liability from an employer/employee relationship is before it starts. It's no coincidence that the mantra of risk managers is "Prevention, Prevention and Prevention."

Let's start at the beginning of employment liability issues. Almost all relationships begin with the applicant's résumé. A résumé is intended to present the applicant in the best possible light, with the goal of earning a face-to-face interview. Applicants will *never* look better than when they are on paper. In the latest "Liars Index," which is periodically compiled by Jude M. Werra & Associates, 23.5 percent of all candidates for sales and marketing jobs overstate their credentials (my guess is that it's much higher). Also, 16 percent of résumés contain false academic claims and or material omissions. Put together, this means that one out of four to five candidates walking in your door are already lying to you.

While thinking about résumés, liability, litigation and awards – keep in mind the legal theory that failure to conduct a background check may no longer be considered a negligent act, but an intentional act. As we discussed earlier – an intentional act is an act that is not generally covered by your insurance. These topics lead us to take a closer look at background investigations.

Conducting the Background Investigation

While preparing to conduct a background investigation you will be dealing with two types of information: claims expressed and claims implied. Expressed claims are those claims represented by the candidate to the employer that would normally be included in a résumé. Implied claims, on the other hand, are beliefs that are unstated by the candidate and unasked by the employer. For example – the employer believes the candidate does not have any existing contractual restrictions that would prevent him from performing the job. The employer often just assumes that there are no active non-compete agreements, no undisclosed felony convictions, no professional license revocations, and no outstanding warrants. Remember, employees are never better than when they are on paper.

Claims Expressed

Résumés or vitae have a familiar progression of personal and professional information. All of the information is stated and expressed by the candidate, and presumed to be true. These claims include education, employment history, age (sometimes), credentials, professional licenses, references and the identity of the applicant.

Education

Read this section carefully. The four or five lines detailing an applicant's education are very telling. Does it say a degree was received, or does it simply state that a university was attended for four years? In *all* instances, verify educational claims.

> When writing my first book, "Due Diligence for the Financial Professional," I carried around 3-inch ring binders and tried to jot down all the information that was whirling in my head. During this period, a dear friend of mine introduced me to a "bellicose bundle of goo" at a lunch meeting. This man went on and on about all of his accomplishments. We could have saved half the day if he had simply avoided the pronoun "I." In this conversation, he bragged about his days at the U.S. Naval Academy. He talked about all the famous officers he had gone to school with, and his lips just kept flapping about all the wonderful things he had done in his life. I excused myself, and picked up one of my binders that had the address and telephone number for the verification of educational credentials at the Naval Academy. In one phone call – and less than three minutes – I was able to verify that (1) he had not graduated, (2) and he had never attended. Actually, he never even applied.

> The operator was very forthright, she said "Thank you for calling sir, we've had several calls about him."

I thanked her and returned to the lunch table, where I listened to a few more fictional war stories. In time, a thought crept into my head. Could I con the con man? I looked at both of my guests and said "This relationship we are beginning to foment requires a fine brandy and hearty dessert." Everyone laughed and agreed. I located the most expensive brandy I could find on the menu, and asked the waiter if he had anything better – unfortunately, he did not. We drank the brandy (which I will add, was excellent). We ate the dessert, and I then took to the side of my friend (who had introduced me to this bellicose tub of goo), looked at our imposter, and said "I never want to hear from you again." I dragged my friend out of the restaurant. When outside, my friend was stuttering – befuddled by my behavior. I told him what I had learned from my phone call to the Naval Academy, and declared our lunch companion to be a liar. As such, I thought it was our duty to stick him with the bill. We had a wicked laugh. I may have just confessed my only quasi-successful con of a good con man (maybe).

It's also important to check the accreditation of the university from which the applicant claims to have obtained his degree. There are hundreds of diploma mills operating around the world. In 2008 the state of Washington raided a diploma mill that had issued fraudulent high school, college and postgraduate degrees to more than 9,600 people. The state of Washington did something very unique and honorable – it released the names of all people it could identify who had patronized the diploma mill. Many of them were working in the government, military and health care professions. It's not enough to check that an applicant has a degree, you must check if the school is accredited, and not a diploma mill.

Side note: While I say that the state of Washington's actions were unique and honorable – I don't mean to be too generous. There are accredited schools all over the U.S. that are little, if any, more than diploma mills. It has been stated that within the Fortune 500 companies, none give any credit for a high school diploma – they privately test candidates. I would agree with that action. A high school diploma issued in the U.S. doesn't even indicate that the recipient can read, let alone do basic math. The high school diploma is now singularly respected by governmental agencies – civil service and military. Others know better. This is more properly addressed as an issue of honesty than qualifications.

There has also been some excellent private work done by a George Gollin, physics professor by profession and diploma scourge by avocation. The trials and tribulations of his efforts against diploma mills and their patrons and the stunning inactivity by law enforcement is an indication that these types of fraudsters will be with us for a long time.

Employment History

This is probably the second most important representation made by an applicant. You need to carefully review the applicant's dates of employment. A gap of any length between jobs is a red flag. You need to inquire about any gaps that last more than a few months. Also, be aware that applicants may use non-specific dates to cover a gap in employment. One position held from 2004 to 2006 followed by a position held from 2007 to 2009 could conceal unemployment lasting nearly two years out of six.

Pay attention to the number of jobs. Frequent changes in employment could indicate that the candidate is difficult to satisfy, uncertain of his or her career path, or easy for another company to recruit (along with all of your trade secrets and training, of course). Look for a description of responsibilities, and if they are not detailed – ask (remember to avoid assumptions and implied beliefs). Did the applicant accomplish anything specific during their past employment? Identify the progression of their career. Don't look for a succession of titles, as it does not necessarily indicate responsibility. A candidate who presents a variety of titles without specifying any achievement may be covering a series of demotions or lateral moves. Check employment history as far back as you can, and compare it to residential history – especially when a former employer can't be located or has gone out of business.
Check the applicant's age to make sure that it correlates with the dates of their education and employment. In several background investigations we've conducted, we found applicants claiming to be in their mid–40s, making it necessary (based upon the dates of

ment and education) for them to have graduated college they were 11 or 12 years old. We have also seen age inflated so that the applicant appears to be 18 or 21, depending upon the prohibition they are trying to overcome. Age deflation is a common occurrence in former senior executives in their early 50s or 60s, who believe that their age now works against them. Age inflation is most common among young people who want to either serve alcohol or drive commercial vehicles.

Credentials

I would like to make a distinction between credentials and professional licenses.

A non-regulatory body generally issues credentials. Credentials, such as those held by a certified financial planner (CFP), are not government issue. Educational experience is a specific type of credential. Professional organizations and associations that attest to an individual's level of skill, or the completion of certain courses, however, award most credentials. Always check an applicant's credentials by contacting the organization that issued those credentials.

A copy of a certificate is no longer sufficient in verifying credentials, given the state of desktop publishing. If the credentials are considered an important part of the applicant's qualifications, check the level of care the credentialing body takes in researching candidates, and if the organization has a procedure for the revocation or suspension of credentials. In many cases, a credential may be revoked if there is a disciplinary action, or suspended if the member fails to pay annual fees. Bodies that have clearly delineated standards for the revocation of credentials should have their credentials held in higher esteem than those bodies that have no method for the suspension or revocation of credentials other than a failure to pay an annual membership.

Professional Licenses

Regulatory bodies grant professional licenses. Examples of regulatory bodies are: a state medical board (doctors), state board of physical therapy (physical therapists), department of real estate (real estate agents), or a state board of accountancy (CPAs). Almost without exception, information related to these types of licenses are a part of the public record and can be obtained for free or for a nominal charge. The information that is available includes the foundation documents that qualify the professional to obtain a license, as well as any and all complaints, disciplinary actions, suspensions and reinstatements. Almost any licensed professional will have a substantial record that may be of great value to the prospective employer – and there are many different professions that require some form of licensure.

The quality of information supplied by licensing bodies is limited. For instance, the state might tell you that it has issued several letters of concern to a doctor, however, unless those letters escalate to some form of punitive or remedial action, the records are not public. You can generally only get a count, and the dates they were issued. As with credentials, professional licenses that have a procedure for suspension and revocation should be held in higher regard than licenses that merely require the payment of a fee.

Other Licenses

Most adults possess a driver's license, possibly a hunting license, a fishing license, a pilot's license, or a voter identification card. A driving record may contain information such as DUI or DWI convictions, and may indicate patterns of reckless behavior, such as driving without insurance, over the speed limit, and other violations. Voting records provide information (at the time of registration) about where the prospective employee lives, as well as his place of birth and telephone number. Whether the applicant is a Democrat, Republican, Libertarian or Independent is not applicable. Party affiliation has nothing to do with qualifications. However, the revocation of a person's right to vote may indicate a felony conviction, which often results in a loss of civil rights – including the right to vote. The absence of a voting record may indicate that the person is not a legal resident of the state or the country, and is not entitled to vote. In several background checks we conducted for a worldwide manufacturer of electrical components, we found that fully half of the candidates that were not registered to vote, either had a felony conviction or were in the country illegally. The pool was split about equally between felony convictions and illegal immigration, with the majority of the illegal immigrants originating from Australia and Canada.

Identity Theft

Fifteen years ago, this subject wasn't on anyone's radar. Now I find myself addressing identity theft almost daily.

> *A local activist in Scottsdale, Ariz., decided to run for public office as a city council member. After an interview with the local newspaper about his credentials, however, Gary Tredway decided to withdraw from the election, claiming he had leukemia. Shortly thereafter, it was revealed that Tredway's true identity was Howard Mechanic. Mr. Mechanic had been on the run since 1970 after being convicted of a federal felony in Missouri, and sentenced to five years in prison. He skipped bail while awaiting appeal. According to federal law enforcement officials, Mechanic obtained his new identity as Gary Tredway presumably from a Black Panther group in Oakland, Calif. With his rich history of convictions, lying, criminal affiliations and deception, what pundit could stifle a chuckle over his run for public office! Sometimes the press actually does its job, and enforces the public sentiment that criminals can run for office only prior to being caught.*

Identity theft is real and it has begun to be used by organized crime and criminal gangs to establish credentials in order to gain access to positions of trust and to orchestrate frauds, usually on a massive scale.

> *Identity predators, in one three-month time span, caused losses in excess of $10 million to several financial institutions in the Boston area. The fraudsters masqueraded as experienced loan officers with exceptional pedigrees. Once they had been hired, they used their positions with the bank to divert large sums of money to their co-conspirators. By the time the problem with the loans was uncovered, the perpetrators had already fled the United States for Europe.*

The perpetrators of this fraud were believed to be members of a Yugoslavian-based crime organization. They specialized in large-scale identity theft, and had operated in several other English-speaking countries, including Australia, New Zealand, United Kingdom, Ireland, Panama and East Africa.

It doesn't take a lot of knowledge to steal another person's identity. All of the references provided by the loan officers in the Boston scandal included names, addresses and phone numbers. An independent check of the references was conducted by one Boston bank. In this case, the person responsible for hiring did not rely on the phone numbers given, instead the person opened a telephone book and contacted the reference at the number listed in the directory. The caller found that none of the referenced institutions had ever heard of the applicant, and the application was denied. The bank thought nothing more about the incident until the story of fraud broke in the Boston newspapers. The fraud had been perpetrated on both the bank's competitors, and less cautious branches of their bank.

Claims Implied

When an introduction takes place, most people make the assumption, absent any evidence to the contrary, that the people they meet are telling the truth and are decent people. We believe this, and yet, we know it isn't true.

Con artists get their name from their ability to gain the confidence of their target. They don't gain people's confidence by being an annoyance – they gain confidence by acting charming, gracious and concerned. They are outgoing and are interested in you, as well as all of the world and all life around them. All good confidence players love puppies, kittens, children and God. That's how they get people to build confidence in them.

Impairment

In the selection process, employers should consider some steps to determine whether a candidate is going to have impairment problems. Many employers do this through tests on urine, blood or hair. Depending upon the risk issues associated with the position, testing is either clearly demanded or subjectively warranted. At the very least, the employer should inform candidates that they are subject to random substance testing. Candidates should also be informed that failing a test may result in termination with cause – and they need to agree with these terms as a condition of employment. This is probably a strong enough policy for low- to medium-risk positions, and can be selectively enforced if problems arise.

I'm not very sympathetic to drug use on the job. I equate abuse of alcohol, prescription medication, and over-the-counter medications to illegal substances. I believe that when someone accepts employment, they have a duty to give their full attention to the job they've been hired to perform. As far as tolerance goes, I'll try to add some reasoning to how I ended up on the far end of the spectrum.

Employers should not hold themselves out to be saints, and they should not hold candidates who are not saints at bay. Everyone should understand that many employers use testing as a method of culling candidates. If you don't address these issues, you will become the victim of adverse selection. Your candidate selection pool will contain a higher percentage of people who cannot work at other locations that do require testing.

I also want to address less obvious forms of impairment. Impairment can come in the form of sleep deprivation or exhaustion. It could come from a long business trip with one hour of sleep before arriving at a morning business meeting. Sometimes people are working two jobs just trying to keep their family together, a roof over their heads, and food on the table. Exhaustion is a real and consistent threat – I would rank it almost as high as drug abuse. People who are sleep deprived should not be driving, or operating any potentially dangerous equipment for that matter. Truck drivers are mandated to take sleep breaks because the federal government recognizes the danger an exhausted driver with a 50,000-pound vehicle presents to the public. And while the federal government recognizes the danger of sleep-impaired drivers, it does not recognize the same danger when it comes to doctors – who are regularly required to perform 24- and 48-hour shifts. Work shifts are not regulated for machine tool operators who may be processing 5-foot wide sheets of steel traveling at 30 miles an hour. Hours are often not regulated for taxi drivers, who will often work 24 hours straight when their leases are due. So, when hiring and scheduling people, be as concerned of the demands of their schedule as you are of substance abuse.

The typical image that Americans have of foreign nationals working in the U.S. is of a low-paid worker, usually in the agricultural, fast food, hotel or hospitality industry. While that is a common perception, there are many foreign nationals working throughout professional communities that have not obtained the necessary visas or permits to do so.

Dr. K. had been working in New York for 11 years as a doctor of inorganic chemistry in the aerospace industry. Dr. K., and the problem of his citizenship, could have continued unknown and unchallenged, probably for the rest of his career, if his group had not been selected to explore non-ferrous coatings in a defense department project dealing with stealth technology (radar absorbing technology). As a matter of procedure, a background check was conducted on every team member assigned to the project. It was found that Dr. K., who had obtained his degrees in the United States, had emigrated from Canada on a student visa. His visa had expired 25 years earlier, and he had not bothered to renew it, apply for a resident alien work permit, or return to Canada. Dr. K. was required to be deported, but his employer declined to fire him, stating that he has been a valuable employee for many years. His employer took full responsibility for (1) not checking the background of Dr. K.'s residency and (2) in having found the discrepancy, working to remedy the situation.

In the process of checking the citizenship of individuals, a check is often made to see if the person has registered to vote. By law, you must be a citizen of the city, state and county in which you have registered in order to vote. In most states, you cannot have a felony conviction, or if convicted, your civil rights need to have been restored. Based upon this definition, many people assume that verification of voting registration is a verification of eligibility to vote. It is not true that registered voters are eligible to vote, or have not been convicted of a felony, because there is no effective mechanism established to suspend the voting privileges of either convicted felons *or* illegals.

Criminal Convictions

Again, it is implied that when one applies for work that one is free of criminal convictions. Please understand that I am not arguing that someone who has a criminal conviction should not be hired. I have hired two people with criminal convictions. I found them both to be excellent workers and excellent individuals. One was convicted of a criminal DUI. It was his wake-up call to stop drinking, to get sober and to become physically and mentally fit and to quit hiding in a bottle. The other person was convicted of a felony for the promotion of gambling. In layman's terms, he was a "bookie," and he got caught. The latter was a bit repentant that he was caught, but not the least bit repentant about running a book (he gave better odds than the state lottery). But what he did realize is that engaging in an illegal activity had been causing his family a great deal of pain and anguish. As such, he became and still is one of the best financial researchers and analysts that I have had the pleasure to work with.

Both of these applicants told me straight out that there were problems in their past. Thus, I made an informed decision of hiring people who had criminal records. Some states, including California, prohibit you from making an informed decision, and in fact have made it a misdemeanor to conduct a criminal records background check prior to employment. Imagine that – a misdemeanor *on the employer* for making an informed decision. As you have, read this has already led to one incident where a man convicted for crimes involving sexual abuse with a minor was looking for work as a janitor while out on parole.

You must conduct a comprehensive check on the background of individuals before you hire them. Included in that check are all public records, federal, state, county and municipal records. Just because an applicant has committed a crime doesn't make him unemployable – it's up to you, the employer, to have the information available to make an informed choice. If you are in a state that makes a criminal background check for employment a chargeable offense, then I would certainly never base a hiring decision upon that knowledge unless it was freely offered by the applicant.

Whose Responsibility Is It Anyway?

Twenty years ago, human resources did it all – hiring, firing, managing benefits and scheduling travel. Today, human resources does little more than manage subcontracts. Placement services are subcontracted, payroll is subcontracted, benefits are subcontracted, and in some cases the entire workforce is subcontracted through employee leasing. So, whose responsibility is it to do background checks on employees? The end consumer of the labor is ultimately responsible to make certain there is an impartial evaluation.

The function of an employee is too important to rely upon a background check conducted by a placement service, a recruiter or an employee-leasing firm. These firms make money when you hire their candidates and retain their employees. Their ability to conduct a comprehensive background check is compromised by their conflict of interest. This is this author's view. If, however, you depend on an interested third party, their claims and responsibilities should be clearly agreed to and defined in your contract.

Placement Services

Placement service companies are paid by the prospective employee to find them positions. It is the function of the placement service company to find a job for their client. Their duty of fidelity lies not with the hiring institution, but with the employee. These firms often claim to perform in-depth interviews and detailed testing for qualifications. I have never worked with a placement service that performed detailed background checks that would result in excluding an employee from being placed or represented by the service. They use "cheap and cheerful" backgrounds

Recruiters

I have had the opportunity to do work for several recruiting firms. Recruiting firms are paid from 20 percent to 50 percent of a prospective employee's annual salary for the successful recruitment and retention of qualified candidates. Recruiters are in high demand by employers for specialized positions and highly technical jobs. The motto of a recruiter is, "The best person for the job is not the one who is looking for a job." Recruiters are keenly aware of the need to conduct background checks. These services are generally detailed in their service agreements, stating that there will or will not be a background check of all prospective candidates by an independent private investigations firm, and detailing who will be responsible for the fees.

Employee Leasing

The conditions, duties, responsibilities and liabilities an employer is exposed to are daily becoming more complex and comprehensive, and as a result many small companies have outsourced all human-relations functions to an employee leasing firm. An employee leasing firm is a firm that will, for a fee, hire your current employees and lease those employees back to you. These businesses perform all of the functions associated with being an employer – except the hiring and firing decisions. The employee leasing firm assumes the function of employer and the liabilities associated with that function, but you are responsible for hiring decisions and the background checks on prospective employees.

General Considerations

Obviously, it is advantageous to hire the best candidate, and not simply the one with the slickest résumé or an ability to interview well. Despite the many hurdles that you may encounter, it is important that background checks are done on prospective employees. There are also legal reasons, such as to protect fellow employees and any third parties with whom the employee may come in contact. While certain conduct may not necessarily expose the employers to legal liability, there is a whole range of employee attributes such as a negative attitude, flash temper, or poor interpersonal skills which may indicate that a particular applicant does not play well with others and ought to be cut before the final round of interviews. The importance of a background check is much more than simply to minimize legal liability. The goal of the employer is to choose candidates with the best chance of success within the organization. It's easy to sort out résumés that don't reflect the experience you desire from an applicant. But how do you proceed with applicants who appear to be perfect on paper?

Analysis of Credentials

As stated earlier, a gap of any length between jobs is a red flag, and nonspecific dates may be used to cover a gap. Total the years of claimed experience, and compare them with the approximate age and level of experience that the candidate has represented. When verifying past work history, ask the employer to provide the dates of employment – try not to simply give them the dates on the application for verification.

Frequent job changes could indicate that a candidate is difficult to satisfy and is uncertain of his or her career choice, or easy for another company to recruit. It may also mean that the person interviews well and has great credentials but is a real pain in the butt to work with.

Look at employment responsibilities. Did the applicant actually accomplish something during his or her terms of employment? Were these accomplishments significant and commensurate with the responsibilities of that position?

On a prospective employee's résumé, you would expect to see a succession of titles indicating increasing responsibilities as they gain experience. Does the position you are filling fit logically into a career progression for this applicant?

Use available databases to confirm a potential employee's Social Security number. Is the person who he says he is, or is he using a false or stolen identity? Try to identify and verify the applicant by name. See additional links at www.feeinc.com for more information.

Most important, throughout the process, scan all available records and information for consistency. This is the real detective work.

Summary

Education: Verify the applicant's educational claims, including fields of study, years attended, degrees received, and all other claims. Do not overestimate the veracity of any applicant, or trust your instincts. Verify.

Employment: Verify all past and present employment history. Verify the employers and their contact information as well. Speak with personnel in human resources, and also ask to speak with supervisors. Speak with everyone you can, including the receptionist. Listen carefully, and try to sense if they are being forthright with their information.

Criminal History: Search federal, state, county and local records for criminal activity or convictions. Courts are subdivided based upon municipalities. A person living in an incorporated city can be subject to the courts of the city, county, justice, state and federal. That's five different courts for one person in one city. The possible jurisdictions are magnified by all of the places a person visits, works, or commutes through. Be thorough in your research. Also check federal and state prison records. Most can be checked online.

Credentials: If a position requires a special certificate or license, you must verify that professional credentials are current and have not been suspended. Verify the type, number, issuing authority, issue date, expiration date, any disciplinary action and current status.

References: Check all references. Personal references are generally going to be more willing to talk with you than past employers. Use reference checks to help build a profile on personality, reputation, character and professional ability. Also do a quick check on the references, ask them about their careers and how they know the candidate. Do the telephone numbers belong to the people you are calling? A reverse phone directory on the Internet can assist in the verification of phone numbers.

Workers' Compensation: According to the Americans with Disabilities Act, a workers' compensation report can be requested once a conditional job offer has been made to an applicant. Running a workers' compensation report helps your company control potentially fraudulent claims, and increases employee safety. The report will generally include, name, address, date of birth, employer and legal representation. Case information includes case numbers, location, injury types, dates and status.

Driver's Record: This is especially important if the applicant will at any time be driving a company vehicle. A driver's record will include driving violations, DUIs/DWIs, accidents, tickets and suspensions.

Bankruptcy Court: A bankruptcy is closely related to the information that is found in a credit report, and can indicate a pattern of financial risk taking. As with a troubled credit report, a bankruptcy needs to be viewed in the context of the circumstances. While checking federal bankruptcy court you can also check civil, criminal and appellate cases.

Other Services: There is a body of modern analysis having to do with more sophisticated employee selection criteria. These selection tools include interviewing, profiling, employee questionnaires, drug tests and even lie-detector tests, all designed to assess a potential candidate for a position. All of these invasive forms of qualifying prospective employees are valid and useful tools, but may not always be relevant. The degree of scrutiny should be commensurate with the amount of contact with the public, the potential effect they could have on the public, the amount and level of contact with other employees within and outside of your company, and the amount of damage or harm that the employee could subject your company to.

Permission: In almost all cases, it is proper to get written permission from a prospective employee before speaking with former employers, requesting copies of credit reports, driver's licenses, and other restricted information. Having written permission allows you to obtain information, it also gives past employers the permission to speak openly without fear of retribution. Requesting consent to do a background check alerts the candidate that you are serious about the representations they have made, that you are serious about confirming them, and are going to be aggressive and thorough in the background research. This does not sound like much. But I am aware of dozens of applicants who, when faced with signing a consent for restricted records, have put up a false front of indignation and stormed out of the interview.

Remember the comment made earlier that one out of four people in sales and marketing have dramatic misrepresentations in their résumé. Our real world experience conducting background checks has shown that one out of seven medical doctors has misstatements in their credentials, and one out of 15 has failed to disclose a material problem in their background. The fatal flaw, in my opinion, is a willingness to lie and misrepresent facts to a prospective employer, a relationship that must be based on trust and mutual respect.

Outsourcing the Background Check

One of the primary functions of private investigators is conducting detailed background checks. Many firms rely on private investigators to handle all of their background checks, usually because they have been burned in the past, and often for hundreds of thousands of dollars. Many human resources departments feel that outsourcing investigations amounts to ceding hiring decisions to the investigator. It should not. A private investigator is a knowledge worker, a specialist in gathering information on people, companies and events. They are information specialists. They are not human resources specialists, and they cannot supplant specialists in hiring decisions. What an investigator can do, relatively quickly, is research the claims made by a prospective employee, determine what needs to be confirmed, and report their findings back to human resources.

To work with a private investigator, it is recommended that the people making the hiring decisions produce a very specific list of their wants and needs. Specific questions from human resources such as, "Should I hire this person?" are inappropriate for the attention of an investigator. The investigator is not a decision-maker, only an information provider. Share as much information with the investigator as possible, the more you share the quicker and less costly the research.

A typical pre-employment background check will cost $100 to $300. A background check known as a "due diligence background check" is primarily associated with insurance, securities, banking, mergers and acquisitions, and can run from $900 to $1,500. The cost for an investigation can be influenced by age, amount and range of experience, and the geographical diversity of those experiences. A young person with little experience living in their hometown will be very easy to research. A person who has traveled extensively, moved frequently, and has had 30 or 40 years of experience with several employers requires more time and energy.

Make it a point to help the private investigator or investigative firm that you work with become familiar with your business and the industry that you operate in.

Follow-Up Background Checks

A follow-up background check is pretty straightforward. Once you hire an employee, that employee's file should be reviewed on a periodic basis.

Follow-up background checks should be part of every employer's policy. The employer, at a minimum, should conduct an annual check on employee licenses, such as driver's license, CPA certification, attorney's membership status with the bar, and teaching credentials. To reiterate, at a minimum, all licenses held by employees to practice the profession they are in should be verified at least every year. A reasonable policy is to conduct a follow-up background check every three years on all employees, annually of key personnel, and before any promotion.

Employees live their lives while they are working in your company. People get into trouble for a variety of reasons, and sometimes, these problems are outside of their control. For example, an employee earning $75,000 per year should not be driving a $125,000 car unless it can be satisfactorily explained. Doctors often have privileges at several different hospitals. Every hospital that has granted privileges to a doctor should maintain an annual litigation review on all of the doctors that have privileges at their hospital. A law firm should ensure that all of its associates and principals have attended the requisite number of continuing legal education courses in a year. A trucking company should verify that drivers haven't had any violations that would have excluded them from being hired in the first place.

One trucking company I worked with was in the process of buying out a smaller firm. When the purchasing company reviewed the driving records of the drivers for the target company, they found that 7 percent of the drivers had had their licenses either suspended or revoked. Some of the suspensions and revocations were for minor offenses, such as failing to pay a parking ticket. Others were for more serious crimes, such as hit-and-run. Follow-up background checks should be scheduled at least annually for any employee required to be licensed in their profession. Check that their physical therapy license is still in place. Check if they are still a member of the bar in good standing. Check to see that they still hold a valid driver's license.

This type of diligence avoids "red-faced" moments. It is not uncommon for a company when it is to be acquired, to have all of the key employees screened. Many have had significant changes in their lives while at the company. If it is an entrepreneurial company being acquired, there may never have been a background check.

How We Fail

You get what you pay for. There are many firms offering $19, $25 and $50 background checks. I have heard them referred to as "cheap and cheerful." If you think that an inexpensive background check will protect you from liability, you are wrong. Some firms offering background checks are simply information brokers. Some are very good, but they work in an unlicensed and unbonded vocation. Information brokers are often used by private investigators as a source for information, just as law enforcement often uses confidential informants. Most of the information brokers I have met would choose to be private investigators if they had the required training and experience, could pass the licensing requirements and could get bonding. Some of these firms may be adequate for purposes such as tenant screening, it simply depends on how highly you value the property. There is a clue here – choose licensed investigators.

When a company is run with cost and revenue centers, usually the center that is hiring a new person is burdened with the costs associated with the hiring process. But, if that person steals information, fondles a co-worker, robs a client, or worse – it is considered an unpredictable event, and rarely is the center charged with the losses. I argue that most events are not unpredictable, and if a department only performs "cheap and cheerful" background checks, losses from bad employees are almost a certainty. I suggest changing the accounting rules so that employee losses are charged to the department that failed in its duty to perform a proper background investigation. What gets incentivized gets done.

In many of the case studies in this book, employers were held liable for the actions of their employees. In at least two cases I know of, judges have thrown out the claim that the employer satisfied their duty of due diligence simply because they had performed an inexpensive "background check" before hiring. As one judge said, "You got what you paid for, and you didn't pay much."

Rants

People often lie in both social and business settings. Usually it's a harmless effort to make others feel better ("Nice tie!"), or to enhance their importance ("I just came from …"). They embellish the condition of their lives, and promote themselves. Humans seek attention, and people pay a great deal of attention to those who have attained positions of wealth, responsibility and fame. As a rule, liars have no special interest in virtuous people. Liars lie because the recipient of the lie is ignorant about the nature of the events and their conditions – leaving them to rely on faith in the person making the claims, and to trust their own interpretations. You cannot stop people from lying, you cannot even stop them from lying to you, but you can check their representations.

Background checks can and do save lives, not to mention money. It is a matter of fact that when the post office ceased conducting background investigations (to save money), all but one of the postal employees involved in a grisly spate of postal shootings would not have been hired. A rapist would not have been hired by a door-to-door sales company. A man who represented himself as a lawyer would not have been hired by a law firm – only to find out seven years later that he was not a lawyer. A drug addict would not have been placed in charge of a hospital pharmacy. I continue these thoughts in the case studies section.

Think about this ...

We must all be careful of what we expect when performing background checks. If we set the standards so high that we only select people with no blemishes, we set ourselves up for a special case of adverse selection. If we select only people who have made no mistakes in their life, we are hiring:

    a) The very young.

    b) Those who take no risks.

    c) Those with a great ability to get themselves out of trouble.

    d) Those who never got caught.

We will be prone to select the young, lazy, glib and corrupt.

I am not dismissing or discounting the belief that many people are genuinely skilled at reading other people's mental states – their intentions, beliefs and emotions. These are the type of people you want working in your human resources department. Never underestimate the value of your intuition and feelings, but likewise never underestimate the capacity of the fraudster to fake sincerity and concoct good fiction. Proper due diligence, supported by a thorough background investigation, will provide protection when our instincts fail us.

Case Studies

If some of the horror stories you have already read don't convince you about the importance of thorough background checks, I have some more!

Mickey Carter, in 1993, was making his rounds as a Kirby vacuum cleaner salesman. He knocked on the door of Dena Kristi Read and worked his way into her home. Kirby salesmen, as part of their sales demonstration, are required to do in-home presentations. The salesmen gain access to the home by virtue of Kirby's name and reputation. Carter used that reputation to get into Read's home and rape her as her children slept in the next room. Carter was not prosecuted for this sexual assault. He appeared before a judge, and all parties involved agreed that it would be easier to revoke his probation on an unrelated charge of indecency with a child than to go through a new criminal trial. In the civil trial that followed, the court concluded that Carter did indeed rape Read, and awarded damages to her in the amount of $200,000, holding both Kirby Vacuum Cleaner and the Kirby Vacuum Cleaner distributor liable.

The court ruled that the Kirby Company should have required its distributor to do a background check before hiring Carter, who had several previous complaints of sexual misconduct – including at least one conviction. Since, it is a matter of course to use the Kirby name to gain access to a home for the purpose of conducting presentations, Kirby's method of conducting their business poses a real potential danger. Quoting Texas Supreme Court Justice Raul Gonzalez, "A person of ordinary intelligence should anticipate that an unsuitable dealer would pose a risk of harm. Any business that hires any independent contractors is subject to a lawsuit if they do something to harm someone else." Kirby argued that it was the distributor who hired Carter that was negligent for failing to check the criminal records of its sales staff. The company further argued that Kirby only had a duty to hire competent distributors, reasserting that it was the distributor's duty to hire competent salespeople. The court rejected that line of appeal.

The $160,000 does little to console Read for what occurred to her, let alone the six years of court hearings.

beldarblogs.com

Dr. John Biskind had practiced medicine in many states; he was licensed, or had been licensed, in six different states. His story is a chilling example of how the public is not protected from professionals just because they are licensed.

Patient 1. Dr. Biskind tried to abort a fetus that he thought was 10-weeks old when it was, in reality, 27-weeks old. For that, Dr. Biskind earned a letter of concern.

Patient 2. The patient was a 26-year-old female from Flagstaff, Arizona. Dr. Biskind began working on her at 10:33 a.m. She didn't see the sunset that day. The coroner ruled the cause of death to be a massive intra-abdominal hemorrhage due to laceration of the uterus during a pregnancy termination.

Patient 3. Dr. Biskind began performing an abortion on a 17-year-old girl. He diagnosed her as being 23-weeks pregnant. She was 37-weeks pregnant. Dr. Biskind ended up delivering, at the A–Z Women's Center in Arizona, a baby girl, 6 pounds, 2 ounces, born with a fractured collarbone and lacerations all over her body.

Patient 4. Dr. Biskind performed an abortion on Lou Anne Herron. The attending nurses kept trying to get Dr. Biscayne to come back to see Lou Anne. They said she looked gray and pale. He refused to check on her. She bled to death in three short hours.

Why does a doctor practice medicine in *six* different states? First, Dr. Biscayne got into trouble in Ohio and several states surrounding Ohio. His former practice partner, Nabil Nashed Ghali, was so sloppy and callous as to cause the death of tens of young women, during or after he had convictions, suspensions, and revocations in Kentucky, Ohio, Utah, Florida, New York and California. So while Dr. Biskind and his practices were known in Ohio and surrounding states, Dr. Biscayne was forced to move his practice thousands of miles to Arizona and commute between Arizona and Ohio in order to keep practicing his brand of medicine.

lifenews.com, highbeam.com

Martin Frankel. He would be remembered as a kind of a goofy, twitty, geeky little fellow if he had not orchestrated the disappearance of between $350 million and $3 billion. Our concern with Frankel's life begins in the late 1980s. The facts show quite convincingly that he was not a financial whiz – but rather a greedy and bumbling fool who traded stocks. The authorities first learned about Frankel in 1988 when John Herlihy, a decorated World War II pilot and retired salesman, contacted them pleading for help. His life's savings were tied up in an obscure investment called the Frankel Fund. The fund's creator and manager, Martin Frankel, was unable to return the money. He was, of course, either the predecessor or student of Bernie Madoff and Sir Allen Stanford – and all were diligent students of someone less known in the current press, Charles Ponzi.

Back to Frankel. The relationship between the broker Frankel and the client Herlihy had grown increasingly strained after Frankel abruptly moved from Toledo, Ohio, to West Palm Beach, Fla. Frankel told his clients he would be better able to manage their money from there. While his clients worried about their investments, Frankel (who previously operated the brokerage firm from a bedroom in his parent's house, and later from a house he had bought across the street) was living in a waterfront home in a fashionable area of West Palm Beach. Queen Anne of Romania, whom he bragged about often, owned the home. He claimed that she and several others of royal lineage, including King Michael of Romania, had invested in the Frankel Fund. He always managed to talk about mingling with people who had a lot of money – but the money that was supporting his lifestyle came from checks he was writing against the Frankel Fund. He used that fund as a personal bank account. Frankel said that during his brief stay in West Palm Beach, he had installed six phone lines for machines to monitor the stock market, and to make trades. According to court depositions, Frankel Fund investors received rosy reports describing the huge gains they were making.

In reality, there was little trading, due to an unusual personality quirk. In a deposition before the U.S. Securities and Exchange Commission, Frankel claimed he suffered from a condition that he called Trader's Block. He described the phobia as an inability to "pull the trigger and put the money on the line." In short, his anxieties were preventing him from trading stock. At one point, he hired another broker to carry out the work. Frankel told SEC investigators that the condition affected his life in other ways too. He never graduated from the University of Toledo, in part, he said, because he would take a course, do the work, comprehend the material, but freeze when it came time to take final exams. "I was always the brightest student in all my classes," he told SEC investigators.

After leaving Utah in 1975, Frankel went 10 years without finding a full-time job. He worked briefly as a busboy and later as a real estate salesman. He finally admitted that he had exaggerated his accomplishments as a money manager. In fact, he admitted that by the mid-eighties he was managing half a million dollars for 10 to 15 clients. He conceded that his grandiose promotional material for Frankel Fund was also exaggerated. The fund was described as a nearly fail-safe and conservative investment fund with limited stock trading. In fact, the fund lost about $130,000 in poor stock trades, most carried out by Frankel's partner, Douglas Maxwell. In actuality, the fund had only a handful of investors – and when a retired oil executive pulled out his six-figure investment, the fund collapsed. By this time, Frankel had returned to Toledo from Florida in a frenzied state. As usual in these cases, Frankel and his partner Maxwell blamed each other – and when the SEC turned its investigation toward Frankel, he was banned from trading stocks. But Frankel wasn't down for long. In 1991, according to lawyers, he paid cash for a $73,000 Mercedes Benz. The broker won the trust of investors, "not because he was slick, but he was disarming and his personality traits made him an unlikely swindler," according to an investor. The Frankel Fund was only an incubator for the monster that came later. As a result of events in Toledo in 1992, Frankel was stripped of his stockbroker's license.

In his last venture, alluded to above, the eccentric "investor" was accused of fleecing between $350 million and $3 billion before he disappeared in May of 1999. Interpol sent out an alert to 160-plus member nations to stop and detain Frankel as a criminal suspect. He was found in Germany, convicted in 2002 and sentenced to 16 years. His maneuvers are truly monumental.

Even after being stripped of his stockbroker's license, he moved to

Greenwich, Conn. (1993-1994), to begin one of the most elaborate frauds in U.S. history. Within a few years, he managed to become the sole investor for several insurance companies. He even set up an unregistered stock brokerage on his four-acre estate to manage the funds. One day, as his limousine was transporting him to the Westchester County Airport, firefighters responded to an automatic fire alarm at his mansion. They found flames in two fireplaces and a file cabinet burning in the kitchen – but no one home. It appeared to investigators that someone was trying to burn documents and records, but never finished the job because the alarm went off. Among the records found were wire transfers and astrological charts with questions such as, "Will I go to prison?" and "Should I leave?" Federal affidavits showed that at least $85 million was wired to Swiss bank accounts in the last eight weeks before Frankel fled.

nytimes.com, cbsnews.com

Robert D. Cornell. Robert Cornell is described as an absolutely charming, disarming and delightful dinner partner. He was a fixture at a Phoenix Baptist church. He began all of his meetings with a prayer, and wished God's blessings upon all who crossed his path. Cornell is an expert in oil and gas, and was a recognized member in good standing of the Oil and Gas Producers Association. He used all of his credentials and charm, along with the disarming prayers, to establish and fund Jet Drilling and American Methane. In this venture, $6.5 million went missing.

Cornell represented Jet Drilling as a company working with American Methane to drill for coal-bed methane throughout Kansas. His companies claimed to have acquired the rights to several existing oil and gas wells on top of a large coal-bed seam that contained methane. Slick brochures, four-color glossy geology reports, and testimony from coal-bed methane experts all added to the hype surrounding the sale of company stock. Records show that Cornell raised money across the country for this scam. Investors included a blind man in Ohio, and a blind wheelchair-bound MS victim in New Mexico. Records also show the money was diverted to the purchase of real estate in Florida, and to several companies incorporated in Nevada and Arizona that functioned as his alter ego. The money raised for this business venture was spent on living expenses. This was a lifestyle ploy, not a business play. Calls to the Kansas Division of Oil and Gas produced very straightforward answers. To quote the head of the Kansas State Oil and Gas Division, "There is no methane associated with that coal, there never has been and there never will be." Further, the rights purported to be owned and controlled by Cornell may have been leased, but none of them were filed. There was no authority given or permits issued which would allow Cornell to drill or access any oil or gas – whether it existed in reality or only in his mind.

None of this should have been surprising to anyone. Cornell was an expert. He was an expert at raising money for companies before driving them into the ground. Investigators were able to find 13 companies that Cornell had looted – all predating Jet Drilling and American Methane.

caselaw.com, findlaw.com

Peter Michaels. There was plot of land between San Diego and Los Angeles that Michaels wanted to develop. But, he wanted to develop the land with investor funds. So, he did what a lot of real estate developers do – he rented some heavy equipment and moved some dirt around. He rented the equipment from Hertz Leasing, and when Michaels didn't pay the lease, Hertz went to the property and picked up the equipment. A lease bill was sent to Michaels, but he wouldn't pay it. At this point, Hertz began researching this customer, and found that several of his credit references were phony. Hertz referred the matter to the county attorney general's office, and a grand jury indictment came down against Peter Michaels and his entity. The county prosecutor didn't understand why this civil matter had turned up on his desk, but he was more than happy to allow Michaels to pay the bill and have a misdemeanor charge against his company. What the prosecutor failed to do was check into the "phony" references. One of them was the Upland Hills Bank. It appears that Michaels had taken out an advertisement in the yellow pages that included a beautiful rendering of the bank, complete with landscaping. The bank, including the provided address, did not exist. The phone number rang on the last line in the rollover at Michaels' office. Anyone calling the Upland Hills Bank for a reference would get a glowing reference on Michaels. The only people who answered that line were Michaels and his secretary. A check of the municipal courts in Orange, Los Angeles and Riverside counties would have revealed numerous debts left by Michaels and his entities.

Building on this pattern of lies and deceit, Michaels needed a new plan to help bury his past "mistakes." He hatched plans to build a bigger enterprise – World Wide Web Casinos. WWW Casinos raised more than $12 million. A small part of that money was used to pay fines and settle with Hertz, leaving the balance for housing, lifestyle, and trips around the world. Michaels was such a bad character that WWW Casinos could not obtain a gaming license in either the former Soviet republics or on the island nation of Antigua. Stock sales of WWW Casinos continued unabated, despite the issuance of official cease-and-desist letters by several states.

Abandoning WWW Casinos, Michaels went on to launch Hop-On Inc. It was promoted as a disposable cell phone company, but was actually displaying off-the-shelf technology from Nokia and claiming it as its own. Michaels was arrested in 2003 on fraud charges related to WWW Casinos. In 2005, he was fined $100,000 and sentenced to eight months in prison followed by three years of probation for a fraud involving more than $12 million.

Assuming that Michaels' probation was over in late 2008, he felt free to make an announcement that Hop-On would introduce an Android enabled phone at the Las Vegas Consumer Electronics Show in January 2009. What is its claim to fame? Hop-On will introduce a mobile casino. On its Web site, the company claims that this new application *"Brings the Excitement of Las Vegas, Macau and Monaco to Cell Phones, PDAs and Satellite TV."*

I would like to inform you that the Hop-On Web site, http://hop-on.com, is still active as of this writing – in case any readers want to invest.

sfgate.com, stockpatrol.com, vcresearch.com

Dr. Lucky, aka Two Thumbs. Investigators were hired to conduct a background check into Dr. Lucky, aka "Two Thumbs," when he was hired by a local hospital. The hospital's insurance carrier informed the hospital that Dr. Lucky could not be added to its malpractice policy, but declined to state why. A background check into Dr. Lucky revealed that he had medical licenses in Arizona, Nevada and California. There were no board complaints against him. Searching the civil litigation records in San Diego and Riverside counties, 15 lawsuits were found featuring Dr. Lucky's name with 14 of them listing him as the defendant, and one as the plaintiff. Researching these cases revealed that the 14 cases against Dr. Lucky were malpractice cases – seven of which had been settled adversely, and seven which were still pending. In the single case where the doctor was the plaintiff, he was suing an attorney who had represented several of the plaintiffs that had won judgments. According to the investigator, the attorney was forthright when he stated "honestly, after several depositions, I got tired of the good doctor making faces at me, yelling at me, and threatening me, so I stood up, grabbed him by the shirt and punched him." The investigator asked, "Was it worth the $25,000 judgment he got against you?" The attorney responded "Absolutely. We just offset it against the other claims we have pending."

One of the more outrageous statements made by Dr. Lucky was that he had fallen off a ladder, injured his arm, and was collecting $17,000 a month in disability. He further claimed that the effects of this disability caused him to keep botching the plastic surgery that he performed on noses and breasts. As the defendant's attorney stated, "It is an interesting defense. Insurance fraud as a defense against malpractice." The nickname 'Two Thumbs' should have raised some concern – as it turned out, he was 'All Thumbs.'

An NASD licensed stock brokerage firm in Boca Raton, Fla., was shut down by the Florida Securities Commission. The state accused the firm of a variety of offenses, including, failing to issue receipts for customer money, unauthorized trading, churning, and several instances of fraud. Following an investigation into the registered representatives associated with the firm, it was learned that all 20 of them had a prior history and similar complaints in the states they had left to join forces in Florida.

Dr. Michael Swango may turn out to be one of the world's most prolific serial killers. It is estimated that he has killed up to 60 people. He has been described as an odd boy – more or less from his beginning. He had a troubled youth, and a troubled life. In a short synopsis of his career, Swango went to medical school in Illinois and Ohio, worked as an emergency medical technician in Illinois, then did residency training in South Dakota and New York. After attempting to join the American Medical Association (AMA), a background check forced him to leave the country, and he spent several years at a hospital in Zimbabwe.

Here's a longer version. While serving as an intern in Ohio, it is documented that Swango poisoned several patients. Some recovered, some sustained lifelong injuries, and some died. When it was brought to the attention of the medical staff responsible for his education and supervision, they conducted an investigation. The investigation concluded that all of the witnesses were somehow delusional or medically incompetent, and thus none of their testimony could be considered material. No outside investigative agency was brought in. Several of the doctors who conducted the did not interview any of the witnesses. None of the physical evidence was identified, secured or stowed.

Leaving Ohio, Swango went to work as an emergency medical technician in Illinois. While there, he poisoned his co-workers. He was found guilty and spent a year and a half in prison.

After forging several critical documents to cover his past, Swango was hired as a resident and practiced at the Veterans Hospital of South Dakota. Several more incidents occurred there. This is when he applied for membership in the AMA, which notified the Veterans Hospital of Swango's past, and he was dismissed.

After Swango's past activities had been identified, and his prior history discovered, he went to New York – where he worked as a resident in psychiatry at the Northport Veterans Affairs Medical Center. This is where the AMA finally caught up with him, and he was discharged.

At this point Swango was well known to the AMA. He began seeking employment in Africa, and he found it in Zimbabwe. Swango continued to poison both patients and those working around him. When he was run out of Zimbabwe, he looked for work practicing medicine in other African nations, but when the Public Health Services in Zimbabwe alerted other African nations about Swango, he was driven out of the continent. Swango was then hired by a hospital in Jeddah, Saudi Arabia, but was picked up on an outstanding federal warrant when he returned to the United States to obtain a visa for travel.

At all times, after leaving school in Ohio, the facts about Michael Swango were available – and most were public records. These records were never checked.

Blind Eye, by James B. Stewart

James Castelano applied for the position of payroll manager at Mesa Airlines. The airline liked him, and the deal was sealed after the placement firm who had located Castelano faxed the results of its reference checks. A representative for the placement firm, Robert Half International, wrote that after talking to a woman listed as Castelano's former supervisor at the REBS Corp., "If you are looking for negatives in a reference, this is not the one you are looking for. She couldn't say enough good. I will keep digging."

The next day, Robert Half International sent over the results from a second reference check, this one from a man listed as controller of REBS Corp. It appeared that Castelano was everything he had touted himself to be (and everything he really was not). The airline found out too late. Castelano was fired within two months after being accused of embezzling more than $30,000 from the airline. The glowing references, it turns out, came from Castelano's wife and a family friend. Both of the telephone numbers Castelano provided for references rang to a voice mail answered by the same person, Janet with REBS Corp. The company had no listed telephone number, and state records show that it was incorporated in 1997, a year after Castelano said he started working there. It appears that just about everything on his résumé was a fabrication. Mesa Airlines remains in disbelief over the costly incident, and point an accusing finger at Robert Half. The airline had paid the firm a $12,000 placement/referral fee for Castelano, and filed a lawsuit against the placement firm alleging breach of contract. They filed a separate lawsuit against Castelano and his wife. Despite the Robert Half representation to "keep digging," Mesa Airlines officials said the firm never really delved in Castelano's background or references. If the firm or the airline had done even a small amount of research, they would have found that Castelano never attended Georgetown University, and he did not graduate with a degree in business management. They would have found that Dream Sports Entertainment, an employer not listed on his résumé, sued Castelano in Maricopa County Superior Court in 1997 alleging the theft of $50,000 in property. Castelano was suspected of staging the theft of the company's computer equipment, was arrested by Tempe police, and accused of filing a false burglary report. According to a Phoenix Police Department report, Computer City (another employer not on his résumé) fired Castelano as a store manager after accusing him of operating a credit card scheme. Castelano admitted to refunding $3,200 in fictitious computer purchases to his own credit card. Toys-R-Us, where Castelano said he served as a payroll manager from November 1989 to May 1996, has no record of his employment. Family members told police that Castelano never worked for REBS Corp. During the time he stated he worked for REBS, his real jobs included a Circle K convenience mart, and his undisclosed positions with Computer City and Dream Sports Entertainment. Castelano could not have served in the Marines for four years, gone to Georgetown for four years, and worked in corporate payroll departments for nine years – all by the age of 31. A Robert Half employee had even noted the number of years next to each résumé entry, but apparently did not notice that they totaled 17, indicating that he joined the Marines when he was 14. A more detailed review of Castelano's past would have revealed a 1989 chapter 7 personal bankruptcy filed in Washington, D.C. Castelano and a former wife listed $15,000 in credit card balances, and other secured debt. In the filing, his military occupation is listed as an administrative clerk – not as a social aide to President Ronald Reagan as his résumé claims. According to the Marine Corps, he enlisted as a private and left as a lance corporal. It is unlikely that he could have ever qualified as a social aide, which is part of the protocol office and includes the responsibility of managing visiting dignitaries.

Castelano's story shows what most con men already know – that employers, especially in a tight labor market, are often lax in checking references and background.

thefreelibrary.com, flightglobal.com, and court documents

Mr. Morris Wolff, a former utilities director for the Arizona Corporation Commission, was fired after the Associated Press found several discrepancies on his résumé. Among other things, Wolff claimed that he had advised former South African President, F. W. de Klerk and the Truth and Reconciliation Commission. Two high ranking South African officials said they had never heard of him.

ap.com, phoenixnewtimes.com

Mr. Smith. In one case I worked on, a Mr. Smith and Mr. Jones got into a row. It seems Smith sold Jones a business. Smith's representations of the business were less than accurate, and Jones felt he was taken advantage of. Jones stated that he wasn't interested in paying the full purchase price for the business, and in fact, he was done paying Smith anything. Smith threatened to get a lawyer. Jones said, "If you sue me, I will kill you." Well, Smith did indeed file a lawsuit, and about 15 days later, the newspaper reported that Jones was arrested for hiring a hit man to kill Smith and one of his co-workers. Smith was nervous for a long period of time after that. During a rafting trip, Jones fell off the raft, sank, and was never heard from again. Smith sued Jones' estate for the deficiency on the sale of the business. The estate, in the meantime, was in bankruptcy court. After several years of litigation, Smith was awarded $5,000, while his attorney's bills were almost $3,000. Smith went to his attorney's office and got a check for $2,000. However, when the attorney deposited the $5,000 check from the bankruptcy trustee, it bounced. The attorney called the trustee, who said, "I didn't issue a bad check. Smith came by and told me that you had lost the original, so I issued him a new one." As a consequence, Smith received $2,000 from his attorney and another $5,000 from the bankruptcy trustee for an overall take of $7,000 on a $5,000 award, of which he was due $2,000. I was hired by a very angry attorney to find out if Smith had any assets. In the attorney's file on Smith were many letters from doctors and psychologists that said Smith was so traumatized by the events with Jones that he could not find work or hold down a job. At the secretary of state's office, I found a trade name for an automobile leasing company registered in Smith's name. At the department of motor vehicles, I found more than 70 vehicles licensed to this entity. These vehicles had an average value of $5,000, for a total of about $350,000. Not only had Smith been working, he was also collecting disability insurance. Since the assets were not in his name, he thought it was untraceable. As a result of the investigation, the attorney collected $7,000 plus collection costs.

– Sanitized case file –

Follow-up Background

Larry Miles was a truck driver for Tri-Ox Shipping and Handling. Tri-Ox had performed a comprehensive background check on him before he was hired. Several years later, he found himself in an unhappy relationship, which he kept trying to work out. He thought that by purchasing his wife expensive gifts, a large home in the suburbs, and expensive vacations, he would be able to hold onto her. His hopes were misplaced, and when his wife left him she sued for alimony and child support. He had been spending $200,000 a year on gifts, vacations, mortgage payments and private schools. He responded to the divorce petition with an affidavit showing that he only made $65,000 per year. After a complex set of legal maneuvers, he finally admitted that he kept his family afloat by stealing cargo from his employer. By his best estimate, he had stolen $5 million worth of cargo and valuables that he had sold for approximately $1.5 million. Occupational theft is real and occurs every day. The average occupational theft, or the amount an employee steals from an employer is $485,000 and occurs over a long period of time. A follow-up background on Larry would have shown that he was living outside his means.

This is the same problem that finally tripped up Aldrich Ames, who stole secrets from the United States and sold them for millions of dollars to the former Soviet Union. He claimed that his wife had inherited large sums of money from her uncle in Colombia. His wife, Rosario, had no uncle in Colombia, which could have been verified by a simple phone call to her father – who was listed in the telephone book. Aldrich Ames was driving a Jaguar that easily cost as much as he made in a year. The CIA did have a protocol for follow-up background checks; the problem is the agency failed to follow it.

Final Note

In most of the preceding cases, any small amount of diligence and care applied to the express claims made by the applicants would have exposed their lies. If employers had used the services of a private investigator, for a fee of a few hundred dollars before or after hiring, they would have likely identified the fatal flaws in these representations.

Chapter 5

Financial Investigations

"The first duty of a man is the seeking after and the investigation of truth."
Cicero

A person's financial life is almost inseparable from other aspects of their life, and to a large degree this entire book is about financial investigations. To dedicate a chapter to it, to segregate it, to bring attention to it – may seem deceptive to the reader. What this chapter contains are a few thoughts that didn't fit anywhere else. This is an overview.

Financial investigations produce value and have applications in many areas.

• Mergers and Acquisitions	• Financing	• Underwriting
• Compliance	• Asset Location	• Verification of Ownership
• Asset Recovery	• Litigation	• Judgment Enforcement
• White Collar Crime	• Money Laundering	• Divorce
• Intellectual Property	• Critical Information	• Trade Matters

Financial investigations have applications in financing activities, financial transactions and financial crimes. The most important technique that I want to emphasize in financial investigations is a multidisciplinary approach. Nobody can understand how information and people will interact. Every researcher brings a different bundle of life skills to their task, and has to rely upon their individual talents. One of those skills should be to understand when you would benefit from the help of people with other skills.

An investigation or due diligence research project is simply researching information that is going to be consumed in making decisions – usually a financial decision. If your research is meant to be completed prior to a decision, it is considered a due diligence investigation. If the research is being done after a fraud is committed, it is considered an asset recovery or litigation support investigation. The work being done and the skill sets used are identical - the research is described based upon how it will be consumed, not upon how the research takes place or what the researcher is doing.

By way of example, the field of economics is simply research and investigations into human activity. As any of you who have studied economics understand, the field has two camps that are diametrically opposed. One group observes what *has* happened, and attempts to explain why – these are the believers in spontaneous order and the hidden hand. The second group has a *vision*, and attempts to explain how to get there – these are people who believe they can shape the world order. As an investigator, you must identify with the former group, as there will be many times you require the help of a hidden hand. As investigators, we are interested in truth, not philosophy.

> *"The curious task of economics is to demonstrate to men how little they really know about what they imagine they can design."*
>
> F. A. Hayek

All research begins with some initial expectations. These assumptions may be taken from an offering memorandum, financial statement or résumé – but they are just as likely to be a conclusion developed by one or more hypotheses constructed by the investigator. The hypothesis is nothing more than a proposed explanation for the fact patterns that are being observed. For example, it appears that Mr. Pinguis Caput Capitis is an able fraudster, and is still in possession of seventy of the three hundred million dollars he romanced out of little old ladies. Taking this hypothesis as an approximation of where your investigation should begin, you can begin to develop tests to conclude whether this information is true. This is a fixed and measurable hypothesis. A more difficult hypothesis would state that Pinguis Caput Capitis is the leader and mastermind of a vicious fraud. In the latter example the hypothesis has degrees of proof, and evidence to support it will be much more subjective. Good questions have only one answer – that answer may force you to recast the hypothesis, it may be arrived at differently, and interpreted differently – but it will be an answer.

The ideal approach to any investigation, even a small one, is a multidisciplinary approach. A useful method is to have one person conduct an investigation and make a presentation to their peers. The investigator should discuss their initial assumptions and hypotheses, the circumstances of the investigation, and what has been discovered. The investigator should then present the details of the work that has been done. I can guarantee that other researchers will have insights that the initial investigator did not. The more diverse the backgrounds of the group, the closer you will get to answering your questions. I cannot stress enough the value of including peers with different skills and backgrounds. An attorney will have one set of insights, an accountant another, a chemist or a plumber even more. Men and women, young and old – they are all different. As long as they can think, use them.

I stress the creation of a foundation and hypothesis along with a multidisciplinary approach to investigations because most failed investigations are due to a lack of perception – the inability of one person to ask all of the right questions.

What is Money?

There is almost nothing as alluring as money. Whatever "enough" is, it certainly is a moving target. In spite of the gains I've made in life, and all the goal posts I've passed, I've never lost the feeling that I could use a little bit more. I think it was J. P. Morgan who was once asked by a reporter in New York, "Mr. Morgan, now that you are one of the wealthiest people on the face of the earth, how much more money would you like?" Morgan responded with a rueful smile, "a little more."

Money represents freedom. This is a universal belief, and it applies to good and bad people without discrimination. It is believed that money provides freedom to do what you want, when you want – and this belief is the trap that ensnares financial criminals. They are only in business for the money – money to free them from their needs, and money to indulge all of their wants and desires. Financial freedom allows them to eat the best food, drive the best cars, and live in the biggest house. It allows them to have a lot of little toys – boats, computers, stereos, snowmobiles, and oftentimes, people. Wealth brings about another intoxicating feeling; people treat the rich with envy and admiration (envy is usually disguised as admiration). No matter how the wealthy have achieved their money, most people will show a degree of admiration. Those who have earned their wealth will usually respond to this deference differently than those who have stolen it. For the honest man, it may be an embarrassment – but for the criminal, it will be an incentive to keep him hunting for more – and to continue flaunting what he's got.

Money criminals are conspicuous consumers of money. They live and spend as if it's not their money, because – *it's not their money!* They will buy a Lamborghini or a Maserati, but never an Annuiti. Money criminals want all the freedom they believe money can buy them, so they spend with reckless abandon. This is a trait to pay attention to! It's natural that the more money we consume, the bigger our appetite gets. Honest people, out of necessity, learn to control that appetite – the criminal rarely does.

While profligate spending is a common trait in those who spend other people's money, it's rarely as indiscriminate as the criminal's behavior. Even trust funds have limits, and politicians must account to voters – the criminal mind recognizes few limits.

Embezzlers and Fraudsters

There is, arguably, a pattern that all embezzlers follow. They always begin by embezzling small amounts of money. Once they realize that they can embezzle small amounts without being caught, they will take more and more until eventually the sums become so large, someone will notice – and they risk being caught. Embezzlers are caught primarily because the amount they have been taking increases to the point where it can no longer escape detection. Why is that? The initial impulse to embezzle is usually prompted by a temporary setback. They simply needed a little extra money to pay their mortgage, so they took a few hundred dollars, and realized that it was pretty easy. Nobody asked them any questions the next day, and everything at work was the same as usual. They don't feel bad, and they begin to rationalize their actions. Nobody cares. It's a big company. My employer is a wealthy man. No one even noticed it was missing.

The criminal's appetites will soon direct his activities. "To get that new car, I would only have to steal a little bit – I can do that. A couple of hundred, or a couple thousand a month won't amount to much." And so it continues.

I worked one case for a few short hours. I received a call from a friend in the medical practice consulting business. He had "run the numbers" for one of his clients, and was certain that there were problems. "Something is wrong, and we think it may be something you can help us with."

I asked one question. "When is the last time the bookkeeper took a vacation?" I heard him ask the doctor. He replied, "She has been working here three years and she has not taken a vacation in the last two." I suggested that two years ago is probably when the embezzlement began. I asked them to shut down the business as normal, and meet me at their offices an hour after closing. In the bookkeeper's computer we found two ghost employees, and three ghost suppliers who, over a period of two years, had been paid a total of $235,000. It was a tragedy. This doctor had been scraping to keep this practice together, to keep people employed. He had to let one nurse go because the practice couldn't maintain the proper cash flow. The doctor had made several large personal sacrifices. Such crimes hurt real people. There is nothing victimless about financial crimes.

Detection

Means vs. Ability Test

One of the best ways to detect money criminals is to look at their means vs. ability. How does their actual lifestyle compare with their stated financial ability? Given their income and financial disclosures, does their lifestyle make sense?

A few years ago, I had a case with an entrepreneur who had raised millions of dollars prior to declaring personal and business bankruptcy. In court he was required to produce the last several years of tax returns. Over the period that he and his wife had operated the business, they jointly reported an income of $3,000 a year. I found this interesting, since they were driving a new Cadillac and living in fashionable Scottsdale, Arizona. None of the attorneys seemed too interested until the couple's bankruptcy disclosure showed that they were making $4,280 per month and needed $5,000 a month to make ends meet. During the deposition, he stated that he purchased the new Cadillac when he traded in his three-year-old Lincoln. He stated categorically that they needed $5,000 a month to live. Yet they only reported $3,000 in annual income. The IRS Criminal Investigations Division (CID) took interest in these disclosures – the bankruptcy trustee and the bankruptcy court, however, did nothing. In the end, with the help of the bankruptcy court, this man shut down the company and frustrated his creditors. In less than a month he was able to set up a new company, purchase the assets of the old company out of bankruptcy, and continue operating free and clear of all liens and debt. Quite frankly, he won! He did not have the stated ability to afford the lifestyle he was living. This is a good example of a means vs. ability test, and why money criminals can be easy to spot.

When conducting investigations you need to look for activity. Activity necessitates transactions, transactions produce documents and other participants. What we are looking for are nouns: cash, cars, houses, boats, bank accounts, art, jewelry and companies. After identifying things, you have to find the activity, the transaction. There will be checks, contracts, insurance, appraisals, sellers, brokers, registrations, licenses, and any number of other leads that you can follow.

Business Types and Uses

In any investigation, it is important to understand that the business structure surrounding a person legally defines their liability. Many structures create "fictitious" people that largely isolate the owner from liability. If you are not familiar with business structures, the following is a summary.

Sole Proprietorship

A sole proprietorship (also known as a "Schedule C business") is wholly owned by one individual. The characteristics of a sole proprietorship are:

1. The owner has unlimited liability.
2. The owner (rather than the entity) pays income tax.
3. The sole proprietorship has a limited life, and
4. Assets of the sole proprietorship are held in the owner's name.

General Partnership

A general partnership is an entity created by agreement (oral or written) between two or more parties to combine assets, labor and/or skills in a business, and share the profits and losses. Profits and losses do not have to be shared equally.

The characteristics of a general partnership are:

1. The partners have unlimited personal, joint and several liability.
2. The partners pay income tax on earnings of the partnership.
3. The partnership has a limited life.
4. The partners have a right to bind the partnership and/or the partners by their individual acts (absent agreement

to the contrary) and.

5. Each partner's equity is reflected in his partnership capital account.

Partnership documents you should expect to find are the partnership agreement and agreements detailing how the partnership will operate.

Limited Partnership

A limited partnership is an entity created by written agreement, having at least one general partner and one limited partner. The characteristics of a limited partnership differ from a general partnership in two significant ways.

1. The limited partner's liability is limited to their investment in the partnership.
2. Each limited partner's interest in the partnership is freely transferable.

Documents you should look for are the partnership agreement, subscription documents for the limited partners, and an operating agreement on how the partnership is to be operated.

Corporations - Regular and Subchapter S

A corporation is an entity created by state law, and ownership is evidenced by shares of stock.

The characteristics of a corporation are:

1. There is limited shareholder liability.
2. The corporation has an unlimited life.
3. The rights of the shareholders are determined by state law and the corporate bylaws.
4. The corporation has centralized management.
5. The law allows free transfer of ownership interest.

Corporate documents include charter documents (or articles of incorporation), bylaws, minutes for shareholder and director's meetings, election documents, and annual reports.

A corporation is generally taxed at a different rate than individuals. If the shareholders of a company elect to be taxed under subpart S of the code ("S Corporation"), the shareholders are taxed directly on their proportionate share of the company's total profits or losses.

Limited Liability Companies

(Being that limited liability companies are a relatively new way to organize a business, I have given more space for an explanation of the entity.)

Origin of the Entity

Even though limited liability companies (LLC) have existed for more than a decade, it was not until 1988 that they began to attract widespread attention. Wyoming enacted a limited liability company statute in 1977, and Florida passed a limited liability company statute in 1982. In revenue ruling 88-76, the Internal Revenue Service (IRS), after eight years of study, ruled that a limited liability company created pursuant to the Wyoming Act would be treated as a partnership for tax purposes.

This ruling marked a significant shift in the IRS policy with respect to entities in which the liability of the owners is limited to each owner's agreed upon investment.

Basic Vocabulary

The owners of an LLC are its "members," and their individual economic interests in the LLC are "member's interests" or "interests in the limited liability company." An LLC is formed by filing "articles of organization." At the time of formation, the articles must indicate whether management authority will be vested in one or more "managers" (who need not be members) or will be reserved to the members. The operations of an LLC and the internal rights and obligations of its members and managers may be governed by an "operating agreement" among the members, which may be written or oral.

Documents you will generally find with a limited liability company are the formation documents, the operational agreement between the unit holders and a management agreement. There may or may not be annual reports. You will also see a tax election on how the members are to be treated for tax purposes either as a corporation or as a partnership.

Cell Limited Liability Companies

This is a new entity in which a company is chartered as an LLC that is able to have specific and distinct cells where assets and liabilities can be booked. Other cells of that cell LLC have no right to the assets and no exposure to the liabilities of the other cells. Very much like several mini-companies under a parent structure. Originally it was designed for the insurance industry where the company can be licensed as an insurance company and each of the cells can undertake the assumption of different risks and premium income streams – primarily directed at risks that have a low likelihood of occurrence but a very high liability if they were to occur.

Documents you will find in a cell LLC in addition to a regular LLC are specific documents that are cell LLC subscription agreements, agreements between cell holders that clearly identify themselves as owners of just cells, and clear language on the purpose of the parent LLC and each of the cells.

General Commentary

I think it is useful to note that this book is not going to go through every single source of information that is available to you. However, we do intend to introduce you to some of the more common sources of information and the more useful sources of information available. On the less-common and less-used sources of information and things you should always check today are the following categories:

Environmental. There are many different regulations governing the environments in which we live, work and provide services. Some of these regulations include exposure levels to things such as radiation, magnetic radiation, hazardous chemicals, cleaning solvents, airflow patterns, and the number of times air cleaners need to be cleaned and maintained (granted, this last example only applies to large office buildings). These are very, very important rules and regulations and each state is so vastly different. Other important environmental issues include such things as gas stations, and any other type of company that uses a petrochemical solvent. These items have to be stored properly, used properly, and disposed of properly, otherwise, they can end up as environmental contaminates to the property or business you are looking to purchase. One of the nasty things about any type of environmental contaminate or problem is that any one in the chain of title of the property is 100 percent liable. Every one is jointly and severally liable for all of the cleanup. I have yet to see an inexpensive environmental cleanup.

Local Government. Many times, people sell businesses because they know the local government is going to put them out of business or something the local government is going to do is going to affect their business. One example is road construction. A small car wash that was purchased by one of my clients discovered, two months after purchasing the business, that a major road widening project was planned. As a consequence, the area in front of the business was blocked off and entry was only available from a side street. My client's business dropped 75 percent overnight. A similar occurrence happened at a neighborhood bar. The city decided to put in an enormous mall, and the heavy construction required the use of the road in front of the bar. As a consequence, there was no parking and the bar owner's business dropped 30 percent. There are zoning rules and regulations that, for a particular business, exemptions may be grandfathered – but if the business is sold, it must be brought up to code. In the town where I live, there are very restrictive zoning codes with respect to parking and landscaping. If a business changes hands, the parking area and the landscaping must be brought up to current code. These laws also apply to signage. My city has very restrictive codes on signage, and if the business changes hands the signage must be made to conform with current regulations. Any time a business is purchased or sold, and you are investigating the value of that business, you need to find out how governments' future plans and current regulations might impact the future of the business. I think it is important to ask neighbors what's going on in the area. Ask the employees, ask the suppliers, ask the customers. Ask questions until you get answers you're comfortable with.

Successful Financial Markets. One of the reasons why the United States' financial markets are wildly successful and out of proportion with its citizens' national savings is because the country's markets are open and transparent. Our markets are open and transparent with respect to the history of the business, to the history of the principals and the actions going on surrounding that business. This transparency acts like an insurance policy to the purchaser and seller, as both parties, more often than not, have sufficient informational resources to make an intelligent decision. Whether they choose to make use of those resources is entirely up to them. You will find some jurisdictions, in places such as offshore financial centers, that have very strict privacy laws, and aren't as successful. Offshore centers may have tremendous sums of money on deposit, but the money doesn't remain on deposit there – it's reinvested in markets where financial disclosure is open. Jurisdictions that are open and transparent can be trusted to be reasonably well-regulated with respect to information available to the investor.

Other Providers of Information

Credit Reporting Services. The Fair Credit Reporting Act restricts the information that you can receive on an individual to a little bit more than their name, Social Security number, date of birth, place of employment and residence. You cannot get any information with respect to the credit history of the individual. <u>You can, however, access that information if the person gives you written permission to do so.</u> I recommend that in any voluntary investigation, in accordance with due diligence practices, you secure permission and get credit information and history. It is an extraordinarily inexpensive way to discover information about past credit behavior (usually, well under $10 per report).

Remember that credit reporting services also have information on businesses. The business credit report is not restricted under the

Fair Credit Reporting Act, and is available to anybody wishing to purchase it. Purchasing a business credit report from TRW will cost approximately $25. That information can be invaluable in the purchase of any size business. The credit report will provide a history that the credit grantors have reported to the reporting agency, along with a history of banking. Recently, we were researching a business for unpaid rent, and for a $25 business credit report, found two banks it used. We recognized one bank, but not the other. We served legal papers on both banks, and found the bulk of the business's funds in the bank we had never heard of. The client and attorney were happy with the results and the speed.

Dun and Bradstreet. Most people think of Dun and Bradstreet (D&B) as a clearinghouse for business information. Much of the information that D&B has secured has come from public sources, including credit grantors reporting to D&B. Much of this information is supplied by the business itself. It is not, in many cases, independent information. That does not negate the value of D&B's reports. If you belong to D&B, the reports are inexpensive, but if you are not a member reports can cost dearly. I have found during many due diligence investigations that D&B provided useful information into the background or history of a company. I attempt to verify all D&B information.

D&B provides several other sources of information such as mapping other businesses in an area that are using the same Standard Industrial Code (SIC) classification. You can sort businesses by SIC code, and you can cross-sort by ZIP code, county, locality to find out what competition exists in an area. Talk to your local D&B representative to learn about the company's myriad of services aside from its credit reporting services.

LexisNexis. It claims to be the largest private database in the world – and having used it, I would agree. This company has both accumulated and normalized an incredible number of data sources, and developed an easy-to-use search engine. Its content is almost universal, and it sells access in degrees. Expect to find law, public records, academic journals, almost any article that has ever been published in the digital age, and a good number before. It is a worthy resource, and in many cases, the only resource.

Public Companies. Public companies are required to file audited financial statements in the form of a 10K and 10Q – 10K is the annual report and 10Q is the quarterly report. Several other documents are filed with the SEC throughout the year. These reports are valuable sources of information on public companies, but they are the beginning of an investigation – not the end. These reports are only on public companies that are "fully reporting." Smaller public companies do not require the same level of disclosure. But I believe it is an important beginning in any research.

A client recently asked us to conduct research into the trucking industry. We found a lot of important information in the 10Ks and 10Qs, including fleet size, expenses and revenue per mile, major customers and company focus. And all of this was extremely important when it came down to verifying numbers another trucking firm was presenting to an investment bank, stating that it could operate routes cheaper and faster than its competitors, based upon fixed criteria. It turned out, as a result of this research, that indeed what the firm was presenting to the investment bank was correct. However, had that investment bank proceeded without that research, taking the firm at its word, and had something gone wrong, the investment bank could have been held liable for damages. Failure of an underwriter to perform due diligence, investigate the history and claims of a company being represented to investors creates a huge liability.

Custom Sources of Information – and Your Investigator

Custom sources of information are those bits and pieces of information that you must develop on your own because you cannot find them from public records or from another commercial source. We faced this situation while researching representations made by a taxicab company.

> *The cab company claimed to have 120 cabs, and that at any given time 100 of those cars were leased out to drivers. It had a well-controlled dispatch center, so that any time a cab came in, it was safety checked and then leased back out. Many of the cabs were rented for a 12 or 18-hour shift, but none of the cabs were rented*

for a 24-hour shift and all cabs had to return to the lot at least once a day. As a consequence, if the company had 100 cabs out at any time of day, then, in theory 200 cabs should go through the release gate in 24 hours. We set up a very simple mechanism, an electric eye, to count the number of cabs that went through the gate. On the first day, there were almost 1,100 cabs that went through the gate. We found that not only taxis went through the gate; drivers also used the gate walking back and forth to a local deli. That was a bad method. We replaced the electric eye with a pressure sensitive tube, the counting mechanism was placed just between the concrete skirt going from the dispatch area to the street. It was placed in such a way that no bicycles could run over it, no traffic in the street could run over it, and only the cabs exiting the dispatch area would run over it. The first three nights we checked it, and found an average of 140 ticker counts. That translates into an average of 70 cars, one count each for the front and rear wheels. This was substantially below what the taxicab company was representing to us. We found a repair facility that housed most of the unused cabs. They were in no hurry to bring those cabs out, because they had leased all the cabs they could. These cabs were being held as spares. Therefore, the revenue projections that came from the cab company were not based on the facts of the operation.

Obviously, not all ideas are good ideas. The electric eye seemed like a good idea and turned out to be a bad idea. All sources of information, including public sources, should be checked, rechecked and verified.

In another case, an investment bank was underwriting a company that produced medical devices. The president of the company had a very unusual nickname as well as an unusual last name. When we did a background check on the president, we found that he was fond of brawling in southern California bars, and usually beat the tar out of the people he taunted. This guy was about 5-feet-8 and weighed 150 pounds. Not one of us could fathom how this scholarly and thoughtful professional could be starting brawls. We confronted him with the information, and he chuckled. He said, "Yea, there is some guy in southern California with the exact same name, starting brawls and beating people up. I have had the police knock at my door a couple of times. They look at me and say 'Oh, it can't be you, *never mind.'" We did some further checking. We obtained one of the arrest reports from Newport Beach, and the man arrested, with the same name, was 6-feet-2, 225 pounds, bald, and had several tattoos on his head. They were not the same person. We knew in our hearts that this was not the person our client was underwriting, but we had to follow the trail to the very end, to provide a complete investigation for the investment bank.*

Investigations are the ultimate sources of custom information tailored specifically to your needs and time frames. Not all transactions require investigators and all investigators are not equal. Seek a firm where the investigators have both the specific skill you are looking for as well as broad and disparate backgrounds. If all have the same or very similar backgrounds they are more likely to miss what may be of value to you.

Chapter 6

Benford's Law

"All progress is based upon a universal innate desire on the part of every organism to live beyond its income."

Samuel Butler

"There is no harm in doubt and skepticism, for it is through these that new discoveries are made."

Richard Feynman

We, as financial professionals use a number of different ratios and models to analyze situations. We use them to compare them to norms, to reach new understandings about our situation in a dispassionate way, and also to detect fraud. There are many of these different ratios and models we can use for different situations. I am taking the time to look at only one as an example. It is also one that I use on a consistent basis to both deter and detect fraud. You will find more ratios you can use in the Appendix.

Benford's law (also known as the first-digit law) defines a somewhat counterintuitive observation that can be very useful in detecting fraud. The law states that in a list of numbers the leading digit 1 occurs with the greatest frequency, the number 9 with the lowest frequency, and numbers between 1 and 9 occur with decreasing frequency. This distribution of leading digits is observed in almost all things that are measured, such as expenses or invoices. The law fails with data sets that are either assigned or random, such as invoice numbers, phone numbers or lottery numbers. Benford's law can be used to observe the distribution of the leading digits in a test population to see if the data conforms to the Benford distribution. If the data you are testing is fabricated, it is highly unlikely that it will conform to the natural distribution. Applying tests to data sets to test conformity of the distribution of natural data as set forth by Benford's Law is a very powerful tool to identify selection pressure or outright manipulation. Manipulated data can be fraudulent expense reimbursements, fabricated scientific data, an indication of stock manipulation, or even tax evasion.

The following table lists the expected frequency of digits in the first four positions as observed from the left-most position and moving right. Be aware that the Benford distribution may not be observed when working with small samples. There is software available that will test not only your data, but will provide a statistical analysis for a preset confidence level.

Digit	First	Second	Third	Fourth
0		.11968	.10178	.10018
1	.30103	.11389	.10138	.10014
2	.17609	.10882	.10097	.10010
3	.12494	.10433	.10057	.10006
4	.09691	.10031	.10018	.10002
5	.07918	.09668	.09979	.09998
6	.06695	.09337	.09940	.09994
7	.05799	.09035	.09902	.09990
8	.05115	.08757	.09864	.09986
9	.04576	.08500	.09827	.09982

While knowledge of these distributions is seen as early as 1881, it wasn't until recent history that there have been tools available that allow us to easily test large data sets.

We can assume that most people are unaware of Benford's law, and will not properly distribute the digits and positions used when fabricating data. Fraudulent data sets will be unnatural, and will most likely be exposed upon analysis. On the other hand, a fraudster who is aware of the Benford distribution would be able to construct a near perfect data set. For this reason, we can use this tool to expose fraudulent data, but not to confirm the integrity of data.

Some examples:

Analyzing data from the payables department at a plastics company revealed a larger than normal number of payables beginning with the digits 1 and 9. The company had a policy that any expense over $2,000 required a supervisor's approval. The spike was attributed to two different clerks in the payables department who were issuing phony checks to phony companies. Oddly enough neither of the clerks knew that the other had landed upon the very same scheme to defraud the company.

In another analysis of expense reimbursements for a sales company, the number 3 appeared too often. The policy of the company was to require receipts for any expenses over $40, and a number of undocumented entries for $38 and $39 were found. They revised the receipt requirement several times, only to find an increasing number of expenses declared just under the threshold for receipts. Their final policy change required proof for all expenses.

Some patterns can be observed simply by visually scanning the data. Check the last two numbers to see if there is excessive rounding. Round numbers beg an explanation, and are worth additional testing.

Just because a data set does not fit the Benford distribution does not mean that it is fraudulent, it simply means that it requires further research, such as comparing tests from data sets that are known to be accurate. Benford tests do generate false positives. One must pay attention to the size of the data set, how it was collected, and any limits in the collection process that may affect the data. The smaller the data set the more likely an erroneous Benford test will occur. Limits on data sets or selection pressure made upon the sample will also increase erroneous results. You, as the financial professional, are required to know all of the history of the data on which you run Benford tests.

Designing Tests

As data sets become larger, the testing methods used need to be refined. It's important to analyze data in subsets, such as shipping or inventory – and to ignore data that has a natural bias. For example, the first digit in payroll checks is likely to be near the same number for all employees and should not be included. You will find a number of free software, shareware and plug-in solutions you can download to begin exploring how this knowledge can be used in your business.

This is a very powerful tool and should not be use too aggressively as in hunting for fraudsters in every department. It is a tool to find data anomalies. Data sets that are expected to fit a natural distribution, but do not, usually can be accounted for with one of four explanations – fraud (internal), theft (external), error or selection bias.

Analysis of situations with ratios and models are powerful due diligence tools for the financial professional. There are many different and excellent publications from Graham and Dodd's seminal work in the 1930's for the stock market all the way to the contemporary writings of Nassim Nicholas Taleb that it would be unwise and a disservice to the reader to try and cover all of the choices. All I intend here is to create an awareness of a particularly useful tool and the role of ratios and models in the due diligence process.

At our Web site, www.aegisjournal.com, you and can click on the DDFP link to see some examples of data sets and links to software programs. You may use these to test your data sets.

Chapter 7

KYC - A Person And Their Data

"Getting caught is the mother of invention."

Robert Byrne

"The very purpose of existence is to reconcile our glowing opinion of ourselves with the appalling things that other people think about us."

Quentin Crisp

If you think many people look similar in person, you should see how many look the same on paper. This chapter is about the care and feeding of a person and the virtual person. It is about how to reconcile the many inconsistencies between the records you'll find and the real person in whom you have an interest. As humans we will make errors, it's almost as if we are coded to do so. Yet we often view data records created by humans as infallible. When research indicates an inconsistency between the record and the person, the data is wrong, the person is wrong, or you have matched the wrong data to the right person. We must be able to reconcile the gross data with the net person.

In the process of reconciliation and verification of data, you will perform the same set of tasks when doing Know-Your-Customer work, front-end control of customers, clients and employees – as when trying to find a person who has caused you or your client harm.

Bill collectors coined the term "skip-tracing." "Skip" refers to someone who has skipped town, and the skip-tracer is the person looking for the skip. Today the term has a broader meaning, and is applied to the process of locating any person for any reason. To reiterate, the same set of skills used by a skip-tracer can be used to deal with a host of KYC issues, the information is simply consumed for different purposes. The primary difference is, in a KYC investigation the process is used to confirm representations made by a person as opposed to locating the person.

This form of due diligence requires you to verify representations made to you, and included in these representations will be addresses for residences and places of business. These are critical representations, assuming that in the future you may have some need to get in touch with those making the representation. One way to approach this problem is to independently verify addresses, and then use some form of delivery service to confirm the postulant's presence at the address.

I am going to present much of this information as if I were trying to locate a person of interest as opposed to performing due diligence in a KYC case. I approach the subject this way because, trying to locate someone who is hiding provides all of the same challenges needed in a due diligence case to verify that someone is where they say they are.

Preliminary Search

When doing due diligence work, we treat everyone equally. We verify everyone and everything. In reality, most people are going to be easy to find – because they're going to be exactly who they say they are. If John Smith tells me that he owns a home at 123 Elm Street, I can attempt to verify that fairly simply. I go to the county recorder's office, and I find that 10 years ago John Smith purchased the house at 123 Elm Street. I also notice that there has been no transfer of title *recorded* since his purchase. What I don't know is if the John Smith who purchased the home is *our* John Smith – and for that matter, how did I verify that *our* John Smith is actually named Smith? How do I know the house hasn't been *recently* sold? Hopefully, I have other information – possibly a copy of some form of identification, a Social Security number, a credit report, recent real estate listings, or even a phone number that is registered to that address. Together, confirming all of this information leads me to conclude that *our* John Smith is *the* John Smith who owns the residence at 123 Elm Street.

But what if I have very little information, and my attempts to confirm what I have provides little additional information – or if the records I do find are inconsistent with Mr. Smith's disclosures? This raises my suspicions. If I can't independently confirm any of the information provided to me, I'm dealing with a missing person – missing from the public record. People attempt to live under the radar of public records for numerous reasons. For some it's simply hard times, and they're looking for a new start. For others, it's to avoid criminal prosecution. More commonly, people who are difficult to find are generally hoping to avoid some obligation they've left behind – monetary or social. In any case, if you've been given the job of finding this person, assume he/she is keeping as low of a profile as he can (or knows how to). The researcher's job, quite simply put, is to locate the missing person. While it's generally a detective or investigator who's given the task, it could just as easily be a debt collector, journalist, pre-escheat locator, or anybody else who has an interest in the missing person.

For the person who's trying to connect this person of interest with their public record, finding inconsistencies in the record becomes a pivotal point in the investigation. You have to ask yourself whether continuing the search is worth it. Whether you want to continue a relationship or abandon a relationship with someone whose past could not be confirmed is a question of risk, rewards and sanctions. Whether you want to continue your investigation is simply a question of risk and reward.

Extending the Search

In the not too distant past, locating people depended upon knowing who to contact for information. Social service organizations, the railway express agent, the postmaster, even the local union hall and grocery store were excellent sources. Contacting these people or organizations is going to the loci of community information. Similarly, professional associations and licensing bodies represent a locus of information for their members. Not much has changed in the process, but today much of the information that was once exclusive to disparate organizations is now available in central databases that have been optimized for information retrieval.

Databases have become so sophisticated that detailed information is readily available to anyone who has access to them, and the reports do not necessarily require a sharp investigator to decipher.

A researcher's job begins with collecting information. Recent efforts to organize and sort information have been growing geometrically, roughly keeping pace with advancements in computer technology, and show no signs of slowing down. This tsunami of personal data is collected, normalized, cross-referenced, and sold on levels we couldn't have even imagined several years ago. It's now almost impossible for an individual to go through life without leaving some electronic trail. Never before in history have we had as much information available for making informed decisions regarding people and investments.

Despite the proliferation of databases, they're increasingly unavailable to private citizens using front-door techniques. Concerns for privacy rights have strengthened laws that restrict access to anyone without a license claiming a legitimate use, or a warrant. To make the best use of your time, it's important to gain access to a consolidated database, which has been designed to provide the most comprehensive access to data based upon your legal rights. Many of these databases are also used for Know-Your-Customer compliance and insurance underwriting.

Technology is a double-edged sword, and can assist the mouse as well as the cat. The same technology that creates an electronic trail can be used to conceal or fabricate a trail. People can easily access cell phones and Internet phones that provide no indication of their identity or location. Phone blockers and caller ID allows people to identify calling parties before deciding whether to identify themselves – or to accept a call. Hundreds of services provide anonymous e-mail accounts. The bad guys have the knowledge and ability to game new systems ahead of the safeguards provided by improved systems. The bad guys will exploit any lack of understanding or failure to review processes by the good guys – they will continue to profit by identifying new system vulnerabilities.

When opening bank accounts in the past, banks needed to know their customer – not just have a computerized record of the person. Today, the customer can show up with a forged identification along with a credit card in that name and open a bank account in that assumed name. The fact that you have a photo ID and a credit relationship provides the bank two forms of vetted ID. The photo ID they can see, the credit card is evidence that some other financial institution knows you, and has given you credit. It is both that preposterous and that easy. Actually when presented with this statement, we challenged the exponent to prove it. He was correct. We tested his boast three times (that I'll admit to) and opened accounts. The exercise proved a point – in the United States, KYC means Konsult Your Computer, and has little to do with any real knowledge. We have erred on the side of convenience, not of knowledge. Our lack of knowledge allows the bad guys to game and take advantage of our systems.

In modern society, people can disappear in many ways. The term disappear is misleading, what actually happens is people attempt to keep all of their financial and personal records from being recorded. For example, if you are driving and get a ticket, it is recorded. If you request credit or apply for insurance, a record of the inquiry and the information you provided will be recorded on your credit report. Tenant screening is captured on your credit report. If you are involved in any litigation, that is recorded. Utility service contracts, phone, cable, power and water are all recorded. All of this information is retrievable. To disappear, there must be a near-conscious choice not to live a life of recorded events. If you live in the cash economy, rent from a landlord who doesn't do background checks, don't drive, and don't work in a licensed profession – you will be hard to find (even if you are not hiding).

Understanding the Information

To understand how data needs to be interpreted and filtered, let's consider cases where a fraud has been committed. Keep in mind that while these new technologies might make it easier to locate a person, it's often these same new technologies that make it easier to commit a fraud in the first place.

Le Charade

> *An electronic identity and fictitious business relationship can be created in minutes using a borrowed address or mail drop, a couple of throwaway cell phones, the purchase of a domain name, and the setup of e-mail accounts. Here's a scenario – I buy the domain SeemsLegitimate.com and create a Web page for my business using a cell phone as the contact number, I then forward the company number to a private answering service that in turn connects callers to my personal cell phone. I tell you that I work for SeemsLegitimate (learn more about us at www.seemslegitimate.com), and you can e-mail me directly using skippy@seemslegitimate.com. If you want to verify my employment and income, you can contact the company using either the phone number or mail-drop address on the company Web site. If you need to contact me directly, here's my personal phone number and mail drop. This all looks pretty legitimate, doesn't it? This entire facade can be created for under a couple hundred dollars. To make it more interesting I'll pay for everything using a prepaid gift card that I register online using any identity I choose.*

If my little charade works, there was a serious lack of due diligence. You probably won't be able to find me, even with subpoenas. It's for these reasons that we have to be just as aware of disinformation as we are of information, and one of the first things to find out is whether or not any of the information we have is real. If you're working in a closed corporate environment where you are responsible for validating information, it's important that you add your knowledge to the due diligence process the company uses when originating a new relationship. It's a lot less expensive to check the accuracy of information a client provides before you establish a relationship than after you find out there has been a fraud.

Assuming we're not dealing with an elaborate case of identity theft, and that we can identify the person of interest, the information collected will almost always identify third parties who can help us. Pretexting employers, neighbors and relatives to learn more about the target is by far the easiest way to locate people. Using public online information resources such as the county recorder's office, assessor's records, criminal databases and corporation filings will often provide a road map to the target's location.

Let's look at a normal case – the ones we see every day. We've run all of the reports we have access to, and searched the public records. We know the person is real, because they had a very public profile prior to their disappearance. Wherever they are currently located, it becomes clear that they haven't contracted for any of the services recorded in our databases. They haven't forwarded their mail through the National Change of Address (NCOA) database, or if they have it's to a post office box. At this point we have to assume that they're rooming with a friend, renting a room, or staying with a relative – but where?

If their last known address is a post office box, we can attempt to confirm that it's active. Sometimes a call to the postmaster of the ZIP code is sufficient. If the box is active, we can safely assume that they're currently in the ZIP code area. This narrows things down a lot. We can also use searches for phone numbers – but in today's world that's only a tentative link to their location, as Internet and cell phones can be set up with the user's choice of area codes.

If we can't narrow their location to a limited geographical area, we need to start making phone calls to get some idea of what city or town they are living or working in. The best sources of information will be family, friends, former employers and known associates. I would start with a simple pretext, such as calling a former roommate or parent, and asking for "Skippy." If the other party seems confused, simply respond "I'm Tracy Goodman, and Skippy gave me this number saying it would be a good number to reach him when I got back in town." That pretext can bring forth a flood of interesting information; you usually won't get an address, but frequently you will get another phone number, a roommate, an employer or a new city. People want to be helpful, and the pretext call is an attempt to exploit their desire. Pretexting for information may or may not be legal, depending upon which state you are in, calling, and how any information obtained is ultimately used. Check with your legal counsel for laws that apply.

If we can't locate our target using family or friends, we need to review the information we do have. Have they lived in, or do they have family in other cities? Where did they go to school? People usually don't leave a town unless they're going somewhere they have a support network. What line of work were they in? People don't change careers easily – especially if they're in need of money. If you know they last worked as a cook for Mom's Restaurant, find out if Mom's is a franchise – call the central office and attempt to verify employment – "And which location was that?" If they managed a Home Depot, check with Lowe's. If you have access to a credit report, don't underestimate its value in determining employment, addresses, and the movements of a target. If you're participating in a due diligence process, don't discount the value of validating this type of information before a problem appears.

Assuming you can't contact the target by phone, but believe you have a good address – delivery services are your friend. Don't spend your time driving around and knocking on doors – let them do it for you. While sending a certified letter might seem to be the correct course of action, people who don't want to be found ignore certified letters – and the post office is less than inefficient at making sure non-certified mail is properly delivered to the addressee. Try using UPS, FedEx, or florists. You might get good results with a few CDs from the dollar store sent to the best address you have, along with an invoice for their Music-of-the-Month club subscription. Make sure the invoice has a prominent phone number for any billing or subscription questions (call 877-SeemsLegitimate). People always open packages and letters that appear to contain something of value – use that to your advantage, and get them on the phone.

There is no end to the creativity that you can use to get information. The important thing is to maintain focus on important information, and discard or ignore all information that is noise. Whenever you have anyone on the phone that is in any way connected to the skip, you have a potential solution to your locate. Be conversational, be polite, and be friendly. Chances are you're not the only person looking for the target, and every other investigator is using the same data that you are. This means that the person on the other end of the phone is already a bit suspicious of anyone they don't know. Be creative, be friendly, and by all means don't sound like a detective.

There are always going to be cases that hit a dead end. At some point you have to consider what value this locate has to you. If it has value – let the project age for a while. Running database checks 30 or 60 days after you've been frustrated by a case will often bring surprising results. As we observed earlier, it's almost impossible to go through life without leaving an electronic trail that will eventually be incorporated into a public database. If your reason to trace the subject allows you the time, develop a procedure to periodically review cases as opposed to closing them. People will surface –eventually. Sometimes people die, leave the country, or land in prison – but more frequently they will get married, buy a home, land a great job, or have other changes in their life that prevent them from living under the radar. Persistence pays off.

In conclusion, this is a game of cat-and-mouse. The mouse has the same tools available to him as the cat, but rarely the same experience in how to use them. This is the difference between a researcher and a competent investigator employing their tradecraft. Due diligence, background checks, and locates often seem like a boring task simply because there are so many dead ends that have to be explored. In our boredom, we often forget that it's this persistence that gives us our experience, and experience is the cat's edge over the mouse.

Chapter 8

Asset Recovery

"Professionals can make mistakes of faith and trust, for they are human. They must forgive themselves now, and believe in recovery from the fraudster."

L. Burke Files

Creditors and victims need to be able to collect what is due to them through legal judgments. Whether the judgments address a debt or fraud it does not matter, either one has caused too much pain and suffering. Compounding the anguish is the difficulty for the victim to either punish the bad guys through the criminal courts, or wrest from them their ill-gotten booty. Our desire is to change this paradigm.

The pain we have witnessed is often simply because the rules of recovery are stacked against the creditor. If you feel or believe that you should be nice in the process of collections, skip this chapter – it will only aggravate you.

In this chapter, as elsewhere in this book, you will see the terms asset recovery and judgment enforcement. These are not interchangeable. Asset recovery speaks of tactics before judgment is rendered to settle an obligation and or freeze the debtor's assets. Judgment enforcement refers to collection efforts after a finding of fact and rendering of a judgment by a court.

Small Judgments to International Fraud Recovery Efforts

The process of recovery is about receiving what is due to the creditor. *This is not an exercise in nice or politically correct behavior.* This is about the mean streets of raw collections from people who do not want to pay an obligation. The facts are simple, the laws do not favor you, the creditor – the laws favor the debtor. The entire process has a number of rules and procedures, and if you don't follow them the debtor can object and turn the tables on you! There are several Web sites and publications dedicated to showing how a debtor can turn you, the creditor, into a defendant.

As one experienced attorney told me, "for the creditor to be successful they must understand that this is a dog-eat-dog world, and the creditor is wearing Milk-Bone underwear." A colorful and accurate statement.

What I am not attempting to provide here is a do-it-yourself guide on collections. No such manual could ever exist. Every collection professional, even those who buy bushel baskets of receivables from lenders and sales companies, know that each debt stands upon its very own foundation and circumstances. Experience and tradecraft count here more than almost anywhere else in litigation. You may win a case, but if you cannot collect on the judgment, why bother?

A note on the Fair Debt Collection Practices Act (FDCPA) - this act only has to do with consumer debt. It does not apply to commercial debt.

> From the Act 15 USC 1629a § Definitions... (3) The term "consumer" means any natural person obligated or allegedly obligated to pay any debt. and (5) The term "debt" means any obligation or alleged obligation of a consumer to pay money arising out of a transaction in which the money, property, insurance or services which are the subject of the transaction are primarily for personal, family, or household purposes, whether or not such obligation has been reduced to judgment.

This is an important distinction and you will need to know if you fall under the FDCPA or you do not.

Introduction

It's you against them. You're the creditor, and they are the: debtor, deadbeat, fraudster, or, if the debtor got a bunch of money – the obligor. However they got to this position, whether through dishonesty, sloth or a series of unfortunate events – there is still a debt. The purpose of this chapter is for the reader to gain a working understanding of the many different ways a claim can be pursued. We will briefly cover strategy and tactics, but not procedure. Procedure varies too much between jurisdictions, and isn't a suitable topic for a generalized overview such as this. The information here is meant for you, the creditor, to understand some of your options and to ask informed questions of your counsel.

Basic Collections
$5 to $100,000

Most collection matters stem from the breach of a contract for services or from an unpaid debt. This covers the vast majority of collection matters, and the debt may range from a few dollars up to millions of dollars. For this portion of the report we are going to focus on the smaller amounts, amounts usually handled by the creditors themselves or by their bill collector/collection attorney.

First, you must marshal and assemble the facts and documentation.

> ★　Is there a contract or agreement? Where is it?
> ★　What court has jurisdiction? International, U.S. federal, state or county?
> ★　What happened, between whom?
> ★　Are there any circumstances either mitigating or aggravating the sums due?
> ★　What is the total due? Will small claims or justice court work?
> ★　If there is a statute of limitations, how long is it and when did it begin to run?
>
> With full knowledge of the facts, you need to make a choice. It doesn't matter how ticked off you are, a realistic choice has to be made as to whether you want to pursue this debt. If you believe that it's a matter of principle, forget all of the facts, and stop there. Proceeding on principle will cause you to pursue debts that are not economically collectable, thus you must have other reasons to continue such as setting an example to others.

If you believe that it is a matter of dollars, continue on. To press on, two additional questions need to be answered:

★   Can all the parties to the agreement be found?
★   Is the collection worth pursuing?

Not everyone can be located with economic efficiency. The debtor may have incurred the debt in one state, where the contract is domiciled, but has moved to another state where the amount is too small to litigate. The debtor's current state of residence may have laws that make it difficult to collect. The debtor may be in financial straits, and without collectable assets. These are just some of the issues to be considered when assessing the collectability of a debt.

If you judge that a debt is not economically collectable, you can table the matter and review it one year before the statute of limitations runs out. In this time, circumstances may change. The risk you face is not being able to find the other party to serve them. Another decision you may make is to serve them now, and place the judgment on the shelf. With a judgment, you can make periodic inquiries into the debtor's financial health and renew the judgment as appropriate. It's a choice you will need to make. If at some point you determine that a judgment is not collectable, you want to document the debt and issue a 1099-C (Cancellation of Debt) for forgiveness of the debt, and send that to the debtor and the IRS. This provides you a means to expense the debt, if you have not already, and requires the debtor to declare the forgiveness as earnings. For more information on debt forgiveness and its consequences, visit www.irs.gov and search "debt cancellation."

Let's assume that you determine the debt is collectable, and the truth is that most debts are, be prepared for the work that's ahead of you. We have aided in the collection of debt for many clients, against debtors who had many other liens and judgments. Our team collected, and the other creditors did not. How? We did our homework.

First Notice

First notice is a requirement under the FDCPA which states that the debtor be given notice of the debt. The laws in some areas of the country say notice must be given before litigation. In other areas, the law recognizes the lawsuit you've filed and served as constituting first notice. The system may already be working against you, and you're just trying to get started. The issue of first notice is a contested issue. The first notice requirement is governed by the FDCPA, and you must know what the courts have held in your jurisdiction, making sure all of the appropriate disclosure is contained with the first notice, whatever it may be.

Who is the Adversary?

The *street debtor* is the person who racks up unpaid bill after unpaid bill. This type lives in an apartment and usually has a car. They are experienced at avoiding process servers and judgments. This debtor is more experienced at avoiding the consequences of the system than the system has teeth to enforce a debt. You cannot threaten street debtors into paying, nor can you cajole them into paying – you must corner them. Put away the old processes you've tried, and approach the problem from a new angle.

> *One process server rapped on a street debtor's door and asked the man who opened it if he was Mr. Mann? The debtor responded, "This is Mr. Steel's home," and shut the door. The process server left without serving the papers. A bit of research by an investigator showed that, yes, it was Mr. Steel's home and that the fellow answering the door was Mr. Mann pulling a fast one on the process server. Photos from the Department of Motor Vehicles (DMV) showed him to be the debtor in question. A second process server returned with a photo of a dog in her hand, she was looking for her lost dog, a truly pitiful sight. When Mr. Mann opened the door she served the papers. Mr. Mann screamed and yelled that this was Mr. Steel's home – many veins puffed up on his head and neck! The process server turned the dog photo around and showed Mr. Mann his own DMV photo. The door slammed. Checking the public records, we learned eight other creditors were trying to serve Mann, but none had done so in three*

months. Please understand, we are not smarter, we just have been doing this a lot longer – it's tradecraft.

The *event debtor* is a lot closer to most of us than we care to acknowledge. These are people who, through a reversal of fortune, divorce, injury or loss of a job find themselves in economic hardship. I know many people who have been at this juncture in life, and it is truly difficult. There is a big difference between those who have been unfortunate and those who never intended to honor their obligations – authenticity. Event debtors will tell you what happened, acknowledge that they cannot pay, and invite you to re-contact them after a period of time. The street debtors will blame everyone else and apply the street skills of avoidance.

We need to think as the street debtor does. Strangers at the door are bad, holiday cards do not arrive certified mail, and nothing good ever happens when answering a collection letter. A kind letter offering a favorable payment plan, possibly some reduction in the debt, and some empathy will go much further than threats. These letters work, and while the percentage response you'll get is quite low, it's worth your effort – since the effort is minimal.

If letters do not provoke a response, proceed with all creditors as you would the street debtor. The difference between them is that in the end, the event debtor is likely to attempt some settlement, be passive, or passive aggressive, like changing jobs when their wages are garnished.

Court

A vast majority of debtors who will not respond to you end up with default judgments against them – somewhere in the neighborhood of 95 percent. Those that respond, but will not deal with you seem to fall into three categories – 1) It's not my debt; 2) It's the wrong me; 3) I'm a constitutionalist.

It's Not My Debt, or It's Not Me

In many cases you will have a contract to work with, as evidence of the debt. Sometimes you don't have a contract – only a debt that was purchased from a large institution. It will cost money to get copies of the contract, but the institution can provide affidavits. A recent court case says that an affidavit of the debt is sufficient – however, some judges want to see the contract. It's better if you know the judge beforehand, but be prepared for anything. You may only have an affidavit to produce along with the proper court citation allowing affidavits. This will address most of the "It's-not-my-debt" arguments. Experience has shown us that most debt is properly tracked – it has simply been so long since anyone tried to collect the debt that they've either forgot, or are going to challenge the system's memory to prove it.

It's the Wrong Me

This can happen. People steal identities and rack up debts. People have similar names, and have lived in similar locations. Parents name their children after themselves, and one or the other is a debtor. It has all happened. Here you must be diligent in proving the debt and the authenticity of the physical person you pursue. Social Security numbers, dates of birth, address histories, and motor vehicle records can all play an important role in properly identifying the debtor.

> *In a recent case we served a Danielle Chris and the debt was in the name of a Dan Christopher. We had served a girl instead of a boy with a similar name. The court found that Dan Christopher had changed his name to Danielle Chris at the time of a transgender operation. Some past and current DMV photos showed they were the same person. The judge was not amused by the high jinks of denial, and specifically stated that the new name and look were insufficient to make the individual a sufficiently different person who could avoid the debt.*

The Constitutionalist

The constitutionalist will require seeing all original documents, and challenge the origin of the debt as well as the authority of the court. These folks can be a real pain in the ass. With the attitude they possess, you know that they are angry and can't hold down a job – so they have all the time in the world to devote to making the collection process miserable. Remember that the laws favor these folks. It can also be a great deal of fun to hound them, but it's expensive and time-consuming. While you do not run into many of them, they always leave a lasting memory and make for good stories at gatherings.

When collecting from a constitutionalist you need to turn good intelligence into iron-clad facts for the judge. Eventually the judge may get as sick of this debtor as you are, and come down hard on him. The operative word is "may." Also, you'll likely need the assistance of law enforcement to collect any assets such as cars or property.

There's a reason people play these games, and it's because most collectors simply give up. Depending upon the size of the debt, it oftentimes makes more sense to offer the person a settlement he should not refuse. If he won't settle, send him a 1099-C for forgiveness of the debt. The IRS has a whole department dedicated to dealing with constitutionalists. Don't just walk away.

Settlement

Sometimes a debtor will offer to settle for a smaller amount than the agreement, or for a payment plan. The amount you settle upon is up to you, as this is a battle that has both costs and rewards. As for a payment plan, always get one when you can – even if it's a small amount for six months – as you can always revisit it at a later date. When you have a payment plan you have a medium of communication between you and the debtor and through this medium you can develop some good intelligence. You'll need this intelligence later, because most of the people on a payment plan fail after a couple of months – it's another stalling tactic. Use the payment plan to develop intelligence on the debtor such as copies of checks, phone numbers, addresses, personal and business vehicles, and whatever else you can learn.

Provisional Remedies

Provisional remedies are available in some jurisdictions, which allow the creditor almost immediate action. The provisional remedy process allows creditors to prove to the court that they have a solid fact-based case, and wish to enforce their collection rights immediately. To do this, the creditor must post a bond with the court to protect the debtor in case the creditor is wrong and causes damage to the other party. This can be a useful method of collection if the judgment is large, or you expect that the debtor may move fast to move or conceal their assets.

Writ of Replevin

A writ of replevin is a prejudgment process ordering the seizure or attachment of property. The writ generally requires a bond from the plaintiff and allows the plaintiff to secure the debt either with the named collateral of the debt, such as with a car or heavy equipment, or with other assets such as bank accounts if it is a contractual debt. There is then a time period, usually up to a few days, under which the debtor can re-replevin the asset by posting a bond with the court, or object to the replevin.

This type of writ is commonly used to take property from an individual wrongfully in possession of it, and return it to its rightful owner. It is a quick fix and the bond, which is required to be posted in case the plaintiff is wrong, can be from 100 percent to 200 percent of the obligation or value of the property. It's an effective tool if you know the location of the asset(s) and direct law enforcement to the asset. It is not a good tool if you have no idea where the asset is, or if there are "issues" that may need to be litigated.

Moving Forward

So you have decided that the debt is collectable and you wish to move forward with collecting the debt. You have a judgment and you are ready to roll – well almost. You can only garnish those funds and assets that are non-exempt.

Exempt Versus Non-Exempt

Certain assets are exempt from garnishment. It differs from state to state and upon the nature of your judgment. In general terms, a portion of a car's value is exempt, a portion of a person's home is exempt, some retirement funds are exempt, some insurance is exempt, a portion of a person's wages are exempt, a portion of a bank account is exempt, some deposits such as those with landlords and utility companies may be exempt, and sometimes some of the marital property is exempt. The rules vary from state to state. If the judgment is a criminal judgment, many of the exemptions may not apply. One is not supposed to be allowed to transfer non-exempt assets, such as those from a crime, into exempt categories.

Also some of the exempt assets such IRAs, retirement plans, annuities, assets under a trust may not be available to your judgment, but may come into play in a bankruptcy. It might be worth exploring whether to band with other creditors and force the debtor into bankruptcy.

Assets

There are a few categories of assets that most people have and can be garnished with relative ease.

There are a number of ways to develop information on assets. The best way for most is to begin with the credit report, any available credit applications along with any and all correspondence to date. You are looking for clues.

Job

Everyone has got to have a source of money and most people work. The credit reports and the original application sometimes give a clue to the debtor's type of work. Were these people licensed, were they in a particular industry, have they always lived in the same neighborhood? All of this helps. If they worked in a licensed industry such as a real estate agent, car dealer, food handler, beautician, medical assistant, etc, check their licenses for leads. Sometimes you get a job and prepare to garnish wages, but the employer says there is no employee working there by that name. How can this be, you saw them there! They could be a contract person, not actually an employee, or they could be working through a temp agency, or they could be a leased employee (a large and growing category) or the employer could be lying.

Bank or Credit Union

Most people used to have at least a small bank account. However, with check-cashing centers sprouting up, a whole sub-nation of the un-banked has flourished. Obtaining bank information is good, how you get it can be bad and possibly illegal. Make sure the information has been obtained without breaking the rules. Check to see if the person works for a company that has a credit union, check to see if they made payments in the past and where those payments were drawn from. All of this can help to pin down a bank's relationship.

Property

For most of us this is the home we live in. Check public records for ownership or refinancing of property that is owned. If the debtor does not own property, are they renting and from whom? Sometimes the landlord can be a good, if unwitting, source of information.

Cars

Cars are part of the fabric of society. Nearly everyone drives and are required to have a license and insurance. Pull DMV records to see if they own a vehicle that is worth more than $1,000 over the exempt amount in their state, if so garnish it. If not, the DMV records can also be a good source of information on where they have been driving and what they were driving when they were ticketed. Many a debtor has received a ticket in a company vehicle.

Trailers and mobile homes are often listed under the same category when one goes to DMV for records. It's a stab when you are getting down this low, but it can really pay off.

> *Nick was an experienced deadbeat, he lived an OK life but no one could figure out how he made money. Turns out, he had fashioned his income stream over the years by first buying and then living in a number of trailers or mobile homes. Once the registration on the unit*

expired, he would rent it out to someone and go buy another. The DMV was littered with old registrations but only a single current one. We went to the location and just watched as people came to his door all afternoon and handed him money and envelopes. We spoke to a few of the people and learned that Nick was their landlord. He had rented out many of the old trailers in local trailer parks and was collecting the rent once a week in cash. The garnishments hit his tenants, and the sheriff hit his trailer home late one Sunday evening. The fit he threw was wonderful, Hollywood quality.

A watercraft can be anything from a canoe to a steamship liner. Most of what we find are Jet Skis and small 10- to 25-foot canoes or fishing boats. When a watercraft is in play, you need to find it and assess its condition before taking action. Not an easy task. Here's a hint, when you look for trailers licensed with the DMV keep an eye out for those that are manufactured specifically for watercraft.

Company shares such as those in a corporation, a limited liability company, or partnership may or may not be able to be found with the particular state registrar. These can be worthwhile or a mess. It all depends upon the entity and the assets of the entity. You may also find that the debtor works for the entity he owns. This can make for some particularly good opportunities to expand the pool of liable parties of a judgment. The self-employed debtors usually do not answer a garnishment served on their own company. Thus, usually through a contempt of court action, the company becomes liable and the creditor can go after the company's customers.

Collectables such as art, movies, DVDs, guns and jewelry can be an option or they can be deemed personal property and possibly exempt. A great deal of this depends upon personal knowledge of the debtor's habits. I know many a debtor that has large collections of DVDs and VHS tapes, books, art, jewelry, etc. These are assets most creditors have never taken the time to go after. There also has to be a sufficient amount of the items at fire sale prices to make it worth the effort. A general economic benchmark is about $1,000 of these assets.

A Judgment Debtors Exam (JDE) is a tool that can be used. This is where you pull in the judgment debtor for questioning. The debtor is required to bring records specified in the subpoena and answer questions truthfully. It should be a time for honest disclosure, but it is not. About half of the time the debtors are no-shows, and while civil arrest warrants may be issued they are not always acted upon even by police. The enforcement of the civil warrant is hit and miss and will vary greatly from jurisdiction to jurisdiction. When the debtors do show up at a JDE, they most always look pitiful and don't bother to bring any of the records. The more effective sessions have the examiner asking many questions of the debtor and showing a reasonable knowledge of the debtor's activities and whereabouts. A good background report of just public information regurgitated by an examiner when questioning, can really rattle a debtor. A well-prepared examiner usually can elicit some form of concession. An examiner who goes in unprepared except for the hope that the debtor will voluntarily give himself up, is wasting everyone's time. Fact − most people do not commit fiscal suicide without a good a push.

> *Debtors have shown up and lied in front of judges, and the judges have done nothing for as long as there have been debtors and judges. Expect it but be ready to force the judge's hand if you can. You can request on the spot jail time for contempt of court. If you don't get it, maybe in the future you should notice the judge since the judge doesn't seem to give a darn. Most judges really do care, some do not. In one case, after many previous lies and no-shows, we requested a JDE in front of a judge. This fellow showed up wearing a new suit, an expensive watch and motoring a new Cadillac. The JDE started and the guy could barely remember his name. After several trip-ups orchestrated by a well-prepared examiner, the judge was red faced, literally red faced. He told the debtor to empty his pockets and remove all jewelry. The debtor froze. A moment later a bailiff walked in and was instructed by the judge to empty the debtor's pockets and remove the jewelry. What was found was the beginning of the recovery trail: several company credit cards, $1,100 in cash, an $8,000 watch, a Rolex with real diamonds, and business cards for his many ventures. The judge tossed him in lockup and held the assets for the creditor. The debtor was released at the end of the day, after the meter on the Cadillac had expired and the car was towed*

– to the most distant lot in the city. Lesson, find the right judge and help the debtor to tick them off.

Effective Collection

It is a process not a place. It is a series of serial events not a point in time. Success depends upon being diligent, persistent, smart, persistent, and possessing expertise, tradecraft and persistence.

The debtors and deadbeats rely on gaming the system and the rules. Don't take it personally, you are just another player to be toyed with.

> *When providing testimony in a case a debtor screamed at me visibly shaking with rage – "How dare you take my money, it was my money you took you thieving B@$!& (%." The calm response from counsel was, "Ma'am, It is not your money, you took it from the bank. The bank tried to get you to pay it back, you did not. A collection agency tried to get you to pay it back, and you did not. When we bought the debt we offered you a discount on the debt or a payment plan, you did not respond. We served you with papers, but you never showed up in court and we obtained a default judgment. After six or more attempts of trying to collect the judgment we are here in court today. For you to argue that we took your money – no ma'am, you took the bank's money and never repaid it. We have no malice; we are just collecting on a debt you did not pay. The money never became yours absent the obligation to repay the money." Her response, "Gee, I never thought of it that way."*

The Fair Debt Collection Practices Act isn't all that it seems. It is your enemy, not your friend. It sets forth many rules that you must follow so the debtors have a chance to honor their debt. While the purpose of the FDCPA was to get debt collectors to behave as humanly as possible, it is my position much of it has gone too far to favor the other side. (My position). The FDCPA obviously was not written by anyone who has had to collect on debts. I am not denying that some people collecting debts have done some bad and dumb things – they have. But such legislative efforts as the FDCPA, the Gramm-Leach-Bliley Act, and rulings by the Federal

Trade Commission are not about how a debt can be collected, they are about how you cannot collect on a debt and what happens to the plaintiff if you break the rules. Thus, learn the rules so you don't break them or retain someone who knows the rules. It is through gaming the system that a wily debtor can frustrate you until you make a mistake. Once you've crossed the line and done something improper you will have your faced rubbed in it. That is how the debtor can become your creditor!

Mid-Range Debt
$50,000 to $5,000,000

The term mid-range debt is a misnomer, but it serves as a category we use in this descriptive process.

This is usually a business debt. Someone has racked up a good deal of money that is owed. It often comes from guarantees and/or the mishandling of funds.

People do not end up with these large judgments because they are dumb. I have seen these come from guarantees at restaurants for liquor and food, guarantees on inventory loans, taking funds held in trust and using them for personal business, personal reasons or just borrowed and not repaid.

Character of the Person/Debtor

People who fall into this range of debt are middle- to senior-level managers, business owners and professionals who fell into trouble. They saw something happening and they tried to take a bit of money or weave a story for more credit. Often, these people had no concept of business and cost structures and were losing 5 cents for every dollar in sale. They believed they could make it up on volume, even though volume actually spun them into the ground faster.

> *I remember looking at a company that was losing about 3 cents for every mile its trucks traveled. The owner was certain that if he could run more miles and deliver more freight, he could work his way out of debt. We were sent in by the creditor to find out what*

was happening to the business. When we ran the numbers and the sensitivity analysis, the owner was dumbfounded, but respected both the process and the results. He initiated several cost-savings programs and raised his rates. Almost immediately he was profitable. The creditor, while pleased, did have to call one of the three loans and while this upset the debtor, the debtor sold the trucks and paid down the loan. The other loans were brought current in about 11 months. It was a unique circumstance because the creditor was a private fund and possessed both the luxury and flexibility of not having to report to the OCC (Office of the Comptroller of the Currency), Federal Reserve or an auditor armed with SOX (Sarbanes Oxley Act) required disclosures.

Nature of Debt

The debt is large and it did not accrue overnight. It usually takes a bit of time to develop a six-figure credit line. This is true of most loans, but I am aware of several loans over a million dollars that went almost immediately into default.

Nature of the Trail of Debt

There will be a trail that will lead to the debtor as sure as the sun will shine tomorrow. The questions are if you can find the trail, what the trail will lead to, and what you will find.

What the trails often tell us is that the debtor saw the fiscal crash coming. The trail began with the realization by the debtor, that troubled times were ahead and cash needed to be sequestered for future use. This is where and when the debtor began planning to sequester funds. This beginning has certain hallmarks, such as: blaming employees for theft, suspicious fires or floods that always destroy records – though little else, or even more absences from the business than would seem appropriate for the situation. I have seen all sorts of ways to shovel money out of a dying business: fake suppliers, side jobs, single premium annuities expensed as insurance, large travel budgets where tickets are full-fare tickets and can be redeemed at anytime for face value, payments to doctors that were covered by insurance where the insurance refunds the payment to the business owner, etc. They are all done in an effort to drain whatever amounts can be redirected from the business to their own pockets before the collapse.

The Plans

Once the failure of a business seems likely, the plans to sequester funds generally set up the business or transaction for failure sooner. A characteristic of this accelerated failure is blame gets redirected at others, while the bad guy squirrels funds away for a recovery at a future date or a good lifestyle in the interim.

> *Carl managed 11 laundromats with limited partners. The business was failing. We were called in to investigate money missing from the "foolproof" money card dispensers at the laundromats used to pay for washer and dryer use. Many tens of thousands of dollars were missing. The research showed that this was indeed the case, but the person named by the owner as the prime suspect, the general manager, was not the culprit. The machines were well designed, and close to foolproof. Their date-time stamp activated every time they were opened, and they had good records of how much cash was in them and when the cash was taken out of them. Many did show date-time stamps from when they were opened and money was removed. This was where and when the theft was occurring. The owner blamed the manager, but on most recorded times the manager was at a different location opening and properly recording revenue. Further, these losses only occurred when the owner or his sons were in town, the only other people who had access to the machines. We pointed this out. We were promptly dismissed as being morons. The business went under about seven months later. The cause of failure? Uncontrolled theft from employees is what he told his partners.*

> *I always love cases where the case has been solved, and we are to provide the report corroborating the preordained decision.*

The Obligation

The obligation must be documented. All of the circumstances and representations at the time of the agreement must be taken into consideration. Anytime you can assert fraud, misfeasance or malfeasance do so, but understand the court really only understands clear and convincing proof on the elements of fraud or statutory fraud. Attorneys, thus judges, and law enforcement professionals do not go to school to learn financial strategies or cash management techniques. Therefore, when presenting a scenario you must be so clear and concise as to be able to overcome the sum total of all of their ignorance and fears. There is nothing wrong with their lack of financial knowledge. Most attorneys did not study business, cash management techniques, fluid dynamics or even medicine. Thus, one must explain the case facts so a high school student can follow, because that's about the time most attorneys stopped taking business classes and began specializing. If this is not your area of expertise either, retain an expert who can help. The story above illustrates that the manager could not have taken the funds, but it does not prove in a clear and convincing way that owner did (though I'll lay money on it). Tie the knot nice and tight around the debtor and litigate like a fiend.

Defense of the Debtor

Bombast, delay and hyperbole are as good as anything. This is what you usually get when there are no facts in the debtor's favor. Be prepared for the twilight zone, anything else is a pleasant surprise. Here's what you should prepared for:

- Can't find the debtor to serve them.
- Lender liability claims from the far side, for example, "If it were not for you lending or investing the money, I would not have to pay it back!"
- An actual claim from the court.
- Counterfeit documents have surfaced in a number of instances. If you don't remember signing a document you may not have actually signed it.
- Intimidations of witnesses and bribery happen.
- When you get the judgment there may be endless rounds of appeals on all sorts of minor things that add up to major delays.

Be ready.

Collection

By this time the debtor has had time to hide and re-title assets. He will have tried to move the assets from non-exempt to exempt status or had them re-titled in other names or entities and even sent overseas.

> *One fellow was a car collector and had some excellent late '50s Chrysler Imperials and New Yorkers. He did not want to lose them so he transferred their titles into his girlfriend's name. So we went after her and obtained a judgment against her for frustrating and impeding the collection of the judgment. It took two more years of chasing her and him, but we got paid mostly from her bank accounts and from garnishing her wages. I believe the relationship ended when the process server showed up at her doorstep. Never did get one of the cars though.*

Strategy

The best strategy after a long litigation is to sit back and take stock of what you know. Hire a good financial investigator, such as Financial Examinations & Evaluations, Inc., the people who helped write this book (so much for subtlety). Then make some choices. Is it time for a full-fledged assault on the debtor, or is it time to wait until another day?

Sometimes it is also a good strategy to look dim, exhausted and ready to quit. Allow the debtor to drop his defenses. Sometimes you need to pounce like a badger and rip into the debtor again and again. The facts, circumstances and budget, including time, money and emotion, are all to be taken into consideration.

Information

Sometimes it is best to come on like a moron at collecting. Things work better when the opposition thinks you do not know what you are doing. In the meantime, you lay back in the weeds and collect information.

Means Versus Ability testing is always good. How is a fellow with millions of dollars in judgments against him living in a million dollar home with no visible means of support?

Actions. What is he doing, where is he doing it, and when is he doing it? This may require extensive research including surveillance.

Third Parties. Can you tie any third parties in to assisting the debtor in the secretion of the assets? If you can, they may become liable for the debt.

Sometimes it is best to be a badger and rip the debtor's carcass and pull it apart limb from limb.

Subpoena bank account records, phone records and e-mail accounts.

Depose their employer and subpoena the personnel file.

Pull a credit report and subpoena every company reporting a relationship with the debtor.

Collect their garbage.

Have them followed.

Depose their dog; some dogs talk more than others.

Process

It will be a slow process; many of these debtors avoided bankruptcy because of the disclosure requirements. Now they avoid it because of both the disclosure requirements and the new mountains of paperwork and requirements that are being enforced on those who choose the bankruptcy route. Fewer marginal debtors are filing and this has changed the landscape. One gentleman, who had gone through a divorce and the loss of a business, took four months and more than 100 hours of labor to file his bankruptcy. It is a changed dynamic for collections. There are often many rounds of discovery, asset location, proving up and garnishing the asset, and doing it again. As mentioned before, maybe it is time to round up some creditors and seek an involuntary bankruptcy.

An ideal process, if there is one, is to have the garnishment process attempt to self-fund the investigations, discovery and future rounds of garnishment.

Sometimes the assets are domestic and sometimes they are overseas, determining which is what and where the assets may be takes time. Be patient and invest your money in information to further the case prior to action.

Large Recovery - Fraud Recovery

This area of recovery usually belongs to the massively failed business or the serial fraudster. They may even be the same person. Most of this section is directed at the serial fraudster.

The world is filled with people looking for a secret get-rich formula. They do not want to think on their own. After all, look where their thinking has gotten them. They just want a recipe, in fact a double secret recipe is even better. Actually, even following all of the directions in the double secret recipe is too hard for them, so they look for an expert who has the special "fix" and knows how to get exactly what they want – money and more of it fast and quick. Such a mind-set maneuvers people into the arms of, and eventual subjugation by, the fraudster. The following disappearance of money is as mechanically predicable as the movements of a watch.

Once the fraudster has the money, some is sprinkled back onto the garden of secret formulas to keep the faithful subjugated and the gullible convertible into the faithful. The rest usually disappears in bursts of activity and lands in many remote countries, far-off locations and changes into many disparate forms. All assets are well concealed from the victim and the asset recovery team by the dishonest obligor. By the way, one is a debtor and a deadbeat when one owes a few thousand, but when one owes millions, one disambiguates into a dishonest obligor.

Concealed Asset Recovery

As the term implies, concealed asset recovery involves the recovery of wealth from a dishonest obligor where such wealth has been laundered, camouflaged or hidden. This simple explanation, however, belies the complexity that accompanies the process. It is a difficult and time-consuming activity. It requires detailed planning and the concentrated labor of a group of professionals. The term encompasses not only the end goal – the actual recovery, but also all stages from discovery through recovery. A successful asset recovery process must be based on a sequential, logical, analysis of what has transpired; an indexing and grading of leads; a calculation of what value has been taken; and the formulation of a model designed to maximize ultimate recovery.

Any effective civil recovery model involving a dishonest obligor and substantial value requires the employment of a professional recovery team. This team should be comprised of financial forensic experts, investigators, multijurisdictional pre-emptive remedy lawyers, information technology experts, and fraud experts. This team must have an in-depth understanding of the fraud and the fraudster.

The recovery of concealed assets involves the management of risk. There is a substantial financial and human capital investment. The risk is a function of the degree of complexity of concealment and how many layers of legal relationships and jurisdictions are interposed between the *corpus* of value taken and the *corpus* concealed. The cost of recovery is not a function of the measure of the value of the obligation. The cost of pursuing a $10 million claim can be the same as a $100 million claim. As more capital is spent on the process, the risk of complete failure declines.

The five cornerstones to a well-constructed asset protection fortress include the following components:

> Trust;
> Company;
> Structuring;
> Multijurisdictional nature; and
> Protection of "confidential" information.

These are all legal concepts. Many jurisdictions seek to superimpose seemingly insurmountable walls around bank, trust and company secrets. These barriers are used to flout law enforcement or to defraud creditors and victims. Abstract legal concepts and relations such as "company," "contract," and "trust" are used by law-abiding citizens and fraudsters alike. The problem is compounded by the fragmentation of events and facts across national boundaries. Limited territoriality of law is a principal strength to fraudsters. There are legal mechanisms used in the concealment of wealth. Legal means may be used to protect wealth – even if the means of acquisition of value is illegal or *male fide* – is fair game. Concealed asset recovery involves a careful deconstruction of the fiscal fortress crafted by the fraudster and his aides to show a link between the assets hidden and the underlying wrong.

Why Are Assets 'Concealed' or 'Laundered'?

The goal of any asset protection scheme is protection. This protection can either be honest or dishonest. In debtor-creditor relations, an *ex post facto* fraud (one that happens after the extension of credit) can be an inference of fraud. Assets are *concealed* for a variety of reasons, some legitimate, many not. The law allows creditors to impute an illicit motive to an impugned debtor or transaction by inviting the court to draw inferences from objective facts and circumstances.

A *male fide* actor must conceal the *fructus sceleris* (the fruits of fraud) to avoid having to account for his wrongdoing. This actor must seek to obscure the fact of ill-gotten gains, their location and their provenance. This is a two-stage exercise: intimidate and hinder. In any successful asset recovery plan, one must remember the primary aim of the fraudster or money launderer is the concealment of the illegal source of funds and their subsequent legitimization. However, any system of concealment has its weakness. A thief knows not to give his plunder to another thief. Rather, the dishonest obligors rely on jurisdictions and legal relationships where obligations are honored. Substantial stolen value may circulate by electronic means through a bank in Montenegro or Macao, but not for long. Much of it will likely be found in London, New York and other centers of law and order. Mind you these are educated thieves and they want to have their money close to where they can use it, not under the control of some third party who could be dodgy or honest – each posing their own specific risks to the fraudster's ill-gotten booty.

Legitimate and illegitimate transactions have the same principal objective in the use of asset protection devices. This is represented by the material and financial protection of the self. The establishment of asset protection offers those who invest, honest and dishonest alike, the means to unshackle large trances of capital from the boundaries of normal legal relationships.

What Manner of Person Is Involved in the Concealment Of Wealth?

The concealment of assets involves and implicates a number of parties. The successful asset concealer does not work alone. The primary protagonists are the first set of parties who become involved in asset concealment.

Advanced plans of asset protection (called "structuring"), employ an array of trustees, nominees, straw men, companies and jurisdictions to act as layers of asset location and information procurement barriers. Such multitiered barriers are calculated to add to the complexity and confusion surrounding the disposition of wealth sought. From strategic and tactical perspectives, every scheme assumes that all victims have scarce financial, human and knowledge resources available to dismantle plans of wealth protection. From the onset, complex schemes woven with a tale of imponderables are concurrently designed to highlight victim's ignorances as well as sap the will of victims to respond to the fraud.

A dishonest obligor will even use members of his family to conceal wealth. These parties are innocent of the primary fraud, but not of the secondary acts of concealment. The distance from the primary fraud does not exonerate the innocent holder of wealth. If tainted wealth is acquired with actual or imputable knowledge of the fraud, the holder can be held accountable under alternative heads of accessory liability. This important fact is often overlooked by asset recovery professionals. Each link along the asset concealment chain must be targeted by the investigation as a possible responsible party and thus a party to the recovery.

The Significance of the Problem

Asset concealment has serious repercussions not only for victims, but for the confidence levels in the capital markets, and the well-being of the world's economy. Concealed assets rarely pay taxes. Concealed wealth is out of legitimate circulation, distorting economic reality. The offshore world consists of more than 60 international financial centers. These attract capital because of bank and fiduciary relation privacy legislation, as well as low taxation on foreign deposits and business enterprises. This privacy legislation purports to criminalize the dissemination of information regarding ownership in offshore banks, trust companies, lawyers or other confidants. Privacy is a major sales point used by the professionals proffering services from these jurisdictions.

The Financial Action Task Force (FATF) helps countries combat money laundering. Money laundering around the globe has increased dramatically over the past few decades. In 2001, U.S. District Courts completed 1,420 money-laundering cases and convicted 1,243 individuals, or more than 87 percent of the defendants prosecuted. Estimates of the size of the problem of international money laundering vary, and some commentators argue that the amounts of money involved are astronomical and unknowable. The germ of the amount of money laundered seems to follow whether a large astronomical number or a small unknowable number further the agenda of the issuer of the amount of money laundered.

In the 1980s and '90s the offshore world took direct and aggressive action to expand asset protection devices to reinforce the flow of capital that was gravitating toward jurisdictions with bank secrecy, minimal reporting and low taxes. An asset concealment device will deter well-capitalized victims; they know there will be considerable expense in recovering hidden assets.

The work of the Organization for Economic Co-Operation and Development (the OECD) and the Financial Action Task Force on Money Laundering (the FATF) have tried to limit the attractiveness of these jurisdictions.

The International Monetary Fund (IMF) and the World Bank have formally added the FATF's 40 Recommendations to its list of standards for which Reports on the Observance of Standards and Codes (ROSCs) are prepared. Bankers, lawyers, trust managers and others who handle money or information concerning assets are compelled by criminal law to report any "suspicious transaction." Much of what may be suspicious is set forth in the guidelines. If suspicious activity is not reported, and thus limited, does the banker and financial institution become one of the parties to the recovery? Some have. The sophisticated criminal is well acquainted with the definition of "suspicious," and what is not. Often the bankers and financial institution managers are not.

For more information on the goals and objectives of these organizations, go to http://www.imf.org and http://www.fatf-gafi.org.

Redefinition of the Victim

The key to the success of any fraud recovery plan is tied to the accuracy and completeness of our understanding of the fraudster. The ability to step into the shoes of the criminal and to absorb his surrounding circumstances proves invaluable to the person who would seek to curtail his activities. One cannot begin to understand the fraudster, the person, until one has had time to metaphorically wear his shoes and walk the same streets. One also needs to be disabused of the concept that this type is talented and could use their skills for good. It would be easier to get a fish to tap dance. This is part of their fiber, part of their inner being, who they are and how they interact with the world. For more on how these people live and behave, please read "Inside the Criminal Mind" by Stanton E. Samenow Ph.D. and "The Sociopath Next Door" by Martha Stout, Ph.D.

Fraud can shatter the world of the victim. One of the benefits of redefining the victim, and the aggressor in an asset recovery case is that it is normally a liberating and worthy change of perspective for them to have, instead of doing nothing to confront the problem. I will also counsel those working with victims of fraud and say they will have to walk a difficult path. That is the path that lies between the two beastie infested swamps of "stupid victim" and "solo recovery." It's the path to meaningful remedy. The choices made by the victims are dicey, their reasoning was flawed, they made an investment of their own volition and chose not to listen to others, that is if they even sought independent advice. This headstrong approach does not miraculously leave them, the very same maker of poor choices remains. Rather than forgiving themselves for the poor choices and working with professionals, the victims continue to make poor choices in what should be a recovery phase. I have seen victims try and negotiate with a fraudster, of the friend/wife/daughter of the fraudster to get their money back. I have seen a victim leak information back to the fraudster about recovery efforts to negotiate the return of their portion. I have seen victims duped by fake fraud recovery teams sent to them by the fraudsters themselves to gather up all of the evidence of the fraud, including original documents, to erase or smudge the evidence trail.

One must understand the fraudster as well as the victim in context. The formulation of any plan requires an answer to the questions surrounding the fraud taking into account environmental, political, economic or social issues or a mixture of all four. Any plan of recovery will involve an investigation to ask and attempt to answer at least some of the questions.

Any complex asset recovery investigation will reach across international boundaries. As individual countries have moved to tackle the problem presented by fraud within their own boundaries, the experienced fraudster will have expanded beyond these boundaries. This expansion has presented bad-faith actors with the opportunity to fragment their conduct across multiple territorial lines and limits. To avoid incarceration and attempts at criminal prosecution, the fraudsters are drawn to conduct a fraudulent business multi-jurisdictionally, to mix it up and confuse the recovery. This increase of international white-collar crime requires the commitment of both financial and experienced human capital.

The initial planning phase is critical in any asset recovery. The first consideration must be to prioritize tactical objectives. Do you have a strong case either for damages or against misappropriated assets? Which jurisdictions are involved and are they favorable to you? Finally, what are the accessible assets and where are they located in relation to your principal legal action?

It is important to remember that the jurisdictions involved can be separated into two broad categories: Those where the assets are currently situated or through which they were filtered, and those where the misappropriation or wrongs were committed. In considering the most appropriate jurisdiction to begin the main proceedings, critical consideration must be given to the availability of extraordinary relief and remedies available with the jurisdictions chosen.

The Team

An effective civil recovery plan will require the employment of investigative professionals, financial forensic experts, multijurisdictional pre-emptive remedy lawyers, information technology experts and fraud experts. These people should have knowledge and understanding of the fraudster, his traits, his modus operandi, and his weak spots and blind spots.

Traditional Methods of Recovery are Flawed

Dishonest obligors anticipate and gear their asset concealment conduct to defeat the widely used and predictable methods of claim enforcement employed by creditors when faced with a major default.

A creditor hires a local lawyer to "get a judgment." The lawyer goes through the normal proceedings and, after many delays, often measured in years, the creditor has a judgment. During this time the debtor has by now, re-hidden his assets even further from view and recovery.

Now the creditor hires a local investigator. The investigator comes up with more questions than answers: No assets in the name of the debtor can be found!

Using this strategy I do not believe that a dishonest obligor can ever be defeated. Further attempts of recovery through even the criminal justice system are rarely successful. To recover misappropriated value, one must invert the fraud paradigm and invert the norm.

The challenge lies in our characterization of the problem, articulation of the issues, and crafting of an appropriate strategy to respond to unorthodox but effective conduct in the province of international economic criminals. A plan of recovery must be developed to move around the thief's strengths. Concealed asset recovery can and should be conceptually as simple as the term suggests, provided the correct approach is both adopted and followed. The collection team must overcome the victim's and many professionals' predisposition toward a retreat to the conventional.

The fraudster is prepared for the victim's response of a traditional recovery effort. It is part of the fraudster's plan.

> *A traditional recovery effort is just like a standing army fighting a guerrilla war. The guerrillas never come and fight in the open; rather they melt into the terrain. They consciously deny the large standing army any attempt at a single decisive battle. Rather, they attack from the front, the rear, the flanks – never forming a front. Slowly their tactics demoralize the standing army. Further, the standing army has to pay for all of its massive troops, armaments, and support infrastructure. By contrast, the guerrillas have few needs, and, with only limited financial resources, can forestall the large army in perpetuity. As we know, no county has the budget or the political will to sustain an army in the field forever. There must be results and an end.*

For the fraudster, the end is using your money for his lifestyle. He and all fraudsters are at their end. All they need to do is raise enough issues to forestall the effort of collection until the creditors run out of will or money to fight.

The fraudsters will put up false fronts and spies into the creditor's camp. For the few dollars it costs, it is a great investment for the fraudster.

When the fraud began to unravel the fraudster gathered all of the investors (victims) together and wove a fascinating tale of woe on how a trader in a larger firm had invested $70 million and disappeared with the money. The trader had gone back to Thailand and stole the funds. As for the other $230 million it was tied up in the trading program and would not be accessible for nine months, as per the agreements everyone had signed. The fraudster was so outraged at this theft of money that he retained the services of an expert fraud and financial theft recovery firm. With that he introduced the expert.

The expert worked diligently, met with all of the victims, empathized with them, and gathered all of the original documents that would be needed for court. The expert worked a magical spell over the investors and would send e-mails with tremendous tales of international financial intrigue and the very dangerous cloak and dagger stuff they were doing to recover the funds.

What had actually happened is the fraudster bought another 18 months of time for a fee of $125,000. The fake recovery specialist was an excellent investment for the fraudster. Further, when the investors realized, yet again, something was wrong, fatigue began to set in and many investors were just giving up the recovery effort. This "investor fatigue" is part of the guerrilla plan. When a real team of experts was hired for the recovery, the fifth column of spies left behind by the fake recovery expert and the fraudster began to actively sabotage the real recovery effort. Part of the sabotage was to claim that the new team was a fake team and was going to steal all of the money. The fraudster earned another seven months with the real recovery team dealing with the spies from within. When the case finally came to court, about $20 million in assets had been frozen and the team had prepared for the final and decisive battle. What did the fraudster do? The fraudster began by contesting the entire basis of the case. The fraudster claimed that all of the documents were forgeries, and seeing that no originals had been produced the case could not go forward, and we had the wrong venue. Our team had prepared for this and won many a battle in court those first few days.

The guerrilla technique is very effective especially when you don't know that it is being used on you. We are so schooled, dipped and dyed in the routine of gathering facts and attacking with force that we miss it. We end up attacking and striking voids. The only effective strategy is to attack the fraudster's strengths. Those strengths are: the money to do battle, the unknown origin of their money, their freedom of international movement, freedom to attack you with no moral or factual impediments, and an ego that has them believing they are smarter than anyone else. Begin any attack by debasing any or all of these strengths and you are on the right path.

The recovery team must work in secret to gather intelligence on the fraudster's empire without the reverse occurring. The team must work to isolate the empire, physically, socially and morally. The team must not respond to the fraudster bit by bit. Its members must maneuver in such a way that each time they strike they achieve an overwhelming victory.

To begin, invert the fraud paradigm. The fraudster has access to a wealth of information and professional advice concerning the obscuring and so called "legitimization" of ill-gotten gains. Both fraudsters and their professional advisors are well-informed and have identified the loopholes and will exploit them accordingly. Often the techniques and devices used by the money launderer are similar to those used by the wealthy, law-abiding citizens, whose objective is the reduction of tax liability or more effective estate management. The recognition and understanding of these facts is core to the ability to deal with the fraudster and the paper trail created.
A lateral approach to thinking about the fraud involves taking a step back and viewing the problems presented from a variety of angles. Lateral thinking does not impose any requirement of proof or truth. Its purpose is as a creator or font of new ideas, and not as a method of testing their validity.

The identification or discovery of concealed assets represents fertile ground for lateral thinking in its unrestrained and varied perspectives. When information and leads appear to have been exhausted, the use of lateral thinking to provide alternatives and new perspectives cannot be underestimated. From an asset recovery perspective, a lateral approach can help detect patterns from what appears to be a chaotic or random construction of facts. Lateral thinking can help us to attempt to rebuild the hypothetical asset fortress, keeping in mind the methods and techniques available within a particular sphere or jurisdiction and an analysis of how the asset secretor has acted in the past. Serious fraudsters seem to possess many common traits and follow similar patterns and modes of operation.

The purpose behind the lateral approach is to avoid a "crises of imagination" and a narrow look at what can and cannot be done. We have all dealt with the naysayer in the room telling us how what we have proposed cannot be done. It is best to invert the argument on the naysayers by asking them "how can a lying fraudster have amassed $300 million from these educated, intelligent and industrious people? On the face it seems impossible, yet here we are looking for paths to a recovery you would opine could not have been committed." The crises of imagination has doomed more asset recovery efforts than any other single event.

An inventory of assets, known and suspected, should be prepared. You should also prepare a set of hypothetical income statements and balance sheets to help in estimating the amount and type of assets missing. A chart should be drawn showing the location of known and suspected assets.

Once you look at known and suspected assets, patterns usually emerge to reveal the means used to hide the assets. After all, the common ways to hide assets are a fairly finite set, and professional advisors, particularly within the asset protection world, usually employ recognized devices.

The value of investigation prior to litigation and pre-emptive remedies cannot be understated. When a picture of the assets and how they are held and controlled is in place, and a pre-emptive freeze on those assets is executed, the fraudster will then act to check his assets. In this effort to check his secreted assets, the actions often reveal additional assets not found during the initial investigation. Further, with pre-emptive remedies, you help deprive him of the fuel that will drive his defense to protect the assets and frustrate your recovery efforts. You attempt to deny him the cash with which to wage war against you! Do you wish to fight a fully funded enemy or one without sufficient funds to hire competent opposing counsel?

Unraveling the Fraudster's Web

The discovery of major loss through fraud or deceit always comes as a shock. Not all victims of fraud, having considered the options, choose to take action. Sometimes the decision is a well-reasoned and objective weighing of pros and cons. Sometime it is cognitive dissonance that prevents them from admitting to themselves they have been conned.

Locating Concealed Wealth

Success with concealed asset recovery requires a clear view of the overarching goal, a well-organized set of action steps, and objectives calculated to reach such a goal. The goal must be worked out in advance. Victims and creditors need to understand the risks and consequences. A written plan should be developed, shared and agreed to at the beginning, setting out known facts, principal goals and objectives, methods to be used, a budget, and a description of the phases of work.

Time and Secrecy are Critical Factors

Quick consideration should be given to recovery. Interim objectives should be set. The elements of surprise and prompt action should not be underestimated. The shear amount of asset protection mechanisms and the ease with which funds can be moved can add frustration to the recovery effort. Any investigation should remain confidential as long as possible. If the target becomes aware of the investigation, assets may be moved and recovery efforts may take longer. A key task is to profile the suspected fraudster. A significant amount of valuable information may be generated from the investigation of the fraud itself. The nature of the alleged fraud must be determined. Legal proceedings to recover assets will require evidence of the fraud and losses suffered by the victim. A judgment sounded in fraud frequently makes the difference between collecting a judgment or not.

Locating concealed assets requires knowledge and understanding of the techniques fraudsters use to conceal. In more sophisticated cases, assets will be concealed in offshore jurisdictions or at least routed through offshore jurisdictions. Many of these developing countries possess legal mechanisms or facilities, or cultures that are to the fraudster's advantage. Discovering where funds or assets may have been hidden requires investigative know-how. Put yourself in the shoes of the fraudster. How would you pull it off?

Defining the Manner of Holding Concealed Wealth

Once concealed wealth has been located, it helps to link the "fruits of the fraud" to the fraudster. Initially, useful information may be found online. More protected information will require experience and knowledge of where to look and how to interpret the data. Asset searching of this kind usually reveals only the tip of the iceberg. Sophisticated methods must be used to give the victim confidence that all assets held by or under the control of the fraudster have been identified, and linked to the fraudster. Interviews with friendly and unfriendly parties can be very useful.

Admissions as to ownership of assets can be obtained if clever pretexts are used. If the fraudster likes to boast, and most do, don't stop them. The objective is to obtain valuable clues as to the use and location of the misappropriated funds. Experienced fraudsters have many methods to conceal assets and keep one step ahead of their victims. In the absence of an investigation, a straightforward asset concealment strategy can prevent or delay recovery efforts.

Attribution of Control Over, or Enjoyment of, Assets to an Obligor

Linking control over, or enjoyment of, concealed assets to an obligor is the most difficult part of asset recovery. Fraudsters know the large task of proving a concrete case against them. Evidence will need to be clear and convincing, and the trail of proof needs to be substantially unbroken in order for the court to reach the conclusion favorable to the victim.

174

The initial "ground-pounding" stages must be carried out with the utmost attention to detail and conviction. All evidence must be clear, correct and convincing. The evidence of investigators will be the crucial missing link. Where extraordinary civil search and seizure or secret document disclosure orders have been obtained, all procedures and their execution must be complied with to the letter. We do not want the obligor to have the opportunity to attack the methods used to obtain evidence. These factors are often overlooked. Many asset recovery exercises have fallen upon a technicality.

These are not desktop investigations that can be handled by a forensic accountant and one lawyer. These are real "boots on the ground" investigations with investigators physically tracing the trail of the fraudster, meeting with people the fraudster met, visiting places the fraudster visited, working aggressively covertly and possibly undercover to get the information. This usually means travel, language ability, local counsel and understanding the difference between intelligence and evidence. Also managing the risks of the investigation both physical and legal. Investigators like this gather information that is not on the Web, on a ledger or a docket.

Pre-emptive Strikes to Preserve Wealth Pending Final Outcome

While there are no guarantees that victims will regain their assets, there are many success stories in asset recovery cases. The key to success lies in the ingenuity and experience of the investigators and lawyers used, and the determination and persistence of the creditor.

Once a clear and convincing picture of asset concealment is drawn by the victim's team, a case may be put to court for such measures of extraordinary relief that can be sought in the different jurisdictions. Such relief may have the effect of maintaining the status quo pending a final determination in the case. It is important to remember that the utmost care and accuracy and completeness of disclosure are demanded in this type of request. All of these applications ought to be made ex parte, that is without the involvement of the defendant. This must be done so the case cannot come under attack in the final inter partes proceedings.

Pre-emptive strikes to preserve wealth should be carried out swiftly and simultaneously. Those strikes in different jurisdictions should be as closely aligned as possible, and each order should be sealed and accompanied by a gag order, so that the fraudster will not be made aware of what is happening, thus encouraging further movement of the concealed assets. The key elements are speed and surprise.

> *In one particular asset freeze, the execution of the orders were timed so that in each of the different countries, there were no holidays that would preclude an execution that day, so that they were filed all about the same time, accounting for day and time differences, and so coordinated on a day when it was known that the fraudster was flying from location A to location B and would be unavailable for a long period of time to react to the freeze orders. This was all done in an attempt to thwart the fraudster's quick reaction to a freeze order in one place or time and moving the assets to another place. It was a reasonable and prudent effort, for when he learned of one freeze he promptly tried to move all of the other assets we knew of, and some we did not. If the orders had not been coordinated many of the assets would have slipped out of our grip.*

Once the wealth is secured by means of one or more ex-parte asset freezing orders, it will be necessary to inform the defendant, within a defined period of time, if he doesn't already know. The victim can expect fierce litigation in an attempt to thaw the freeze, prior to the hearing on the merits.

One of the tactical consequences of pre-emptively freezing assets is that the obligor is placed in a position that may induce a proper settlement. Care should be taken in policing the asset freezing relief. The obligor is ordinarily allowed a certain "stipend" for living and legal expenses; it is supposed to be "reasonable." With the pre-emptive freeze in place, the victim is now in a stronger position to consider his options. At this stage, the victim's team must concentrate upon building its case in advance of the final hearing of the merits.

The Fundamentals of a Civil Asset Recovery Plan

Selecting the Place of Judgment

In constructing a model to recover concealed assets that have been fragmented, the selection of the location for the principal proceedings represents an issue of single importance. A judgment will, with some basic requirements, be enforced abroad if it can be proven the defendant (a) was a resident in the country of judgment at the time that the proceedings were instituted, (b) was served with process while he was physically present within the court's territorial jurisdiction, (c) submitted to the jurisdiction of the court by voluntarily appearing in the proceedings, or (d) entered into a contract prior to the institution of the proceedings which gave rise to the judgment, agreeing to submit to the jurisdiction of the court in question. Some courts apply the notion of "extended jurisdiction." This permits the court to exercise its power over defendants who are abroad when it is deemed appropriate for a trial to take place locally.

Once the question of jurisdiction has been considered, there are other issues to be considered before concluding where the principal asset recovery proceedings should be venued. If the judgment would not be recognized in certain countries, the proceedings should not be launched there.

The Harmonization of Multiple, Concurrent Proceedings

The next issue to be considered when designing multijurisdictional proceedings to recover assets is how multiple litigations are to be managed and harmonized to achieve objectives set for each satellite proceeding, as they relate to the principal action.

In a prejudgment context, multijurisdictional litigations are launched in three waves. Some may overlap and be run concurrently:

(a) Pre-emptive discovery litigation to compel the disclosure of confidential records under court-sanctioned seals and gag orders;

(b) Pre-emptive asset freezing or preservation litigation; and

(c) The principal or centerpiece proceedings to obtain a final and conclusive judgment capable of being enforced in each of the jurisdictions where assets have been preserved by judicial decree, abroad.

Historically, in the English speaking world, there was no way to freeze assets provisionally or pre-emptively, without launching a full-blown lawsuit, locally, where the asset sought to be preserved was domiciled.

In contrast, in civil law countries the courts have the power to issue orders of asset arrest that are purely satellite to an outstanding foreign civil litigation on the merits. In the United States, if an obligation can be properly characterized as a debt, state pre-judgment attachment statutes afford a satellite remedy to a plaintiff who might commence a principal proceeding elsewhere. To freeze assets before judgment in America, an interlocutory application must be brought within the context of a full-blown litigation and/or bond for freezing orders under the laws that provide for provisional remedies.

In Europe, a plaintiff in France has the right to compel an English court to provisionally freeze a defendant's assets that are situated in England and Wales, so long as the relevant standard of review and elements of proof required are met or established.

There are other risks to be managed when launching litigations the world over. It is important that the plaintiff, when speaking to multiple courts, does so with a clear and consistent voice. All draft pleadings and forms of evidence must be reviewed carefully to ensure consistency of method of expression and content, legally and factually, throughout the chain of foreign counsel, experts and fact witnesses. In the absence of this consistency, the defendant will discover and exploit inconsistent statements. If this is allowed to occur, it weakens the integrity of the overall effort on behalf of the claimant.

What was harder is becoming easier. As more multinational fraud recoveries are undertaken, the body of law supporting them has grown and is better understood. Further developments have been made and are continuing to be made on laws and treaties dealing with corruption as well as the frauds and money laundering that occur concurrent with the fraud. These international developments of law and treaties were originally aimed at corrupt potentates and functionaries, but are having a very desirable spillover effect in the assistance with civil recovery efforts.

Blocking Devices

For multiple satellite asset-freezing proceedings to hold together, the overall plan must be designed to sustain the stress of multiple and sustained attacks by the defendant. Once assets have been discovered and preserved by means of multiple ex-parte freeze orders, and once the defendant has been served, it is in the interest of both sides to attempt to stay all satellite litigation pending the outcome of the principal proceedings. The defendant may find tactical advantage in rejecting this notion. The defendant may try to burn out the other side financially, by filing a snowstorm of motions. The defendant may also object to the plaintiff's first choice of venue. The plaintiff would be well advised to have a plan ready to be launched to aggressively force a stay of proceedings in each satellite jurisdiction.

Building The Foundation to the Case – Introduction

All successful civil fraud recoveries start with a solid foundation. Setting out the primary allegations of material fact in support of the relief sought, which fall under legal categories called "causes of action." A "cause of action" is defined as "a factual situation that entitles one person to obtain a remedy in court from another person." The way a claim is framed from the beginning can have a major impact on its meaning and effectiveness. If fraud is properly pleaded and proved from the outset, it links the primary and secondary fraudulent conduct into a continuum of deceit. What follows is a summary description of a number of the causes of action used when building the grounding pleading to recover value for an apparent victim of economic crime.

Fraud at Law – Deceit

The deceit or fraud at law is a false statement of fact, which is made by one to another, with the intent that it should be acted upon. This tort is of no use to a victim of an act of non-disclosure, unless the party remaining silent can be shown to have had a duty to speak (as would a fiduciary).

The most significant problem with the deceit is that it requires an examination of the state of mind of not only the wrongdoer, but also of the victim. It involves pleading and proving the necessary mental processes of both the maker and receiver of the material. These notions are difficult to prove and are incomprehensible to most juries.

Fraud at law is capable of covering a multitude of situations involving fraud. False statements of fact may be made in verbal or written format. This too is not easy to prove, but may be easy to refute.

Fraud at Equity

Fraud at equity is often referred to as "constructive fraud" in the sense that it is not readily defined, but may be construed from objective circumstances. Constructive fraud encompasses the following headings:

> (a) Undue influence;
> (b) Unconscionable bargains;
> (c) Abuse of confidence; and
> (d) Fraud on powers.

Courts have refused to define the boundaries of this extended (or constructive) fraud. As a result, the concept of fraud at equity is capable of expanding to fit a variety of circumstances of fraudulent conduct which might otherwise fall foul of the requirements of actual fraud or fraud at law.

Fraud at equity offers the equitable remedies of rescission, specific performance of declaratory relief. Another remedy for the wronged party is a declaration lifting the veil of a company that is the instrument of a fraud. The legal analytical basis for doing this was the notion of fraud at equity.

Statutory Causes

There are a variety of legal bases available for a victim of fraud. These can include consumer protection laws, securities fraud, insider dealing in the United Kingdom, and in the United States, state and federal securities and civil racketeering statutes.

Tracing or 'Tracking and Attributing' Ownership to Concealed Wealth

Tracing refers to the process whereby assets may be "traced" by their owner from their point of departure through to their current location. It provides an answer to the question of who the true owner of wealth may be, and if it has been misappropriated or lost due to some form of wrongdoing. Tracing is neither a claim nor a remedy, it is a fact trail based on evidential process. It is the process taken by the original owner of assets to identify those assets in the hands of a third party and to justify his claim. Upon completion of the identification process, the original owner will be entitled to a remedy.

English law contains two separate legal systems, common law and equity. Each system recognizes a different kind of ownership of money. The rules of common law recognize legal ownership or legal interests in money. The rules of equity recognize beneficial ownership or beneficial interests or equitable interests. Tracing rules, generally, are the legal rules by which a court decides whether the money that the defendant holds or has received is the same money taken from the victim of the fraud. If a victim claims that he remains the legal owner of the misappropriated funds, he will have to show this under the common law tracing rules. If he is claiming that he has an equitable interest, he will have to rely upon the tracing rules of equity.

Tracing at common law suffers from the fact that the victim of fraud loses legal title to the money when it passes through the banking system. Under common law tracing rules, legal ownership of money is lost when it is mixed with money that belongs to someone else. When the victim loses legal ownership of the money, it is still possible to claim an equitable interest under the tracing rules of equity.

Tracing at Equity – Requirements

For property to be traced in equity there are three conditions:

(a) The property must be traceable;
(b) There must be an 'equity' to trace; and
(c) Tracing must not produce an inequitable result.

If these conditions are satisfied, the claimant will be entitled either to the assets into which his property has been traced, or, if there are others who have a claim upon them, to a charge.

Equitable relief is only available where legal remedies are either not available or have been exhausted. A victim's money will be regarded as trust money if it was held under special duty, or fiduciary duty, when he parted with it. Fiduciary duty exists because of the relationship between the victim and fraudster prior to the fraud. The most common example of fiduciary relationship is between trustee and beneficiary. Other fiduciary relationships are, agent and principal, partner and partner, solicitor and client, and director and company.

Fraudulent inducement is when the victim is tricked into entering into a contractual loan or commission arrangement, or where large numbers of victims are tricked into buying worthless securities; through fraudulent representations. An example could be when a fraudster presents forged documents to a confirming bank under a letter of credit or issues a fraudulent demand under a performance bond.

The victim must establish a "proprietary base." The victim must first establish it was the victim's money to start with; and that the defendant received that money. The next questions are whether the victim can claim that the defendant received the money and what happens if that money has changed hands.

Property can be traced only if it is traceable. In the asset tracing process, a series of rules have been developed.

They are:

> The Mixed Fund Rule;
> The Rule in Re Oatway;
> The Lowest Intermediate Balance Rule;
> The Overdraft Rule; and
> The Rule in Clayton's Case.

These are worth reviewing with your asset recovery team.

Investigative Methods, Extra Judicial

Investigations to discover the whereabouts and manner of holding of concealed assets must be conducted under the protection of utmost secrecy.

The use of private financial investigators has increased in recent years. The use of a private financial investigator is the most efficient method of gathering necessary evidence in a time-sensitive fashion. In the face of serious fraud, it is imperative that an investigative team be assembled as soon as practically possible.

It is the lawyer's responsibility to coordinate with the investigative firm. It is important that there is a mutual understanding between counsel and the investigative firm. A written agreement between counsel and the investigative firm is essential. The investigative firm should be appropriately licensed. Otherwise, in those jurisdictions that impose a licensing regimen, the lack of a license may damage the credibility of the investigation.

A complex investigation involving serious fraud must be conducted in a thorough and legal manner, free from conjecture, unsubstantiated opinion or bias. The professionals involved must be receptive to all evidence, exculpatory, as well as incriminating.

Judicial Discretion to Exclude Certain Evidence

The admissibility of evidence wrongly obtained is an issue. Judicial opinion frowns upon illegal or improper methods of obtaining evidence. The court has a duty to reject evidence, which is not relevant and not admissible. It must be remembered that there is no rule that automatically excludes evidence, which has been obtained by improper or illegal means. The general rule is that where evidence is relevant it is admissible, many times regardless of its provenance.

Pre-Emptive Strikes to Freeze Assets – the Old and the New Ways

The Old Way

Freezing Orders/Mareva Injunctions

Courts in the British Commonwealth have moved to respond to the dishonest dealer who may seek to avoid his obligations by concealing evidence, dissipating or transferring assets, and resorting to delaying tactics. The ex parte Mareva injunction and the Anton Piller order represent two of the most important accomplishments of modern English legal reform. These remedies put the victim of financial crime in a position of obtaining meaningful pre-emptive and pre-judgment asset freezing and evidence search and seizure relief. These remedies are special – and have been abused.

Given the serious damage that can be done by the grant of a Mareva injunction, English courts have imposed very strict requirements upon parties seeking this relief. The victim must demonstrate possession of a good and arguable case on the merits.

Today, British Commonwealth Courts will grant a Mareva injunction that has worldwide effect but must be based upon a solid case and well-documented facts.

The New Way

Mareva by Letter or Creating a Constructive Trust

A Mareva by Letter is also known as a Freezing Order by Letter. In order to successfully preserve assets through freezing or restraining orders, detailed affidavits and pleadings must be prepared and filed with the appropriate court coupled with requests for sealing and gagging relief where relevant. One can also construct a detailed proof of the origin of funds held by a third party and raise the issue of a "Constructive Trust" that this third party, now being made aware of the origin of the asset, has been placed. There should be no expectation that the funds will be released to you, but the objective is that the third party will not release the funds to the frauds until orders from a judge are issued and received.

Financing the Cost of the Asset Recovery Process in the United States

In the United States, there are two methods to finance the asset recovery process: (1) attorney contingency fees and (2) third-party investment.

Investigators, forensic analysts, and local counsel must be retained, often in multiple jurisdictions, and paid on an ongoing basis, though you can string along the private investigators for a long time without paying them. A party that has suffered a loss of millions of dollars may be wary to invest additional funds.

Attorney contingent-fee arrangements are lawful in order to allow indigent plaintiffs with meritorious claims access to the judicial process. In the United States, attorneys working under contingent-fee arrangements are permitted to advance costs.

In the absence of "finance" through the attorney contingent-fee model, the most practical method to finance asset recovery plans is through access to the capital markets. In the major financial centers there are numerous financial entities that take positions in situations where the likelihood of success is unclear. Investment in asset recovery plans is a natural addition to these markets.

These businesses provide advances to plaintiffs of pending personal injury lawsuits or judgments on appeal in return for a high rate of interest or a large percentage of the award.

Where Asset Recovery Cases Fail

There are several enemies to successful asset recovery. Honestly, when a fraud to merit an international recovery effort has been effected, we by definition have a fraudster that is smarter and more cunning and ruthless than the obligor. The obligor must admit to themselves they were conned. This hump is one of the most difficult to get over for the obligor. The obligor has to come to the realization that their personal decision-making system is flawed. For some people, it is easier to walk away from the money than to admit they were wrong and implement corrective action.

Time is on the fraudster's side. The longer any actions are delayed, the longer the fraudster can spend and enjoy the obligor's money. The more time they have the more layers they will construct to frustrate and impede collection efforts. The two biggest time-wasters are getting the obligors to admit they have been taken, and then arguing amongst themselves as what should be done. Committees of angry defrauded people decide little and often turn on one another.

Stories are what fraudsters tell as to what happened with the funds all coming to the same end: The money is gone and it wasn't my fault. Some of these stories and ruses can be elaborate and convincing. But they are just ruses to get more time.

Law Enforcement

There is nothing wrong with calling law enforcement when a crime has been committed. The problem is that criminal prosecution and asset recovery are two different goals. Prosecution is revenge, and asset recovery is about getting some of the funds back to the victim. It's not to say they are mutually exclusive either. While one works on asset recovery you build a very fine case for law enforcement later. When law enforcement personnel build the case, they don't share information (they really can't), and several years later the fraudster has spent all of the funds defending the criminal matter and there is nothing left to recover. Also, new and growing threats to asset recovery are "proceeds of a crime" legislation. The assets of the obligor in the fraudster's hands are proceeds of a crime. It is not unknown for the government to file to seize all of the proceeds of the crime, depriving both the fraudster and the obligor of the assets, and converting them to government assets.

However, when a victim is covered by insurance, the insurance carrier may require that the incident be reported to law enforcement. Failure to do so may bar the victim from making any recovery of the loss from the insurance carrier. This is most often the case under embezzlement and employee related frauds. Make sure that if the victim is a company, that its insurance policies are checked immediately to see if there is any coverage from insurance. After all, what we are trying to do here is recover a loss and if the client has insurance coverage that will cover the loss it makes more sense to be made whole by the insurance carrier instead of mounting a recovery effort. Leave that up to the insurance carrier.

Means Versus Ability

Most of the big frauds bring money in and send money out. It is part of the seeding process to keep the fraud going. If $100 million was invested and $80 million paid out, the ideal corpus is $20 million. But fraudsters spend money like it is not their own, because it is not. Thus a reasonable spend rate must be surmised from what we know. If we surmise that they are spending $3.2 million per year, and the intake of funds stopped three years ago, the target for recovery is $10.4 million or 100 – 80 – 9.6 =10.4 million.

Failing to know and understand how these items inject themselves into an asset recovery plan may allow them to trip you up.

Qualifying And Quantifying the Assets

It helps with all asset investigations to make a list of assets known and presumed. It is also helpful when setting up a plan of recovery to prioritize the task of asset recovery as part of the recovery effort.

Assets can be roughly divided into five categories:

Cash and cash equivalents such as cash on hand, demand deposits in bank accounts and brokerage accounts. Marketable securities and other marketable investment vehicles fit into this category since once controlled they can be sold for cash.

Real estate is another category; this includes not just land, but condos, time-shares, co-ops. These are title assets and both common and civil law have excellent means for both of these assets as well as means for forfeiture and freezing.

Equipment such as cars, boats, planes heavy equipment, boys toys and like. But do not forget valuable equipment such as printing presses, scientific equipment, mining equipment, etc. These items may be part of a class of equipment that does not have any title or registrations or they may. The issue of title or registration can be a subcategory of this, if one chooses.

Ownership of entities and rights by contract. This includes more familiar assets such as common stock, LLC units, bonds, partnerships, etc. that are not listed or readily marketable. It also includes assets such as rights like warrants, options, rights of succession, and rights of action. This also includes beneficiary status on insurance policies, if the fraudster actual ever did buy insurance, or is the beneficiary of a policy where they control that status. This also includes items such as copyrights, patents, trademarks, and all other forms of IPCI.

> *As our economy has left the Knowledge Age Economy and has entered the Age of the Intangibles, new assets are brought to life by the body of law that both defines these assets and help protect these assets. A lease with a right to purchase can be a valuable asset in a robust real estate market, stock options are a common part of many compensation packages, the rights to Web sites are often over looked, istockphoto sold in Feb of 2006 for 50 million dollars, we have even seen some simple web sites sell for 15 to 20 thousand dollars. The content on one blog was so narrow and deep that it sold for $45 thousand just so the copyrighted material could be re-tasked into a book and movie. Sometimes, these assets may have no immediate*

value, but ask yourself how much would this company's competitor pay to possess the information? Now you're getting a sense of how to recognize and develop the value.

Inchoate assets or interests. These are assets that are not yet fully formed. The inchoate interest becomes an asset after a triggering event such as death for heirs, or meeting performance goals for bonuses, or an heir reaches a predetermined age to receive a distribution from a trust. It is best to think of this asset in as broad as terms as possible and to involve a multi-disciplinary approach to seek and indentify inchoate assets.

> *This is, at least conceptually, the most difficult of the asset categories to wrap one's mind around. There is a right to an asset, but that right is not yet fully developed to the point where that right may be exercised. This concept was made clearer to me in a case where a young lady disappeared. She and her boyfriend had a dispute and she left him, never to be seen of or heard from at least now ten years as of this writing. All suspected her boyfriend and while he did enjoy some of her money at first after her disappearance that ended when the police arrested him. He was charged with several counts of fraud having to do with his actions before the two met. The family, or prospective heirs, should she be declared dead, immediately requested the courts to appoint a conservator/custodian for the assets. The assets were to be protected, should she be found later alive or for the heirs should she be found to be, or declared, dead. The conservator/custodian sold off the assets and pursued several parties who had defrauded the young lady, shortly after she disappeared. The inchoate rights were developed with the court authorized conservator/custodian. The tangible assets were liquidated and held in cash and cash equivalents. Five years later she was declared dead by the courts and the funds were released to the heirs. If these rights were not exercised a home full of artwork would have been foreclosed upon and lost, a car would have rotted away and the assets held by the banks and brokerage companies would have escheated to the state.*

All of the identified assets should be weighted based upon the availability of the assets to satisfy the claims of the creditors against the fraudsters. These assets are roughly colored by distance from initial legal action, nature of the assets, and efforts required to turn those assets into cash.

The first condition of assets we can call the immediate assets or low hanging fruits. These are the assets that can be recovered the quickest and turned into cash. These assets are key to deal with and aid in funding the recovery. Victims of fraud are already in both emotional and fiscal fatigue. They have realized that the investment opportunity they have been given was nothing but a pack of lies and a circus if chicanery. These are intelligent people that have been dumped and need to have some recovery for their emotions as well as for their wallets. These can be any of the assets mentioned in the list of the categories of assets. Boats titled locally may be easier to turn into cash than cash sitting in a foreign bank account. Do not let the category of the asset color the condition of the assets.

The next group of assets are those assets that while not as easily recovered can be correctly identified. These can be any of the assets described but for some reason, either titling or the domicile of the assets, they cannot be seized - but they can be frozen. The freezing mechanism can be a Mareva injunction – enjoining the parties to the assets from moving or retiling those assets. In the U.S. this can be a court order, or part of other legal proceedings. In civil law jurisdiction in can be the arresting of the asset pending the outcome of any litigation. The victims are not going to gain immediate access to the assets but the use of the assets is denied to the fraudster.

The last action you can take on the assets is impairing the title or the fraudster's use of the assets. This tactic requires the cumulative creativity and life skills of the asset recovery team. You cannot grab or freeze the asset, but you can impair either the transfer of the assets or the ability of the fraudster to enjoy the asset. Two examples of this are first a letter to a bank that may have a large deposit of funds that originated from the actions of the fraudster. A detailed letter to the banker letting them know that the funds contained in the account are most likely the proceeds of a fraud and rightly belongs to the victims of the fraud. This creates a condition of constructive trust placing the banker into the role of custodian of funds that may belong to the victims of the fraud. Does this mean you get the funds? No. However, the banker is not about to let the fraudster have the funds either. The banker will not let the funds move until a judge tells him what to do. The second example is the ownership of a significant asset such as art, or collectable cars etc. Registering the item with the Art Loss Registry will more or less ensure that the item will not be able to be sold at any reputable auction. It does not stop the sale; it just prevents the item being sold at or through reputable channels. Also any open and notorious disclosure of the provenance of the asset will affect the transferability of the asset. You are altering the marketplace and there may be a problem with the title of the object and cloud the presumption of an arms length sale of the item. For an example, if a printing press or company was purchased with proceeds of a fraud it is possible to place an advertisement in trade papers that the assets may have a clouded title.

Prioritization and Valuation

The assets now need to be prioritized. What assets represent the low hanging fruit of the recovery. What assets can be harvested as expeditiously as possible to help self-fund the recovery process? Cash in a local bank account is always good, but it may not be the easiest target. Experienced asset recovery attorneys and investigators need to assess and prioritize each asset based upon ease of recovery for the victims and cost and time involved in executing the recovery plan that is different for each asset and each legal domicile of the asset. Also what is the net value of the asset? What is the value of the asset accounting for the current value of the asset, minus the cost of recovery of that assert discounted to the present value of the asset reflecting the time cost during the recovery process?

> We had identified several assets of a fraudster including bank accounts in Manhattan and the proverbial Swiss Chalet, actually a $2 million plus condo in Gstaad to be more exact. It took less time in Switzerland to obtain title and sell the condo in Gstaad than it did to get through the clogged courts of Southern Manhattan and deal with the appeals process in the U.S.. Our experienced counsel was well aware of how much the Swiss dislike financial fraudsters and how expeditious their legal systems become when they are fighting fraud.

Asset Recovery Planner

Asset / Action	Cash & Cash Eqiv	Titled	Not Titled	Inchoate
Immediate	*NPV*			
Freeze				
Impair				
Declare				

The table is a way of thinking about the assets and the recovery process. It is not a difficult process and intuitively is not a difficult process. But is a process that is more
ignored than it is used. The use of, or failure to use, this or a similar process is a failure of the management of the asset recovery team to plan an efficacious recovery model.

Final Thoughts

This report is directed at anyone thinking about collecting upon a debt or obligation. It is not a cure-all or a road map, but a primer to get the reader to think about the process whether it be little or large.

> *The creditors in planning an asset recover strategy and its related support tactics must be given no refuge other than to think about the process and the plan.*

There are overlaps in the presentation, some smaller obligations may be fraudulent and some very large one may not be. I get it, but it is a useful manner of presentation to get the reader to think about the process.
May you never lose money to a debt or a fraud, and that this information forever remains just a curiosity.

I want to give some credit and thanks to three true gentleman who have worked in recovering money and from whom I continue to learn.

Joseph F. Musumeci, Esq. of Arizona has an entire legal practice dedicated to getting thousands people to pay what they owe pursuing them doggedly and fiercely, but always as a gentleman.

Peter J. Rathwell, Esq. of Arizona is a man of letters with the gift, or honed skill, of possessing a near foolproof B.S detector. His wide-ranging experiences litigating in state, federal and bankruptcy courts make him a formidable adversary. Peter understands how to use the law married to collection strategy and tactics to produce results few others will ever achieve.

Martin Kenney, Esq., of the British Virgin Islands, either through working with him on cases or from his writings – some of which serve as the kernel for the international asset recovery portion of this chapter, has always been a generous mentor. Much of my thinking on large scale international fraud and fraud recovery has come from working with Martin on unusual cases in some of the strangest courts and countries I have ever known.

Chapter 9

Resources

"Knowledge exists to be impaired."
> Clyde Allen Smythe-Howlett, aka CASH for short
> of which he never is...

What follows are several example of resources that may assist you, the financial professional, in locating answers and information. Some of the records have story embellishments to highlight how they can be used.

Public records can be used to support information contained in résumés, including identity and address verification. Public records can also be searched as part of a background check on many other claims and representations that we may encounter in our personal and business lives. Understanding what records are available, helps us search for professional affiliations, licenses, criminal records, judgments, liens, corporate affiliations and bankruptcies.

Public records are increasingly becoming available online for free or for a small fee. For some records you may need to visit the custodian of the records, and possibly identify yourself along with your purpose in requesting the information.

The following list is in no way exhaustive, it is simply a representative sample of common public records that may be available to you, and contains some examples of how they can be used. It is to stimulate the thought process as you pursue what information may be available in your area on the person you are studying.

Municipal Records

Municipalities have many records that can be of assistance in one's research. Building permits, construction inspections and occupancy permits carry information about owners, insurance policies and contractors, including contact and bonding information. Meetings at city hall range from the regular gatherings of representatives to the occasional meetings of boards and commissions, but they all produce records involving the first public discussion of issues. Locations of cell towers, zoning decisions, utility line placements, rights of way and planned construction projects can all help in your research. The police and fire departments also have records that are of great assistance.

> *A man was selling a dry cleaning operation for a relatively cheap price. A review of the city's records showed a significant development project was planned and budgeted. Its location affected the corner where the dry cleaner was located. The project was to redo the water and power lines while widening the road by one lane. The project was expected to take 11 to 18 months. We confronted the owner of the dry cleaning shop with this news. We learned he knew about it already, and that he was selling his shop because he expected the project would cause his revenue to drop by half. There was no negotiation on the price, he figured someone would not do his or her homework and would give him what he was asking – he was correct.*

> *An employee of a horseracing track was required at the end of every day to deliver a very time-sensitive cargo to a laboratory – horse urine from the winning horses of that day's races. One day he showed up an hour late to the lab claiming he was delayed by a huge accident with fire trucks and ambulances, etc. A very reasonable excuse, but his manager made a call to the fire department just to check. On that day there were no calls for service anywhere in the city. Driver – fired!*

Sales Tax

Depending upon the state and local community, sales tax reports are generally unavailable to the public. These records can be used to confirm sales activity in a business. When buying a business, one of the best ways to find out the level of activity is to review the sales tax reports filed with the city or state. Require the seller to grant access to past sales tax reports filed, don't rely on what the owner represents – get the records from the city.

Water Department

Water usage and hook-up information is often available for both business and residential customers. I have often found the water department to be helpful in locating people. These records can help with verification of ownership, and determining the level of activity in many businesses. Water usage can be very important in analyzing certain businesses. In two businesses I have investigated (a brush and squirt type car wash, and a beauty salon), the volume of water use was directly correlated to sales.

Examining water usage is a good example of investigative technique. The water department is not on any list of resources I would use in most investigations. But this is an example of how to stretch your mind and to think of other sources or locations with information. In doing your research you need to look for any source that will add information to the corollary – including secondary, tertiary and tangential sources that you can use for inference. It's almost always discordance in the expected pattern that exposes false information (or assumptions).

County Recorder's Office

County recorder offices are an especially good asset, as they are the repository for legal documents from a wide array of sources. Recorders' offices are tasked with maintaining official records, including, but not limited to: mining claims, judgments, purchase or sale of real property, purchases and sales of businesses, tax liens, declarations of homestead, powers of attorney, and the filing of trust documents. These records are extensive and can reveal many items of issue, fact and interest. Take your time when you go to the county recorder's office and read, read, read.

Country Assessor's Office

The assessor's office is responsible for the maintenance of maps, sales records and tax assessments for a given county. Uses of the sales records can support property valuations or discredit them if you can document that many of the comparables were between conspiring parties to drive up land prices – not that that has ever happened. One can also access information on the payment of taxes on a parcel and sometime see proof of that payment in the form of an imaged check. The level of access will vary, but at least you now know one of our favorite ways of finding accounts on people who have property. If the property taxes are paid by a title company, then we can use discovery powers to work our way back to see how the homeowner pays the title company.

Board of Realtors

The Board of Realtors is the licensing body for real-estate agents and real-estate brokers. Brokers are different from Realtors. These records will show if the individual is, or has been, licensed with the state to engage in real-estate transactions and whom they are licensed with. Some states also maintain a real-estate recovery fund to indemnify people from financial harm caused by a Realtor. To emphasize, each state is different and to highlight this fact, here is a little story.

> *Mr. Smith was offering in the newspaper a 20 to 25 percent rate of return, fully collateralized by property. Mr. Smith would get people to buy property, then he would rent that property out. The property he would have the people purchase would be inexpensive properties. For example, he had one of my clients purchase a townhome for $25,000. The fair market value of this townhome was $18,000. As a consequence, Mr. Smith made, how much, $7,000 on the transaction before the provision of his managerial services. When he rented out the property, he would collect the rents for a little while, pay the people and then say the real-estate market has turned, or there are other problems, blah, blah, blah, blah, blah. In short, the investment is not going very well. The investors would have a first position on the property, but nevertheless, by the time they foreclosed on the property, and sold it and went through the legal rigamarole, they would have little or nothing left. Oddly enough, this Mr. Smith purchased properties for his investor victims that were just the right size. These properties would cost him just as much to go through and foreclose and sell as it was to just let them be. Mr. Smith many times offered to pick up these terribly dilapidated properties*

from his beleaguered for just a few thousand dollars to assuage the investor. He made money on the purchase of the property, on the management of the property, when he collected the rents and kept the rents (not paying them to the investors) and than when he took the property off the investors hands. He was insulated against legal action since all of the investments were small enough that legal action did not look appealing to the investors. He had offices in Tampa, Philadelphia, Chicago, Littleneck, San Jose, Phoenix and Houston. Not surprisingly, all the calls were forwarded to his home in Phoenix. There were no other offices in any of these other locations. It was nothing but a business presence purchased at a suite of offices.

Contractors Board

A state contractors board licenses a variety of contractors and may maintain a recovery fund for victims of these contractors. These records will show if the individual is licensed, the type of work he is licensed to perform, and bonding information. All types of contractors are licensed through contractor departments. Contractors such as cable TV installers, landscapers, roofers, builders and cement layers may have to be licensed with the state by the contractors board. An investigator can obtain a lot of information about an individual or a company if either one is registered with the contractors board.

Corporation Commission / Secretary of State / Corporations Division

A corporation commission maintains records for all of the corporations and limited liability companies within a state (in some states these records may be kept by the secretary of state's office). The corporation commission's records will include who is incorporated, annual reports that show changes in management and structure, and possibly the corporate balance sheet. Only application and termination information is kept on limited liability companies. I am using the state of Arizona as an example because that is where I live and perform most of my investigative work. Records and procedures are different from state to state and in federal territories. Most of the important information you will find, will include the name of the statutory agent, the names of the officers and directors, who the major shareholders are, the standard industrial code under which that business operates, articles of incorporation, and annual reports. You may also be able to run an asset search on the corporation. Many states allow searches by major shareholders, officers and directors. Once you have a person's name, you can cross-reference names and corporations.

Department of Motor Vehicles

A state department of transportation maintains records on both vehicles and their drivers. These records will show if a person has a driver's license and what citations have been issued in the last five years. The records will also show all vehicles, including trailers and mobile homes that are registered to an individual. Following up on tickets is always a good idea because the person may have been cited while driving a company vehicle, or the information on the citation may give you their new address, phone numbers – and lists of witnesses and passengers, if they were in an accident. For people trying to hide, getting in contact with those whom they know may be the only way to locate them.

> *I had an interesting case that came to me from Germany. Mr. Vonsmith owed a very large sum, several million Deutsche Marks which translated into a little over a million dollars. The client bank had pursued him all the way to the United States. The bank's representatives were particularly upset that Mr. Vonsmith took out a loan and left the country. Hey, he was out of money, he had to get the money somewhere! I was asked to see if I could find Mr. Vonsmith and find out what assets he had. I pulled his driver's license. That was the only bit of information I could find on him in the state of Arizona. What I found is that Mr. Vonsmith had received a few tickets. I pulled the ticket information and found the vehicles he was driving at the time he received the tickets. They were in the name of a business. I checked other cars in that business's name and found two brand new Range Rovers, a relatively new Mercedes and a Rolls Royce Corniche Convertible. He had to do something with the money. By continuing to check on the name of this business, I went back and found out that Mr. Vonsmith had purchased a very*

nice house in an expensive neighborhood in Phoenix. As luck would have it, I went up and drove past the house and noticed that the house was for sale. I called the Realtor and asked if the Realtor would be kind enough to show me the house. Notice, I did not say buy it! The Realtor was more than happy to oblige. Myself and another investigator posing as my wife went to the house. The female investigator kept the real-estate agent busy while I wandered around the house looking at all the documents left out on the table. Without opening or touching anything, underscore, nothing was opened or touched, we got information about all his credit cards, the several businesses he owned, all of his insurance policies and his impending move to Southern California. The information was turned over to the law firm and within about four months, they were able to seize the home, all of the automobiles, the businesses and the insurance policies since it was all purchased with stolen money.

Insurance Department

The state department of insurance maintains records on insurance companies, insurance agencies and insurance salespeople. These records will show all of the affiliations with insurance companies and all of the insurance companies' agents and sales people. They also maintain licenses on the individual people who are licensed to sell in that state.

Fairly recently, an insurance agent began drawing workers' compensation for an injury he received while on the job. Apparently, he slipped and fell on some water that had leaked from a water cooler. This man was a very good and aggressive agent, and after this accident, he requested workers' compensation. The state began to pay it and ding the company for the cost. The company strongly disagreed. But neither the state nor the former employer could find any information to support the company's position. The agent seemed to live for the most part at his house in Arizona. I was hired to find what the insurance agent was doing. A check of insurance licenses in California, Nevada, Utah, New Mexico and Colorado found the individual active in California. In fact, he was so active that he had received several awards for all of his insurance sales in California. He had been working with an associate over there and he was calling *all of his buddies here in town asking for referrals to companies in California. Needless to say, the workers' compensation claim was denied for the period of time that he had requested assistance because he could not work. During this four-month time period, he earned more than $60,000 in commissions.*

Liquor Board

The liquor board licenses individuals and their establishments to sell alcoholic beverages. These records will contain lots of information on an individual including useful background details if the person has ever been issued a liquor license. I cannot underscore how much information is available from this licensing board. You will find that the investigation involves a great deal of individual disclosure before the license is issued. There can be information about the spouse, prior employment and any major lenders or silent partners in the bar.

Just a side note, a story on bars. I'm not sure it is necessarily pertinent to financial investigations, but I'll tell it all the same. I have been hired several times to take a look at bars and find out if the operations are doing any type of skimming. For the first operation I was asked to look at, I walked into the bar, and there was not another person in sight. It was absolutely desolate. I sat down at the bar and the bartender came out and asked me what I was doing there. I said I came in for a drink. He said "I don't think I want to serve you. Get the hell out." I did. The bar was shut down about six months later for laundering money. That is one good way to keep the complications low. Have great sales and no patrons. Cuts down on overhead.

Another note, on any type of bar skimming, usually what you will see is a row of registers. For example, a row of three registers with one register that rings up "no sale" the whole night. That is the unimaginative way. The other way I have seen, operates at the front of the bar or near the door where a young person warmly greets arriving patrons and offers them say a long neck beer or a drink for a very nice price. A price just a little bit below what they are serving at the bar. Kind of a "welcoming" gift. Usually, what happens in those situations is that the owner or the person selling the drinks is buying the drinks retail and selling them at the door. At night's end, they split up the cash, go back and start up all over again the next night. That complete, off-income statement transaction is run out the right and left front pockets of the owner.

Medical Licensing Board

The state medical licensing board licenses most health care practitioners. Records here will show if an individual has been licensed as a medical care practitioner and their most recent professional affiliation. With the medical licensing board, you will find licensing history, complaints, if there is any malpractice that has been submitted to medical board arbitration. You will find complaints there, but you will find most of the medical malpractice claims filed in a nearby county or state court. I find it interesting that there is more information on a person with a liquor license than on a doctor or medical practitioner.

Professional Licensing Board

Many professionals require licensing with governmental agencies. These include accountants, attorneys, medical professionals other than doctors, therapists, technicians, beauticians, food handlers, barricade workers, and all sorts of people such as securities dealers, commodity brokers, realtors, pest control workers, etc. Check with the local and state regulators to see if the profession of the person you are investigating requires any type of professional licensure requirements.

State Bar

The state bar is a professional licensing board for attorneys-at-law and certified legal assistants. Records here will show if the individual is either an attorney or a certified legal assistant and the most recent professional affiliations of that attorney. It also maintains information about complaints, disciplinary actions, arbitrations, etc.

As a private investigator, I specialize in finding assets. In this particular case, I was hired to find assets for an estate. After the assets had been found, the attorney decided that she was going to claim a contingency fee. A many million dollar contingency fee, all for herself. Well, it ended up in arbitration. The individual said that she would not accept less than her several million dollar fee. The client said "my private investigator found those assets, not the attorney." The arbitration was quite, quite amicable (I was while I was deposed by 13 different attorneys over the course of an afternoon), and in the end, the attorney was awarded only the several hundred thousand dollars for her actual work. The dispute arose over ambiguities contained in the contingency fee agreement. The attorney claimed the fees on the grounds that I worked for them to preserve attorney-client privilege, but I was paid by the client so the client considered me his man, which meant the attorney did not find the assets I had found and was not entitled to a contingency fee. The arbitrators, I think, got it right, giving the attorney her fee on what she found and exempted what I found from the agreement.

There was a fellow running around the neighborhood, an attorney called Mr. Smith, who was a defrocked, disbarred attorney in a couple of states, but he was still practicing law. He was charging exorbitant fees for trust work and still representing himself as an attorney. As you can tell, the local bar did not have jurisdiction and law enforcement saw it as a civil matter. In the end the client constructed a Web site resplendent with the ex-attorney's background and current waves of misrepresentation. Had some nice photos of him at the seminars Mr. Smith was hosting. Smith threw quite a tantrum – but in the end just left town.

Attorneys are people, and are subject to the same temptations and failings as any other group. No more, but certainly, no less.

State Board of Accountancy

The state board of accountancy is the professional licensing board of certified public accountants. These records will show if the individual is a certified public accountant and their most recent professional affiliation. CPAs must not only pass an exam, but also maintain their dues with the licensing body. If they do not pay those dues with the licensing body, they are not a CPA. There is also separate registration for auditing public companies and tax work.

A little note about financial statements, there are really four different types of financial statements: 1) internal, 2) independently complied, 3) independently reviewed and 4) independently audited. The audited is the most rigorous. There may be no common control, there may be no other interest in the company by the accountant that audits that company. There should be no commonality at all between the owners and the auditors. No common ownership or control. Further the auditor should not be performing other services for the company, other than tax work. The accounting firm should not be involved in consulting work of any kind. A couple of other things, the major regulatory body for accounting is the Financial Accounting Standards Board (FASB), which promulgates Generally Accepted Accounting Principles (GAAP). The Public Company Accounting Oversight Board governs registration and auditing of public companies.

Department of Game and Fish

The department of game and fish maintains records on hunting and fishing licenses, and boat registrations. These records will show if an individual has a hunting license, a fishing license or boat. Again, it varies from state to state on how hunting and fishing records are kept as well as boat registrations. In some states, boats are a part of the motor vehicle licensing apparatus, or even have separate and distinct licensing processes.

> *Everyone likes to recreate. Money criminals are no different, they just want to recreate a little bit more than the rest of us. And I will tell you, a money criminal has always got to have a boat. All right, that is an over-broad and generalized statement, but it is true. Boats are a sign of wealth and affluence and are a great deal of fun to have. I have played with other friends' boats, and I know how much fun they are. I am glad they are still other friends' boats. An individual may have stuck his car under a sister's name, or have stuck his house under a trust name, but he won't think of things like boats and airplanes and toys. These things can be easily identified and garnished. Also, if you are looking for someone and you happen to know that they like to hunt, you will find that if they have been issued a hunting license, it will give all sorts of information about their residence and*

where they are going to be hunting. I have tracked down two people that have owed back child support through hunting licenses in the past, and had them arrested on the outstanding warrants when they showed up at the designated location and time for their hunt. I stayed way behind the law enforcement officers – way behind.

Abandoned Property

Many states have an abandoned property section where items such as insurance refunds, stock certificates, tax refunds, etc. are deposited when the sender cannot find the recipient. After a certain amount of time, the property will revert to the state or county but in the meantime, that information about that asset is public information. I have found in the past when doing an asset check on an individual that has intentionally kept a low profile because there were judgments against him, that contacting the state abandoned property division is very fruitful. This is because these people, on average, are due everything from insurance refunds to apartment rental refunds to state tax refunds, and it's all the types of information that can usually be found at the abandoned property office of the state. We have also been successful in finding information and directing our clients in garnishing those assets that may be at the abandoned property office.

Department of Agriculture

The department of agriculture maintains records on registered livestock brands and transactions under that brand, which can show if an individual has been actively engaged in the purchase and sale of livestock. The department also maintains information on farms, farming and farming programs. When applicable, these records can be a valuable resource.

Records may also be kept on the application of fungicides, insecticides and weed killers and the licensing of those for both commercial and residential applications.

A client who was in a divorce case maintained that her husband was doing lots of business in cattle. None of the other investigators *could figure it out. Well, once you know the source of information it becomes relatively easy. By contacting the state department of agriculture, I found out that he had three brands registered under his name, and that he was doing lots of business under the two new brand names that he had registered and none under the old brand that his wife was familiar with. How much more? He had over 400 cow calf pairs and six registered bulls – more than $1 million in hoofed assets. When this was presented in court, we raised his net worth and gross income substantially.*

Banking Departments

State banking departments license banks, finance companies, pawnshops and collection agencies, among others. Their records are useful because they provide the financial status of a company and identify the principal owners. In many cases the banking department supersedes other regulatory agencies with respect to rules governing financial transactions and businesses engaged in financing activities. For example, if you own an automobile dealership and wish to provide financing, your business needs to register with the state banking department and obtain a finance license (in addition to a dealership license).

Credit Reports

A credit report is an important background document to review when hiring any employee who will have access to a company's cash, bank account information, inventory or leased property. A credit report will generally reflect an individual's ability to responsibly handle funds. We must be aware that people can have financial problems in their lives, as a result of an automobile accident, a medical emergency, a divorce, a death in the family, or for many other reasons. If there are problems in a credit report, see if you can identify what those problems are, and try to put problems of an extraordinary nature into perspective. In any case, an employee who is under financial pressure is far more likely to cause a problem than one who is not. Access to a credit report requires either the applicant's written permission or a credit granting relationship with the subject of the credit report.

Federal Licensing Bodies

The federal government licenses many different types of activities and their key personnel, including interstate transportation, securities offerings and banking institutions. These records will show if an individual is licensed or registered to transact business in a regulated field. The Interstate Commerce Commission maintains records on shippers and truckers. The Securities and Exchange Commission maintains records of securities offerings and issuance. The National Association of Securities Dealers maintains records about securities dealers and registered representatives. There are many federal licensing bodies that may be of assistance to you if the person you are researching is required to be licensed. For current links to various federal Web sites, visit www.feeinc.com.

Federal Aviation Administration

The Federal Aviation Administration maintains records on pilots and aircraft, both are public records. For information you can contact the Airman Certification Branch office in Oklahoma at (405) 954-3261. The FAA maintains very complete records. People who steal money generally spend it on lifestyle and status, and one of the most prized symbols of status is a private aircraft. If they can't own, they will rent – but in either case, they will need a pilot's license.

There was a case that I worked on where a very wealthy dealer in scrap glass, paper and iron had gone through several business turnarounds and was being sued for a substantial amount of money. While his business deteriorated, his lifestyle didn't seem to change. I began my investigation knowing that the dealer was fond of airplanes, and quickly found his pilot's license. I contacted several of the fixed base operators (FBOs) in the area to find out if the dealer was a frequent renter or an aircraft owner. One FBO told me that the dealer owned several planes parked at his location, and pointed them out to me when I visited him. I noted the registration numbers of the aircraft (tail numbers), and went to the FAA to find out who owned the planes. The owners were a scrap metal dealer in New Mexico, another dealer in Utah and a third in Nevada. The target of the investigation owned all of these operations. His love of flying, his pilot's license, and the information from the FBO allowed us to locate substantial assets, all which were previously unknown.

Mineral Rights and Production

Each location has its rules and regulations, but generally you will find subsurface rights registered with each specific country recorder. You may also find production history stored with the state, for example in Texas it is the Railroad Commission, in Oklahoma it is the Corporation Commission, in California it is part of the Department of Conservation. Subsurface rights can include gems, ore bodies, caves, helium, natural gas and oil, geothermal, coal, peat moss and water. You may also find subsurface rights-of-way for pipelines and utility lines.

Military Records

These records may be limited to the branch of service, dates of service, and the current status of the enlistment. Call Military Records Service at the Pentagon in Virginia for further information (703) 545-6700. They will not give you a full history for an enlistment, but they will talk about the date of induction, date of discharge, and whether it was an honorable, general or dishonorable discharge. If you are checking attendance at one of the military colleges, such as West Point, the Air Force Academy, or the Naval Academy, these institutions will release information about an individual's attendance. Again, no grades – just attendance dates.

A very prominent citizen in Phoenix claimed to be a decorated war veteran. He said he had received several medals for bravery and his actions in combat, and frequently appeared in uniform. After a couple of drinks, he used to regale people with one story after another of his fighting days in the Korean War. There was, however, a problem. When his wife divorced him, she applied for her portion of his military benefits and found out he had never served in the military. The revelation was a big embarrassment to the city's major newspapers – their high and mighty, opinionated and self-righteous publisher had concocted his stories of a military career.

Be aware of what you're reading when you review records. I'm aware of a man who was hired as a part-time security professional with an armored car company. He had recently been discharged from the military and received, not an honorable discharge, but a general discharge. The general discharge was a result of this man stealing money from other people in his barracks – but he was never caught in the act. As a consequence, he agreed to accept a general discharge from the military, rather than face prosecution. The person who conducted the background check was unaware of the distinction between an honorable discharge and a general discharge.

Courts

Justice or Municipal Courts

These generally handle small offenses and things specific to that jurisdiction. Misdemeanors and traffic tickets are the norm – but occasionally they will deal with some of the lighter felonies. What is dealt with in a particular court all depends upon that state's and county's customs and choices.

> *Municipal court is where I find most of my "deadbeats." People who owe a few thousand dollars and skip from apartment complex to automobile contract to partnership. They default on money they borrow and don't repay. … It seems that it is just a matter of time before they stiff someone else and they have a lawsuit filed against them, which includes the whereabouts of the deadbeat. I will use that information to find the deadbeat. Also, municipal court needs to be checked any time you conduct due diligence on a company. It is very important even though the lawsuits are under $10,000, a company, or an individual, could have many small lawsuits. Recently, I looked into an acquisition of an automobile leasing and finance company. There were no complaints against the company in superior court whatsoever. It looked as pristine and pure as the driven snow, but unfortunately, in municipal court, the owners had drifted. It seemed that on a number of occasions, they had leased cars or repossessed cars or had been particularly nasty in their dealings with their customers. They had been sued time and time again in municipal court, and many of the actions were still pending. The*

total of the lawsuits was more than $100,000, in 18 individual actions. Not only could this be devastating to the company, but it is also very expensive to litigate 18 different cases. Please check small claims court always.

County Superior Court

The county superior court is the main court for most legal actions and will contain records on an individual if that individual has ever been a plaintiff or a defendant before the court. These records will contain the nature of the cause of actions and a list of the parties to the action. The superior court is where most litigation above $10,000 occurs, again depending upon the state. The cases and complaints can be pulled and read in full, along with their exhibits, and can be quite useful to the investigator.

> *In one particular case, in a divorce case, I was asked to take a look into a husband's assets. Three years earlier, the husband had been involved in a long, protracted litigation process with a former partner. Schedules of income and assets were filed in that prior case. Income and assets, in the current divorce case, that the husband said he did not seem to have. When it was shown that just a few years prior to this, he had all sorts of income and assets out of the United States and in other states, he was ordered by the court to describe and produce documents showing what had happened to the income and assets. He could not. Instead, he amended his financial disclosure statement to include these "lost assets."*

State Court

State court maintains records on cases that have come before the court. These records will show if the individual is either a defendant or plaintiff in a case that has come before the court and the nature of the case. Most state court cases are appellate cases. As such, the primary trial or issue of fact has been decided or adjudicated in a lower court. At the appellate court, the case comes down to a decision of law, not the facts.

Federal Court

The federal court will involve cases primarily with federal law and enforcement agencies or information on disputes that may cover several state jurisdictions. The federal courts consist of the civil, criminal, bankruptcy and appellate courts. These records will show if the individual is either a defendant or plaintiff in a case that has come before the court and the nature of the case. You will find that the disputes in federal courts, other than bankruptcy, will primarily involve tax issues, patents, trademarks and copyrights.

My client owned a business that specialized in manufacturing weapons, handguns and rifles. He was interested in purchasing another company that had several patents for the design and manufacture of a semiautomatic weapon system. There were approximately 18 patents. It was very impressive, and it appeared to be a substantial bundle of this individual's life. He asked me to check out the individual and the patents. Well, I was given a nice large retainer to do this, and I ended up refunding 80 percent of it because I tripped across enough evidence in one day's worth of work to recommend that the transaction not go through. Specifically, what I ran across, in federal court, was four lawsuits where this individual had sold the exact same information to other weapons manufacturers. The lawsuits maintained that the equipment did not work. A little further checking would show that this individual did not pay an annual maintenance fee on his patents, which is required. As a consequence, all 18 patents were public domain. There were no proprietary rights associated with the semiautomatic systems whatsoever. It was public information. Needless to say, the transaction did not go through.

Federal Bankruptcy Court

The Federal Bankruptcy Court maintains records on entities and individuals that have declared one or another form of bankruptcy. In these records, the individual is required to list all of the assets and sources of income available to him at the time the bankruptcy was filed. This may show other assets and sources of income. A previous bankruptcy petition is a very good source of information on people and persons who were not paid by the target of your investigation. You will find out that an unpaid debt has a memory longer than a private investigator holding a grudge. I have found many times, that the people who were stiffed in the past have an inkling of what this individual is doing now.

> *In one case, I found out that the fellow I sought was now a muffler king. He owned several muffler shops in Northern Arizona. We were then able to tie him to those muffler shops from a lead on an old bankruptcy petition. Once we tied him to those businesses, we were able to garnish the bank accounts of those muffler shops in Northern Arizona to satisfy my client's lien.*

Tax Court

Tax courts are special courts set up in some counties and states as well as the Federal Tax Court to hear matters involving tax disputes. It is very specific to tax matters and interpretations of tax obligations and sums due.

Administrative Hearings

Many departments of both state and federal government have administrative enforcement abilities as well as hearings. Some examples include, the Securities and Exchange Commission, the Occupational Safety and Health Administration, Department of Education, Department of Commerce, Department of Transportation, Industrial Commission, etc...

Other Sources

Colleges and Universities

These institutions not only grant degrees, they maintain records of attendance. They are excellent resources to assist you in your research. If you are lucky enough to live near a Federal Depository Library, you have a rare gem – a treasure trove of information at your fingertips. It may seem silly, but always check to see if a person who has a university or college degree is from an accredited institution, as opposed to a diploma mill.

Newspapers

There is a great deal of information contained in local newspapers. The local papers cover all sorts of events and people and when information does appear it helps to color the more dry facts you have assembled.

But Wait, There's More!

This is to give you an idea of the resources that are available and can never be a comprehensive list. There are so many places to look, such as minutes of public hearings, labor relations boards, bid awards, industrial commissions, permits for the use or discharge of something, occupancy permits, building inspections, approved material lists tied to a manufacturer you can decode from those labels you can never remove from furniture. The idea, as is it everywhere in this book, is to spur you on to think more about what you need to know and where you may find the answers you seek.

Chapter 10

Frontiers of Fraud

"When a true genius appears in this world you may have to know him by this sign, that the dunces are all in a confederacy against him."
Jonathan Swift

"Where there is an open mind there will always be a frontier."
Charles Kettering

"Fraud has restraints but no frontiers."
Apologies to Lloyd George

The frontier is that area just beyond civilization. Whether physical or virtual, it is an undeveloped area with few rules. It is on the frontier of fraud that swindlers, wholly focused on parting you from your money, spend day and night probing for weaknesses they can exploit. Without rules, or any compunction to honor any of society's norms, they work to find flaws in the systems honest people use to transact business.

Some frauds become extremely popular, eventually becoming well known to the public, and consequently less profitable to the fraudster. Once you see organized seminars by law enforcement and professional associations discussing a topic of fraud, it is no longer of much value to the fraudster in its current form. The knowledge of a fraud is the intellectual property of the fraudster, and like all intellectual property that cannot be legally protected, once the knowledge is diffused, it is of little use. Exposed methods of fraud get shelved, waiting to be repackaged in a less-recognizable form to come back another day. And they do come back – they're dusted off, given a new twist, and become a new source of revenue for the fraudsters. This cycle has been going on for a long time. Every conceivable fraud that can be committed has been committed – only the packaging changes.

Counterfeiting is a popular fraud. The ancients Mayans used seeds as their currency, in particular, the seeds of the cacao tree, from which cocoa and chocolate are made. The Mayans were buried with this currency for the afterlife. Archeologists have found cacao beans in pots in the ruins of undisturbed burial sites, with some pots filled with mud instead of seeds. An act of counterfeiting, or a relative no one really liked?

Bribery is not a modern crime. Bronze utensils from the roughly 2,800-year-old Shang Dynasty show what appears to be China's oldest known bribery. According to a 2006 report in Hangzhou's *Metropolitan Express* newspaper, the utensils detail how an aristocrat, Diao Sheng, avoided tax-evasion charges by offering the investigator a precious bronze pot and a large piece of jade. The charges against him were promptly dropped. This incident predates Judas and the bribe of silver by almost 800 years.

Related to my work as a financial investigator, I have many friends who study in some strange fields, and I get to hear some wonderful stories. One friend, who is an expert on things old and obscure, recounted this story of maritime fraud he remembered from his research.

> *A shipment of goods from Athens to Argos was reported lost at sea. It was reported that the ship, captain and cargo were all lost. Four weeks later, the shipper discovered the missing ship in port at Athens with the expected return shipment from Argos – no captain, but the same crew. The captain had passed away en route, so the crew chose to dump the captain, take his ship and cargo, as well as the return cargo.*

Almost all maritime law developed out of what economists and sociologists today refer to as the principal-agent problem. And nothing much has changed over the years. When a principal hires an agent to advance the interests of the principal, it's very difficult to align their interests – and one of them is likely to have an advantage in information. Almost all frauds contain the elements that define a principal-agent struggle.

Advances in technology and markets always change the way that criminals will game the system. People want to steal and be successful at it – that's no change. What changes with technology is how criminals game the new system.

Some of the biggest changes in recent years have been in the electronic clearing of checks and drafts. Another big change has been the opening of closed markets, or state-controlled markets. With the opening of these previously closed markets, many people are being beset by frauds they've never seen before – but which are old in the Western world.

Electronic Check Clearing – ACH and EFT

Automated Clearing House (ACH) is the name of an electronic network for financial transactions in the United States. ACH processes large volumes of transactions between bank accounts. The rules and regulations governing the ACH network are established by the National Automated Clearing House Association (NACHA) and the Federal Reserve System (the Fed). In 2002, this network processed an estimated 8.05 billion ACH transactions with a total value of $21.7 trillion. ACH, as its uses expand into uncharted applications, is also a big arena for fraud.

ACH credit transfers include direct deposit payroll and vendor payments. ACH direct debit transfers include consumer initiated purchases, as well as a variety of recurring payments on items such as insurance premiums, mortgage loans, cell phones, dues and memberships. Businesses are increasingly using ACH to collect from their customers, rather than accepting credit or debit cards.

Debit transfers also include new applications such as the point-of-purchase (POP) check conversion pilot program sponsored by the Electronic Payments Association. FedACH is the Federal Reserve System's centralized application software used to process ACH transactions. Both the government and the commercial sectors use ACH payments, with the Electronic Payments Network (EPN) as the only private sector ACH operator in the United States.

The Federal Reserve Banks are collectively the nation's largest automated clearing house operator. In 2005, the federal system processed 60 percent of commercial interbank ACH transactions, with EPN processing the remaining 40 percent. EPN and the Federal Reserve Banks rely on one another for the processing of some transactions in which either the Originating Depository Financial Institution (ODFI) or Receiving Depository Financial Institution (RDFI) is not their customer. These interoperator transactions are settled by the Fed's banks.

In accordance with the rules and regulations of ACH, no financial institution may simply issue an ACH transaction (whether it be debit or credit) toward an account without prior authorization from the account holder (known as the receiver in ACH terminology). An ACH entry starts with a receiver authorizing an originator to issue ACH debit or credit to an account. An originator can be a person or a company (such as the gas company, a local cable company, or one's employer). Depending on the ACH transaction, the originator must receive written (POP, prearranged payment and deposits PPD, or accounts receivable entry ARC), verbal (TEL), or electronic (WEB) authorization from the receiver. Written authorization constitutes a signed form giving consent for the amount, date or even frequency of the transactions. Verbal authorization needs to be either audio recorded or the originator must send a receipt of the transaction's details before or on the date of the transaction. A WEB authorization must include a customer reading the terms of the agreement and typing or selecting some form of an "I agree" statement.

Once authorization is acquired, the originator then creates an ACH entry to be given to an ODFI, which can be any financial institution that does ACH origination. This ACH entry is then sent to an ACH operator (usually the Fed) and is passed on to the RDFI, where the receiver's account is issued either a credit or debit, depending on the ACH transaction.

The RDFI may, however, reject the ACH transaction and return it to the ODFI with the appropriate reason, such as that there were insufficient funds in the account or that the account holder indicated that the transaction was unauthorized. An RDFI has a prescribed amount of time in which to perform returns, ranging from two to 60 days from the receipt of the ACH transaction. However, the majority of transactions, if going to be returned, are done so within 24 hours from midnight of the day the RDFI receives the transaction.

An ODFI receiving a return of an ACH entry may re-present the ACH entry two more times, or up to three times total, for settlement. Again, the RDFI may reject the transaction, after which the ODFI may no longer present the transaction via ACH.

ACH And Fraud

Many ACH frauds are occurring through the use of huge databases of stolen account information. For the bank's customer, the ACH transfer can only be disputed for three days after the transaction. If this same customer doesn't have other methods of monitoring his account, he may not see any transactions until the end of the month. One firm lost $4.5 million on more than 1,500 transactions in a two-week time period. Governments and municipalities are being hit hard by frauds of this type.

In another fraud, the perpetrators will steal or counterfeit a company's letterhead, and use it to contact customers, suppliers and banks. The fraudsters use the letterhead to open a bank account in the company's name. Once the account is opened, the company's customers are sent a request on the fabricated letterhead asking them to re-route their payments to a new address and/or utilize ACH with their new account.

One of the most interesting frauds involving ACH is with prepaid debit cards – also know as stored value cards. Fraudsters obtain these cards and use them to move stolen funds. These cards are to bank accounts what a cell phone is to a land line – functional with total freedom. After a fraudster has gained access to the victim's bank accounts, he can transfer funds to the prepaid card and use them to get cash from ATMs anywhere in the world. Stored value cards are being abused in other ways, but essentially they are being used to move stolen funds from the locale of the theft to another nation for collection of the funds.

The following are some variations and permutations of classical frauds, along with some others that are simply interesting.

The Bait Check

I'm sure you've seen them in the mail, those pesky little checks for a few dollars. You assume it was some rebate check you had forgotten about, so, you deposit it. What you may not have been aware of is that the check had an endorsement on the back. It said that if you deposit this check, company X will debit your account using ACH for "Y" dollars every month for its service.

The problem is, once ACH debits start they can be almost impossible to stop without closing the account. At the very least, this is a pain in the neck for an individual, but imagine a large corporation that receives one of these checks in its payment lockbox, where all the checks are swept and deposited several times daily without anyone really looking carefully at them. Changing one of these accounts may take months, and tens of thousands of dollars in man-hours, not to mention check reprinting and other costs.

How do you prevent the deposit of one of these ACH debit checks? For a person, it's simple: Read what you get in the mail, and don't deposit them. For a large corporation, only a few choices are available. One of them is ACH blocking and filtering. Many banks allow you to set up your business account with options to post no ACH entries, post only ACH credit entries, post only ACH debit entries, post only certain ACH debit and/or credit entries, and to automatically return unauthorized items to the originating company. This last option is commonly referred to as positive pay.

ACH blocking aside, it is prudent to set up your accounting so that deposits are made into one account only. Once deposits clear, the funds are transferred out to other accounts, which are used for payments and which do not accept any deposits other than your own transfers. Never set up a tax account that would accept direct deposits, particularly without ACH blocking. Can you imagine trying to get 50 states and all of the municipalities changed to a new account just to solve your ACH withdrawal problem? Yikes!

There is an interesting question as to what law governs these restrictive endorsements. Is it the Uniform Commercial Code (UCC), or Commercial Contract Law or perhaps the National Automated Clearing House Association (NACHA)? Is this a corporate-to-corporate debit? While there are agreements in place there is very little case law. It is much better to be aware and prepared than to litigate.

Errors With EFT

A client came to us with a problem. He had inadvertently sent an electronic funds transfer (EFT) payment to the wrong vendor and had been unable to retrieve the funds from the vendor. Does he have any recourse through the banking system?

NACHA does allow the recall of a file. In banking terms, a file is not an individual transaction – if more than one transaction was initiated at the same time, the file is the entire batch of transactions. However, if the EFT was the only transaction initiated at that time you can reverse the transaction through an EFT debit by requesting a reversal from the receiving bank. The receiving bank will request permission from the account holder whose account received the funds. If the account holder consents, the EFT reversal will be granted, and the receiving bank will return the funds. If the receiving account holder refuses permission, you have the option of going to court.

Another question came from a client concerning how to prevent fraudulent check and ACH transactions on their accounts. The answer is that you cannot prevent them from posting to your accounts. You can, however, prevent those accounts from paying out. What you need to do is to set up an account that is for deposits only. All of the credit, cash, checks, ACH and other deposits go into that account. That account is a check- and ACH-blocked account. The funds are then transferred into other accounts to be used for purchasing, payroll and other expenses. On these expense accounts you use positive pay to monitor the activity and stop unauthorized debits. If you are a large enough depositor, the bank will allow you to add some magnetic ink character recognition (MICR) lines at the bottom of the check and you can use a single account. The MICR lines will contain coding that automatically assigns that amount to a cost account. You will need an accommodating bank to use this option.

This opens up a whole new area of risk management for already stretched treasury staffs. A study by the Chicago Clearing House showed that 38 percent of large corporations had experienced unauthorized debits to their accounts. Fraudsters realize that they can now do with ACH transactions what they did with checks in the past; all they need are a couple of numbers. Even NACHA had its own account hit with unauthorized debits after the association put account information online for bankers to pay conference registration fees. Attempts to defraud corporations almost always start with someone getting account information from a check. EFT advocates argue that ACH security will improve when more companies stop writing checks and use ACH transactions exclusively.

Payroll checks are the greatest vulnerability. Some crooks will work for a company one or two days just to get a paycheck, which has the company's account number and transit routing number on it. They then try to hit the account with fraudulent debits. In one classic case, a debtor being hounded for a credit card bill gave the collector a checking account number with permission to debit. The account information was from his paycheck, his employer's payroll account, which was successfully debited. It wasn't for a large amount, and he got away with it three times before he was caught. You're vulnerable if you don't reconcile accounts regularly.

Time is not on your side when disputing electronic transfers. The window to dispute a transaction is only three days – and statements come out monthly. If you wait until your statement arrives, you're out of luck.

The best way to avoid these pitfalls is to work with a bank that has a positive pay module, which lets you authorize the checks you have written – and only for the amount authorized.

These few examples are related to technology that we only have a few years experience with. Whatever the future holds – technology will certainly present more problems. The reason the operating systems on our computers have almost daily updates is because criminals never relent. As financial professionals, we need to be at least as strategically efficient and technologically aware as the fraudsters.

ACH Frauds

There are a number of criminal organizations now specifically targeting small banks and small businesses for ACH related attacks. They generally begin with an e-mail to a bookkeeper of the business with some guise of legitimacy; some have even come as software patches. These malicious codes plant the seeds for a future attack and are prepared to harvest the login information when you enter a bank or credit union's Web site. The business account is then debited by the malware by adding several new payees to the company's chart of accounts payable. The money is sent to money mules, legitimate companies, or innocent dupes that believe they are doing processing for international payroll before they send the funds overseas. These attacks have become so sophisticated that in one scenario the fraudsters initiate a DOS attack on the ACH processor to prevent an already sent transfer from being recalled. The fraudsters tend to target small organizations and banks since these organizations are less likely to have up-to-date fraud detection control. This is not an issue of firewalls – it is not a hack of the bank, it is a hack of the client's computers that issue orders to the bank to disburse funds using ACH. In the U.S., it appears that $1.5 million to $2 million a week is being lifted from customers' accounts.

Click Fraud

Bad clicks, or false positives, are a real problem for Internet advertisers. Rates are frequently based upon the number of times someone clicks on an ad or link. Several fraudsters have developed bots to generate false clicks on ads to either develop revenue, make the link appear more valuable than it is, or burden a competitor. Some research estimates that approximately 11 percent of all clicks are false positives, or fraudulent. The typical bad actors are industry competitors who want their competition to pay for useless advertising, publishers who want to make it appear that the competing publisher is padding revenue, and friends of the publisher.

Bust-Outs

This is an old trick that is back in vogue with the continuing state of the economy. It is typically used by people or businesses that are nearing an end. The owners realize this, so they work very hard to generate credibility by wearing a mask of success. I have seen such masquerades put to use a great deal with apartment building shams in which rent is paid by phantom tenants so the building looks to be 97 percent occupied. What's really happening is the owner has a loan based upon cash flow, makes a few payments and defaults. In reality the apartment complex is only 50 percent rented. The bust-out is about getting as much leverage as you can before going belly up.

Mobile Devices as a Gateway to Fraud

The algorithm that protected the cell phone network has been broken and published. The only secure system of cell conversation is the 3G and 4G networks. The downside is that those phones set up to access and use the 3G and 4G networks have been under attack from malware and viruses that are spread by Bluetooth, texting and Short Message Service, and simply by answering the wrong sort of call. Almost 95 percent of all cell phones and PDAs have no protection whatsoever from these types of attacks.

Data – of All Forms

The attacks will continue because it is from data on people, businesses, accounts and Intellectual Property and Critical Information that contain the chink in the armor that fraudster find and use as an entry point for their data theft. With records lost in batches of 10,000 to 100,000 records or more, the expense of cleaning up the mess after a breach is becoming severe. While we as a global society are getting better at detecting attempts we are losing much more when we fail.

Intellectual Property and Critical Information

Another frontier for fraud is Intellectual Property and Critical Information. IPCI is simply a form of currency, but it's a form that doesn't enjoy the same guarded attention that most people give to money. As IPCI becomes an increasingly large part of our economy, fraudsters are seeing the value in targeting this low-hanging fruit.

The theft of IPCI is raging. The number of companies inadvertently leaking IPCI is even larger. In the last two years there have been more incidents of theft involving operating data, patent technology and research work than were reported in all prior years. Educating law enforcement and the courts to understand the complex issues has been an ongoing problem – as the theft of information does not leave the same void that a missing car does. In the theft of IPCI, the owner loses the exclusivity of use and his competitive advantage, not a physical asset. While espionage used to be a tool of governments, more and more disgruntled or unaware employees are selling or leaking information. This is by far the biggest trend in frauds, as many company assets are increasingly, and sometimes exclusively, comprised of IPCI.

One day on the bus, I met a fellow who was very drunk, two gents riding on an all-day pass (apparently with nothing else to do), and one other fellow trying to sell a memory stick for $2. You get to meet the best people on the bus. I purchased the item for $2 (less than a bottle of water). At the office, I plugged the memory stick into our forensic computer port. What I found were all of the records for a small business with about 20 employees. It had the business plan, marketing plan, account information (including sign on and passwords), and all data on the employees – I mean all of the data. In the hands of a fraudster – it could have meant an easy $50,000. Easy.

I called the owner, introduced myself, and described to him how I came into possession of the memory stick. He was not amused, and threatened to call the police. I suggested that he call if it would make him feel better. My offer was to deliver the memory stick to his office, and I asked if I could speak to him about the loss – after all I am a financial investigator. He agreed, and calmed down when I arrived. He knew how the memory stick was lost, and intended to fire the employee responsible. However, not being able to find anyone to replace the errant employee, the best he could do was to soldier on – and encrypt his data.

The same tools that make it easier for us in the workplace make it easier and quicker for a fraudster to game the system. Transferring files allows us to work at home or on our laptops – but it also allows a lot of critical information to escape the protections we've built into our systems. An alarm system, security guard and password-protected workstations are simply an illusion of security if critical files can walk out the door on a key chain.

A point that deserves repeating is that you need to periodically test your own systems to see how easy it is for unauthorized people to steal information. You then need to see what security measures are being used to prevent leaks and transport data by those who are authorized.

To add emphasis to the value of IPCI, many companies that have chosen to outsource parts of their manufacturing to far-flung locations have found people in those locations copying their intellectual property. This piracy has been seen in everything from industrial parts, fashion and accessories, to software and pharmaceuticals. The costs of piracy and IPCI theft have led to a new trend to in-source production in order to secure the IPCI.

Virtual Worlds

Many new opportunities for fraud lurk in the virtual world. Virtual worlds are persistent environments in which multiple individuals from around the world can interact simultaneously in real time. In order to make these environments persuasive, these systems always present to the players an illusion that encourages the acceptance of familiar concepts, such as places, inhabitants and objects. Massively Multiplayer Online Role-Playing Games (MMORPG) is the environment I'm describing. Players in these virtual worlds refer to virtual items in the same way that we refer to real items such as a house, store or car, rather than as an interpretation of computer code. This can be seen, for example, in Second Life's recognition of intellectual property rights for virtual assets created by subscribers, and its laissez-faire policy on the buying and selling of Linden Dollars for real money on third-party Web sites. Virtual economies can also exist in browser-based Internet games where your money can be spent and user-created shops opened.

We are now seeing the foundations of a real currency emanating from the virtual world. The fact is that virtual currencies have developed a de-facto exchange rate with legitimate currencies. This is facilitated with fixed exchange rates and the ability to buy and sell items but exchange those items using a debt card for currency. Several of these virtual sites have already been used to commit crimes and launder money from crimes.

Many virtual worlds allow characters to interact with one another to buy and sell virtual goods. According to our concepts of the economic value of goods and services, virtual economies have a demonstrated value – because players in these games are willing to exchange their time and money for the virtual resources, thus demonstrating their utility to the user.

This is probably the most elusive example of IP, and it is currently in its infancy. These games are like the portals we visited in the early days of the Internet, which has evolved into a system of unexpected scope. The Internet is spontaneous cooperation. And so, we have to ask ourselves, what will these virtual worlds evolve into? Their proven potential to develop a loyal following, to cross international boundaries, to bridge language barriers, and to establish as well as regulate a currency should, at the very least, give us pause.

For organized crime, the sale of virtual goods would be a spectacular money-laundering tool. If you think selling Pet Rocks was a brilliant business model – consider what you could do selling *Virtual Pet Rocks*. It doesn't even require an inventory that can be checked against revenue.

In October of 2008, a ring running between Korea and China was busted. About $38 million was laundered through the virtual world and transferred into China. This was done through "Gold Farming." In the virtual world, gold farming involves doing a task to earn points or virtual currency. This can be done by killing a monster, reaching a certain skill level, or performing a mundane task over and over again to "earn" the points. It is not unusual to have people set up a sweatshop-type operation, playing video games all day long, so the owner can move and exchange the points (virtual cash) for real cash. The world is changing – these are realities, and we need to be aware of them.

Fraud in the Secondary Market

At one time, secondary sales in online auctions represented a high percentage of online fraud. Someone in a far-off land would login to a server in the United States through a proxy, make purchases with a stolen card, then resell the items on the secondary market. Organized crime is involved, and it's anonymous.
Another fraud involves the use of stored value cards, or prepaid debit. Using micropayments and small ACH transactions, the fraudster can credit his card and draw the cash off through ATMs each and every day until the card is turned off. There have been several cases where a stored value card has been reloaded with many micro-transactions and ACH transfers, all under $20, and then cleared of thousands of dollars in cash every day. None of these frauds are large, they are small and they are persistent.

We also have to consider organized crime on the frontiers of fraud. There are well-funded and predatory groups that evolve faster than the countermeasures to stop them. Cocaine is now being smuggled into the U.S. with semisubmersible craft that are almost undetectable to radar.

Cyber Narcotics

This is a term applied to a host of devices that can produce desirable effects without running afoul of too many laws. A device that is placed on the skin, inducing the body to produce more endorphins is sold over the Internet, and reloadable for additional uses. Scientifically designed patterns produced on a computer screen help bring about a feeling of well-being or increase energy. These highs can be every bit as addictive as designer drugs. Virtual reality drugs by means of the Internet are already on the radar of law enforcement in the U.S. and the U.K., where preparations for Cyber Narcotics are under way.

Phishing

In a nutshell, "phishing" is the use of a fraudulent Web site in order to trick visitors into revealing confidential information. The fraudsters, or phishers, generally use fraudulent e-mails to lure unsuspecting recipients to a counterfeit site. Any method of driving traffic to the fraudulent site will work, such as using a common misspelling of the target domain name, registering the misspelling as a new domain, and pointing the domain to a fraudulent site. While a misspelling of the target domain might drive a limited amount of traffic with no additional effort, it is most common to use a highly misleading URL, or the target domain as a subdomain name, which convinces the casual user that they are in fact at the target's Web site. Phishers generally use e-mail to drive that traffic.

The term phishing, clearly a variant of fishing, was created by "phreaks," a slang term used to describe people who study and experiment with telecommunication systems. Phreak was coined to describe people who were previously known as "phone freaks," however, most phreaks have turned to the Internet as a more lucrative and feature rich communication system. There is widespread belief that the "ph" in phishing is an acronym for "password harvesting" – which, while untrue, certainly does accurately capture the phisher's intent.

This section is going to focus on what you can do if you're the target of a phishing attack. There are many Internet articles on phishing, and there's no point in duplicating that work – as tactics change rapidly. You can find a lot of detail about the devious and ingenious methods used by the fraudsters by doing an Internet search. Our purpose here is to provide you some background that may help you understand how Internet sites and e-mails may not be what they seem to be.

The trends in phishing attacks are not encouraging for small and midsize businesses. The fraudsters are no longer attacking only large commercial banks – they're now going after smaller companies as well. And that means that all hosts who deal with critical information need to be concerned. While Internet hosts are the targets, it's their clients who become the victims. I strongly encourage all hosts dealing with critical information to dedicate some space on their Web site to educate their clients about phishing. Publish a policy statement, display it whenever a client signs up for service, and most importantly – follow it. Education is the only line of defense that will ever eliminate these attacks. If none of your clients respond to a phishing attack, it will stop.

If your site is the target of an attack, your first response is to get the offending e-mail with all header information. It's important to get the full e-mail with headers so you can analyze its source. If you are unfamiliar with e-mail headers, you can use the following link to get instructions for your e-mail software.

http://www.spamcop.net/fom-serve/cache/19.html

From the body of the e-mail itself, we can see where the victim is being directed to (the phishing host). For those who want to learn more about e-mail headers, e-mail servers, and how e-mail works in general, the following link is an excellent source.

http://www.stopspam.org/email/headers.html

After determining the e-mail's sending source, the next step is to determine the site where the fraudster is attempting to lead people. Reading the body of the e-mail (or the source code of HTML mail), you will find the hyperlink(s) or the target that identifies the phishing host. This is the server that captures sensitive information from the phishing victim. If you plan to view the link on the host to see what information they are gathering, use a non-critical computer system that is isolated from your network. After all, you're intentionally visiting a criminal site – who knows what it has in store for your system.

Armed with information about the source of the e-mail and the address of the phishing host, you can begin fighting back. Stopping the e-mail will stop the problem from growing larger, but the only way to end the attack is to shut down the offending server.

Your first step should be to notify your clients. Only you (we hope) have access to your complete client list. Protect your customers first, and send them an e-mail letting them know that there are people attempting to compromise their personal information as it relates to your site. Remember to follow your own e-mail policies when you contact your clients – you want them to read it.

After notifying your clients, you want to go after the host. Most phishing sites are hosted on compromised machines, and the server you're looking for may be in another country. Know that the owner of the server may not even be aware of the problem, so you don't necessarily want to blacklist or cut off the IP address – just the domain name pointing to the IP address, and the offending software.

Contacting the host of the Web site is almost the only way to proceed. Using the IP address or domain name of the phishing site, you will need to find the party responsible for the server.

Here's a brief description of Internet architecture and hierarchy. The Internet evolved from an unregulated network of independents that developed a peer-to-peer networking agreement, and this is substantially where it remains today. Internet Protocol (IP) addresses are broken into four parts, with the highest order given to the first part, the network ID (e.g. the IP address 208.109.67.29 has a network ID of 208). Much like phone numbers that are broken into area codes, exchanges, and unique phone identifiers – the three numbers following the network ID are the host IDs, and are in a decreasing order. What this means to you, is that if you cannot identify the owner of the unique host with the number 29 in the example IP, you will need to identify the owner of 208.109.67, as this is the provider who issued 208.109.67.29 – and if you can't find 208.109.67, you will need to identify 208.109. Because the highest order is to the left, as you go from right to left you are identifying an upstream provider. Enforcement of Internet policies are handled in the same hierarchal manner, with every provider responsible for those downstream of their "tier" of ownership. Therefore, from an enforcement standpoint, if we can't get resolution we have to keep finding providers upstream.

If all you have is the IP address, you can do a reverse lookup on a Windows system by using the "ping -a" command or the nslookup command to find out the hostname associated with the IP address. Open a command prompt (usually on the Accessories menu), and type one of the following:

ping -a 208.109.67.29
–or–
nslookup 208.109.67.29

where 208.109.67.29 is the IP address. If the IP address has a domain name associated with it, you can use a whois server to find the owner of the domain. If there is no domain name associated with the IP address, go to DNSStuff.com (http://www.dnsstuff.com) and enter the IP address to determine who owns the address. You will find e-mail and contact information allowing you to report abuse to the issuer of the IP address containing the offending site.

In the previous example, the command ping –a 208.109.67.29 returned the following result:

Pinging ip-208-109-67-29.ip.secureserver.net [208.109.67.29] …

The primary domain is defined by the last period in the name, to the left of the last period is the domain name, and following the period is the Top-Level-Domain, the TLD (e.g., EDU, COM, NET, ORG, GOV, MIL). It's important to *correctly* identify the domain name, in this case it is secureserver.net. One of the easiest methods of phishing is to subdomain an address to make it look like the address it is pretending to be. For example, you may get an e-mail that represents itself as being from eBay. The domain may look something like the following:

eBay.com.customerservice.helping.us

The primary domain in this example is actually <u>helping.us</u> (US is another TLD).

Once you are able to identify the owner of the offending server, your first step should be to make a phone call – it couldn't hurt. You will probably find this solution to be less than satisfying, and language barriers may limit your ability to get it resolved. Continuing to identify upstream providers, you will find increasing sophistication and more likely resolution of your problem.

Your response to the e-mail issue is similar to the hosting issue, except that you will want to cut service to, and blacklist the domain responsible for the offending e-mail. Closing the account can only be done by the service provider, but that doesn't prevent the fraudster from simply finding another provider – and may only disrupt outgoing mail access for hours.

To check if a domain is on a blacklist, go to http://www.mxtoolbox. com/blacklists.aspx, to report e-mail abuse, go to http://www. spamcop.net.

After the e-mail source IP appears on a blacklist, the *subscribing* mailservers will start blocking e-mail from the source. How effective this is depends largely on the number of subscribers using the list and how frequently they update their lists. This may be the hardest part of the problem to solve – which is why going after the server first makes the most sense.

One thing to remember is that both the customer (Internet client) and business provider (host) may be unaware that data has been collected for a long period of time. As an example, once the fraudulent server has a client, it displays a normal login page copied from the target Web site – usually requesting a username and password. After the client has entered this information, the fraudsters can collect the data for themselves while redirecting the client to complete a legitimate login. From the client's perspective, everything proceeded as normal – and he has no reason to suspect that his information has been harvested. From the host side – this can be prevented. The host site should monitor the submitting page's header and verify that the data was submitted by a page which originated on the host server.

To report fraudulent e-mail, Anonymous Postmasters Early Warning System (APEWS) is an organization that compiles a list of areas on the Internet assembled from personal experience by, and anonymous reports to, system administrators, ISP postmasters, and other service providers. This list is used to deny e-mail, or all network traffic, from ISPs and domains that are known sources of spam. The site is located at http://www.apews.org.

One of the problems with blocking mail or all traffic from sites known as a source of spam, is that the problem is so pervasive. It has been reported that APEWS currently lists about 40 percent of routable address space. Most of this is in IP blocks that could essentially shut down entire countries. This is usually an unacceptably broad (though tempting) solution for a commercial ISP serving a broad range of customers. Don't expect quick resolutions or for everyone to be cooperative.

Spam detection is improving both at the clients' and mailservers' locations, but as spammers constantly change their techniques, there is no 100 percent solution. Due to these limits, spam will always be sent, some will get through, and a percentage of it will be opened.

There is a need for both the targeted institutions *and* their clients to fight phishing attacks. Unfortunately, to properly secure clients, the combination of education and added security measures would frequently outweigh the savings they enjoy from e-transactions.

The client is simply not likely to be sophisticated enough to understand the degree of and points of vulnerability that are presented by both mail-based and browser-based applications. This leaves the targeted institutions as the primary source for security. Digital signatures have been offered as a solution – and work well when all people in the loop have some degree of sophistication with computers. In most scenarios, digital signatures break down at the client level. Again, it's an education issue.

While law enforcement should be notified (FBI in the United States), expect their actionable response to match a glacial pace. In the end – it's your fight. This may seem like vigilante justice, but taking responsible self-help actions to protect your business and clients is the most realistic approach. Standing in the middle of "E-Street" complaining that you're a victim will do you no good.

Institutions should educate their clients as much as possible. At the very least, customers should expect to see their names in any correspondence initiated by their transaction partner. Since phishing scams generally rely on casting a wide net to catch a few clients – this would limit their potential targets to e-mail addresses whose owners are known to them. Institutions need to incorporate policies, communicate their e-mail and Web site policies to their clients, and follow their own policies.

These are some of the issues you need to be aware of if your business is the victim of a phishing attack. With good practice and an effort to educate your clients about e-mail policies, you can make it a lot harder for fraudsters to harm you or your clients.

In early 2010, finextra.com reported that phishers net 3 million euros in an attack on the international carbon market.

> *Account holders at emissions registries were targeted last week when e-mails linking to a fake Web site were sent to market participants, says the German Emissions Trading Authority (DEHSt).*
>
> *The European Commission says the Web site that the e-mails directed victims to, asked for user identification codes and passwords and had its "visual identity and appeared genuine."*
>
> *The e-mails were sent to thousands of firms around the world, with seven German companies known to have been duped into handing over registration details. Of these, six were subject to theft, with 250,000 permits stolen worth EUR 3 million, before being sold on to unsuspecting parties.*
>
> *It is believed illegal transactions also occurred in the Czech Republic.*
>
> *-finextra.com, February 4th, 2010*

Credentials and Identities

Once you understand how a phishing attack works, you can begin to see how these same tactics can be used to misrepresent credentials in many other types of frauds.

The truth is that most Web sites are visited because the user has clicked on a link, not because they typed a known URL in the address window of their browser. Who provided the link? Without looking closely at the URL we are clicking on, or confirming the site address by using a trusted third party or search engine, we really don't know who the link represents. It is really quite simple for a fraudster to copy a legitimate Web site, edit the content, and then host the revised content on another server.

If a person wants to represent himself as a board member of a large corporation, he can copy the corporate Web site, insert his name, picture and assumed title in the content pages, host it, and send you a link in an e-mail, such as:

LargeCorporateName.boardmembers.us/index.html

If you use the link provided to you in the e-mail to do your due diligence, you will see everything that the fraudster wants you to see. If you call the number on the Web page, it will be an untraceable number going to the fraudster's agent. Toll free phone numbers can be anonymously secured in a few minutes for only a few dollars a month, and programmed to ring at whatever location you choose.

This type of a fraud can be used to create references with companies or people that may not even exist, or to falsify a corporate identity. When performing your due diligence, be suspicious of all information that is *provided* to you.

The same tools that seem to make our lives easier, can trip us up. The fraudsters also understand these tools – better than most people. They also understand how people misuse the tools, and they exploit unsophisticated users. Phishing attacks have been going up by hundreds of percent annually – estimated up 600 percent between

2008 and 2009. What used to simply be a browsing threat is now showing up in Short Message Service or texting. If you are an early adapter of new technologies, beware – so are the fraudsters.

Future

There are many new changes on the horizon, including Mobile Commerce (mCommerce), micropayment processing, and a continued move away from cash transactions. Big changes in financial systems such as what we're currently witnessing always occur slower than proponents predict – and always go further than what was predicted. In the virtual world KYC will evolve into Know Your Avatar, we will be slim, tan and rich. Expect new frauds to appear along the way.

Chapter 11

Money Laundering

"He that is of the opinion money will do everything may well be suspected of doing everything for money."

– Benjamin Franklin

All the rules surrounding international and financial due diligence are directed at the shadow economy. All Know Your Client (KYC) rules are directed at the shadow economy. In particular, they are targeting participants who are trying to avoid detection, taxation and supervision. The source of targeted funds can be the underground economy, cash-based businesses, or those employed in the shadow economy. Funds may originate from people participating in financial frauds that are using the proceeds from their crimes to further their own personal goals – or could be the proceeds of more serious crimes, violent crimes (such as kidnapping), arms trafficking, drug trafficking and sales, as well as financial fraud. It is estimated that the shadow economy comprises about 6 percent to 8 percent of economic activity in the developed nations, over 20 percent in emerging nations and approaches 80 percent in failed nations.

The definition of money laundering is fairly straightforward. It is a process designed to move ill-gotten gains into a visible, legal form. There are three steps a money launderer must accomplish to re-channel money and cleanse it of its pedigree. These steps are really abstractions that allow us to understand the process and comprehend what colors a transaction and makes it suspicious. These steps are not always discrete, and are not always linear – but they always exist.

The three actions necessary to launder money are:

> Placement;
> Layering; and
> Integration.

Placement

In the placement stage, the form or origin of the funds is converted. In most modern criminal activity, particularly in fields such as drugs, gambling, prostitution and weapons, the initial medium of exchange is cash. Therefore the placement stage usually involves the conversion of currency into another form, or the physical movement of the currency. For example, a large amount of cash received from the proceeds of a crime can be converted into cashier checks and then deposited, through multiple transactions, into a bank account. The form of the money has been changed from physical currency to an electronic entry that can, and will, move around the world. Money can also be converted into items that have high residual value, such as appliances, automobiles, airplanes, art, jewelry, gold, numismatics, etc. The process of converting tainted cash into items of value relies upon "legitimate" dealers that deal in cash and act as a clearing intermediary for the cash. Though cash is anonymous, and it leaves no trail, as it becomes deposited in the financial institutions of the legitimate dealers it begins the process of creating a paper trail. Large cash transactions are also subject to reporting requirements imposed by international and domestic financial standards, which can bring unwanted attention to the money launderers if the legitimate dealers are complying. Placement mechanisms are designed to position the funds in a bank or financial institution and to avoid required disclosures.

The placement of tainted funds into a financial institution creates a dilemma for the launderer. Once the funds have been converted into an electronic signature on some computer in a vast sea of money, the electronic trail has been seeded. That trail leads in two directions, not only forward to where the money is going to be used – but backward, showing how it arrived into the system.

Layering

In the layering stage, the launderer is attempting to obfuscate the origin of the money – to eliminate a paper trail. As the name implies, the launderer will use layers of transactions, multiple transactions involving many different business entities and front corporations to confound the source of the funds. There are numerous other concealment mechanisms and strategies in the layering stage. One of these layers may involve multiple jurisdictions, including places where bank secrecy laws make following the money trail difficult or impossible. Another signature of layering activity is the velocity of transactions and the number of entities used. The money launderer wants to get his money back into the system where he can make use of it as quickly as possible. The longer funds remain in the system during the layering process, the longer the funds are at risk of loss by forfeiture.

Financial institutions maintain transaction records that are required by law enforcement and defined by the legal and administrative actions taken by their government. These requirements might include a money log of any transaction greater than \$3,000 or even a lower threshold set by the financial institution. In the United States, currency transaction reports are required for any transaction greater than \$10,000. Passengers who travel internationally and are carrying financial instruments with a value of more than \$10,000 are required to report to the customs and immigration services. The purpose of these requirements is to begin creating a paper trail for large transactions. The theory is that every large transaction will be traced from the time the funds leave the financial system up until the time when they are fully integrated back into the system. This "recording" of fund transfers is what a lot of the legal actions in the '70s, and '80s focused on – trying to identify laundering methods by following the path the funds were taking. Over time, the transaction volume and amounts increased, and what was thought to be a manageable amount of information became an overwhelming network of transactions too difficult to track.

Some common layering mechanisms include: purchasing items of high value, such as real estate and vehicles and then selling them to another intermediary. Thus, as the funds from the sales are integrated into the system, they appear as the proceeds of a common and legitimate commercial transaction.

As you can see, placement and layering are closely related – and both can be done in a single transaction if the launderer has a legitimate, but untraceable source to use in placing the funds. Examples of this could include a carnival, a casino, or an auto salvage yard, where large amounts of cash could simply be merged into the daily receipts. This activity also includes the final stage – integration.

Integration

The integration process uses the same financial institutions and instruments employed in the placement and layering stages, but with a different objective. In the integration stage, the apparent source of the funds is the main focus. The launderer needs to make the funds look like their origin is legitimate, resulting in some rather creative schemes and explanations.

> *One of the better-documented cases I have been involved with included a very successful entrepreneur living in the inner city. This man always had the ability, as a street thug, to see things a little differently than everyone else. His skills allowed him to take advantage of those around him. He began his criminal career by shoplifting, moved up to automobile theft, and then had his career interrupted by a short period of incarceration. While he was in the penitentiary, he had the opportunity to learn about identification theft. After leaving the penitentiary he took up with a young immigrant woman who worked as a nanny, and he convinced her to steal the identification cards of two young children in her charge. He then began the process of slowly assuming the identification of one of the boys. He would have had trouble getting employment using his true identity, as he had worked for many fast-food outlets in the city and had embezzled money from most of them. It was time to begin using his new ID.*
> *He applied for a job at a fast-food franchise, and he quickly gained trust and confidence – just as he had done in the past – rising to the position of assistant manager. He always volunteered to do any job necessary, to take on the most difficult and loathsome tasks, and to close at night after cleaning up. Of course, closing is the time when a restaurant is at the most danger of theft. One night, just as our boy was getting ready to liberate the day's receipts, the owner approached him with a novel opportunity. The owner was old and tired, and he told this young man that he would be willing to make him a partner in the enterprise. The thief was stunned. He thought about it, and*

concluded that this was his opportunity to make things right. The owner gave the young man profit participation, and in return he worked diligently to make their restaurant the best in town. Our boy soon found that building the business was an arduous task, and his profit-sharing plan wasn't as profitable as he had hoped. He convinced himself that his competitors were newer, better equipped, cleaner and had better advertising. So, resorting back to the experience of his youth, he decided that the best solution was to put the other restaurants out of business. Old habits die hard! He had their power turned off, he had fights break out in front of them, he contacted some of his friends from the hood and had windows broken. Finally, after they didn't get the message over a period of two years, four fast-food franchises burned down within a five-mile radius of his restaurant. Of course, more business came his way as a result. During this period, the two co-owners of the restaurant prospered, and prospered legitimately (albeit with some improper advantages). This wasn't enough for this young man. He wanted more.

One day the old man became ill and couldn't come to work. After a short period, the young partner decided to try and force him out completely. Just as the young man was ready to make his move, the old man passed away. In his will the old man had arranged for his young partner to buy out his portion of the restaurant for the sum of one dollar – as he was so enamored with this young man's attentiveness. So, just as he was on the verge of stealing the restaurant, it was given to him. Again, success followed, and the national franchise board recognized our young man for his ability to successfully run a restaurant in such a troubled neighborhood. He soon became a turnaround specialist in the region. Over time additional opportunities were offered to him, including a franchise empire. What the franchiser didn't know was that our boy was building his business by terrorizing neighboring restaurants. After all, that's his business model. Threats, intimidation, and well-scripted bad publicity targeted at competing locations seemed to control the competition. The franchiser didn't know that a large part of his earnings were made through the back door, by cloning his restaurant at several different banks.

Our young man's hoodlum friends knew who he was. A convicted *drug dealer and car thief operating under an assumed identity is not a difficult mark. He was soon in the money laundering business. He charged approximately 9 percent of the funds he laundered. What he did was clone his daily restaurant receipts for four of the five banks he used. He deposited the actual receipts of his day's activity into bank A, and then he deposited an identical amount into banks B, C, D and E. Most of his time was spent laundering the money, not minding the restaurants – but his fame continued to grow and he was offered more and more restaurant opportunities. He purchased additional restaurants, not because they were particularly good investments, but because it provided him additional opportunities to launder money for the local drug dealers.*

This is a good example of how a combination of identification theft, and the use of a cash-intensive business allowed the laundering of substantial sums of money on a daily basis. It was placement, layering and integration. The cash was deposited into banks with the provenance of proceeds from retail sales. The funds were then layered out of these money-laundering accounts into business accounts in different jurisdictions as the proceeds of a retail transaction. The funds were sent to companies that had similar names as the restaurant suppliers – a bakery, a meat supplier and paper suppliers. In fact these businesses were nothing more than front companies that all funneled the money (again under the auspices of buying supplies) to another location in another country. This came to an end in the '80s when many banks merged due to competitive pressure. Imagine the surprise to the banks when their transaction profiling software found several accounts with identical names, deposits and withdrawals. Suspicious activity reports (SARs) were filed. The young man was not caught by due diligence, but by very simple and valuable pattern matching software.

You can envision money laundering as two funnels connected by a pipe. One of those funnels is the placement of money, the pipe where the funds speed along is the layering process, and the final funnel is the integration – where the funds are distributed far and wide. The difficult problem for all money launderers is the layering process. In the process of layering, visualize a small spigot on that pipe with a valve that opens to account for the costs. The loss will be anywhere between 5 and 15 percent, either for structural costs or because that's what other people charge to do it for you. The process of money laundering is like carrying water in a leaky bucket.

"Pecunia non olet" is a statement attributed to Emperor Vespasian after he raised taxes on public toilets. More recently it has been paraphrased by a Swiss banker friend who said that "money has no smell." Pecunia non olet means "money does not stink."

This has been the predominant attitude in financial and criminal justice systems for many, many years. While a crime may be heinous, more often than not the proceeds of the crime are very quickly assimilated into the legitimate economy. This attitude is reinforced by the fact that most of our criminal courts have a very difficult time understanding financial crimes or tracing the proceeds of crimes. Unless accompanied by some type of violence, or an overt action has been taken by the other party, rarely is any action brought to court. In fact, one prosecutor in New York had the "seven-stitch rule." He figured that if the victim didn't get seven or more stitches, it wasn't a crime worth prosecuting.

Over time, the perception of "victimless crimes" has evolved. Criminal activities such as prostitution, drug use and financial fraud generate huge profits. Using the law to remove the profit seemed to be the only legal strategy that could assure offenders were deterred. The legal strategy is to confiscate the funds as the proceeds of a crime. The laws that were put in place to deal with the instruments of a crime and the subjects of a crime did not deal with the profits from crime until the mid- to late 1980s. A full-coordinated effort against these types of crimes didn't begin until 1988 with the United Nations Convention Against Illicit Traffic in Narcotics and Psychotropic Substances. It gained momentum with the 1990 Council of Europe Convention on Laundering.

Leading up to the mid-1990s, most nations had passed some form of law that allowed for confiscation or forfeiture of proceeds from criminal activity. This is the period where the detection of money laundering activity began to rise to the level of a science. Criminals who had amassed large stores of wealth needed to give these funds a legitimate appearance. They needed to "launder" it. To the criminal enterprise, money laundering has essentially two goals: preventing money from being connected to the crimes that generated it; and ensuring that the money can be used without any danger of confiscation. The interest of authorities in detecting the link between the offender and the proceeds of the crime is twofold. First, detecting that the crimes were committed in order to bring the perpetrators to trial, and two, in identifying the proceeds of the crimes so that they can be confiscated. The deterrent philosophy is that if you remove the economic benefit of the crime, in theory you eliminate the incentive to commit the crime in the first place.

It is important to note that most forms of money laundering have the intent of injecting dirty money into the legal economy, and to obtain this goal you need the cooperation (knowing or unknowing) of third parties. These are the "gatekeepers." The cooperation provided by these third parties is what allows the launderer to alter the provenance of the proceeds of the crime, giving the proceeds a legitimate appearance. Without regard to the specifics of the laws, and the legislation in this field – the criminalization of money laundering can generally be defined as economic legislation aimed at disrupting the cooperation of the gatekeepers.

Most laundering activity has its roots in high-yield investment frauds and organized crime. Understanding the enormity of the profits in these activities helps explain the logic behind an approach that focuses on the gatekeepers. The corruptive power given to anyone who controls these funds provides the corrupt organizations the political and economic leverage they need to make things happen. There is a direct relationship between the influence organized crime has with politicians, civil servants and law enforcement authorities, and the belief that the most fundamental pillars of modern society, i.e. the rule of law and democratic government, can continue to exist. The ability to launder the funds and bring them into the legitimate economy is truly the lifeblood of any organized crime or financial fraud syndicate.

Author's note:

Here, I would like to make a note on the author's perspective.

When I use the term "corrupt organization," I am referring to an organization that is involved in illegal activity. There is no possible way to navigate this subject without understanding that there are people inside the law, and those outside the law. Because of that, I use the language from the perspective of the legislators. And while I realize that many people do not consider certain activities criminal, especially in areas commonly known as "victimless crimes," I am taking a position on the side of the legislators, but only for clarity.

When I refer to the corruption of politicians, civil servants and law enforcement authorities – here I take my positions on the law with complete conviction and sincerity. Among the examples I could give are Bolivia, and how the government was completely corrupted by the cocaine trafficking industry. In these cases, I find all too often that the legislators agree with me, but only for clarity.

The move toward forfeiture laws was based on the belief that classical crime-fighting tools had completely failed in the fight against organized crime. Governments throughout the world consider the confiscation of the proceeds and incrimination of the money launderers as a more effective tool in dealing with organized crime than the pursuit of the individuals. There is practical merit in this view. These beliefs are the underpinnings of a great deal of the legislation. These new instruments are part of a strategy against organized crime that are clearly aimed at the structure of the crimes rather than at directly deterring individuals from taking part in the schemes. The philosophy is to take away the incentive to organize crime, and more importantly, to disrupt the profit-making function of the group.

Since the introduction of legal confiscation mechanisms and the criminalization of money laundering, these strategies have been more broadly interpreted and expanded in scope. Where the criminalization of money laundering was once specifically targeted at the proceeds from drug trafficking and organized crime, many legislators and courts have broadened its application to include the proceeds from any offense, the interpretation not at all limited to drug offenses or activity by organized crime. This means that the group of predicate offenses is not any longer limited to drugs, and the application of the law is no longer limited to "organized crime." The confiscation of the proceeds of a crime, whatever that crime might be, and the charge of money laundering, however funds have been laundered, are tools that have undergone a profound evolution. Confiscation, far from being just an instrument to fight organized crime, has now become a tool that can be used in almost any case. The broadening of this interpretation means that many profitable forms of crimes, such as trafficking in arms, environmental crime, illegal trade in cultural property, tax evasion and capital flight are now all subject to different geopolitical interpretation. This explains why many of the Mutual Legal Assistance Treaties (MLATs) discussing these criminal matters cover offenses not even remotely related to organized crime.

Money laundering clearly constitutes the Achilles' heel of any criminal organization, as it forces criminals to cooperate with regulated institutions in their efforts to move funds into the legal economy. Criminals must co-opt institutions with technical skills and access, such as banks and other financial institutions, to work on their behalf. This necessary alliance demonstrates the corruptive influence of money generated by criminal activity.

Soft Laws

There is some international harmony in the meaning of money laundering, and in the adoption of measures to counter money laundering activities – but there is also a fair amount of discordance. The international community relies upon statements of agreement in principle, and acceptance of international goals, with an understanding that every jurisdiction is free to determine the degree and method it will use to incorporate these principles into its legal structure. These quasi-legal instruments, which have no universal legally binding force, are known as "soft laws."

Soft laws are instruments that have been created by international organizations, but lack a formal international authority or jurisdiction. Soft laws can take the form of legislative measures, codes of conduct, or regulatory measures – and generally address the actions of banking supervisors and financial regulators. While this practice of generating soft laws has been subjected to a great deal of criticism, many look upon it as a useful practice in that the persuasive force of a rule is often more important than its actual binding nature. We witness this with the Organization for Economic Cooperation and Development's Financial Action Task Force list of Non-Cooperative Countries and Territories in the fact that these countries were blacklisted for failing to adopt the FATF's set of 40 recommendations on money laundering originally proposed in 1990. This came on the heels of the first international instrument to address the issue of money laundering. Specifically, it was the Basel Statement of Principles, Number 12, issued in December of 1988 by the Basel Committee on Banking Supervision.

Soft laws, such as the Ethical Banking Principles, Good Banking Practices and Know Your Customer rules, are not legal documents. Basel is a non-binding charter and its statement is only indirectly binding upon financial institutions in various countries. Different techniques, such as drafting laws, amending regulations and updating professional codes of conduct are used to implement the spirit of the international soft laws on a domestic level.

Domestic implementation of these soft laws comes in two forms, legislation or industry standards. When drafting legislation, the legislature will often refer to the statements and directives contained in these soft laws. If the legislature is not taking an initiative or the professional community wished to pre-empt the law-making process, they too will reference these soft laws when amending their code of conduct.

The Financial Action Task Force was created at the 1989 Paris Summit of industrialized nations (the G-7). The FATF was charged specifically with three objectives, to improve national systems that combat money laundering, to increase the role of the financial systems, and to promote international cooperation. More generally they were to assess the results of cooperation already undertaken in order to prevent the utilization of the banking system and financial institutions for the purpose of money laundering, and to consider additional preventive efforts in this field, including the adaptation of legal and regulatory systems to enhance multijurisdictional assistance.[16]

Shortly thereafter in 1990 the first FATF report was issued detailing 40 recommendations to strengthen the fight against the use of capital derived from criminal activities. The report contained not only an analysis of the extent and nature of the money laundering process, and an overview of programs already in place to combat money laundering, it also contained the recommendations. These 40 recommendations were the most extensive and influential part of the report. It argued effectively that countries should embrace the legal fight against money laundering and enhance the role of the financial system to fight money laundering. The recommendations were no more and still are no less than recommendations, non-binding soft law. It was a deliberate choice not to cast the recommendations into the mold of a treaty. This was to avoid the elaborate ratification procedures that would have followed if it were to be a treaty.

Flexibility was a true motive behind the loose structure of the FATF, which is merely a working party supported by the Organization for Economic Cooperation and Development's (OECD) secretary in Paris. Since 1991, the FATF has issued annual reports with evaluations carried out by other FATF member states of the legislative and regulatory measures member states have put in place to fight money laundering. The FATF recommendations often functioned as de facto provisions, which help shape domestic legislation and professional communities with regard to money laundering.

The recommendations further yield their unifying influence through the European Union Council Directive of June 10, 1991 on the prevention of the use of financial systems for the purpose of money laundering. No less than 15 FATF recommendations found their way into the EC directive which made them binding into law for EC member states.

The 40 recommendations were revised in 1996 to reflect the years

---

16 Group of 7 Economic Declaration of July 16th 1989.

of experience they had and the changes in the way money was being handled and transmitted. After the terrorist attacks of Sept. 11, 2001 in New York, eight new recommendations were added to more specifically combat the financing of terrorism.

The FATF has put together an international response to money laundering that looks remarkably uniform from nation to nation. Thus, various international organizations have engaged the fight in international money laundering essentially setting up a de facto international regime on drafting conventions, issuing recommendations and directives, and producing a foundation for future laws and action on given items such as money laundering. Without going into greater detail, much of the international foundation for anti-money laundering activities are contained in:

1) The 1988 UN Convention Against Illicit Traffic in Narcotic Drugs and Psychotropic Substances.

2) The 1990 Council of Europe Convention on Laundering. Search, Seizure and Confiscation of the Proceeds of Crime. Further, at the end of 1999 the Money Laundering Convention as it became heretofore known thereafter, was ratified by 28 states.

3) The 40 recommendations of the Financial Action Task Force on Money Laundering, the EU Council Directive of June 10, 1991 on Prevention of the Use of the Financial System for Purpose of Money Laundering.

4) The Wolfsberg Principals on Anti-Money Laundering published in 2000 and revised in 2002.

There are many more guidelines and laws on AML – but these are the foundation from where much of the rest has grown.

AML is an important part of the framework for both governance and finance. Pablo Escobar laundered his money and slowly took control not only of the financial institutions but also a portion of the government in Columbia. It was simple, he offered a bribe and you took it or you died. In 1989 *Forbes* Magazine listed him as the seventh richest man in the world. He did not get this way overnight. Little by little he used his profits, laundered through local businesses to gain power over the local communities and businessmen. Once you had taken money – you are compromised – you either do what you are told or a) you die, or b) you're turned over to the government.

What was going on is an extreme example of why allowing a little money laundering is a problem. Money laundered from the proceeds of crime is reinvested back into the crime game. The reinvestments are deployed in three directions, illicit commerce, and protection in the form of arms and subverting the government. If you subvert a good portion of the government – the criminals now run public life. Government's claim of sovereignty is that it has the sole exclusive use of violence to control the population. The criminals have supplanted the government. While other corresponding factors such as corrupt and inefficient governments, and tax revenue completely subverted by an underground economy, all aid in this transition from licit to illicit government, this transition would and could not occur without the predicate offense of money laundering.

Politically Exposed Persons

In the process of background checks you will occasionally come across a person who is designated as a "politically exposed person" or PEP. Although this designation needs to be noted, it is not derogatory. View the designation of PEP in light of the dealings you intend to have with this person.

In researching the origin of the term politically exposed person, the earliest reference I find is in an English translation of a Brazilian document on money laundering from 1998. There is a term in the document that could have been translated as "potentate," but was given more color in the translation as politically exposed person. The term refers either to a government official who can directly influence state spending, or someone close to that official. The designation PEP raises suspicion of government corruption, specifically, the ability to abuse power for personal gain.

"I know a guy" runs through my head every time I hear the term PEP. In its first use, this designation was focused on heads of state who were brazen in their corruption. Leaders such as Ferdinand Marcos of the Philippines, General Sani Abacha of Nigeria, and Vladimiro Montesinos Torres of Peru serve as examples. PEP identification was directed at heads of state, their families and related business enterprises. The Swiss were the first to realize the exposure the banking system could face by abuse from foreign politicians. In 1998 the Swiss adopted rules dealing specifically with these types of persons. This was followed in 2000 with the Wolfsberg Group's Anti-Money Laundering Principles where the 12 international banks of the Wolfsberg Group committed themselves to higher standards on Anti-Money Laundering and specifically identified senior politicians as a specific risk category requiring special attention. In 2001 the Basel Committee and the USA Patriot Act followed suit, and in 2003 the FATF added to its revised list of 40 recommendations the identification of PEPs. In 2005, the Third European Union Money Laundering Directive addressed PEPs.

To understand the identification and designation of a PEP, we need to go back to the origin of the term, understanding the problems it addressed at the time. Heads of state were systematically looting their countries of hundreds of millions of dollars. I have been told, from people affiliated with the United Nation's Stolen Asset Recovery (StAR) program, that trucks used to back up to the Nigerian Treasury that were physically loaded with cash for Abacha. The history of Marcos' corruption is well documented, and the videos of Montesinos Torres negotiating his assessments can now be found on the Internet. These were not subtle forms of corruption – this was open and notorious. Corruption of this type is damaging to the infrastructure of a country, and has long-term consequences that negatively impact development and foreign direct investment. This level of corruption all but ensures that a majority of the population will remain poor and destitute. These are the long-term consequences of corruption. The international community needed to develop a way to deal with the issue of corruption, and the designation of PEP was created.

A PEP needs to be a "natural person" in a position of power and influence, defined as "senior political figures" or those overseeing "prominent public functions." While neither of these definitions is completely or clearly defined, I believe this to be by design. The need to be a natural person is clear when you understand that they are delivering access for large sums of money to those who are willing to pay-to-play. These are personal choices made by PEPs for their personal benefit. The key to this designation is the PEP needs to be *able* to profit from their position of influence or control. There are many titles they may hold, president, prime minister, military head, minister, chargé d'affaires, governor of Illinois or contract administrator. Their title gives them access, but control is the real issue. I believe the definition is vague because control is ambiguous. The title is not foundational, the economic influence the PEP wields is.

There are many people with titles down the hierarchal ladder of influence who do not have the access to deliver real counter-value to bribes that may be offered, nor do they have the opportunities for systematic looting that is required for a PEP designation. These limitations also tend to eliminate committees, political parties, international organizations and most charities from being designated as a PEP. These types of entities have their own different and specific requirements.

Initially, the PEP designation was aimed at foreigners with accounts outside of the government in which they hold office. The prime minister of Cashistan would not be a PEP in his own country, but if he had an account in Creditstan he would be designated as a PEP there. The mere fact that a leader of one country finds it necessary, or desirable, to hold funds in another country should be considered suspicious – and while many cases support this suspicion, it still should not be used as a general rule. PEP started out as a term directed at corrupt leaders or potentates, but has rightly evolved to include anyone involved in politics with influence or control.

The actual designation of a person as a PEP has been left to financial institutions, with some very open guidelines. PEPs are delineated in many pieces of legislation, but not always clearly defined. Thus, there is understandably a fractured and uneven application to the designation of PEP by financial institutions. Although it is in the public's best interest to identify PEPs, putting the responsibility for designation and policing on the private sector has not brought about a balanced effort. Financial institutions are required to define who is a PEP, and can be severely fined if they interpret the intent incorrectly. Identify too many PEPs, and it affects the cost structure of the financial institution – get it wrong, and the financial institution exposes itself to fines and loss of reputation. There is no master list of PEPs, which leaves a gap in the identification of peripheral PEPs such as relatives of PEPs and their business affiliations. These relationships, unless disclosed, will generally only be exposed in background checks.

After a financial institution designates someone as a PEP, special monitoring of the accounts will be required. Significant deposits or withdrawals need to be explained and documented. PEP designation leads to considerable additional expense and effort for the financial institution.

Private investment companies (PIC), such as limited liability companies (LLC), corporations, trusts, partnerships, cell LLCs, hedge funds, etc., pose a second problem for the financial institution. The financial institution is required to identify all of the beneficial owners of a PIC. This may be an easy affair, or it may require digging though several layers of documents and ownership to find each of the natural persons who are beneficiaries. This can be as frustrating and mind-numbing for the financial institution as it can be for the PIC. I have seen banks take weeks to drill down to each of the natural persons who were beneficiaries, and do a fine job of it – all while both the institution and the prospective customer were shouting at each other. I have also seen the identity process go horribly wrong. When a clerk demanded to know the natural persons behind each of the owners of a fund that traded short-term U.S. government funds, it was explained to him that the fund's only subscribers were central banks of small nations. The clerk then demanded copies of the passports and reference materials for all of the presidents of the central banks and the leaders of those countries. I will not quote the fund manager's response. The financial institution lost a $3 billion account, admittedly a small account, to another institution that took the time to understand the issues and not to simply fill in check boxes. PEPs in PICs are not easy, they are hard and require thought.

De-PEPing, re-PEPing, Family PEPs, and Connected PEPs (aka, "I Know A Guy").

Generally a PEP is no longer a PEP one year after leaving a PEP post. They can be re-PEPed if they continue to play a substantial role in the government, but this becomes a judgment call. Family PEPs, business associates, and connected PEPs are the hardest to identify. The most straightforward way to find out who these people are is by asking the PEP. For known business associates you also may need to ask those in the same community as the PEP. Discovering who the PEP associates and socializes with is a beginning.

How many PEPs are there in the world? Not many. IMF, World Bank, FATF and OECD sources estimate 250,000 to 500,000 worldwide. Each PEP has its own exposure and thus, as we have seen, no one model or checklist is going to work. Institutions need a risk-based assessment for each PEP, covering two areas of interest. The first area is with the account – know-your-customer (KYC). Before the account is opened, designate the owner as a PEP, and monitor that account. In KYC you need to assess the PEP's domicile, the risks of the domicile, their individual reputation, and their function in office. The second area of interest is the steps taken when the account is opened and designated as a PEP account. The financial institution must undertake a review of the services requested, demands on services such as confidentiality, i.e., are the requests reasonable in light of their position, and the types and volume of transactions. A periodic review of the account should include assessments, and if needed, SARs should be filed. If you choose to close a PEP account, you need to have an internal and authentic reason. If the cost of monitoring is too high, so be it. Tell this to the PEP, and give him time to make accommodations elsewhere. If the closure has to do with the PEP's actions, you will need to file an SAR and ask specifically, from the appropriate regulatory body, if you can close the account. Demand a response from the regulatory authorities in writing. Many times the authorities do not respond immediately, or at all. Liability is with the financial institution, so keep after the regulatory authorities and given them notice that you, the financial institution, may choose to close the account without their direction. It is a heavy hand you are wielding, but you could be held liable for future actions – even after filing the SAR(s). After informing the PEP that you will close the account, you need to block additional deposits, as well as limit withdrawals to closing type activity. Withdrawals, all in cash and deposited in trucks, is probably not the proper way of closing the account.

The idea of the traditional PEP account as we know is gone. People are more sophisticated when it comes to structuring their transactions to obfuscate both control and beneficial ownership. I do not expect the FATF is going to be comfortable with either the current definition of PEP or how beneficial ownership is being established. I expect that periodic reviews will be implemented whereby PEPs will have to prepare an income declaration under penalty for falsification so a bank can make a required comparison to the activity in that PEPs account. Not only is it expected that PEPs will have to disclose their ministerial salaries but also the source of their "consulting" payments. There will be little or no distinction between foreign and national PEPs. Also, once a PEP always a PEP should be expected, and that de-PEPing a person will occur only after 5 or 10 years after they have left their position of control. In time both civil and criminal penalties will be proposed for those institutions that fail in the KYC to find PEP if they exist. I find this an egregious economic burden on banks and institutions, but I understand the desired impact to eliminate corruption. As long as corruption is economically viable to the huge extent that it is, it will remain a barrier to civilized government and the development of many, many nations. I expect that many banks will treat PEP designation as a red flag / fatal flaw and they will choose not to deal with PEPs. This is sure to result in a concentration of PEPs in those institutions, who either barely comply or exist outside the FATF guidelines.

PEP designation is directed at dealing with the reality of corruption. Very few people earn the PEP designation, and of those very few are corrupt. As a wise doctor told me, "When looking at diagnosing a patient's ailments, think horses not zebras, and you'll be accurate a vast majority of the time. But when you find a zebra – deal with it."

Scope of Money Laundering – Gravitational Model

How big is the problem of money laundering? Earlier we gave an estimate that the shadow economy comprises about 6 percent to 8 percent of commerce in the developed nations, over 20 percent in emerging nations, and approaching 80 percent in the failed nations. At the very least, it includes all illegal activity, including (when illegal) drugs, prostitution, gambling, kidnapping, arms trafficking, tax evasion and financial fraud. Many people have attempted to define the scope of the problem, but the answer is elusive. One of the more interesting theories I've read suggests that a model of money laundering activity should follow the properties of a gravity model. If this is true, an empirical study in several selected jurisdictions may be able to generate a worldwide analysis of the scope.

The Gravity Model for Measuring Money Laundering and Tax Evasion –
Brigitte Unger, Professor of Public Sector Economics, Utrecht University
School of Economics

$$\frac{F_{ij}}{M_i} = \frac{Attractiveness_j}{Distance_{ij}{}^2} \quad \text{when}$$

$$\frac{F_{ij}}{M_i} = \left(\frac{GNP}{capita}\right)_j \left(\frac{3BS_j + GA_j + SWIFT_j - 3CF_j - CR_j + 15}{Distance_{ij}{}^2}\right)$$

Where GNP/capita is GNP per capita, BS is Banking Secrecy, GA is Government Attitude, SWIFT is SWIFT member, CF is Conflict, CR is Corruption. M_i represents the proceeds of crime in the sending country. In the receiving country, the "mass" is welfare (GNP per capita). All the variables relevant for money laundering have been captured in the remoteness variable. The gravitational "masses" of the two objects country i and country j have been assumed to be GNP per capita and money generated for laundering, respectively.

Gravity models are models that mimic the relationships identified by Isaac Newton's law of gravity. Newton's law established that gravity can be represented by using a few constants combined with the variables of mass and distance. In the 1960s, Dutch Nobelist Jan Tinbergen proposed that the flow of trade between two countries could be identified with a gravity model using gross domestic product (GDP) to represent mass, and the distance between the two countries' capitals to represent their relative distance. By identifying the constants that completed the equation, it turns out that Tinbergen was quite accurate in his analysis. While it may seem counterintuitive on first glance that a law in physics could be applied to human behavior – the accuracy of his predictions really only revealed that the GDP of trading partners and the distance between them were the primary factors that determined their trading behavior. Gravity models have since been used in attempts to predict migration, traffic and other problems involving human behavior.

In more recent years, it has been suggested that a gravity model could be applied to money laundering activity between nations, using a method similar to that used in analyzing trade flow. The idea is that the flow of funds among and between nations that exceed what the gravitational model predicts is from the shadow economy. The proposed formulas actually have little in common with a traditional gravity model, other than being based upon the assumption that mass and distance are the most important factors defining commercial activity between nations. Among the many other considerations used to build these models are banking laws, safety, corruption, court systems, taxes and language. Further, money itself has become a trade good and seeks the best opportunities. Changes in opportunities will change the flow of funds. I find these models to be highly suspect, but they do force the researcher into building a framework that reasonably defines the rational behavior of international commerce with the excess standing as an indication of money laundering and the money launderer's attempt to maximize his wealth.

One of the more peculiar aspects of these models is the necessary assumption that low tax rates create an incentive to launder funds in that jurisdiction, because paying taxes is an important aspect of legitimizing funds.

It is unlikely that the actual scope of the shadow economy will ever be accurately known, yet estimating its scope appears to be a much simpler task than determining its location – where the proceeds are laundered. While a criminal transaction may take place in the shadows, it will still leave evidence – and illicit goods still respond to the market forces of supply and demand. Money laundering, on the other hand, is the process of integrating those proceeds with legitimate funds, actively seeking the light of day to give them legitimacy.

Asset Forfeiture and Perverse Incentives

While Anti-Money Laundering (AML) laws are important, there is a strong case that asset forfeiture laws create a perverse incentive to law enforcement, as the seizing agency gets to keep all, or a lion's share of what it confiscates.

One of the inherent dangers in anti-money laundering legislation that has been put in place is the attractiveness of confiscation without litigation, and without the presumption of innocence. An unintended consequence of these laws may be policing for profit. In the United States, after the passage of the 1984 Comprehensive Crime Control Act, U.S. federal law enforcement agencies were allowed to retain the proceeds of asset forfeitures, and rather than having to deposit them in the Treasury's general fund, a specific asset forfeiture fund was set up. Money seized by federal agencies must normally be transferred, after deduction of expenses, to the federal Treasury. The Federal Equitable Sharing Program provided state and local police agencies with a significant share of the seized or forfeited property, even if federal agencies were involved in the program. With this new incentive for law enforcement, harsh and sharp criticism was leveled at the process. The line of criticism was fundamental fairness – it is wrong to investigate and prosecute criminal activities with a view toward financial profits. Can justice be served when police officers, prosecutors and judges carry out their task with a pecuniary interest in the outcome? From a due process point of view, it is required that courts be completely and totally impartial. According to the U.S. Supreme Court, even a possible temptation suffices to disqualify a judge under the 14th Amendment.

Why should these principles not also apply to the police and prosecutorial agencies? These issues have reappeared in many cases and, in fact, have resulted in the reversal of the burden of proof. Many legal systems have introduced legal techniques intended to make it easier to demonstrate the criminal origin of proceeds, and consequently to order the confiscation. The reversal of the burden of proof should be distinguished from other ways of tinkering with normal standards. For example: A young man was living at home and involved in an illegal activity known as a "sports book." He was arrested, and a plea bargain was entered with him taking responsibility for the book-making activity. The very next day, law-enforcement officers took an action against his parents, grandparents, aunts and uncles, claiming that more than $175,000 of assets they collectively held could only be explained by their profiting from this young man's illegal book-making activity.

It cost his family $22,000 in legal and expert witness fees to show that the state had made a substantial and serious error in its prosecution. First, the expert had systematically miscalculated the amount of money that could be explained as illegal proceeds, almost $62,000 of *incorrect addition*. This total represented 33 errors by the government. Assuming an honest error, half of the errors favoring the state and half favoring the defendant would be the norm. However, all 33 errors were in favor of the state's assumptions! The probability that this would occur by chance is 1 out of 2 to the 33rd power (1 : $[2^{33}]$ = 1 : 8,589,934,592 = One out of 8.5 billion). The odds of winning the national PowerBall lottery is roughly one out of 195 million, about 44 times more likely than the state's expert honestly making those errors. There was a common practice in this family, the defendant's mother would do the marketing – buying groceries, blankets and other household items for the extended family. The mother would often make these purchases with a credit card, and be reimbursed in cash. This family came from a place in the world where banks regularly failed and the communist government could not be trusted with their funds – so they kept cash in the house and in safety deposit boxes. Any effort at an impartial investigation would have revealed this, and not required this family to spend thousands of dollars defending themselves. The state, based only on a theory, seized the assets, reversing the burden of proof on the family to show and prove the origin of the funds (which they did prove).

I'm not arguing that asset forfeiture is a bad idea – asset forfeiture tied to a crime is an essential tool. I argue against the perverse incentive created by making law enforcement and prosecutors the beneficiaries of assets they confiscate.

There is a real risk to law-abiding citizens when the burden of proof for the origin of seized assets is shifted from the state to the accused. Many gatekeepers have insufficient documentation and records to be able to prove either way whether the proceeds held in their trust are the proceeds of a crime or the proceeds of legitimate business and investing. It has been demonstrated in many cases that there is little or no protection for innocent owners of property that get caught up in forfeiture actions. Further, many of these laws provide for not only the confiscation of the proceeds of a crime, but also the confiscation and freezing of all assets allegedly associated with a crime. Many accounts have been frozen on international orders after the proceeds in question have long since left the account. Accounts have been frozen months later, in many cases completely shutting down small brokerage firms and financial service providers that were only remotely associated with the proceeds in question. At that point, law enforcement is no longer confiscating the proceeds of a crime, its officers are confiscating the proceeds of legitimate businesses and investors who simply happened to place funds into an account that may have previously been tainted.

These experiences punctuate the risk management principle of "know your customer – know your customer's origin of funds."

U.S. AML Laws

1970 – Bank Secrecy Act (BSA)

Established the requirements for record keeping and reporting by private individuals, banks and other financial institutions to help identify the source, volume and movement of currency and other monetary instruments. It is the foundational law requiring banks to report cash transactions over $10,000 using the Currency Transaction Report (CTR), properly identify persons, and keep appropriate records of financial transactions.

1986 – Money Laundering Control Act

Established money laundering as a federal crime, as well as structuring transactions to evade CTR filings.

1988 – Anti-Drug Abuse Act

Expanded the definition of financial institution to include any business essentially dealing in items with concentrated value. Also added the verification of identity of purchasers of monetary instruments over $3,000.

1992 – Annunzio-Wylie Anti-Money Laundering Act

Origin of Suspicious Activity Reports (SAR), and established the Bank Secrecy Act Advisory Group (BSAAG).

1994 – Money Laundering Suppression Act

Required banking agencies to review and enhance training, develop anti-money laundering examination procedures, required each Money Services Business (MSB) to be registered by an owner or controlling person of the MSB, and made operating an unregistered MSB a federal crime.

1998 – Money Laundering and Financial Crimes Strategy Act

Required banking agencies to develop anti-money laundering training for examiners. Required the Department of the Treasury and other agencies to develop a national money laundering strategy, including setting up the High Intensity Money Laundering and Related Financial Crime Area (HIFCA) Task Forces to concentrate law enforcement efforts at the federal, state and local levels in zones where money laundering is prevalent.

2001 – Uniting and Strengthening America by Providing Appropriate Tools to Restrict, Intercept and Obstruct Terrorism Act of 2001 (USA PATRIOT Act)

Note: Title III of the USA PATRIOT Act is referred to as the International Money Laundering Abatement and Financial Anti-Terrorism Act of 2001. Criminalized the financing of terrorism and augmented the existing BSA framework by strengthening customer identification procedures. Prohibited financial institutions from engaging in business with foreign shell banks. Required financial institutions to have due diligence procedures (and enhanced due diligence procedures for foreign correspondent and private banking accounts). Expanded the anti-money laundering program requirements to all financial institutions. Increased civil and criminal penalties for money laundering and provided the Secretary of the Treasury with the authority to impose special measures on people, matters and places of primary money laundering concerns.

2004 – Intelligence Reform & Terrorism Prevention Act of 2004

Amended the BSA to require the Secretary of the Treasury to prescribe regulations requiring certain financial institutions to report cross-border electronic transmittals of funds.

Chapter 12

Doo Doo Diligence

"You have to understand that being wrong is part of the [investment] process."

Peter L. Bernstein 1919-2009

"It seems to be a law of nature, inflexible and inexorable, that those who will not take risk cannot win."

John Paul Jones 1747 - 1792

Our first lesson is, we simply do not know what the future holds. This seems evident on the surface – but our actions, especially in the face of error, often contradict this truth.

I'm reminded of a brilliant satire in *The Onion*, October 16th, 2002.

FAA Considering Passenger Ban

WASHINGTON, D.C.—Seeking to address "the number-one threat to airline security," the Federal Aviation Administration announced Monday that it will consider banning passengers on all domestic and international commercial flights.

"In every single breach of security in recent years, whether it was an act of terrorism or some other form of crime, it was a passenger who subverted the safety systems on board the aircraft or in the terminal," FAA administrator Marion Blakey said. "Even threats that came in the form of explosives inside baggage were eventually traced back to a ticketed individual. As great a revenue source as they have been, passengers simply represent too great a risk to the airline industry."

It's a logical conclusion. All of the complaints come from customers, all of the fraud comes from customers, all of the threats come from customers, and only customers lose luggage. A logical series of deductions and conclusions would have the due diligence and know your customer (KYC) departments shut down air travel to avoid risk. The missing element, obviously, is the revenue generated by carrying the passengers.

There is dynamic tension between teams responsible for customer acquisition, KYC, and compliance. In the past, many institutions erred on the side of customer convenience – the current trend is to err on the side of mindless due-diligence checklists that erect significant barriers to relationships and commerce.

> *A hedge fund had a trading account with the same New York broker-dealer for more than 20 years. There were no incidents, problems, errors or complaints. When pattern-matching software was installed, it was noted that nearly all of the transactions of this hedge fund were between small and arguably dodgy (in their eyes) countries such as: Surinam, Bahamas, Guyana, Transnistria, Bolivia, St. Christopher, Western Sahara, Trinidad and Tobago. As per standard operating procedure, they flagged the account for enhanced due diligence. The brokerage required that the hedge fund share its KYC files with the broker-dealer. The hedge fund's response was simple: "We trade U.S. government securities for the central banks of small countries whose needs do not allow them to purchase these securities directly. Here is a list of the central banks we deal with." The hedge fund manager thought the issue was resolved – he was wrong. The broker-dealer required that the hedge fund have on file the identification documents of all beneficial owners of the funds. The hedge fund replied that the beneficial owners of the funds for each of the investors amount to the entire populations of the countries under which the central banks are chartered. Thus, we the hedge fund cannot comply. In place, we can offer you the identification of the leaders of these countries who can be found in the CIA World Factbook online. The broker-dealer was not in the least bit satisfied with the answer, and ordered the fund to produce the records immediately. The hedge-fund manager called the broker-dealer in New York, and quite rightly asserted that: 1) the clients are protected by diplomatic immunity, and 2) if they intended to freeze the funds – it would be an act of war. The hedge fund manager was*

unable to dissuade the broker-dealer's insatiable appetite for complete checklists, and moved the $20 billion fund to a broker in Europe, dumped U.S. treasuries and began buying European treasuries. No more problems.

I do understand the due diligence department's fears. People in that department have a gnawing distress about something going wrong on their watch. I can easily address that fear – something *will* go wrong.

Back to our first lesson – we have to stop deluding ourselves into believing that we can know what the future holds. A belief that the future can be known will not lead to small failures; it will lead to massive failures. You need to be humble about your ignorance of the future, and comfortable with this position. Once you accept the fact that you cannot know, predict or prevent the future, then, and only then, will you be in a position where you can responsibly think about the future.

The people you will be investigating are entrepreneurs and risk-takers. Managing risk is how they make their money. To paraphrase the quote at the beginning of this chapter, *it is a law of nature, inflexible and inexorable, that those who will not take risk cannot win.* All of these people have made mistakes, have taken risks, and have assumed obligations that you may find nonsensical, or even foolish. That's the point. Your checklists are going to exclude a large number of these people because they have made errors. They have taken risks, and sometimes they will have lost.

Great men and woman do not dawdle, their idle speed is simply set too high – they are built for speed and action. They carry too much sail, and they take great risks. This is who they are. The more timid clerks who err on the side of caution will trim the sails whenever they see a storm approaching, and look for a safe harbor. These ships of commerce commanded by men and women of action are not going to put up with mindless checklists and oppressive requests for information meant to paper a clerk's file. These souls, these entrepreneurs, will go where their innovation and actions will not be hampered by mindless clerks. The generic response of the clerk is, good riddance.

I was called on the carpet by a bank's due diligence department for errors in the documentation I submitted to open a broker account for a captive insurance company. The bank's representative raised these issues: 1) The certificate of good standing and the insurance license were not notarized as true and original copies; 2) The audit report was not notarized as true and original copies; 3) No business plan was submitted, and 4) The utility bill, although notarized, looked as if it was printed on a personal computer.

My response? 1) They did not need to be notarized as true and original copies – they were the originals; 2) The audit was a copy obtained from the government of the location of the captive insurance company. See the seal? Is it notarized as a true and original copy by the government? 3) Was a business plan requested, needed or required? The company had been in the same business for 20 years; 4) the utility bill was printed from a personal computer. It's called paperless billing, and no I cannot get a hard copy. This is what it looks like when you go to the utility office. And by the way, take a look at the detailed enhanced due diligence research report on the principals of the company. The principal has lived in the same house for 23 years. I asked if the bank's due diligence department could just call the regulators in the county of origin and verify over the phone that the certificates are originals and the audit is from their archives. The answer from the bank was no.

Continuing with my full-throttled rant about checkbox due diligence, I want you to think about who will survive this selection process. I discussed this with several of the investigators in my office, and the answer was clear. The financial firm will be left with nothing but those most desperate to get an account opened or a transaction completed. The consequences of this mindless "enhanced" due diligence will have the opposite of the intended effect on the financial firm. To test this hypothesis, we fabricated a person and a company. We created impressive notarized documents and submitted them with the KYC forms and applications to financial firms. Within three weeks both nonentities were cleared to open accounts.

Empirical evidence, of our own making, has shown that strict mindless due diligence does not decrease the likelihood of a disaster, it increases it – since those willing to put up with the paper assault are those who are desperate to get an account opened. Desperate people will put up with a mindless deluge of paper requests, and they will game the system.

What is the likely response to an increase in troubled accounts? Probably an increase in due diligence requirements and more intrusive screening techniques. *The Onion*'s solution is beginning to take hold in financial institutions.

I suggest offering a minimum of good screening and excel at working with your customers. Getting to actually know your customers and their business is more important than participating in the farce of enhanced due diligence checklist screening. Get off your backside and go see your customer's business. Not only will you get a good feel for the voracity of the client, you will gain a great deal of goodwill. Trust can quickly be translated into more business. You need to challenge your customers, and ask them to educate you about their business.

> *From a due diligence seminar in Uzbekistan:*
>
> *But Mr. Files, we here in Toshkent do not have sophisticated property registrars or credit reporting databases; we have to go on our gut and the potential client's reputation. Yet this too fails, I loaned a great deal of money to a fellow called Sergei against his tractors. He did not pay, and when we went to get the tractors they were gone, and no one in the community knew who Sergei was.*
> *My response: This is exactly my point. In the future take a stack of business cards and go visit all of Sergei's neighbors. Find out what tractors he does and does not own, if he is a good farmer, and is knowledgeable about his crops. Find out who Sergei buys supplies from such as seed, fuel and fertilizer. Find out who is buying Sergei's products. In the end, you will have an excellent profile of Sergei, and 20 potential customers on your doorstep, all because you cared enough to go and visit.*

Due diligence is about doing your homework and knowing something about your clients – it's not about completing a checklist.

By taking my advice and reaching out, this banker in Uzbekistan quadrupled his business and reduced loan losses to near zero in less than six months. If I am fortunate enough to return to Uzbekistan, I am told I have a lamb dinner waiting for me.

The Regulatory Effect

Due diligence is an important part of intelligent business processes and gauging future risks. It is well understood that there are limits to what you can know; historians don't even understand the past. Due diligence must be incorporated in your decision-making and risk assessment, with the understanding that you cannot reduce risk to zero.

Regulators require that every financial-services business has robust KYC and due-diligence procedures in place as part of their efforts to prevent money laundering. The problem is, you cannot prevent money laundering – it can only be detected after it has occurred. This is a subtle distinction. Many accounts transact legitimate business for a long time before they are re-tasked for money laundering. There are very distinct patterns of activity that arise in money laundering, and you are required to detect and report these activities.

One downside of these requirements is the levy of fines on banks and financial institutions *after* a self-disclosure event. This is a damnable dilemma the regulators have created. You, as the financial institution operator, have detected money laundering. If you report it, you could get fined or administratively disciplined. If you don't report, and simply close the account, odds are you will skate. The regulatory institutions need to have more forgiveness when events are self-disclosed. The act of penalizing financial institutions for self-disclosure is also counterproductive. These actions incentivize institutions to remain quiet and deprive the regulatory bodies of what could be valuable information and intelligence.

I understand that you have third parties to deal with – auditors, government regulators, clients, customers and suppliers. If you can be as open and authentic with them as I recommend, it will benefit you. If they have a checklist you need to follow, fill it out, and then do the real work.

Doo Doo Diligence Under a Black Hat.

Due diligence is also used as a ploy to get one company to reveal secrets to another company during the underwriting or acquisition process. Here, due diligence is used to get the other party to disclose its competitive advantages, its most profitable activities, and its gold collar workers (who, if they were to leave the company, could jeopardize its future).

I have seen this tactic work with great effect on small companies, especially those working in a narrow field of technology.

> *A securities underwriter picks a target and shores up the company with a minimal amount of money. The underwriter then launches a comprehensive study of the competition and competing technologies to the company he is going to fund. A key part of this study is identifying what technologies could compete with the company to be underwritten and who the gold collar workers are in the competing companies. Those companies that possess reasonably similar technology that agree to be acquired are acquired, or just the technology is acquired, along with noncompete and non-disclosure agreements from the once-competing company. The second option is a strategic move to thwart and undercut the competitors, whereby the underwriter handicaps the other companies and technologies. Knowing the identity of the gold-collar workers in the competing companies, the underwriter does his level best to hire away from the competitors these gold-collar workers for two to three years at ridiculous sums. When the underwriter has diverted all of the brainpower that was once at the competing companies, they often wither. The last stratagem is to license competing technologies for a period of time in such a way as to be able to stall their development as the newly funded company accelerates the development of its technology. It's called buy early, hire gold and stall the others.*

Due Diligence Done Right

Due diligence is a process of gathering information to make informed decisions about commercial relationships. When due diligence interferes with the commercial process of the business as opposed to supporting the commercial process – it is being done incorrectly. You cannot have all of the information you need to make a decision, because you cannot collect it. If you could collect it all, you will never digest it. Another reason you can't have all critical information is because some of it is stale – certain classes of information are only compiled periodically. There is a difference between information and wisdom. A collection of facts that often passes for knowledge is an enemy of the holistic approach that all due diligence should follow. A brain stuffed with facts does not make it smarter, just more crowded.

I urge all practitioners of due diligence to use the checklists at the back of the book as outlines, not as mind-numbing marches in search of riskless opportunities. (Hint: there are none.) For those in KYC, I strongly encourage you to get up off of your backsides, meet your clients, and get to know them. Those involved in underwriting need to learn about the company, its principals and its environment. (Ratings companies are not a substitute for your shoe leather.) Thus, I suggest that you do your work openly, notoriously and transparently.

Chapter 13

Transparency

"A word is not a crystal, transparent and unchanging, it is the skin of living thought and may vary greatly in color and content according to the circumstances and time in which it is used."

Oliver Wendell Holmes, Jr. 1841-1935

After something unforeseen has gone wrong in financial markets we regularly hear about "transparency," and how increased transparency is going to increase opportunities, decrease risk and save the day. A careful look at transparency presents some interesting dichotomies – not just between secrecy and full disclosure, but also between constructive disclosure and destructive disclosure. This perception of transparency is a remarkable feat of human knavery.

A definition of "transparency" mined from Wikipedia and Webster's:

> *Transparency, as used in the humanities and in a social context more generally, implies openness, communication and accountability. It is a metaphorical extension of a "transparent" object, one that can be seen through. Transparent procedures include open meetings, financial disclosure statements, freedom of information legislation, budgetary review and audits.*

Transparency is therefore an authentic way of conducting business or living your life. Authentic, to me reflects more than just being honest, it means being forthright. It is an easy lifestyle to have and a hard one to fully embrace. Very hard. Conversely, a lack of transparency implies deceit, breach of trust, or unfair advantage.

The adjective transparent is an attribute we apply to things. Yet, when regulators ask us to be more transparent they use it as a verb, and it inherits all of the properties from the humanities and social context. With this understanding, we can see that *being transparent requires a relationship between two or more parties* – such as the relationship between providers and consumers of information. In the commercial world this relationship may be between a single buyer and seller, or among multiple participants in markets and exchanges. To a provider of information, this relationship creates a problem, because they don't know who the consumer of their information will be. Not knowing the sophistication or experience of the consumer, a provider can offer information that is fully transparent, while doing nothing to promote communication. Chaos theory, after all, is fully transparent to anyone who can understand it.

The problem with all efforts to legislate transparency is that they will attempt to address these relationships by setting rigid standards of assumed sophistication and disclosure. By nature, such legislation will define who can trade with whom, set minimum disclosure standards, and proscribe some methods of presenting information. After the regulators have standardized disclosure and risk limits, the proverbial square peg will once again be morphed until it fits into the round hole set by the regulatory boundaries. Do AAA-rated mortgage-backed securities ring a bell with anyone?

Information

If information and access to information is transparency, then our world is more transparent today than it was yesterday -- and will be more transparent tomorrow. Every day we get closer to the sum total of human knowledge being cataloged and made available online. Personal information, where we have been academically, professionally and physically, can be harvested from massive databases of public and private records. Add to these sources all of the personal information we voluntarily add on social networking sites such as Facebook, MySpace, LinkedIn, Twitter and blog entries. It isn't only in the U.S., European Union countries, and developed nations where these changes are occurring; they're taking place worldwide. Information technologies have also altered the way people interact around the world. The distance between countries shrank dramatically with the introduction of air transportation, and more with modern jet travel. As our commerce becomes digital and

IP based, there is less to physically transport. As the Internet has matured, distance has become, in many ways, insignificant.

I want to take another detour here. I'm sure you've heard all of these metrics before, but I want to recap them to create a quick timeline of the Internet, and then to add some commentary.

> ARPANET was started in 1969. CompuServe offered e-mail in 1979. It was in 1980 that the first Internet Service Providers started forming, TCP/IP protocols were adopted for the Internet in 1983, Windows 1.0 was released in 1985, Yahoo was founded in 1995, Google was incorporated in 1998, and the Internet did not surpass 100 Internet hosts until 2001. As of 2009, the number of Internet hosts is near 700 million.

The rate of change and access to information has been astounding. It was at the turn of the century that markets were nearing the top of the Internet bubble – and we were saturated with information explaining how these new technologies would transform our lives. When the market bubble burst, many people believed that the promise of these transformative technologies burst with it. In reality it was only our misconceptions that burst.

The reality is we had not learned how to make intelligent use of this new technology. In the last decade developers have standardized and enhanced both the Internet browser and e-mail services, which solved a lot of cross-platform issues. Database formats, graphic formats, and methods to access data have been standardized – making it easier to share data and develop distributed applications. Open source software has been developed that makes access to many of these developments virtually free. All of these changes were necessary before we would see the worldwide use of technology that we experience today. The integration of hardware – merging audio, video and telephony with the PC – has created a tool that can transform itself and emulate what at one time represented thousands of specialized hardware systems. These changes multiply the effect technologies have on our lives. The past 10 years has brought us some very interesting tools, and has slowly transformed the way businesses are managed and commerce is conducted. We have only begun the next revolution – the intelligent application of these technologies.

> *"Why does this magnificent applied science which saves work and makes life easier bring us so little happiness? The simple answer runs: Because we have not yet learned to make sensible use of it."*
> – Albert Einstein, 1931

Integration

This seamless integration of technology is what computer scientists refer to as transparency – another definition for transparency. What scientists mean by transparent is that the user of the technology does not perceive the process. The systems all speak the same language, and follow a standardized set of rules.

It is these same transparent information technologies that are creating transparency in all of our lives. Events that at one time we could choose to forget, such as an unfortunate office party event, may now show up on the Internet complete with photos and video. Transparency should be considered a foregone conclusion for all of our futures. We used to be able to remake ourselves after an error in life. An ugly divorce, a business failure, or a rough and tumble adolescence could all be swept under the carpet by placing physical distance between where it happened and where you went to remake yourself. The information access and the storage capacity we possess today make such a transition nearly impossible. For those over 40, think of all the fun (excuse me, socially irresponsible, or better) things we did as adolescents. Those events and records are now behind us – thankfully – and we have been able to remake ourselves as adults. Future generations may not have this opportunity.

The advent of modern information technology has also made it easier for regulatory agencies to require disclosure. We no longer have to print cases of documents and distribute them to the requisite parties, they can be prepared in a reasonably automated fashion, formatted, posted to a secure Web site, or distributed via e-mail. The cost for the dissemination of disclosure material to achieve regulatory transparency has evaporated. This reduction in distribution costs may be more than offset in the cost of compliance and exposure to different perils.

Secrecy vs. Privacy vs. Transparency

An eternal truth is that we are more likely to try and get away with something when we think no one is looking – or if looking, could never find. In the private sector, I can think of a few dozen massive frauds as examples, and in the public realm I can think of no better examples than the hacked e-mails exposing the suspect or even fraudulent science promoted by climatologists at the Climate Research Unit (CRU), the embarrassing disclosure of Member of Parliament's expenses in the U.K., or the governor of Illinois trying to sell Barack Obama's Senate seat for $1 million (Note: In an open and transparent market he could have demanded and received much more.)

Secrecy is the process of hiding information with the intent to use that information to your benefit. It's important that we have secrets, and keep some information from being disclosed. Nations have a legitimate need for secrets, to craft informational and strategic advantage over other nations. The same is true for companies that wish to keep their Intellectual Property and Critical Information (IPCI) secret along with operational efficiencies, proprietary technology and future plans. Individuals too have legitimate needs for secrets.

Privacy is the concept of depriving others of information about you, thus selectively revealing who you are, when you wish and to whom you choose. Samuel Warren and Louis Brandeis defined privacy in the context of information and technology, with a focus on protecting individual liberty – a "right to be left alone" (Warren & Brandeis, 1890). While this definition prevails in North America, definitions and the meaning of privacy are closely tied to cultural norms. Privacy is not anonymity, and it doesn't have much to do with security. Privacy is a concept in social conduct as well as in law. When a person compromises their privacy, they normally do so in exchange for a perceived benefit. The Fourth Amendment to the

U.S. Constitution guarantees "the right of the people to be secure in their persons, houses, papers, and effects, against unreasonable searches and seizures." This is probably the best statutory definition we have, for now.

Information that is private means that it is not secret – it is private though it is accessible and is usable by a third party. For example, your tax returns are private – not accessible without your permission or a court order. Driver's license information is private, and only available to you and a select cadre of government departments and private parties. As Warren & Brandeis observed in 1890, privacy rights are inextricably intertwined with advances in technology. This is clearly as true today as it was then, but current technologies are challenging the interpretation of that relationship.

Why so much discussion of privacy vs. transparency? Because for businesses, privacy concerns several aspects of their operation, including their list of investors, their formulas for providing returns, their strategies, and their communications regarding future investments. One underlying assumption in the laws and regulations affecting transparency is that a company will be trading privacy for a perceived economic benefit. What benefit is provided is undefined – but legislators always assure the public that there will be a benefit. These types of laws and regulations force businesses to make a choice about government licensure. Will the costs of licensure be outweighed by the economic benefits? If not, the follow-up challenge will be how to restructure the company or recast its activities to be exempt from licensure. This challenge may include a choice that requires a departure from the present system of laws and regulations under which current operations exist, i.e., moving to another country.

Among the questions that need to be asked are, what are the economic benefits of transparency and what are the costs associated with the regulations? Are the rewards worth the costs?

As fodder for thought, the U.S. is where you will find the most draconian disclosure rules. The year after the Sarbanes-Oxley Act (SOX) was passed, the number of initial public offerings (IPOs) dropped, and the number of companies going private increased 22 percent. The number of publicly traded companies was already in decline, and now even IPOs are dropping to new lows. In 1996 there were more than 600 IPOs, in 2008 there were less than 35 (this was across all public markets.) According to many people I have spoken with the regulatory requirements on disclosure and accounting simply make it too expensive to go public in the U.S. According to a study by the SEC on capital formation 28 percent of funds go to marketing, commissions and other costs associated with an offering.

Chapter 14

Risk of Transparency

"Charm is a way of getting the answer yes without asking a clear question."
Albert Camus

The best risk management practices will be open and transparent, as it makes them totally defensible. The market recognizes risk and is, in fact, a barometer for risk. The market is a place where one assumes and accepts risks in exchange for reward. Metrics such as Maximum Peak Exposure (MPE), Credit Value Adjustments (CVA), Potential Future Exposure (PFE), and Expected Positive Exposure (EPE) are all methods used to digest risk and its impact. The market knows this, understands this, and will expect both disclosure and open discussion. Those companies and funds that disclose and discuss how risk is assumed and managed will earn the highest possible valuation by the markets.

Conversely, losses sustained in vehicles that had less than transparent disclosures will continue to make headlines and be springboards for litigation. The difficulty is establishing what you knew, what you could have known, and when you could have know it. Many very smart people have miscalculated risks that look obvious to us today, but the risks were not obvious at the time.

Those companies absent from the headlines are the funds making money and disclosing as little as possible. Without considering this paradigm we cannot calculate with any degree of certainty the optimum balance between disclosure and preservation of IPCI. After all, no matter how much we disclose there is never a safe harbor from litigation. It will cost more to attempt to include all of the risks instead of just the operative risks – and in the end, over-disclosure may actually expose you to additional liability.

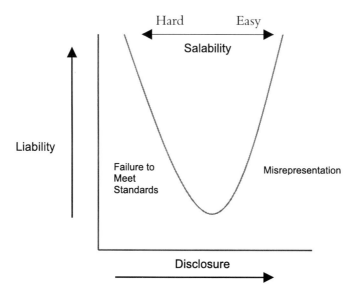

Disclosure Liability Risk

The underlying assumption of the regulators is that with full disclosure, in real time, people can somehow prudently manage risk. In reality, any study of decision making will show that, as humans, we are anything but prudent – we are likely to respond to a host of biases, misperceptions and misinformation that will color our expectations and decisions. After all, what is a failed investment? It is simply an investment that has failed our expectations.

Full Transparency and Litigation

First of all, it's impossible to provide full disclosure – since all risks cannot be known at the time of investment. It is impossible. I have on my desk, as I write, a three-and-a-half pound set of documents for a multifamily Real Estate Investment Trust (REIT). It's a massive set of documents, disclosure and information that is beautifully written, documented and printed. I'm guessing that this sales and disclosure tome cost several million dollars to author and publish. Even after all of that work, there are five supplements correcting or updating the information. If I've ever seen full disclosure for a REIT – this is it. However, this attempt at full disclosure poses another problem. That is, it serves as a solid foundation for litigation. Several securities litigators I spoke with really liked the investment, and made comments along the line of:

> *"This is a no-loss investment for me, whether they do what they say they are going to do or not. If I get a return along the lines of my expectation, I'll be happy. If not, and the investment appears to be failing or coming up short, I'll comb through the offering documents - because I will not read the many hundreds of pages before I invest - no one does. I will look for where their representations at the time of investment are incongruent with their subsequent actions - as they always will be. No one can craft a prospectus with full disclosure and adhere to the model throughout the term of the investment. Markets change, and the economy changes, requiring adaptations in the management of the fund. But, it's sufficient grounds for litigation and recovery."*

The calls for increased transparency assume that more informed choices can be made, resulting in less fraud and risk of litigation. This is a simplistic analysis, and acting upon it may be counterproductive, unless it offers managers and administrators some form of statutory safe harbor.

Regulatory Regime Response

In an effort to promote transparency, regulators are exploring the standardization of investment contracts and agreements, as well as an independent exchange to trade these contracts.

I disagree with standardization. That should be a market choice. Many of these contracts are used to manage risk, and to manage *specific* risks. Standardized contracts make hedges more imperfect than the parties may like, and they cause other problems when dealing with the management and disclosure of risk. What was once a risk that could be close to perfectly hedged, is now imperfectly hedged – and may add new risk as opposed to shifting risk.

An independent exchange is a must. Prices mean very little if transactions are not conducted on an exchange that allows participants a thorough understanding of what is being traded. Further, an exchange acts as a mechanism to enforce the settlement of contracts and agreements. Industry and corporate governance require a bona fide independent marketplace to ensure the viability of contracts. The exchange will provide for pricing and information transparency while the parties will still possess a degree of privacy for their economic positions. The exchange will enforce settlement through its own exchange rules and requirements, along with an explicit warrantee.

An efficient independent exchange will moderate the debate on valuation (mark-to- market versus mark-to-model versus mark-to-fantasy) revealing volume and prices while ensuring enforceability and settlement.

Endnote

Legislative efforts on transparency inevitably follow some event that "no one saw coming." The efforts are reactive, and designed "to prevent this from ever happening again." Facts are assembled, experts are empaneled, chests are pounded, and fingers are pointed. In the end, laws are passed that restrict the manner in which two parties can interact which restricts the flow and application of capital. Regulation is often a short-term solution to a long-term problem. Bad facts and haste make bad law. Legislators are all too willing to pass laws before the problem the legislators intend to address is fully understood. Intervention in complex systems doesn't always have the desired effect, and often creates new and unforeseen problems. SOX was the right idea, with ham-handed execution.

All laws limit choices, so new laws should only be passed when the problems they are meant to address are adequately understood, alternatives have been reviewed, and the potential consequences discussed. The entire legislative process requires diversified input. Advice should be solicited from those outside the political process, including those involved in industries the legislation might affect. This process, too, needs a degree of transparency.

From the standpoint of due diligence, transparency can be both private and public; it can be either disclosed or observed. While due diligence is about creating a transparent relationship between you and your client, public transparency mandated by regulated disclosure may create risk. And due diligence is also about eliminating risk.

Chapter 15

Individual Questionnaire and Instructions

"Truth is like the sun. You can shut it out for a time, but it ain't goin' away."

Elvis Presley

The instructions for this questionnaire guide the user as to the relevance and significance of the information, interpretation of the information, and where that information becomes important in the process of the investigation.

Going through the questionnaires, point by point by point, and telling you exactly what each section means would be an insult to your intelligence as well as a waste of ink and paper. The following is only a brief overview.

Background Information

This section of the questionnaire deals with general information about an individual. This is information that helps define the person – socially, fiscally and geographically. The first section of the questionnaire helps define the individual, where to contact him/her, what he is doing now, and his current relationships. As part of your investigation, you will request the person's Social Security and driver's license numbers, as well as authorization to pull his credit report and driving history (an authorization form is posted at the end of the individual questionnaire). While most credit reports contain errors, they will tell you a lot. They will indicate if bills are paid on time, show some residential history, and provide some information on the spouse. Primarily, a credit report will tell you how well a person is regarded in the credit granting community. A driving record will show you if there is a reckless disregard for the law, or a history of accidents. All of this information is important, as it reflects on the overall character of the individual.

In the section discussing the relationship this individual has with the company, as well as other companies that may contract with the company, you need detailed information. This information should expose any conflicts of interest. These relationships are important, as excess payments directed to outside vendors is a common method of theft. A questionnaire should simply be used as one of many tools to locate potential areas of occupational abuse.

The personal financial information will provide some information about financial needs. If this individual has an expensive lifestyle and no savings, they are getting money from somewhere to support this lifestyle. Is money from the company funding the cash-flow-lifestyle gap? It is a question you need to ask and be answer. Does this gap mean the person will steal from the company? Does this mean he has to find additional employment? Does this mean that because he cannot support himself at this company, that he will not be with this company for a long period of time?

The important point is, means vs. ability. What are the person's means in terms of expenditures and what abilities does he have to cover those expenditures? If there is a shortfall between the two, that shortfall has to be accounted for, either from investment, savings, trust disbursements, spousal income, investment income or embezzlement.

Licenses, Credentials, Awards and Significant Achievements is a section in which an individual has an opportunity to demonstrate to you what he believes to be important. Many of us have received Who's Prominent acknowledgements and the blankety blank nominations. Once you have been nominated, you pay your exorbitant fee, and you are Who's Prominent. I don't believe that to be a significant achievement. I know I have a few of those plaques. I do however; weigh the individual's professional membership or recognition in their industrial and professional groups as significant peer acceptance or acknowledgement of their abilities. Those are the ones that I would look for to be important to the individual as opposed to the pomp and circumstance of a Who's Prominent or similar type award.

Legal Proceedings

Any entrepreneur worth their salt has made mistakes and has gone through litigation. How they dealt with those problems, on the other hand, is a real test of an entrepreneur's mettle. Litigation, by itself, shouldn't be a disincentive or dissuasion for a person to have business dealings. Litigation reflects how an individual deals with adversity, it is publicly disclosed, and provides a rich record of their activities to be harvested and read.

> *In one particular case I worked on in California many years ago, an angel investor hired us to perform a comprehensive background check on an entrepreneur prior to funding a real estate management company venture with him. We located more than 42 potential lawsuits to which the entrepreneur was exposed. As a longtime entrepreneur and developer, he had gone through a crash in California real estate, and afterward he chose to start his new business in property management. However, he had failed to effectively deal with his old problems, and as in the course of our due diligence investigation, we discovered that if these lawsuits were successful, he could have approximately $20 million in judgments against him. Second, these disputes were likely to result in judgments because he was not defending himself. Now, not all of the claims against him were valid – but he had enough of a real estate business to make him a target, and sufficient frustration with litigation that he chose to ignore it in hopes that it would all go away. As a consequence, the angel investor decided to withhold funds until he had settled all potential disputes. The entrepreneur finally had to declare bankruptcy. It was a sad day for him and his creditors.*

> *After the bankruptcy, the angel investor contacted the entrepreneur and said, "Now that you have all of your problems cleared up, let's talk again about investments in real-estate management." I don't know if it was ever funded, or where it went from there, but it was a real object lesson in doing your homework.*

Ownership

The section on ownership is important because understanding the ownership and control of the company is important. It should be simple to understand, well stated and correctly stated. Whether this individual controls shares through proxies or relatives or close friends, or whether the individual controls all the shares in his own name. There is not a significant difference with respect to the SEC and SEC Disclosure, nor is it a significant difference in how the company would be run. So as a consequence, you need to find out what shares this person controls over and above the shares issued in his own name. Remember to look for who is the beneficial owner and who has control of the vote of the shares.

The Certain Practices section goes into activities that are blatantly illegal and asks the individual if the individual or the corporation has ever been engaged in such activities. Some examples are: kickbacks, excessive political party contributions, fees in excess of the reasonable value of services for consultants or agents, donating money to the individuals of the corporation so those individuals in mass can donate to a political party, any type of off-balance sheet or income statement activity. This is important activity to be disclosed. If it has happened, it is not necessarily a pass or fail for the individual; however, it is something that needs to be disclosed within the scope of activity of the company to any potential investor. The issue needs to be forced. If the answers are no, an active declaration affirming that no such activities have taken place must be made – passive assurances are no longer sufficient.

The Indemnification section talks about how officers and directors will be indemnified by the company for their actions when taken on behalf of the company. Please note, the company cannot be held liable or be required to indemnify an officer or director of the company if the action that the individual has taken is outside the scope of authority of that individual or if that activity is criminal in nature.
The National Association of Securities Dealers (NASD) section is important to be included for any individual who is a subject of a due diligence investigation of a company that is going public or intends to go public within the near future. Going public means offering its shares for sale to the investing public.

Affirmation. This is where the individual affirms all of the answers in the individual questionnaire to be true and correct and that he understands that he could be held liable for any mistakes, errors or omissions.

The last section is called the Acknowledgment. In most cases, you should get five to 10 originals of the acknowledgment for when you are performing any public records search in which is required the written consent of the individual to gather that information. Specifically, records such as driver's licenses and credit reports, require this type of personal consent for the due diligence practitioner to gain access to these records.

Individual Questionnaire

I.   Background Information

    1. General Information

        a.   Personal Information

Name – First, Middle, Last – also any other names used including aliases and maiden names.

Age, Date and Place of Birth

Social Security Number

Driver's License Number

Address, State and ZIP Code

Citizenship

Passport Number

2nd Citizenship

Passport Number

Work Permit / Green Cards Held

Marital Status

Name of Spouse

Age, Date and Place of Birth

Social Security Number

Driver's License Number

Address, State and ZIP Code

Citizenship

Passport Number

2nd Citizenship

Passport Number

Work Permit / Green Cards Held

Children's Names and Addresses and Current Employment

Residential Address: Street, City, State, ZIP Code

Business Address: Street, City, State, ZIP Code

Home Telephone

Business Telephone

Cell Phone Number(s)

Voice Over Internet Protocol (VoIP) Number(s)

b.   Education:

For each institution you have attended from high school onward including college, university, trade schools, professional and technical certifications etc.

Institution

Field of Study

Months / Years Attended

Degree or Certification Used, If None State So.

c.   Employment Foundation

    i.   Please state your current position with the
            company and the length of time you have
            held that position. (Please discuss and attach
            agreement.)

    ii.   Were you (or will you be) selected by the
            company pursuant to any arrangement or
            understanding between yourself and any
            other person? (Please discuss and attach
            agreement.)

d.   If you are not an employee of the company, please
        describe your principal occupation and the name
        and principal business of your employer. (Please
        discuss and attach agreement.)

e.   Briefly describe any arrangement or understanding
        between you and any other person or persons
        pursuant to which you were or are to be selected
        as a director or officer of the company and identify
        the person or persons with whom you have any
        such arrangements. (Please discuss and attach
        agreement.)

f.   State the nature of any family relationship between
        you and any director or officer (or person nominated
        or chosen to become a director or officer) of the
        company or any affiliate of the company. (Please
        discuss.)

g.   Please   describe your business experience up to,
        together with the dates, and including the present
        time, including your principal occupations and
        employment during that period and the name
        and principal business of any corporation or other
        organization in which such occupations and
        employment were or are being conducted, and,

if you are an officer of the company, describe the nature of the responsibilities undertaken by you in your prior positions with the company including where applicable, the size of the operation, number of personnel and annual budget supervised. Please complete on a separate sheet. Include, principal occupation, name and principal business of employer, period of service, and an explanation of the duties and postings held.

h. List the name of each company in which you currently serve as a director. Please indicate whether (i) each company has a compensation committee on its board; (ii) you serve as a member of the compensation committee, if any; and (iii) each company is a "publicly held company" (any company which has a class of securities registered with the Securities and Exchange Commission pursuant to Section 12 or Section 15 of the Securities Exchange Act of 1934 or any company registered as an investment company under the Investment Company Act 1940).

i. Please list all business, civic, trade or other organizations to which you belong, including any offices or other positions held in each.

j   Are you now, or have you been since the formation of the company, an officer, director, employee of, or do you now own, or have you owned since the formation of the company, directly or indirectly, in excess of a 1 percent equity interest in any firm, corporation or other business or professional entity:

(1) which has made payments to the company or its subsidiaries for property or services during the company's last fiscal year in excess of $10,000;

Yes ___   No ___

(2)   which proposes to make payments to the company or its subsidiaries for property or services during the current fiscal year in excess of $10,000;

Yes ___   No ___

(3)   to which the company or its subsidiaries were indebted at any time during the company's current fiscal year in an aggregate amount in excess of 3 percent of book value;

Yes ___   No ___

(4)   to which the company or its subsidiaries have made payments for property or services during such entity's last fiscal year in excess of 3 percent of such entity's gross revenues for its last full fiscal year; or

Yes ___   No ___

(5)   to which the company or its subsidiaries propose to make payments for property or services during such entity's current fiscal year in excess of 3 percent of such entity's consolidated gross revenues for its last full fiscal year?

Yes ___   No ___

k.   Do you possess (other than through your position as director), or indirectly, the power to direct or cause the direction of the management and policies of the company, which through the ownership of voting securities, by contract, or otherwise?

Yes ___   No ___

l. Did you have during the past five years a principal occupation or employment with any of the company's parents, subsidiaries or other affiliates?

Yes ___   No ___

m Are you, or is any member of your immediate family, or any associate of yours, currently engaged in any activity that is similar to or is in any way competitive with any of the present or proposed business activities of the company? (Please see glossary for definition of "immediate family" and "associate.")

Yes ___   No ___

n. Do you, or does any member of your immediate family, or any associate of yours, have any direct or indirect ownership or other interest in, or family relationship with, any person or entity that currently is or in the future may be engaged in any activity that is similar to or is in any way competitive with the present or proposed business activities of the company?

Yes ___   No ___

o. Please provide all of the screen names and posting names you have used when working with any of the many forms of social media such as but not limited to: e-mails, blogs, posting boards, Twitter, Facebook, My Space, etc. Please attach this information.
For all "yes" answers to any of the above questions, please describe.

2. Residential History: (Give all addresses for the last 10 years, starting with current address, and be specific with street, city, state, ZIP Code and time period of residence.

3. Financial Institution Relationships

    a.   List all deposits with financial institutions including but not limited to: banks, savings and loan, credit unions, brokerage firms, insurance companies and trust companies either domestic or international. Include the name, address, type of account, account number and balance.

    b.   Please prepare a letter to each of these institutions authorizing them to confirm these balances to [Insert Name]. Attach the letters to this questionnaire and return with questionnaire. Credit lines and borrowing capacity including credit cards and insurance polices. Please be specific for each financial institution and include contact person's name, telephone number and details and terms of the relationship.

    c.   List all debt with current maturities (amounts, dates):

    d.   Discuss any "buy-sell" agreements or other buyout options in existence (Please attach agreement):

    d.   Are you bonded? <u>If so, please discuss and attach a copy of the bond.</u>

4. Licenses, Credentials, Awards & Significant Achievements

Please set forth a list of all designations you have – either by achievement, membership, license, award or other, and please include a list of all publications along with dates for all.

5. Intellectual Property and Critical Information (IPCI)

    a.   Are you bringing or have you brought to this company any items of IPCI that are deemed to be your own or that of a third party?

Yes ___   No ___

b.   Does your agreement with the company clearly state who is the owner of the IPCI generated by your efforts for this company?

Yes ___   No ___

If you have answered "yes" to any of the questions above, please supply the information related to the questions(s) on an attachment to this questionnaire.

II.   Legal Proceedings

1.   Please indicate whether:

a.   A petition under the federal bankruptcy laws or any state insolvency law was filed by or against, or a receiver, fiscal agent or similar officer was appointed by a court for, your business or property, or any partnership in which you were a general partner at the time of filing or within two years before the time of such filing, or any corporation or business association of which you were an executive officer at or within two years before the time of such filing.

Yes ___   No ___

b.   You were convicted in a criminal proceeding or are a named subject of a pending criminal proceeding (excluding traffic violations and other minor offenses but including all felony charges).

Yes ___   No ___

c. You were the subject of any order, judgment or decree, not subsequently reversed, suspended or vacated, of any competent jurisdiction permanently or temporarily enjoining you from, or otherwise limiting any of your activities.

Yes ___   No ___

d. You were the subject of any order, judgment or decree, not subsequently reversed, suspended or vacated, of any federal or state authority barring, suspending or otherwise limiting for more than 60 days your right to engage in any activity described in subparagraph 3 above, or to be associated with persons engaged in any such activity.

Yes ___   No ___

e. You were found by a court of competent jurisdiction in a civil action or by the Securities and Exchange Commission (the "Commission") or any state securities commission to have violated any federal or state securities law, and the judgment in such civil action or finding by the Commission or any state securities commission has not been subsequently reversed, suspended or vacated.

Yes ___   No ___

f. You were found by a court of competent jurisdiction in a civil action or by the Commodities Futures Trading Commission to have violated any federal commodities law, and the judgment in such civil action or finding by the CFTC has not been subsequently reversed, suspended or vacated.

Yes ____ No ____

g. A lawsuit has been filed against you, any business or property of yours, any partnership in which you were a general partner, or any corporation or business association of which you were an officer or director.

Yes ____ No ____

h. You, any associate of yours or any affiliate of the company are or may be a party to any pending or contemplated legal proceedings, including administrative proceedings and governmental investigations in which you or such associate or affiliate has an interest adverse to the company?

Yes ____ No ____

i. Are you aware of any pending legal, arbitrations or administrative proceeding to which the company is a party which may have an effect upon the earnings or financial conditions of the company?

Yes ____ No ____

j. At anytime have your civil rights been suspended, and if so have they been restored?

Yes ____ No ____

k. At anytime have you been the subject of, or been required to request the courts for any type of protective order?

Yes ___   No ___

l.   Have your wages or assets ever been subject to a garnishment or an assignment for any reason?

Yes ___   No ___

m.   Have you ever employed casual labor such as childcare, or handyman work, etc., where the annual compensation for an individual has been more than $800 in the year?

Yes ___   No ___

n.   Have you issued a 1099 for that (those) person(s) as required by current tax guidelines?

Yes ___   No ___

o.   Are your state and federal taxes current?

Yes ___   No ___

p.   Are you aware of any of the control persons, officers and directors, promoters or key persons that would be required to answer yes to any of the questions in this Section II?

Yes ___   No ___

If you answered "yes" to any of the foregoing questions, please explain the circumstances, including any mitigating circumstances, in detail on a separate sheet of paper. For purposes of this questionnaire, the date of a reportable event shall be deemed the date on which the final order, judgment or decree was entered, or the date on which any rights or appeal from preliminary orders, judgments, or decrees have lapsed. With respect to bankruptcy petitions, the date shall be the date of filing for uncontested petitions or the date upon which approval of a contested petition becomes final.

III. Ownership

1. Please list the number of shares of all classes and types of stock, of the company beneficially owned, directly or indirectly, or controlled by yourself.

Number of Shares	Voting Power (Sole or Shared)	Investment Power (Sole or Shared)
Shares owned by you.	_____	_____
Shares owned by your spouse, minor children or relatives living with you. Provide details.	_____	_____
Shares owned by you as trustee, custodian, or in some other capacity for the benefit of another person. Provide details.	_____	_____
Shares owned by a corporation, partnership, or other entity of which you are an officer, director, or 5 percent shareholder. Provide details.	_____	_____
Shares which you have a right to acquire (by		

option, contract, or
otherwise) after the date
of this questionnaire.
Provide details.   _____   _____

Any other shares over
which you possess voting
or disposition power.
Provide details.   _____   _____

-

      a.   If you listed any shares, please explain the details of ownership.

      b.   If you listed any shares over which you share authority to vote or dispose with another (e.g., with other directors, pursuant to a voting agreement, with other trustees, or otherwise), explain the details of the shared-power.

      c.   If you wish to disclaim beneficial ownership of the above shares
of common stock, please furnish the following information with respect to the person or persons, who should be shown as the beneficial owner(s) of the shares in question. Include, name of actual beneficial owner, relationship to you, number of shares beneficially owned, and the reason for the disclaiming of beneficial ownership.

2.   Do you have any right to acquire beneficial ownership of any of the company's securities, whether through the exercise of any option, warrant, right, convertible security, or otherwise?

      Yes ___   No ___

      If "yes" please set forth the title of the securities,

the number of shares associated with such rights and date such rights become exercisable.

3.   Do you know of any person or entity which owns beneficially in the aggregate, more than 5 percent of the outstanding security of the company?

Yes ____   No ____

If the answer is "yes" please state the name and address of such person or entity and state the number of shares beneficially owned. Be specific and include security holder, number of shares, type of ownership, and anything else that may be material.

4.   As to securities indicated as being beneficially owned in answer to question 3 a or b, does any person other than the person identified as the beneficial owner have:

a.   The sole or shared power to vote or to direct the vote of any such securities?

Yes ____   No ____

b.   Or the sole or shared power to dispose or to direct the disposition of any such securities?

Yes ____   No ____

If "yes" please set forth below the name and address of each person who either has such power or with whom the indicated beneficial owner shares either such power, together with the number of shares and relationship to beneficial owner and the limits on the power to vote or dispose of these shares.

5. Do you have knowledge of any arrangements, contracts or agreements of which you are aware, including any pledge, hypothecation, or voting agreements of the company's securities, that may at some future date result in a change of control of the company or of the ownership of the equity securities of the company presently beneficially owned by you?

    Yes ___   No ___

6. Do you know of any arrangement through which the company's common stock is held or is to be held in voting trust or other similar agreement?

    Yes ___   No ___

7. Do you or any associate of yours have any interest, direct or indirect, by security holdings or otherwise, in the proposed issuance of securities by the company?

    Yes ___   No ___

8. Do you have any interest in or affiliation or association with [name of company asking questions]?

    Yes ___   No ___

9. Do you intend to sell any shares of common stock pursuant to a registration statement other than the registration statement to which this questionnaire relates?

    Yes ___   No ___

10. Do you own an interest, either public or private, domestic or international, in companies other than

this one?

Yes ___   No ___

11.   Do you have obligations to other companies as an officer, director, employee or significant person? This list is to include all companies, even family enterprises and trusts.

Yes ___   No ___

If you have answered "yes" to any of the questions above please supply the information related to the question(s) on an attachment to this questionnaire.

IV.   Certain Practices

In your response to these questions, the following instructions apply:

- Each of these questions is to be read as relating to the activities of the company and any of its affiliates, as well as to the conduct of any person who has acted or is acting on behalf of or for the benefit of any of them.

- Each question is to be read as relating not only to activities or conduct within the United States, but outside the United States as well.

- The terms "payments" and "contributions" include not only giving of cash or hard goods but also the giving of anything else of value, for example, services or the use of property.

- The term "indirectly" means an act done through an intermediary. Payments to sales agents or representatives that are passed on in whole or in part to purchasers, or compensation or reimbursement to persons in consideration for their acts, are examples of acts done through intermediaries.

- Your answers should consider not only matters of which you have direct personal knowledge, but also any matters of which you have reason to believe may have existed or occurred, (for example, you may not "know" from your own personal knowledge that contributions were made by the company to a political party, but based upon information which has otherwise come to your attention you may nonetheless have "reason to believe" that such contributions were made. In such case, your response would be "yes.")

Do you know or have reason to believe that any of the activities or types of conduct enumerated below have been or may have been engaged in by the company, directly or indirectly, at any time since the formation of the company:

1. Any bribes or kickbacks to government employees or their relatives, foreign or domestic or any other payments to such persons, to obtain or retain regulatory approvals, licenses, or otherwise to receive favorable treatment with regard to business;

   Yes ___   No ___

2. Any bribes or kickbacks to persons other than government employees, or to relatives of such persons, or any other payments to such persons or their relatives which might be deemed questionable, to obtain or retain business or to receive favorable treatment with regard to business;

   Yes ___   No ___

3. Any contributions, whether or not legal, made to any political party, political candidate or holder of

government office;

Yes ___   No ___

4. Any fees paid to consultants or commercial agents which exceed the reasonable value of the services purported to be rendered;

Yes ___   No ___

5. Any payments or reimbursements made to personnel of the company for the purpose of enabling them to expend time or to make contributions or payments of the kinds or for the purposes referred to in subparts 1 through 4 above;

Yes ___   No ___

6. Any bank accounts, funds or pools of funds created or maintained without being reflected on the corporate books of account, or as to which the receipts and disbursements therefrom have been reflected on such books.

Yes ___   No ___

7. Any receipts or disbursements, the actual nature or amount of which have been disguised or intentionally misrecorded on the corporate books of accounts?
   Yes ___   No ___

If you have answered "yes" to any of the questions above please supply the information related to the question(s) on an attachment to this questionnaire.

V.   Indemnification

Is there any arrangement under which any control person, director or officer of the company is insured or indemnified in any manner against the liability which he may incur in his capacity as such?

Yes ___   No ___

If "yes" please describe such provisions:

VI.   National Association of Securities Dealers (NASD)

If this questionnaire is being completed in connection with an offering or due diligence review of an existing public company, the company is required to furnish certain information to the National Association of Securities Dealers, Inc. (NASD) relating to its security holders, and provide disclosure to current and potential shareholders.

1.   Indicate below whether or not you have any information pertaining to underwriting compensation and arrangements or any dealings between any underwriter or related person of the NASD, person associated with a member or associated person of a member on the one hand and the company or controlling security holder thereof or an affiliated company on the other hand, other than information relating to the proposed underwriting agreement to be entered into in connection with the offering.   If you know of such information, please describe below.

        I know of no such information _____

        I know of such information _____

2.   State below whether you are a member of the NASD, a controlling stockholder of a member, a person associated with a member or associated person of a member, or an underwriter or related person with respect to the offering.
        Yes ___   No ___

3.   State whether (i) you have made any sales or disposition (including contracts to sell or to dispose) of securities of the company during the last twelve (12) months to any member

of the NASD or any person associated with a member or any underwriter or related person with respect to the offering, or (ii) you contemplate any such sale or disposition to be consummated in whole or in part within the next twelve (12) months, other than a sale or disposition in connection with the offering. If your answer is "yes," please describe below.

Yes ___   No ___

If your answer to any of these questions is "yes" please describe.

VII.   Affirmation

The answers I have supplied to the foregoing questions are true, complete and correct, to the best of my information and belief. I understand that material misstatements or the omission of material facts in the registration statement may give rise to civil and criminal liabilities to the company and to each officer and director of the company signing the registration statement. I will notify you and the company of any misstatements of a material fact in the registration statement or any amendment thereto, and of the omission as soon as practicable after a copy of the registration statement or any such amendment has been provided to me. I shall advise the company's counsel promptly from time to time if any event occurs that to my knowledge would require any change in my answers to the foregoing questions in order to make such answers correct. I also understand that all of the attachments and appendices are herby incorporated by reference into this questionnaire and form parts of the answers I have given.

Dated: _____

_____
Signed

_____
Typed or printed name of Signee

THE INFORMATION PROVIDED ON THIS FORM IS COMPLETE AND ACCURATE. I AUTHORIZE VERIFICATION OF THIS INFORMATION VIA A BACKGROUND INVESTIGATION AND I AUTHORIZE A FULL CREDIT, EDUCATIONAL, EMPLOYMENT AND PUBLIC RECORDS INVESTIGATION EITHER DOMESTIC OR INTERNATIONALLY.

_____
Signature

_____
Date

★ THIS FORM MUST BE NOTARIZED

ACKNOWLEDGMENT

STATE OF _____

COUNTY OF _____

On this _____ day of _____, 20_____, before me, _____the undersigned officer, personally appeared ___ _____to me personally known and known to me to be the same person(s) whose name(s) is (are) signed to the foregoing instrument, and acknowledged the execution thereof for the uses and purposes set forth herein.

IN WITNESS WHEREOF I have hereunto set my hand and official seal.

_____
(Notary Public)

(Notary Seal)   My commission expires: _____

Chapter 16

Corporate Questionnaire and Instructions

"Corporation, n. An ingenious device for obtaining individual profit without individual responsibility."

Ambrose Bierce, *The Devil's Dictionary*

This corporate questionnaire can be used both for corporations, sub-chapter S corporations, limited liability companies, limited partnerships, general partnerships, and to some extent, sole proprietorships. This is a questionnaire for the business.

General Information

The general information on the corporation is information that helps us find and identify the corporation. This would include: the legal name, stated formation, tax ID numbers, any city, state, county or federal licenses and permits, the dates of incorporation, what type of business this corporation is, what type of business this corporation is engaged in and the identity of any subsidiary corporations. If the company has subsidiary corporations, the questionnaire must be applied to each of the subsidiaries. If the corporation in question is a subsidiary, then the questionnaire must be applied to every sister corporation as well as the parent corporation.

Organizational

A corporation as a legal entity has certain requirements. Those requirements include keeping the articles of incorporation in good standing within the state jurisdiction where it was incorporated, keeping its shareholders' and directors' meetings current, and adhering to the bylaws of the corporation. A corporation is not a living, breathing entity, it is the sum total of the efforts of people who work for the corporation. The organizational portion of this questionnaire goes into the status of the enterprise as well as what contingency plans are in place to deal with the loss of key people.

Litigation

All corporations that are active and transacting business will eventually be sued or will have to sue someone else. Some corporations, by the nature of the type of business they conduct, are prone to litigation. In my experience, one of the businesses most prone to litigation is an automobile dealership. Dealers are not particularly liked, and when something goes wrong customers have few reservations about escalating their dispute. From my experience serving on the board of dealership leasing and finance company, it is virtually impossible for a dealership and finance company to escape litigation.

Does litigation indicate a bad company? No, quite to the contrary. An automobile is likely to be the first or second largest investment a person ever makes, and they are less than uniform. Every automobile is unique, even if the year, make, model and color are identical – they're still different. While a company may do its very best to satisfy the customer, some people are never satisfied. It is important to understand the nature of the company, the nature of the business, and the nature of the litigation. In today's world, litigation is simply another cost of doing business.

If a business has been involved in either bankruptcy or criminal proceedings, it requires a closer look. If there is criminal litigation, the status of the litigation and the circumstances surrounding the incident that propagated the litigation must be researched. If an individual or corporation has declared bankruptcy, it should be determined whether the collapse resulted from a general business risk, sensitivity to market conditions or a management problem. I have known many successful executives who resisted cutting payroll during an economic crisis. Their motives were truly genuine and caring, but it is almost always an unfortunate decision. In the long run, a bloated payroll leads to bankruptcy and everyone loses, not just a few. Executives are there to make difficult decisions – decisions that affect many lives – and they have to make the right decisions. A bankruptcy requires special attention to the management activity that preceded the filing.

Financial

The financial portion is one of the most important sections of the questionnaire. The enterprise was formed to make money. Companies need to have a current income statement and balance sheet. The accountants and financial experts should be readily available to the investigator, and prepared to answer pointed questions when asked. The questions are fairly self-directing and general in nature. Every enterprise will require inquiries specific to the nature of its business, which obviously cannot be covered in a manual.

Ownership and Securities

This section covers basic information – whether the company is publicly or privately owned, and what securities have been issued. In the process we need a description of the securities, whether they are common shares, different classes of common shares, preferred shares, or debt instruments, who the owners of those instruments are, and what rights are conveyed to the owners of those instruments.

If the company is publicly traded, there is a very specific set of questions dedicated to public companies and those seeking to become public.

Records

Corporate record-keeping is part and parcel of a well-organized, well-run company. Records are essential to understand business activity and should be well-maintained, current and well-protected at all times.

Acknowledgment

The acknowledgment needs to be signed by an officer or director of the corporation that is actively directing its operations. In 99.99 percent of the cases, this is the president along with the chairman. Add as many signature blocks and verifications as you think are necessary to get the proper scope for understanding the operations of the company.

Document Checkoff List

There are many documents that are required to be read (and understood) in any due diligence investigation. The documents most frequently required are on the attached checkoff list. No list can be all- inclusive, and the investigator must consider any special circumstances or risks involved. If the business you are investigating is a refinery, you will need all of the permits with respect to pollution control and EPA compliance. If the company is involved in importing and exporting, the necessary import/export licenses to transact business need to be included.

At the end, there is an affirmation of corporate information questionnaire. This should be signed and notarized in a number of original duplicates by all of the people who acknowledged and affirmed the corporate individual questionnaire. The several duplicate originals from each individual are needed for, or required by, third parties to disclose information relevant to your investigation.

Corporate Questionnaire

This is a list of questions to be answered in the report to the inquirer, with copies of requested documents to be attached as appendices to the report and organized by section.

1.   GENERAL INFORMATION

Legal name of company.

Type of entity – sole proprietorship, general partnership, limited partnership, limited liability company, cell limited liability company, foundation, other, and tax elections.

Tax ID number, state.

Tax ID number, federal.

Date and place of formation.

Nature of the company business.

Nature of business of parent and subsidiary entities.

Articles of formation for all entities.

Governance documents such as bylaws or operational agreements for all entities.

Records of the meetings for the security holders and guidance bodies for the entities.

Current and past addresses for all entities.

All trade names, brand names and service marks owned, and uses.

List all acquisitions and divestures.
City and county permits and licenses.

2. ORGANIZATIONAL

Structure chart of parent and subsidiary entities.

Organization chart of each of the entities.

Records of the meetings for the security holders and guidance bodies for the entities.

Current and past addresses for all entities.

What is the organizational status of the company, and who are the responsible people? (Attach résumés.)

Who are the key persons to the corporation, internal or external? (Attach résumés.)

What is management's plan for dealing with the loss of a key person, for any reason?

What has been the total number of employees, today, one year ago, five years ago?

Is the corporation in good standing?

Yes ___   No ___
If no, please explain why?

Have any officers or directors resigned from the company? Why?

Yes ___   No ___

In a merger or acquisition, is it the plan of the current board of directors to maintain or give up control?

What are the board's expectations and conditions?
List all present officers and directors of your company, their current annual salary and other compensation, including all

bonuses paid or expected to be paid during the company's current fiscal year, retirement, health, travel, options and others.

List names, titles and annual compensation of all salaried employees of your company with salaries greater than $_____ per year.

List all employment and consulting agreements, and copies of all such agreements.

Are any of the workers of the entities represented by unions? If yes, name the union along with contact information and an assessment of the relationship with the union(s).

List any collective bargaining or other union contracts, if applicable, and copies of all such contracts.

Describe any loans to or from officers, directors, agents or stockholders of the company.

Describe how you recruit new employees, i.e.: advertising, open applications, recruiting and others.

Describe your selection and screening process for all new hires.

Describe inquires into prospective new hires if their spouses or life partners work at competing firms.

Describe any problems with workers' compensation, or any other employment problems concerning compensation, termination of employment, or other reason.

Are there employee benefit plans, pension, retirement, disability, medical, dental, other health, life insurance or other death benefit plans, profit sharing, deferred compensation, stock options, stock purchase, bonus or other incentive plans, vacation benefit plans, severance plans or other employee benefit plans or arrangements?

Yes ___   No ___
If yes, please attach copies.

Does your company lease employees or make use of temporary services? If so, attached those agreements as well as the method used for vetting their workers.

Describe your procedure for the termination of employees and exit interviews.

Please share a copy of your disaster recovery plans.

Please share copies of all anti-money laundering and know-your-client guidelines.

3.   REGULATORY MATTERS

Most entities possess operations and professionals that require licensing and permits from a variety of licensing and regulatory bodies.

List licenses held by the company, the licensing body, the status of the licenses, and the annual cost and activities required to maintain these licenses. Attach copies of all licenses.

List all of the employees, direct or leased, that possess licenses, the status of the licenses and the annual costs and activities required to maintain these licenses. Attach copies of all licenses.

List all past investigations and their outcomes, as well as pending investigations by the licensing and regulatory bodies. Also discuss potential outcomes both positive and negative and the resulting costs internal and external such as legal representation and fines.

4. INTELLECTUAL PROPERTY AND CRITICAL INFORMATION

Seventy-five percent or more of the value in a modern company is Intellectual Property and Critical Information (IPCI). This section addresses IPCI.

Please provide a list of the following:

Patents, with number and expiration date and status as well as all jurisdictions where the patent has been filed.

Trademarks with number, expiration date, and status as well as all jurisdictions where the trademark has been filed.

Service marks with number, expiration date, and status as well as all jurisdictions where the service mark has been filed.

Trade secrets – with a list of what they are (without disclosure of actual secrets).

Copyrights – a list with expirations, and discussion of how these rights were created and how they have been protected.

A list of all critical information. This is information you would not want your competitor to have such as business plans, marketing plans, lists of suppliers, customers, employees and other information.

Please supply your IPCI asset elements registry.

Who in you company is charged with the responsibility for assembling the IPCI asset elements registry?

Do your employment agreements clearly list the company's IPCI and how it may or may not be disclosed? If so please provide the sample paragraph in the employment agreement.

Do agreements with third parties clearly list the company's IPCI and how it may or may not be disclosed? If so please provide a sample paragraph to these agreements.

Do the agreements with both employees and third parties clearly state that all work product generated is the property of the company?

What disclosures or compromises of company IPCI have occurred?

Do you have IPCI defense insurance?

Please describe your operations security (OPSEC) program and those who are responsible for the OPSEC program.

What training have the employees had on IPCI and OPSEC?

5.   **LITIGATION**

Is there any present or pending litigation on behalf of, or against the corporation?

Yes ___   No ___
If yes, briefly describe.

Have any of the officers or directors of the entity been involved in any of the following legal proceedings:

A petition under the federal bankruptcy laws or any insolvency filed by or against you, or a receiver, fiscal agent or similar officer appointed by a court for your business or property, or any partnership in which you were a general partner within two years prior to the time of such filing, or any corporation or business association of which you were an executive officer within two years prior to the time of filing?

Yes ___   No ___

Have you ever been convicted in a criminal proceeding or are you presently the subject of a pending criminal proceeding (excluding traffic offenses and other minor offenses)?

Yes ___   No ___

Have you been the subject of any order, judgment or decree, not subsequently reversed, suspended or vacated, of any court of competent jurisdiction, permanently or temporarily enjoining you from, or otherwise limiting the following activities:

(A.)   Acting as a futures commission merchant, introducing broker, commodity trading advisor, commodity pool operator, floor broker, leverage transaction merchant, any other person regulated by the U.S. Commodity Futures Trading Commission; an associated person of any of the foregoing, or as an investment advisor, underwriter, broker or dealer in securities, or as an affiliated person, director or employee of an investment company, bank, savings and loan association or insurance company, or engaging in or continuing any conduct or practice in connection with such activity?

Yes ___   No ___

(B.)   Engaging in any type of business practice?

Yes ___   No ___

(C.)   Engaging in any activity in connection with the purchase or sale of any security or commodity or in connection with any violation of federal or state securities laws or federal commodities laws or those of any other nation?

Yes ___   No ___

Were you the subject of any order, judgment or decree, not subsequently reversed, suspended or vacated, of any federal or state authority barring, suspending or otherwise limiting for more than 60 days the right to engage in any activity described in paragraphs A, B or C above, or to be associated with persons engaged in any such activity?

Yes ___   No ___

Were you found by a court of competent jurisdiction in a civil action or by the Securities and Exchange Commission to have violated any federal or state securities law, and the judgment in such action or finding by the commission has not been subsequently reversed, suspended or vacated?

Yes ___   No ___

Were you found by a court of competent jurisdiction in a civil action or by the Commodities Futures Trading Commission to have violated any federal commodities law, and the judgment in such civil action and finding by the Commodities Futures Trading Commission has not been subsequently reversed, suspended, or vacated?

Yes ___   No ___

If any of the answers to the preceding questions are "yes" please explain; giving the case name, number and court of jurisdiction wherever located.

Are you, or any corporate officers, directors or affiliates of the company currently involved in any

Securities and Exchange Commission's formal or informal inquiries, investigations, hearings, temporary or permanent injunctions?

Yes ___   No ___
If yes, please explain.

Describe any disputes which could lead to financial or legal impediments in the operation of the company.

6.   **FINANCIAL**

Are all tax filings and payments current?

Yes ___   No ___
If no, please explain why?

Please list all accountants for the corporation along with contact information.

Does the company have any usable tax losses?

Yes ___   No ___
If so, how much and explain?

Is there a list of customers, dealers, distributors, employees, friends, relatives or others who are most likely to invest in your firm?

Yes ___   No ___

Describe all encumbrances, mortgages, liens, etc. on any of your company's assets.

Describe all insurance policies that cover fire, liability, directors and officers' liabilities, and any other insurance which your company maintains, including the name of the insurer, the nature of the coverage, the risks covered, the amount of coverage, the appropriate deductible, term of the coverage, and the annual premium.

List all banks and other financial institutions with which your company has bank accounts, and list all representatives of your company who are authorized to act or deal in connection with those accounts.

State the representatives of your company who work with these institutions.

Describe any pending tax audits or results of any closed tax audits.

List all intellectual property such as copyrights, trademarks, patents, trade secrets, and rights of similar effect used in connection with your company's business, and supply copies of all documentation of any of these items.

List and provide copies of all material contracts, options, deeds, agreements, guarantees and other arrangements of a contractual nature exceeding $10,000 to which your company is a party.

List and provide copies of all permits, authorizations and other governmental orders applicable to the operation of your company's business, safety, environmental, building, zoning, health and others.

Describe any contingent liabilities applicable to your company.

Provide the fiscal year of the company, including all subsidiaries.

List all creditors, secured and unsecured, of the company over $2,000, including names, addresses and telephone numbers, along with an aging of the debt.

State the net before taxes for the last fiscal year, and attach statements of operations concerning all revenue-generating properties, with profit and loss statements.

7.   OWNERSHIP & SECURITIES

Is company's stock publicly traded?

Yes ___   No ___
If yes, answer all questions below.
If no, proceed to question [blank] and continue.

Please complete the following table regarding persons known by the corporation to be beneficial owners of 5 percent or more of any one class (or combination thereof) of the corporation's outstanding stock:

NAME & ADDRESS	NUMBER OF SHARES OWNED	PERCENT CLASS	OF CLASS
_____	_____	_____	_____
_____	_____	_____	_____
_____	_____	_____	_____
_____	_____	_____	_____
_____	_____	_____	_____
_____	_____	_____	_____
_____	_____	_____	_____
_____	_____	_____	_____
_____	_____	_____	_____
_____	_____	_____	_____
_____	_____	_____	_____
_____	_____	_____	_____
_____	_____	_____	_____
_____	_____	_____	_____
_____	_____	_____	_____

Are there any pre-emptive rights?

Is cumulative voting allowed?

Please complete the following table with respect to the beneficial ownership by each director and nominee, and by all present directors and officers as a group, of the corporation's stock.

NAME & ADDRESS	NUMBER OF SHARES OWNED	CLASS	PERCENT OF CLASS
_____	_____	____	____
_____	_____	____	____
_____	_____	____	____
_____	_____	____	____
_____	_____	____	____
_____	_____	____	____
_____	_____	____	____
_____	_____	____	____
_____	_____	____	____
_____	_____	____	____
_____	_____	____	____
_____	_____	____	____
_____	_____	____	____
_____	_____	____	____
_____	_____	____	____
_____	_____	____	____
_____	_____	____	____
_____	_____	____	____

If interested in becoming a public company, what is the shareholder-of-record date to be?

What is the total number of shareholders?

In how many states is stockholder distribution?

In what city and state is the greatest concentration of shareholders?

Please list the stock transfer agent(s), with address and contact information.

Please explain how you perceive market-making activity in your company stock taking. Identify who your market makers will be, who the main supporters of your market will be, whether you plan to hire a public relations firm to assist in those activities on a full-time basis, and what trading range you would realistically like to see your stock at in the next year, two years, three years, and show your plan to accomplish these goals.

List all stockholders and option holders of your company, setting forth shares of stock or options owned by each of them, and in case of option-holders and holders of convertible preferred stock, the number of shares of common stock which the holders have a right to acquire.

A description of any proposed use of proceeds/assets, approximately $_____ immediately, and approximately $_____ through the exercising of all warrants of the candidate.

Is the company prepared to provide an audited financial statement prior to the post-effective amendment filing of any outstanding warrants with the Securities and Exchange Commission?

Is public status the result of a merger or acquisition?

Yes ____   No ____
If yes, between what companies? Explain.

What was the merger date?

What was the date of public offering?

What was the type of public offering?

Who was the underwriter?

Who was the investment banker?

Under what form were the securities registered?

What was the initial selling price?

What is the highest price at which the stock has traded?

What is the lowest price at which the stock has traded?

What is the current price at which the stock is trading?

Have the securities been registered with the Securities and Exchange Commission in the states where traded?

Yes ___   No ___
If no, what exemption from SEC registration is being relied upon?

Are there stock warrants outstanding?

Yes ___   No ___
If yes, state the class, type, terms of exercise and expiration dates.

Is the company listed, and current in its listing information, with any registered manual such as Moody's Investors Service, Standard & Poor's, Value Line, Walker's Manual, Fitch, Dun and Bradstreet, others?

When were the securities last active in trading?

What are the total number of authorized but unissued treasury shares?

What are the total number of free trading shares currently issued and outstanding?

When was the last annual report released?

What are the total number of shares optioned or escrowed?

Are there certified statements available?
Yes ___   No ___
If yes, what is the most current date?

What are the classes of stock authorized?
 Is the stock assessable or non–assessable?

What is the par value of the stock?

What is the total number of shares authorized?

What is the number of shares issued and outstanding?

8.   RECORDS

Do you have the following corporate records:
Stock certificate books and stubs;

Yes ___   No ___

Stock ledger journal;

Yes ___   No ___

Shareholder list;

Yes ___   No ___

Financial accounting records and ledgers;

Yes ___   No ___

Corporate minutes (complete and current);

Yes ___   No ___

Brief history of company;

Yes ___   No ___

Bylaws of the corporation;

Yes ___   No ___

Certificate of good standing;

Yes ___   No ___

Articles of incorporation;

Yes ___   No ___

Canceled stock certificates for the past;

Yes ___   No ___

The corporate seal;

Yes ___   No ___

Records of any amendments;

Yes ___   No ___

Attorneys' opinions of the status of the corporation, assets, debts, public offerings, and ability of shares to trade;

Yes ___   No ___

Securities Exchange Commission correspondence and file.

Yes ___   No ___

Are any stock certificate books lost?

Yes ___   No ___

Is there any danger of forged stock certificates showing up?

Yes ___   No ___

Are the stock records complete and up to date?

Yes ___   No ___

What was the date of the last shareholders meeting?

What was the date of the last board of directors meeting?

Has the board been active?

Yes ___   No ___

Authorization (Sample)

In accordance with the Privacy Act, Freedom of Information Act, the Fair Credit Reporting Act and other applicable laws, I authorize, _____ or its agents to contact orally, or in writing, any third parties to obtain information or analysis which _____ ___ deems necessary and appropriate. I hereby waive any rights or claims I might have against _____ or its agents, as well as any company, agency representatives or other persons providing or analyzing such information and acting with regard to the acquisition, use, retention or disclosure of such information. A photocopy of this authorization shall be as valid as an original.

I understand that a material misstatement or the omission of material facts may give rise to civil and criminal liabilities to the company, its officers and directors. I will notify _____ of any misstatements of a material fact necessary to make any statements contained herein not misleading.

I confirm, represent and warrant to _____ and its agents, that I have necessary board authority to act for and on behalf of the corporation in making the foregoing statements, and that they, to the best of my knowledge and belief as of the date herein, are correct, and that no statement of fact is omitted from this questionnaire which is necessary in order to make the statements herein not misleading.

_____
Signature

_____
Please print your name

_____
State your title or position

_____
Date

Document Checkoff List

*The following documents should accompany this
work sheet as backup information to enable processing:*

__ Certificate of incorporation and amendments.

__ Articles of incorporation and amendments.

__ Bylaws and amendments.

__ Organizational minutes.

__ List of shareholders, number of shares held by each and
date that shares were issued.

__ Corporate and shareholder minute book.

__ Résumés or profiles on each director and officer.

__ Copies of patents, patent application, trademark
registration, trademark application copyrights and any
other registered or registration application on IPCI
belonging to corporation.

__ IPCI assets elements registry.

__ Contracts with management (employment agreements,
stock options, others).

__ Contracts with manufacturers, distributors, affiliates,
associates and others.

__ Lease agreements for premises occupied by
corporation.

__ License agreement(s) for the use of any proprietary
rights not owned by the corporation.

__ All other material contracts.

__ Financial statement(s) for the previous three years, if available.

__ Literature, catalog sheets, specification sheets, on products/services offered by corporation.

__ Test results on any products offered by corporation.

__ Copies of all insurance policies carried by corporation, such as liability, key man, health, warranty and others.

__ List of any litigation current or pending facing the corporation, whether known, or pending, real or asserted.

__ Business plan for corporation to include 36-month sales and profit and loss projection.

__ Copies of any and all independent appraisals and/or analysis of business or properties.

__ Corporate certificate of good standing.

__ Qualification certificate to transact business in any other location.

__ All documents that relate to your facilities and properties such as, but not limited to: lease, title, bills of sale, appraisals, environmental studies, others.

__ Legal and accounting opinions.

If you have any questions whatsoever, please contact _____ __ at (XXX) XXX-XXXX.

CORPORATION INFORMATION QUESTIONNAIRE

_____

NAME OF CORPORATION

_____

DATE OF QUESTIONNAIRE

This information provided to:

BLACK AND WHITE, INC.

The data was prepared by: _____
_____

Who serves in the capacity of: _____
_____

With the above-named firm: _____
_____

_____
(Signature of Preparer)

STATEMENT OF PRINCIPAL

I, _____, warrant that the information provided herein is accurate and complete, to the best of my knowledge, and that any material changes in this information will be relayed immediately to the due diligence department of Black and White, Inc. I authorize verification of this information via a background investigation and a credit investigation.

_____   _____
(Signature of Principal)   (Date)

★ THIS FORM MUST BE NOTARIZED

STATE OF _____

SS.

COUNTY OF _____

On this _____ day of _____ , 20 _____, before me, the undersigned officer, personally appeared _____ _____ personally known to me to be the same person(s) whose name(s) is (are) signed to the foregoing instrument, and acknowledged the execution thereof for the uses and purposes therein set forth.

IN WITNESS WHEREOF, I have hereunto set my hand and official seal.

_____
(Notary Public)

(Notary Seal)   My commission expires:_____

IMPORTANT: This report, if on a partnership must be signed by a member thereof, an executive if it is a corporation or an empowered member, manager or trustee if another form of association.

Chapter 17

Professional Services Questionnaire and Instructions

"Nihilism is best done by professionals."

Iggy Pop

The Professional Services Questionnaire is for professionals that are providing more than just basic services to their clients. Professionals such as investment advisors, trust officers, attorneys, accountants, estate planners and some insurance professionals can benefit through the use of this questionnaire.

I understand that asking a high-net-worth client to fill out a questionnaire is likely to elicit a less than pleasant reaction – and sometimes there will be good reasons to be more discreet in how you seek the information. In these cases I can suggest that the Professional's questions be asked verbally. The question and answer session should than be summarized in a letter to the client for their acknowledgement. The objective is to memorialize the client's positions for your records.

The recognition that you need to grill some clients a bit more rigorously is not a new insight, what is new are the sanctions and license revocation proceedings for a failure to do so. The foundation of this questionnaire goes back to before the first edition of this book in 1996. Its origins began with an attorney who is a very near and dear friend of mine. It seems he had a client who lied to him. Imagine that! What was stunning is that the bankruptcy court held him, as the attorney representing the liar, responsible for all court costs and fees. The story goes as follows:

> The client owned a business, sold the business, and carried a note on the balance of the sale price. He then sold the note to his mother and declared Chapter 7 bankruptcy, representing no assets – including the note.

There was only one problem, he did not sell the note to his mother. He was using a lie and a ruse to protect the note from his creditors.

The bankruptcy trustee and one of the opposing attorneys learned of this when the mother, unbeknownst to her son, filed bankruptcy, and listed no note from the sale of her son's business. In her deposition, she stated that she knew nothing about a "note" and that she hadn't purchased anything from her son. She knew better than that!

The bankruptcy quickly turned ugly when opposing counsel informed my friend of his client's misdeeds. He withdrew from the case as soon as possible, but the opposing attorney and trustee pursued him, demanding attorney's fees and sanctions. They won a judgment for over $150,000. This was done under the legal theory that he, the attorney, could have and should have known what his client was doing – and thus, the legal assistance given to the client constituted assistance to a fraud upon the creditors.

There was no amount of due diligence from public records that could prove the client was lying. Even though he received an "Affidavit of Facts and Representations" from his client, the judge ruled that he could and should have known the truth. A no-asset bankruptcy taken for a few thousand dollars in legal fees turned into a several year battle and a $150,000 liability.

Clients

Clients come from all walks of life, and all have unique histories and goals. You cannot assume that you "know" your client without spending a lot of time with them, or by doing your homework.

A client asked me if I did asset searches for a "piece of the action." I had done some work on this basis, and was always interested in a good deal – what did she have to offer? The client was a developer and had sold a custom home. She had carried a second mortgage to help with the closing on the property. After three years the buyer defaulted on the mortgage and disappeared. The developer wanted me to find the buyer and "get the money." The case had good definition, a contract, the scope was clear, and most importantly, it was clear how I was to get paid. I took the case on contingency. I found the buyer living in a large home a couple of states away. His fortunes had improved substantially. He was ripe to be garnished.

I contacted the client and let her know that I had found the debtor and their attorney could begin garnishing wages and assets. The developer refused to hire an attorney to domesticate the judgment in another state or to spend one $#★@ dime on attorneys. According to the client, since I knew where the assets were it was my job to go and get them. I declined. I didn't want to go to jail for theft. She also refused to assign the judgment to me so that I could hire an attorney. I really did not see this one coming.

This client was a developer that lived on action, and could not be bothered by the legal technicalities. I spent several weeks trying to resurrect the arrangement or to work out some form of relationship where I could garnish the assets. The client would not cooperate if it involved an attorney.

If I had spent a little amount of time investigating the client I would have found that this wasn't the first time she had done this. There were several lawsuits in Superior Court where the developer had failed to pay attorneys.

Agendas

I've had many conversations with attorneys, consultants and accountants about "client agendas." Many times a client will come into their office and state that they want to do X, claiming they are aware of what they are doing, and understand the consequences. The client may do better with other options – only a professional will know – so to gain a foundation, the professional needs to ask questions.

Consider the earlier example of the bankruptcy case. The client really just wanted to keep the note from the business he had sold. He chose to file a Chapter 7 bankruptcy, a full liquidation of assets, but a Chapter 13 bankruptcy, a consolidation of debt and reorganization, may have allowed him to keep the note and pay his creditors. He may not have lost the note in a Chapter 13 bankruptcy. He did lose the note as a result of his fraud (and then some). Here, the client's real agenda was to protect, at almost extraordinary lengths, the note from the sale of his business. This is an example of agendas differing from actual and stated goals. The attorney got caught in the crossfire.

People Lie

I would be out of business, and most attorneys would be out of business, if people did not lie and engage in improper conduct.

> *We were asked to review a limited partnership that, by all accounts, should have been making money, but year after year the business just broke even. The general partner regularly complained to the investors about the real-estate market and the cost of repairs.*
>
> *The real problem for the limited partnership was that the general partner had been building a summer home and charging his costs back to the limited partnership as repairs to the apartment complexes the limited partners owned.*
>
> *The summer home project got a little out of hand. The general partner faced a dilemma; if he quit building the limited partnership would suddenly have a substantial positive cash flow that would have to be explained. To resolve this, every year he had another project at his summer home to drain the cash out of the limited partnership. After 10 years of doing this he had a multimillion-dollar home with an Olympic-size heated swimming pool, tennis courts and a five-car garage. It is worth noting that the pool was open year round in northern Michigan. Not to worry, the limited partners paid the gas bill too.*
>
> *When the facts were revealed as a result of our investigation, his defense was that it couldn't possibly be true. All of the partnerships had audited financial statements. He was correct, they did! He had duped the auditors. The receipts for the work on the property were altered, changing the address from his summer home to one of the rental buildings. The accounting firm was added as an additional defendant in the limited partners' lawsuit.*

I have a bundle of these stories. Some are more complex, and some are simpler. There are plenty of stories. Any professional with just a few years of experience will have many stories. It is best, if you accumulate your stories as an observer. Do not be taken in by a nice face, a large wallet or a good pedigree. Good breeding, white teeth, tailored clothes, and a slight foreign accent are not reasons to believe in your client. Check your clients out; the prevention is cheaper than the cure. To paraphrase J.K. Galbraith, do not confuse good manners and good tailoring with integrity and intelligence.

Guilt by Association – aka Reputational Risk

Many firms have had unpopular clients or high-profile clients that have embarrassed them. It's a part of living, learning and doing.

A more complex problem arises from working with, or having an association with bad people, and not being aware of it. The definition of a "red-faced moment" is a trust professional who finds out one of his clients is a multinational fraudster from the morning's *Financial Times*. It's only a matter of time before people ask, "How is it you didn't know?" or "When did you find out?" The litigation will revolve around the question, "When should you have known?"

This may sound a bit dramatic, but when it happens, it is traumatic. I assure you, it does happen. It happened to me back in the early 1980s when a client our broker/dealer chose to underwrite appeared in the "Heard on the Street" column of *The Wall Street Journal*. The story painted a very disturbing pattern of bad behavior. We were fortunate that we were not further along in our relationship, but it still cost our underwriting firm many thousands of dollars in legal bills explaining to regulators why we didn't know until the article was published. In our defense, we addressed the issue immediately and terminated the relationship that afternoon. We acted as soon as we became aware of the issues.

I have met many people who will refuse to do business with a firm based upon "stories" they've heard from their friends. People enjoy gossip, and they will tell their stories to everyone that will listen – and the professional-services provider may never know. Conversely

I have seen many clients brag about a deal they did with a famous so-and-so, or how they were involved in a big international transaction. Do not be swayed by gossip or bragging rights – be persuaded by facts developed from your due diligence.

If you associate yourself with people you shouldn't, you may pay the price and never know what the costs are. Once reputational damage is done, you'll never know how many potential clients never contact you – you'll be off the list. Check your clients out. The prevention is far cheaper than the cure.

I. BACKGROUND INFORMATION

1. General Information. When investigating a person, you need to have as much basic information as possible. Basic information is a full name, including middle name, and a date of birth. If you are investigating someone with a common name, you will need both the middle name and date of birth to disambiguate that person from the others with similar names. If you're interested in how common your name, or any name is, visit www.howmanyofme.com and enter the name for a statistical analysis.

Social Security numbers were never designed as a national identification number. In fact, the law specifically stated the number would not be used as identification. However, during the intervening years the number has become a de facto national identification number. Most information in public databases is cross-referenced by name, date of birth, and Social Security number. Without the Social Security number, you may be unable to locate all available information.

The driver's license and the driver's license numbers are a key form of personal and commercial identification. When asked for identification, the driver's license is the most common form of ID presented. Because the driver's license is the most common form of ID, it is generally the method used by private firms to record check fraud.

You need enough general information to be confident you know who this person is, that you would be able to contact them if necessary, and you could disambiguate them from others with the same name when doing research.

1.a. Education. A person's educational background will give you some idea what level of communication is required (or possible). If you are describing complex legal terminology or sophisticated financial concepts to a person whose education ended at high school, you may have communication issues. While profession specific speech and jargon provide an economy to those who understand the terms, it will sound like a foreign language to those who do not understand it.

1.b. Employment. Employment information and employment history will provide some information about a person's sophistication, responsibility and the trust other people place in them. A work history will give you some idea how this person got their current position. If they are the son-in-law of the owner, and have no independent training, there is an increased probability that their decisions may be second-guessed, or even reversed.

1.c. Business Experience. We all have a unique bundle of job, business and life experiences. The breadth and depth of these experiences will provide clues about the background and ability of the individual with whom you are about to contract.

1.d. Outside Directorships. While outside experience and service adds to a person's base of experience, it can also increase their exposure to liability.

1.e. Trade Organizations. Trade organizations are usually the first place that industry information is recognized, disclosed and discussed. It is usually a benefit when people participate in trade groups within their specialty.

1.f. Control. If motivated, does this person possess the ability to sway, move, cajole or vote a company in the direction the person desires? It's important to know. If not, you may not be dealing with the key decision-maker.

1.g. Affiliations. This person may have worked for several different companies, all owned by the same company. This pattern is common when management is grooming an employee for an upper-management position. It represents an expanded base of experience.

1.h. Similar Activities. Similar activities performed with more than one company or group may represent a conflict of interest, which should be addressed and disclosed.

1.i. Future Similar Activities. Future activities, similar in nature, with other companies or groups that may represent a conflict of interest. Plans should be addressed and disclosed, as well as any non-compete agreements currently in force.

2. Residential History. This information will provide some indication of their geographic experience and stability. The information will usually indicate whether they rented or owned, and how transient they are.

2.a. Professional Licenses. Many professions currently require some form of licensure or registration. It's not just doctors and lawyers any longer, all sorts of professions and jobs require some form of licensure. Examples include, massage therapists, X-ray technicians, private investigators, accountants, day-care operators, auto mechanics, barbers, manicurists, and food handlers – and the list is expanding. Check with your local government to see if the subject of the questionnaire requires a license. If so, the license application will provide useful information on the individual. Application information usually includes all of the basic information found on a job application, including education, employment, and professional history.

II. Legal Proceedings

The purpose of this section is to perform a broad-based exam of the individual's legal experience. When answered correctly, it should provide you, the professional, with a good idea of what the person has been up to.

III. Purpose of Engagement

1. Purpose. This section provides your client with the opportunity to state their clear purpose in engaging you and your firm.

2. Preparations. The client will need to prepare documentation and records for your use and review. What preparations have been made by the prospective client in anticipation of this engagement? This will help you determine the scope of your work.

3. Selection. Have the client tell you why you were selected for this engagement and what were the key factors in making that determination. The key factors indicate what is important to the client, and what they will expect in the performance of your services.

4. Material Factors. Why is this person or company using an outside source, and not handling the matter internally? If it's because they lack the expertise, have never experienced the need before, or require a third-party presentation, that's normal. But, it could also be that they need a scapegoat if things go wrong, and want an outside person to "help" them. It's always easier to point a finger at an outsider than to accept responsibility. Consider their motivations in light of the particular project and potential liabilities.

5. History. This section prompts the client to begin the process of supplying you with the necessary information not contained in "document" form.

6. Documents. This prompts the client to organize and supply you with the necessary documentation you will need to perform your function.

IV. Affirmation

This certifies that the information and representations provided to you are true and correct. This is important if you are performing any type of service that requires your third party impartiality or professional assurances. It is also important if the engagement has a "change of scope" – as there will necessarily be changes made on both sides, and they will need to be justified.

<u>**Professional Services Questionnaire**</u>

I.   **Background Information**

     1.   GENERAL INFORMATION

         a.   Personal information

Name – first, middle, last – include any other names used, including aliases, nicknames and maiden names.

Age, date and place of birth

Social Security number

Driver's license number

Address, state and ZIP code

Citizenship

Passport number

Second citizenship

Passport number

Work permit / Green cards held

Marital status

Name of spouse – first, middle, last – include any other names used, including aliases, nicknames and maiden names.

Spouse's age, date and place of birth

Spouse's Social Security number

Spouse's driver's license number

Spouse's address, state and ZIP code

Spouse's citizenship

Spouse's passport number

Spouse's second citizenship

Spouse's passport number

Spouse's work permit / Green cards held

Children's names, addresses and current employment

Residential address, street, city, state, ZIP code

Business address, street, city, state, ZIP code

Home telephone number

Business telephone number

Cell phone number(s)

Voice over Internet Protocol (VoIP) number(s)

b.   Education:

Provide for each institution you have attended, from high school onward including college, university, trade schools, professional and technical certifications, etc.

Institution

Field of study

Months / Years attended

Degree or certification, state if none.

c.   Please state your current position with the company and the length of time you have held that position.

d.   Please describe your business experience, with dates, up to the present time. Include your principal occupations and employment during all periods, and include the name and principal business of any corporation or other organization in which such occupations and employment were or are being conducted. If you were or are an officer of the company, describe the nature of the responsibilities undertaken by you in those positions including, where applicable, the size of the operation, the number of personnel, and annual budget supervised. Please complete on a separate sheet. Include principal occupation, name and principal business of employer, period of service, and an explanation of the duties and postings held.

e.   List the name of each company in which you currently serve as a director. Please indicate whether (i) the company has a compensation committee of its board; (ii) you serve as a member of the compensation committee, if any; and (iii) if the company is publicly held.

f.   Please list all business, trade, or other organizations to which you belong, including any offices or other positions held in each.

2. Residential History. Provide all addresses for the last 10 years, starting with your current address, and specify street, city, state, ZIP code and time of residence.

3. Licenses, Credentials, Awards & Significant Achievements.

Please provide a list of all designations you have, whether by achievement, membership, license, award, or other event, and include a list of any publications including dates for all.

II.   Legal Proceedings

Please detail all legal proceedings or administrative processes you have been involved in, are contemplating, or may currently be threatened with.

III   Purpose of Engagement

1.   Please state the purpose for the engagement of this firm's professional staff.

2.   Please discuss what preparations you have made to assist this firm in its provision of services.

3.   Please discuss all of the material factors you considered in making the decision to seek this firm's professional help.

4.   Please discuss all of the material factors involving yourself or your business that require the assistance of our firm's professional staff.

5.   Please assemble for our staff a brief narrative history of yourself and/or your company, and all relevant information and representations necessary for us to provide the services you are requesting.

6.   Please assemble for this firm's staff all of the necessary documents needed for this firm to provide its services. Attach these documents or exhibits to the questionnaire, and identify any that you will be providing at a later date.

IV.   Affirmation

The answers I have supplied to the foregoing questions are true, complete and correct, to the best of my information and belief. I understand that material misstatements or the omission of material facts may give rise to civil and criminal liabilities to myself and or the company. I will notify you and your firm of any misstatements of a material fact in the questionnaire or any amendment thereto. To my knowledge my answers to the foregoing questions are correct.

Dated: _____

_____
Signed

_____
Typed or printed name of signee

THE INFORMATION PROVIDED ON THIS FORM IS COMPLETE AND ACCURATE. I AUTHORIZE VERIFICATION OF THIS INFORMATION VIA A BACKGROUND INVESTIGATION AND I AUTHORIZE A FULL CREDIT AND PUBLIC RECORDS INVESTIGATION.

_____   _____ __
Signature   Date

★THIS FORM MUST BE NOTARIZED

ACKNOWLEDGMENT

STATE OF _____

COUNTY OF _____

On this _____ day of _____, 20_____before me, _____ the undersigned officer, personally appeared _____to me personally known and known to me to be the same person(s) whose name(s) is (are) signed to the foregoing instrument, and acknowledged the execution thereof for the uses and purposes therein set forth.

IN WITNESS WHEREOF, I have hereunto set my hand and official seal.

_____
(Notary Public)

(Notary Seal)   My commission expires: _____

Chapter 18

Checklists

"Enough organization, enough lists and we think we can control the uncontrollable."

John Mankiewicz, *House, The Socratic Method, 2004*

I get it, everyone has a checklist: David Letterman has his Top 10, St. Nicholas has his list of who is naughty or nice, there's Noah's list of animals, the Ten Commandments, etc.– I get it.

> *We pilots live by checklists. Sometimes the checklists are lengthy, and sometimes they are short. For the little airplanes I fly, the landing checklist – a fairly critical checklist – has four items, abbreviated as GUMP. But what about a big plane, like a 747? Are there a lot more? Not really. The reason for this is that landing is a critical time, and you only want to be distracted by having to check a few critical items. As an example, landing with the gear up is bad, big plane or little, and will make every landing checklist. Due-diligence practitioners are in a similar position. There are an unlimited number of pieces of information that we would like to have to support our choices, but we really only have time and budget to look at the most critical of these.*
>
> ÆGIS, June 2009

By definition, all checklists are static and lack the interplay with reality that thought provides us. Thus I intensely dislike checklists because they're often not seen as a plot outline but a task assignment that is to be completed and closed. Tacky little tick boxes. I cannot tell you how many times when I begin a postmortem at the start of a financial fraud investigation to discover what went wrong and someone on the client's acquisition and analysis team says: "... but we followed the checklist."

Furthermore, any checklist, in the attempt to be comprehensive, has to be created on a specific company for specific legal domicile at a specific fixed point in time.

I know that if I compile a checklist it will be used like a checklist. Why then do I do it?   It is what our industry demands to see. What I would like from you is for you to use these checklists as thought outlines. These checklists are constructed as an overview for many different types of companies and people. The depths of the questions are only deep enough to get you to ask the remainder of the right questions, focused on the business, the people and the interplay of economics and facts. The due-diligence practitioner has to learn to ask the right questions.

I suggest that you take the extra time and effort in your business processes to look at these checklists that pertain both to your knowledge needs and are outside of your knowledge needs. Doing so will stretch the curiosity of the process and of the participants. This is done in order to draw you out of your comfortable thought processes and to meet a requirement in the performance of proper due diligence. Continually ask the question "what if," and look for an answer. It is OK that you cannot find a satisfactory answer. It is not OK to fail to ask the question. Also question your process, find where your answers fit, but look to find out what other answers may fit.

Get comfortable with the fact that you will never have all of the information you will need. You must seek that information that in its economic form provides tested substance for your choice. You will also learn about "Fatal Flaws." If you have 20 problems to overcome for a project, and you can overcome 19 worry about the last problem, for that is the "Fatal Flaw" that if not overcome, your efforts on the other 19 are for naught.

Our merchant fleet wasn't built for a quick sail in the harbor, it was built to sail the world, assume the risks of such a journey and return home with a profit. Due diligence is not about eliminating risks, it is about identifying them and being able to manage, assume or transfer those risks. These thought lists are just that – lists, and not all will apply to all that you will be called to review, but they will get you to think about the process.

Chapter 19

Mergers and Acquisitions

"Romance is dead. It was acquired in a hostile takeover by Hallmark and Disney, homogenized, and sold off piece by piece."

Lisa Simpson
(Matt Groening – Creator of *The Simpsons*)

"TAKE, v.t. To acquire, frequently by force but preferably by stealth."
Ambrose Bierce – The Devil's Dictionary

This is an outline not a checklist. As such it is not designed to be comprehensive for all situations but to be thought-provoking for the practitioner. For example, under legal construction – if the entity you are looking at is not a corporation, then adapt the thought-list for the nature of the entity.

1. Legal Construction. Due diligence needs to begin with understanding the legal underpinnings of the company you are running or acquiring.

> Corporate charter documents
> Subsidiary charter documents
> Special purpose entities "SPEs"
> Board minutes
> Shareholder minutes
> Voting / Cumulative
> Authority for action and contract
> Authorized positions
> Share issuance / Transfer agent
> Options and their pricing
> Ownership of company and subsidiaries
> Intellectual Property Critical Information (IPCI) elements list

It is not unusual to find significant gaps in corporate documentation and operations. This is especially true for smaller or closely held companies. The documentation of subsidiary companies is also very likely to have been ignored. If you are dealing with a parent company that has recently completed a round of acquisitions, it may be murkier still.

Problems you are likely to encounter include: delinquent filings, revoked corporate status, actions taken by parties that lacked the authority, failure to hold shareholders meetings, acquisitions not fully digested, and out-of-date corporate manuals.

2. Corporate Governance

Standing committees
    Audit
    Compensation
    Finance
Poison pills
Pre-emptive rights
Outside directors
Background of directors
Family matters in a closely held business
Takeover defenses
Plans for transition and sudden vacancy
Continuity planning
Disaster planning
Management style
    Personality cult
    MBO
    TQM
Prior mergers and their integration into operations
Legal counsel

3. Strategy

Vision of the company – does one exist and is it communicated?

Mission statement
Projections and forecasts
     Nature of projection
     Assumptions
     Reality
     Independence
     Compensation tied to achieving measurable goals

4. Senior Management Team / Gold-Collar Workers

Backgrounds – verified
Conflicts of interest
Spouses or close family members working for competing companies
Work for hire / Protected IPCI
Clearly defined scope of responsibility and accountability
Organization chart and structure
Benchmarking
Business process / Re-engineering
Performance evaluations / internal and third party
Succession for key persons
Use of consultants
Compensation
Perks
Politics
Power, formal and informal

5. Human Resources

Corporate culture
Adult learning and training
Employee litigation
EEOC issues
Sexual harassment / Hostile work environment
Employee morale
Employment agreement
     Terms and duties to be performed
     Work for hire to protect IPCI
     IPCI clearly identified

Payment for performance / commission or productivity
Contract workers
    Terms of contract
    Work for hire to protect IPCI
    IPCI clearly identified
    Payment for performance / commission or productivity
    Background check performed by contractor
Benefit – clearly defined and accessible.
Pension
    Level of funding
    Compliance with current local and federal rules
    Employee Stock Ownership Plan (ESOP)
    Portability
    Disability
Health
    Dental and vision
    Medical
    Catastrophic medical
    Level of self-insurance
    Plan administrators
Comp time
Vacation
Family leave
Holidays
Sick leave
Whistleblower protection and tips lines

Treasury along with human resources usually handle benefit plans. Often you will see some benefits bundled with other providers to help deliver benefits – such as in group plans. Check if benefit and retirement plans are fully funded, and if not, that the shortfall is well documented. Verify that the annual reporting requirements required under Title I and Title II of Employee Retirement Income Security Act (ERISA) and the IRS tax code have been completed. This is done on Form 5500. Clearly set forth the responsibilities for custody and management of benefits with the responsible party or division identified.

Labor. This is very important when working with unions. Clear understandings need to be documented before proceeding. This also becomes an issue when dealing with compliance thresholds. Many small companies are exempted from certain labor practice requirements. It's important to consider how current plans may affect these exemptions, growth or acquisition may mean these companies are no longer exempt.

Professional. Most professional licenses follow the employee, not the employer. There are often some benefits, professional insurance for example, that may or may not follow the professional to a new company. Licenses must be current and verified. The same is true for professional accreditations and the associations behind the accreditations.

Recruiting. What are the recruiting practices? Do these practices induce a bias into the selection of employees, such as advertising only in a single paper, or using only one medium? Does the company make use of professional recruiters for filling high-level positions? Does the company have a contingent of temporary workers or leased workers? How are temporary workers screened?

Authority to Work. Do the applicants and employees have the authority to work in this country, the required licenses, accreditation, and training to work at the job they will be performing?

Background Screening. What level of background screening is performed? When were the practices put in place, and which employees were hired under different screening standards? Does the firm perform follow-up background checks? Background screening is one of the most effective ways to eliminate future workplace problems and fraud.

Employee retention
Performance evaluations
Compensation evaluations
Americans with Disabilities Act (ADA) compliance
Discrimination, age, color, sex, religion, gender
Employee manual – what is included? Is it up to date?
Employee termination
Exit interviews
Employee layoffs
Outplacement opportunities
Non-compete and non-disclosure agreements post
termination

6. Marketing

List of products and services
Marketing efforts for individual products and services
Image advertising
Lead advertising
Measuring impact of advertising
Brand ID and loyalty
Business cycle
Marketing plans
Price management
News and reviews
Types of advertising
     Outdoor
     Transit
     Television
     Radio
     Internet
     Print
     Viral
     Other
Advertising agency
     How long has it been around?
     Do the agents listen?
     Do they do –
          – real marketing?

- try and sell products? or
- simply place ads?
How close are they to those who selected them?

7. Market Analysis

Barriers to entering a market
Business intelligence
Cost of customer acquisition
Customer feedback
Demographics
Industry trends
Market trends
Market share

8. Sales

List of sales people
Training and continuing education on products and services
Productivity
Sales leads and customer list controls
Order-takers versus salespeople
Incentives
Technology
Sales cycle
Market research and knowledge of competition
Client entertainment
Authorized and unauthorized gifts and expenses
Relationship with clients (CRM)
Buyer programs / rewards

9. Products and Services

Business model for each product and service
Use of Internet in delivery of products and services
Distribution channel management
New product assessments
Product / Service differentiation

Product / Service features
Product / Service liability
Product / Service life cycle
Product and service obsolescence curves
Profitability of product / Service
Reliability
Value / Utility
Warranties – and trailing liabilities
Use of Critical Path Method (CPM) and Program
Evaluation and Review Technique (PERT) in development
and implementation

10. Finance

Chief Financial Officer. Must have a thorough understanding as well as ability to design and implement controls over all operations for which they are responsible. This includes systems knowledge such as billing, inventory, cash management and treasury operations. This position also requires an understanding of IPCI and its uses.

The CFO should have a good handle on the internal customer operations and reporting needs. You need an assessment of the technology used in the financial operations of the target.

It is highly recommended that all senior positions within finance and treasury have current Association for Financial Professionals (AFP) certification.

Treasury. An overview of the functions should confirm that treasury is acting as a custodian of value for the company. An in-depth knowledge of operations is required to understand all of the costs for treasury services, including analyst's fees, investment-management fees, letter-of-credit fees, surety bond fees, and any other third-party fees. Treasury is a vital operational division, but must also be a profit center.

Cash Management. Payments and Collections are a vital function in every business. There must be a detailed understanding of when and how bills are paid. These processes may include lockbox processing, non-lockbox receipt processes, deposit clearing processes, Automated Clearing House (ACH), credit card, and other systems as well as how they are integrated into the company systems.

The acquirer has to understand the cash forecasts, both short-term and intermediate, which are used to give direction to managers and coordinate the budgeting process. Look at historical cash forecasting and see how closely the forecasts correlated with actual cash operations. Understand the components of working capital in order to understand their impact on the cash forecast.

As a final thought – as the acquirer, your people need to get the cash flow and accounts as soon as possible. You are too ignorant of the newly acquired operations to manage from a distance, and the new employees may not feel secure. This gap of knowledge fosters a near-perfect environment for frauds to occur. Be aware of how and when revenue is booked – for example, if customers have return rights, revenue should not be booked until after the return period has expired.

Payables. Requires a high level of familiarity with the system. To understand the accounts-payable system you must understand the clearing process, ACH and wire transfers. You need tight controls over who is permitted to initiate payments.

Fund Transfers. The acquiring team needs to be familiar with regulations, NACHA rules, and compliance issues. There are many new payment systems emerging, and an awareness of where and how they can be used is an important part of remaining competitive.

Receivables. The two companies have to match their policies and practices. The systems for processing and collection need to be normalized immediately. One of the most common forms of fraud during an acquisition involves receivables being embezzled by the staff of the target company – assuming that the acquiring company can be bamboozled, or that the transition will be so sloppy that records will be lost. Direct, clear and complete instructions must be communicated to all customers, present and past, informing them of the acquisition, the terms for payment, where payments are to be sent – and where payments are not to be sent. You need to get control of funds immediately.

Rating Agencies. These entities used to be more important than they are today – but if you are a rated company, you should have a representative meet with the rating agency. Your purpose is to provide fair and appropriate disclosure, protecting your rating and ensuring it is performed on a fair basis.

Banking. This is one of the very first contacts an acquirer needs to initiate during the process. The acquirer must understand the cash management services being provided, the pricing, and what products and services are offered – whether they are being used or not. It's important to develop a good understanding of the trust in custody operations, credit agreement issues and the banking operation.

Credit. Review all credit-granting agreements looking for covenants that may be breached as a result of the acquisition. These breaches can be triggered by ownership changes, changes in debt to equity, and even significant changes in management. Agreements may be domiciled in jurisdictions where you plan to cease operations or no longer have operations.

Capital Operating Leases. All operating leases should be thoroughly reviewed; an analysis of lease-versus-buy presented, and tested to ensure compliance under Statement 13 of the Financial Accounting Standards Board (FASB).

Public Company Matters. For publicly traded companies, there are a host of requirements imposed by federal and state regulations, and an additional layer of exchange regulations. Compliance with these regulations is imperative. You must have a seasoned team for a public company Merger and Acquisition (M&A) to work. This includes knowledge of disclosure requirements detailing when you can and cannot share information with the public. At least one team member should possess a thorough understanding of the Sarbanes-Oxley Act (SOX) requirements, in particular SOX 404.

Investments – Cash Positions. What short-term instruments are being used? What are the counter-party's risks or collection risks if X occurs? Review your understanding of the capital-market instruments that are being used, be conversant with the investment policy of the company, and familiarize yourself with how its reporting fits into the general ledger. Be sure to cross-check FASB 157 and FASB 115.

Portfolios. The acquired company could possess an investment portfolio that may contain things such as financial derivatives, interest rate swaps, forward future contracts, as well as stock positions. These must be fully documented and compared against what is reported. What was the purpose behind each investment, and what are the plans to add or eliminate these positions?

Position Limits. Commodities and equities regulators impose position limits. There are position limits dealing with risk exposure that are often imposed, by contract, from lending agencies and insurance companies. There may even be rating agencies that track your open positions. All positions of the "to-be-combined" companies must be reconciled and cross-reference against statutory and contractual position limits as well as rating agency thresholds.

Opposing Positions. It is not unknown for two companies to have economically opposite positions in the market and have value in those positions that, when combined, is substantially less than the two positions standing alone.

Hedges. Explore the different exchange-listed hedges, marketplace hedges, and tactical hedges. Look for more efficient means of hedging risk as well as avoiding double hedging – in which case you are no longer transferring risk, you are assuming the risk of a position opposite your economic position. Also, look at enforcement of your hedging contracts. Exchange traded contracts survive in a different enforcement environment than private contracts.

11. Tax Matters

Sales. The first concerns with sales tax are, that they have been timely paid, that there is proper documentation for any exemptions made, and that the tax continues to be collected and remitted on a timely basis. The next concern is how the acquisition will affect future tax liability. The acquirer may now have purchased or introduced a physical presence in states that were previously exempt from sales tax. Internet sales originating in New Mexico generally do not collect sales tax from New York sales, and vice versa. Once a business has a physical presence in a state, it is liable for taxes. Several states consider an employee who lives in the state or a sales affiliate in the state sufficient presence to create a sales tax liability. Tax avoidance is a crime and will be used, in some cases, as the predicate crime for money laundering charges which bring more severe penalties.

Use. A use tax is a type of excise tax, and is often assessed at the same rate as sales tax. If the acquisition moves property from one state to another, a use tax may be due in the destination state, and there may be a tax credit in the state of origin.

Payroll. Payroll tax needs to be continually withheld and remitted until the taxing authorities are informed and acknowledge whatever changes may have been made in structure and employment status if there is a transition to the acquirer's payroll. Failure to timely remit will result in onerous penalties.

Property. There are many formulas for property taxation; most of them are based upon the value of the underlying property and it is generally collected on a semiannual basis. The acquiring company needs to make sure that the target's taxes are current, and that the change of ownership or use does not adversely impact the acquirer's enjoyment of the property. In several states tax is established at the date of purchase, and the property is not reappraised until it is sold. Acquiring a piece of property may trigger an appraisal of the property. There can be large tax changes when changing the use of property. As an example, we worked on a large property that was used for grazing, and the taxes were $4,122 per year. When the cattle were removed from the land, the taxes jumped to more than $186,000 per year! In some foreign countries there is no annual property tax, instead they levy a tax on the transfer of property. This tax rate can be high, and it's not unusual to see rates of 10 percent to 15 percent on the price of the property.

Offsets. The merging of two entities that have been paying taxes are more likely than not to present some opportunities for tax offsets.

Base. The tax base is an appraised value to which tax rates are applied. Acquisitions can trigger the adjustment of a base, and taxes due can be altered as a result of an acquisition. Taxes that are particularly sensitive to a change in ownership are use taxes, property taxes and asset taxes.

Tax Reporting. Both parties should assemble a comprehensive list of taxing bodies being reported. Is there a systematic approach for integrating the reporting requirements of the two companies?

Tax Incentives. Tax incentives are, more often than not, quirky and heavily restricted tax reductions and/or remittances to taxpayers. A tax incentive program designed for a medium to small business with less than 100 employees will cease to apply if a merger results in an entity with more than 100 employees. There are many documented incidents where business success results in lower profits because of lost tax incentives. It's often a surprise to all parties.

12. Intellectual Property and Critical Information (See chapter for more information)

An IPCI Asset Elements Registry represents all of the intangible assets of a company. It represents not only the intellectual property, but also the knowledge the company possesses to act efficiently. The first step is to create a comprehensive list of all IPCI including the date of creation, details of all applications for protection, the date exclusivity expires, all infringement events (real and alleged), and all defense claims. Special attention to detail is important for IPCI that is licensed.

You need to document a foundation for each major item of IPCI – the seeds and sprouts that are the evidence of creation. Patentable concepts generally are not born fully developed. The evidence of creation should offer some proof that the IPCI was created within the enterprise, and not stolen or laundered.

An IPCI Asset Elements Registry is a requirement.

Patents
Date of application
Date of issuance
Date of expiration
Maintenance fees current?
Ownership clear and undisputed
Key patents or parts of a defensive patent system
Infringement issues and responses
International issuances

Trademarks and service marks
Date of first use
Date of application

Date of issuance
Date of expiration
Maintenance fees current?
Ownership clear and undisputed
Infringement issues and responses
Local, national, international scope

Copyright
Date of creation
Was it filed or assumed?
Clearly identified
Infringement issues and responses

Trade secrets / Critical information
Date of first use
Date of creation
Ownership clear and undisputed
The information is secured from leakage and diffusion
Clearly identified in the employment agreement and agreements with third parties.

Defense. Is there an OPSEC program in place to protect the IPCI? Is there a method to detect an IPCI leak and calculate the cost of impairment?

13. Insurance

Assemble copies of all property-casualty, errors and omissions, life and health, as well as any other policies. Secure letters from the underwriters verifying the terms of the insurance. Determine whether the insurance will survive the merger, and if the policies represent duplicate coverage. If a policy does not survive the transition, attempt to get a refund or credit. Look specifically for duplicate coverage issues, gaps in coverage, loss of coverage, and self-insure options.

Review all warranties, both purchased and offered.

14. Information Technology

Computers have become a commodity, and as such are applied directly or indirectly in everything we do. These systems not only hold an enterprise together, they represent windows that expose critical information and pathways for leakage. Be certain that you have employed experts who are well acquainted with the specific systems you are intending to integrate. The following list presents some areas that need to be addressed. This list can never be exhaustive, as these systems are pervasive – if you don't trust your knowledge, be very careful to ensure that you are receiving a qualified assessment.

Key application and application dependency mapping
Enterprise software
Application service providers
Backup – operations and data, with an eye toward continuity planning
Process integration
Security for the system, physical, virtual and operational
E-mail and archiving procedures
Continuity planning
       Disaster backup
       Equipment replacement
       Facility replacement
       Supplier replacement
Internet
       Connectivity
       Business presence
       E-commerce
           – Shopping carts
           – Processing and tracking
       Web presence
       Affiliate programs
Intranet – access control and privileges
Management Information Systems
License of software and compliance with license

Company's information available or disseminated over the Web
    Web page content
    Web casting
    E-mail
    Employee blogs
    External blogs
Web hosting
    Internal / External
    Updates and Upgrades
Threats from third parties
    Phishing
    DOS targeting
    Hacking
    Tunneling
    Packet sniffing
    Others

15. Competitive Analysis

Who are the competitors?
How do they compete?
Monitoring of competition
Condition of competition, financial and otherwise
Competitors' market shares
Competitive intelligence
Threats from competition

16. Operations

Safety. Local fire departments and OSHA primarily enforce safety compliance, and both will generally provide free audits.

Health. Regulated by OSHA and a myriad of public heath agencies. Request an audit if there are any concerns, as the rules are often arbitrary and indecipherable.

Materials. A material handling license for sensitive or regulated materials is generally issued to a company, its ownership and management. These licenses may or may not need to be renewed, and new management may require background checks, certification, bonding or other proof of skills and ability to make reparation.

17. Manufacturing

More often than not production managers will be well aware of the relationship the company has with their customers, and often participate in contract details. The production team is generally not as familiar with sales issues such as territories, pricing and competing vendors. If an enterprise is wholly located in Tennessee, and as a result of acquisition the home office is moved to Ohio – this change can disrupt the personal relationships between management and production as well as disrupt exclusionary provisions in supply contracts. The combined entities may be in violation of their exclusive supply agreements. It's important to ensure communications between management, sales and remote production facilities are intact – and to include these costs into your plan. Here are some areas of concern:

Automation
Manufacturing equipment
        Condition
        Downtime
        Serviceability
        Automation
Dealerships
        Network
        Education
        Support
        Tracking
Demand chain management
Distribution
Capacity management
Finished goods
ISO standards
Receiving

Just in time – management and tracking
Logistics
Manufacturing personnel
    Skill
    Language
    Licensing requirements
    Union / Non-union
    Third parties under contract
Manufacturing flow
Purchasing
    Capability maturity model (CMM) level – What level?
    Single sourced dependencies
    Raw materials
    Electronic payment due when? Before or after inspection?
    Tracking quantity and quality differentials
Quality management programs
Dialogues with suppliers, expectations of buyers, and ability to supply
Scrap
    Recycling
    Security
    Sale
Shipping
    Land
    Sea
    Air
    Rail
    Internet
    International / Export controls
Work in process monitoring and quantifying
Work-flow automation – success and shortcomings

18. Shipping / Receiving

One hard and fast rule is that shipping and receiving should be as separate as possible. An open bay is an opportunity. Items not logged in often leave with employees or contract workers, and if not monitored it's not unusual for several truckloads of cargo to disappear before signs appear. The more redundant and automated the systems are, the better control you will have. Decentralization creates problems that must be addressed with robust systems that ensure proper accounting and reduce opportunities for theft.

Shipping
        Tracking matches content
        Quality control – signed off
        Efficacious method of shipping chosen
        Regular bid process to check rates
        HazMat license and disclosure acknowledged
        Material Safety Data Sheets (MSDS) compliance
        Insurance
        Tracking
        Secrecy concerning high-value cargo
Receiving
        Description matches contents
        Damage and testing completed before acceptance
        Immediate logging of arrival, log in after acceptance
        Upon arrival, contemporaneous notification
        Accounting notified of arrival
        Properly placed into inventory

19. Regulatory Compliance

Rules and regulations along with their ambiguities are the service end of governmental activity. The bigger and more complex an operation is, the greater the likelihood it will wander into the shadows of their purview. Here are subjects to consider:

Professional Licenses
        Accounting
        Legal
        Medical
        Technical
        Trade

Materials
    Radioactive
    Biohazard
    Restricted
    High value
    Art and antiquities
Discharge permits
    Land
    Air
    Water

Location. Functions are permitted in the location where they are performed.

Grandfather issues. Does a change of ownership trigger requirements for retrofits or compliance with new standards?

International. Are you compliant with laws and regulations concerning the exportation or importation of prohibited substances or technology? Familiarize yourself with the Foreign Corrupt Practices Act (FCPA) and its implications, or find a qualified person to help you.

20. Physical Facilities

At this point it cannot have escaped your attention that you need to make a distinction between real and virtual property, visible assets and hidden assets. There are long established rules for appraising the value of real property, insuring title and recording ownership. These processes work quite well when markets are stable. Be very wary of appraisals in markets that are transitioning. See the list on property.

21. Environmental

The environmental regulations a company may be subject to are strongly influenced by the industry and where it is physically located. Visibility is definitely going to increase the cost of compliance. What is compliance? Nobody knows. If you have concerns, an audit would be advised. Almost all environmental risks are excluded from standard insurance policies, but there are insurers who specialize in environmental and regulatory risk – these insurers are your best source for information.

States regulate the workplace under a number of legal acts that deal with general office space and industry specific regulations. Federal regulations may be enforced by a number of administrative bodies. The acquirer must consider how compliant the acquisition is, and how a merger might affect the regulations under which it currently operates.

City, county, state, federal, international. There appears to be no end to the number of legal authorities that can and may interfere in your operations. Do not assume that their rules will make sense or be consistent – they will often be senseless and contradictory. These are real risks, and when present need to be researched.

22. International Business

The due-diligence process must be performed by each and every unit of the company, in every jurisdiction in which the company or its subsidiaries may operate. You may be subject to the laws of the U.S., Mexico, Oman, Malta or admiralty laws. Remember that complexities arise quickly when bridging civil law, common law, Dutch civil code, administrative law and private law (jurisdictions that offer whatever law you can afford).

Foreign Corrupt Practices Act
Anti-money laundering
Countries on black lists
Office of Foreign Asset Control
Specially designated national
Countries not signators to treaties

Intellectual property
Service of process
Human rights
Human trafficking
Environmental
Labor / Labour
Standards
ISO 9000
Accounting

23. Other Things

ISO Standards – there are very many of them
Listed companies
Auditors
International Standard Book Number (ISBN) and Stock-keeping Unit (SKU) issues

24. Legal Matters

License agreements, rights and options
Arbitration
Lawyers vs. barristers and solicitors
Insolvency rules
Regulatory compliance
Protection for IPCI
Access to court
Class action matter
Authority to act and bind the company
Certificate of Incumbency
Escrows and escrow agents
Contracts, forms, agreements
In-house counsel
Ability to negotiate
Attorney-client confidentiality
Regulations and relationship with regulatory agencies
Corporate structure and subsidiaries

25. Acquisition Teams

Board Level. Does the CEO have a coherent plan to effectively integrate new board members? Has the board's audit committee been kept fully informed of the information harvested in the due-diligence process, in particular information that is incongruent with representations made by the other company.

Legal. The legal team has a number of responsibilities. Its members need to ensure that all of the corporate records and documentation are intact, and if there are exceptions that they are identified and dealt with. If the acquiring company and the targeted company are in dominant positions within their industry, antitrust issues have to be considered.

Strategic. Is there a clear strategic purpose to the acquisition? If so, does this acquisition meet that purpose?

Finance. What is the best way to finance the acquisition, and what are the parameters for a successful financial acquisition? Consider debt, equity and assistance with public incentives.

IPCI and OPSEC. Intellectual Property and Critical Information represent the real value of every company. Identify the necessary actions both parties need to take in order to secure the IPCI and guard against leaks from employees. The process of protecting IPCI is called Operations Security (OPSEC), a well-documented process.

Investment Bankers. Try to involve an investment banker with in-depth knowledge of similar transactions. Make certain that there is no conflict of interest in the ensuing relationships.

Technology. Most acquisitions are targeting talent or technology to fit into the acquiring company's mix of goods and services. The acquisition team must be confident that these assets can be integrated and that all obvious opportunities to exploit the assets have been considered. This responsibility needs to be placed with the most qualified person available, probably a senior engineer or product manager.

Marketing. Marketing needs to participate with the acquisition team, understand the marketing messages of the target company, determine which messages have been successful, and offer advice for product integration.

Transition Team

Senior Management. Senior management of both companies should be brought together to interact in social settings. They will need to share experiences to help the companies integrate as quickly as possible. The transition team's role is to lead and guide these introductions.

Tactics. What are the procedures for integration? What is the strategy to integrate operations? How will you best leverage the combined talent?

Management Plan on Integration of Acquisition. There must be a written plan stating the intentions of both parties. The plan should be open and easy to understand. The more secrecy surrounding your plans, the more likely that gossip will fill the information void. A lack of clear intentions will create uncertainty and fear in both entities.

Legal. Legal representatives of both companies need to meet, share information and analyze all matters requiring legal interpretation – including employment agreements, rental agreements, regulatory disclosure, joint-venture agreements, facilities agreements and conflicts of interest.

Tax. No transaction can occur without tax consequences. It may be as simple as getting the correct parties and addresses on the tax forms. On the other hand, it may include resolving unpaid taxes, penalties and fines. These issues must be addressed in the transition process.

Human Resources. Human resource departments often outsource many of the functions traditionally handled in-house. These departments in both companies need to share their standards of practice and any key suppliers they rely upon.

It's unlikely that all employees of both entities will survive the merging of the two companies. Both human resource offices can be helpful in the process of trimming staff. The earlier these decisions are made, the less tension there will be in the entire process.

Third-Party Agreements

Media Professional. When transactions are contemplated and consummated, information must flow to the stakeholders and public. Messages have to be crafted to address the concerns of the audience. Employees need more detailed information than the media. Vendors need specific information that is distinctly different from what customers need. A media plan should be developed and professionally executed.

General. Companies are a party to all sorts of agreements. The agreements most overlooked are the common agreements, such as phones, utilities, rentals, credit cards and licenses. All agreements and contracts need to be reviewed and summarized, including all options the company has to terminate, modify or extend the agreements.

Credit Agencies, Rating Agencies, Business Reporting Services.
These are third-party commercial agencies in the business of gauging your credit and fiscal worthiness. They often rely upon public data and data-mining to form opinions. It's always better to explain transactions and provide them

with information as opposed to trying to correct it after it is misinterpreted.

Governmental Bodies. Many businesses have investment tax credits, development agreements, tax increment financing, tax holidays and other agreements with governmental agencies. It's wise to review these agreements and obtain permission and or concessions in advance of any transaction.

Customers and Clients. These relationships are the most important to the enterprise. All client agreements should be reviewed for triggering events that allow the client to terminate their agreement. Where language like this exists, address the issues before the transaction. Communicate with clients explaining what changes they should expect. Clients do not value surprises.

Suppliers and Vendors. More often than not, suppliers are well aware of what is happening with their customers. Issues will be infrequent, but may include a battle over territories or commissions. As a new entity, you may choose to renegotiate your terms. It is a potential problem, and it's the vendor's problem. Awareness is important if you want to have a seamless integration.

27. Fraud

You need to be prepared to deal with fraud both before and after the closing. If you encounter a problem, don't immediately assume fraud – remember that fraud, third-party theft, and errors can all look a great deal alike.

Some highlights: You need to get access to transaction histories, not just samples. You will need access to all information, transactions, system configuration data and operational systems – everything. No exceptions. When looking for fraud, you are not looking for data that will appear in samples – you are looking for the anomalies. Sampling only allows you to estimate errors within a population, not find specific instances of fraud.

Be diligent in your analytical techniques. Set statistical parameters to identify anomalies, break out and classify the data to see if you can find trends and anomalies within those trends. Use as much digital analysis as you can, including Benford's Law, population tests, ratio analysis, and pattern matching. Match data to bodies. Identify ghost employees and/or ghost suppliers. Test for duplication in payments. As you develop information, graph the transactions – sometimes what doesn't appear in numbers will stand out in a graph.

28. Post Acquisition

Spend some time with the acquisition teams over a period of many months to assess what worked and what should have been done differently. Document everything. Intranet blogs provide a useful platform where everyone can provide input. These records will be invaluable when looking at future acquisitions.

Chapter 20

Background Check – Checklist

"There are two kinds of people, those who finish what they start and so on."

Robert Byrne

Between 70 percent and 80 percent of all frauds and thefts are performed by insiders, your employees. Yet we as business owners fail miserably again and again in performing a proper background check on prospective employees. We claim that each employee is an individual yet we treat them as some standardized labor unit at the time of hiring, performing only a modest background check – if that. Beware of the cheap and cheerful report.

As said before not all items in a background check are applicable or even appropriate for every hire. Each position you are filling is as unique as the applicant.

Best advice for all hiring, let every applicant know that you perform a detailed background check of their claims, credentials, education and work histories. This is often enough to scare off those you would not hire, and leave you to perform the detailed inquiries on applicants you might hire.

Consent Form for Background Check

> Each state and industry has different requirements and standards along with the federal rules. Make sure the consent form to perform a background check complies with the many laws on background checks and pre-employment screening.

Personal Information

Citizenship

This is a requirement for all hires, even casual labor. An excellent form of proof is a passport or certified birth certificate tied with a corresponding photo ID. For non-U.S. citizens, verify that all immigration papers are authentic and accurately filed.

Fingerprints

Some positions and licenses require fingerprints to be taken and submitted for screening. As an employer, check to ensure the ID submitted at the time the fingerprints were taken corresponds with the fingerprint card submitted.

Verified Copy of Government Issued Photo ID

Obtain a copy of a government-issued photo ID and verify the information on the photo ID.

Residential History

People live, work and play in many locations. A full and complete history of residence for the period of time corresponding to the application is important for when you go searching civil and criminal records.

Civil History

A civil court history gives an indication of how this person is performing within the community. Civil records are found at the city, county, state and federal levels. Civil court records contain complaints for commercial disputes, contract enforcement, mis- and malpractice issues, etc. ... You should check the different courts that correspond to the residential history of the applicant.

Criminal History

A criminal court history gives an indication of how this person is dealing with the government and its laws. Criminal records are found at the city, county, state and federal levels. Here you find complaints dealing with everything from minor traffic violations to heavy felonies. You should check with all the courts that correspond to the applicant's residential history.

Some locations do not allow criminal records to be reviewed as part of a pre-employment background check. These are unfortunate laws – but worth checking on before you proceed.

Note of Court Records: Just because you have an applicant's name on a lawsuit does not mean it is that same person, or that he had any responsibility in the matter especially if he is one of a number of litigants, he could have just been in the room – so to speak. The court case must be pulled, the applicant and the name on the case matched and the case read to understand the particulars. Also not all people get in trouble in the location of residential history. We have had people checkout cleanly, but turn up felony convictions and prison time served in other locations. The gaps in employment and residential history help to indicate the possibility of such problems.

Credit Information with Written Permission Only

This may only be obtained with written permission. Once you have a credit report, if you are not a pro at reading it get the appropriate help so you can understand its information and context.

Publications Search

As Andy Warhol said, one day everyone will have their 15 minutes of fame. Check publications for information about the applicant, this can be done online with simple searches of publications in their area – geographical or professional, as well as through many specialized suppliers of this information.

Medical

When medical histories or certification are required, double-check with the medical professional the contents of any report issued by that professional and confirm that the professional is licensed.

Professional Life

Verification of Education

When you verify educational credentials, some schools are helpful and some are very difficult. We have had schools refuse to verify the attendance of students as a matter of policy – thus you have to get a copy of the person's diploma and verify with the school that it is a legitimate diploma. Check to ensure that the degree is not from what are called diploma mills. These are schools set up to issue certificates and diplomas for a fee – no education required.

Verification of Credentials

Credentials are the second part of an education and are given by professional bodies. Check those credentials and verify their dates with the professional bodies that issued them. There is a great deal of overreach with credentials. Just because you are a member of a professional association does not mean you have the credential proffered by that association.

Verification of Professional License

All licenses must be verified. For each license, check the expiration and other dates, look for any past, present or pending discipline. Also, if continuing professional education is required, check applicant's status on those requirements.

Gaps in Employment

For reasons, sometimes well beyond our means to control things, we have gaps in employment. All of these gaps must be explained. It could be a series of unfortunate circumstances, a sabbatical or a prison term.

Personal Reference

These are almost uniformly positive, but you still need to check them and the contact information given for them. Also inquire where these personal references work. Try to avoid the trap of relatives and paid informants. If the phone number is a rollover line at the current employer, or the candidate's home or neighbor's home, give the recommendation the proper weight.

Employment References

Here are some of the favorite references we have heard over the years: "Works well when cornered like a trapped rat," and "Somewhere he is depriving a village of an idiot." But today you may only get verification of the dates of employment or simple monosyllabic answers. When this occurs ask this: "Would you rehire this person? If yes let me know, if not just remain silent." This seems to get the former employer over the hump of the fear of litigation.

Interview Information

If you conduct an interview of the prospective employee, keep the notes in the applicant's folder. Notes, information and forms concerning the candidate are restricted and should be kept confidential.

Secure the Final Report and Documents

The final application with all of the information should be secured in one location. If that person is hired, the file most likely will move to the personnel folder. If the person is not hired, check and comply with all policy and laws for records retention. Let the unhired applicants know during the application process that their records will be kept on file for X number of months for consideration against future openings and then destroyed.

Record

Employment applications contain sensitive information about a person. Even though an applicant is not hired, the records, prior to destruction, should be kept in a manner congruent with your other personnel records. Document the date and location of destruction.

Chapter 21

Real Estate Due Diligence

"It is not the size of the land, but what you do with it."

Paraphrased from Someone

Real Estate
Due Diligence Checklist
Investment / Commercial Property

The purpose of due diligence is to determine the specific opportunities and risks of the investment, including market factors; identifying, quantifying and managing the risks of the investment; providing support for the underwriting assumptions; acquiring the documents, data and knowledge that will be required to manage the asset, and confirming that the investment meets the investment criteria of the intended buyer.

- Property Ownership
    - Address of property, parcel number(s) and full legal description.
    - Map of property – including all buildings, utilities, piping for property and transit piping such as natural gas, sewer, water, etc.
    - Summary of site history/ownership/development.
    - Summary of mineral/water rights tied to the property.
    - Documentation of waterway, railroad, pipeline, air, etc., access rights tied to the property.
    - Request copies of environmental impact reports.
    - Seller background and brochures.
    - Proof of point person's ability to act (e.g. corporate resolution) on behalf of selling entity.
    - Request copies of ground/master leases, joint venture agreements, lease agreements, contracts, etc.
    - Request copies of debt and security instruments.

Request copies of commitments to finders and/or brokers.

Seller's financial statements.

Consent agreement, decrees and orders to which seller is a party.

Agreements that require third-party consent.

Copies of any appraisals or estimates of market value done for the seller in the last 12-months.

Check for protected or historical structures on property.

- Title, Survey & Zoning

Current preliminary title report with copies of underlying title documents.

Uniform Commercial Code and judgment lien searches.

Updated American Land Title Association (ALTA) and/or as-built survey.

Subdivision and parcel maps.

Copies of restrictive covenants, easements and agreements.

Description of ownership and operation of adjacent land uses.

Flood plain and seismic zone location.

EPA watch sites in vicinity.

Local improvement district information.

Verification of zoning use for property and copy of permitted use under the local zoning authority.

- Property Operations

Current certified rent roll.

Standard form of current lease agreement.

Background on tenants to see if any are involved in litigation, especially bankruptcy or on-site claims that may involve the owner of the building.

Check on license status or requirements for tenants that may require a liquor license, water discharge permits, hazardous material handling, etc.

Certified operating statements.

Schedule of tenant escalation billings.

Copies of utility bills.

Copies of most recent tax bills and related information (including any special assessments).

Monthly rental delinquency report for a minimum of one year of operation.

Capital-improvements schedule including those completed and those budgeted.

Operating, service and/or leasing agreements.

Property management and/or leasing agreements.

For retail property, monthly tenant sales volumes for retail property.

Copies of all leases and amendments.

Tenant correspondence files.

Copies of tenant guarantor financial statements.

Tenant profile and background.

Copies of tenant insurance certificates.

Copies of estoppel certificates.

Summary of pending leases.

Copies of pending leases.

Schedule of vendors historically that have used the property.

Copies of any rent-control regulations and compliance.

Copy of state and local laws that affect landlord-tenant relations, if any.

Review tax laws affecting the property.

Confirm with all relevant government bodies that obligations such as taxes and fees are current and that there are no enforcement proceedings current or contemplated.

Insurance items to think about, fire, flood, public liability, plate glass, business interruption, rent insurance, mechanical failure, as well as look at self-insure and risk-management matters.

• Property Physical Information

Copies of "as-built" plans and specs including electrical, mechanical and structural.

Existing environmental studies.

Existing inspection reports (e.g. roofing, HVAC, termite, deferred maintenance, etc.)

Soil reports.

Copies of building permits, licenses, certificates of occupancy.

Construction contracts and subcontracts (if within last six months, ask for copies of lien releases).

Engineering plans, specifications and inspections for the property and the buildings.

Building warranties and guarantees.

List of personal property and trade/service names.

Copies of liability, casualty and all other insurance and review of historical and/or ongoing insurance claims.

Site plans, leasing brochures, maps, photographs and all other marketing materials.

Determination of compliance with the Americans with Disabilities Act (ADA).

Environmental issues to think about such as, lagoons and ditches for water, pipelines, previous disposal of items on site, wastewater, air emissions, asbestos, PCBs, radon, lead, CFCs, radiation from a linear accelerator, biohazards from the gene lab, and what may have gone on next door that no one has told you about.

• Position in the Market

Compile summary of recent comparable sales.

Compile summary of recent leases of comparable properties.

Create a financial model from specific and realistic data derived from an understanding of the property's position within the market.

Interview and identify candidates for ongoing management responsibilities.

Identify future position of the property and steps necessary to achieve that position.

- Miscellaneous but Important
  - Interview tenants for what they know.
  - Interview neighbors for what they know.
  - Check with police and fire to see what calls for service they have had to respond to at that address for as long as their records go back. You may learn about old fires, hazardous material events, or injuries that occurred because of the design of the building.
  - Check with local reporters and review newspapers for stories on the property, buildings and the tenants.
  - Check with previous insurance carriers for all claims paid and reasons why. You don't need the claimant or defendant, but you need to know why.
  - Check with the local historical society – just because your building is not on the list of protected or historical buildings does not mean it will not be soon.
  - Check with the pertinent municipalities for all infrastructure renovations, installations, and construction that will impact your site.
  - What is the relationship between the seller, the broker and the representative at the title company?

I know I have not seen it all, but I have seen a lot.

One of my favorites was in a town with an artificial lake where the developer wanted to put in a harbor for the boats. The harbor would be 20 feet deep. The only problem was that the major crosstown sanitary sewer was located just beneath the location, and was only 18 feet down. Neither the city nor the developer caught this. The contractors, who just happened to have done the excavation work 20 years earlier, caught the error.

I remember a buyer of apartment buildings. He liked to buy buildings in foreclosure, or from the note holders. He always ordered an asbestos inspection before negotiating on a property. In all cases, the inspection report described the asbestos problems, and locations, along with an explanation of how asbestos may be a problem for the property. In fact, there was never any asbestos problems. He was hiring the same company for all of the inspections. All of the sellers lowered their price significantly upon reading the reports. The operational word was "*may*."

All properties have problems and opportunities. It is the process of thinking through the due diligence process to help you clearly identify both.

Residential Real Estate

In any residential real estate purchase, be sure to order your inspections, title history, check with the local police about crime, ask the fire department about calls for service to that location and check your real estate agent's background. Use a proper escrow and title insurance company. I strongly caution against the buyer and seller using the same real estate agent or having bankers and title people who work together too closely.

On residential property order a C.L.U.E. report either directly from Choice Trust, a LexisNexis Company or through your insurance company

C.L.U.E. stands for Comprehensive Loss Underwriting Exchange, a database used by insurance companies to share histories of claims or damage reports on property. Typically it contains information from the last seven years. A seller of the property may be wholly unaware that something had happened in the past before they owned the property. It is one of many valuable tools.

Insurance underwriters use this report as well as others in assessing rates based on risk of claim… e.g. three water claims, higher risk. Buyer then has the opportunity to ask the seller to provide proof of repairs, which can be forwarded to the insurance underwriters to lower the rates. Also, since Katrina, property near a navigable river or within a "high wind" district (five miles from the coastline for the U.S.) are rated higher unless they have hurricane-rated windows and/or hurricane shutters, or are constructed of poured reinforced concrete, such as many homes in the Caribbean.

Also avoid properties on top of old pet cemeteries or haunted ground - it may damage resale.

Conclusion

This is not an exhaustive list by any stretch of the imagination, and the items set forth may or may not be appropriate for the location you are thinking of acquiring.

It is also more effective if you establish a single point of communication between the buyer and seller. This eliminates many of the known communication problems and the many other unmentionable problems that will occur.

Remember this is not a checklist, it is a thought list.

> Thanks to Wendy F. Brown Broker of Rhode Island,
> who is a Certified Real-Estate Instructor with nearly
> 40 years experience in real estate,
> for her help in compiling this list.

Chapter 22

Asset Recovery Checklist

"OWE, v. To have (and to hold) a debt. The word formerly signified not indebtedness, but possession; it meant "own," and in the minds of debtors there is still a good deal of confusion between assets and liabilities."

Ambrose Bierce - *The Devil's Dictionary*

It is about distortion – debt from a contract or fraud – it is simply "Lies, Losses and Law" – stop thinking any harder.

Distortion and debt are the more civil form of losses in which a borrower or someone in charge of your money has had problems or errors, or distorted the environment in such a way that you put your money in and are taking a loss. While you may think there is a fraud, it may be a change in business conditions, a risk issue not considered, or bad luck. This is the civil form of what has gone wrong.

Lies and losses are at work when you are induced to invest your funds in, or with, an entity after being lied to about the opportunity, or how the funds were to be used, or were just taken on a jolly good but fraudulent ride.

The thought list on documenting the damages for both is the same, with the exception of some procedural differences for lies and losses, preemptive recovery and scheme liability issues.

In the beginning

> Assemble all of the promotional material on the investment.

> Assemble all of the correspondence dealing with the relationship. From before the relationship through the good times to the current date.

Assemble all letters of intent, agreements, schedules and modifications.

Document the inconsistencies in the relationship. Don't be blind to your own inconsistencies either, no one is perfect. It is best to own up to your failure immediately as opposed to having the other side open with them in court.

Assemble any information you may find in the courts or on the Web.

Where is the venue for the dispute?

Qualification of Losses

How did the loss occur?

A very clear narrative must be set forth that describes the relationship between the parties. It must show how the agreement was to benefit both parties and how it was that agreement failed.

Specifics must be cited from the agreement to the correspondence to the modification to the first indication of rupture to failure.

Beware of the expectations trap. All agreements fail because they failed one side's expectations. Read the agreements and correspondence clearly. Was this a real breach or just a breach of unexpressed expectations?

Quantification of Losses

What was lost – in specific amounts?

What are the ongoing losses? If a company's return on capital is 3 percent or 20 percent, the losses caused by this event have a multiplier effect. What is the multiplier effect on damages? Don't forget to include the cost of experts and attorneys on that multiplier effect.

What default interest rate does your agreement provide?

What does the agreement say about attorney's fees and court costs?

Present different loss scenarios and damages to the recovery team.

Who were the parties in the transaction?

There are the main parties to the agreement. There are intermediaries such as introducers, brokers, escrow companies, bankers and lawyers.

You must ask how these parties could have failed you. Also, is there a reasonable expectation on your behalf that there is a duty of these parties to care? Most of the time the exercise is a wash, when it is not, it opens up some of the parties to what is known as scheme liability. The places to check for this are:

> • The agreements. Did the parties do what they were supposed to in the agreement?
> • The professional code of conduct. Did the professional follow the professional code of conduct?
> • Regarding conduct: Did the enterprise follow its own internal guidelines on this such as know your client, or anti-money laundering?
> • Did the parties engage in activities that were outside their scope of authority of licensing?

You can see the theme, what were they doing that they should not have been doing either by contract, professional conduct, international guidelines, scope of authority, licensing requirements, etc.

We are looking for those affiliated with the transaction that were not doing what they were supposed to be doing. We are looking for other bad actors with deep pockets that can be included in the scheme of liability so we can enlarge the list of entities to recover from.

The danger in this is you can be too successful and find yourself battling many lawyers and companies. It is a risk.

Who are the parties to this loss that you are looking to hold responsible?

Full legal name; is it the person's real name?
Nationality; does the person have more than one?
Age
Health
Known places of visitation and dwelling
Unique identifiers – such as date of birth, Social Security number, cedula number etc.

Assets
       Property and location with encumbrance
       Bank accounts
       Security accounts
       Insurance
       Annuities
       Vehicles, boats, aircraft
       Collectables such as art, jewelry, guns, other
       Credit cards
       Overdraft – or lines of credit
       Corporations, partnerships, trusts etc.
       Intellectual property
       Liabilities
       Liens
       Judgments
       Forfeiture orders
       Ex-spouses
       Taxes

Income
> Declared income
> Income declared on credit or loan applications
> Tax refunds
> Other sources of income

Expenses
> Living expenses – get them all in
> Fraud expenses

Outside Professionals

Retain an attorney for recovery, so all research on the recovery process can be protected by attorney client privilege.

Before letting the attorney pursue the debt, hire a financial investigator to find assets and create a picture for recovery of those assets. I must stress, hire an investigator who does nothing but financial investigations. Many think they can do financial investigations, but few can. With the asset profile, you need to make a choice of whether you pursue or withdraw.

There is also a partial test. That is to file the lawsuit and proceed with discovery with the attorney and the financial investigator working together. Sometimes the financial discovery, with directed subpoenas can unveil a great deal of information only suspected, or not.

Choose to go forward or not to go forward. Set certain benchmarks for re-choosing at dates or events in the future.

Stones and a good investigator and attorney can overturn to find clues:
> Telephone numbers for toll calls.
> Credit report.
> Records of credit card charges and how they were paid.
> All credit granting applications for asset disclosures.
> Frequent flier programs.

Follow the money

> It is trite and true. Use investigators and subpoenas to follow the flow of funds from your account to the account of the other party. Follow the funds from the account of the other party to where they went and for what.

International

> Many larger frauds involve an international component, as do larger civil recoveries. It is best to engage a competent financial investigator and a competent asset recovery attorney to give you some clue as to how you will fare in the courts in the foreign lands.

> In the case of frauds, most of the world allows for Mareva injunctions in commonwealth countries, and civil arrest for the assets in civil law countries. This is where you need a lawyer steeped in asset recovery to give you correct information based upon your specific fact pattern.

> Seek jurisdictional advantage when you can and avoid areas of jurisdictional concern.

Reality of Financial Litigation.

> All of your documentation needs to be clear and convincing. All areas of gray must be clearly explained.

> In both civil and fraud cases, there are a number of expedited remedies. Pre-emptive remedies for civil ligation often require a bond to be posted – in case you are incorrect in your recovery efforts. In fraud cases you have the opportunity to use, when permissible "Constructive Trust Theories" and injunctions and civil arrest of assets as prejudgment relief.

> Read more on this from the chapter on Asset Recovery and discuss the option in detail with your asset recovery attorney.

Bankruptcy / Insolvency

Make sure you file a proof of claim.

Ensure your documentation is peerless, clear and convincing.

Choose with legal counsel the merits of pushing for a nondischargeable debt.

Strategy and Tactics

You need to work with your team to understand what is best for your recovery based upon a specific fact pattern.

What is nearly always against you is time. The longer it takes to affect a recovery the more changes and time the target has to secrete the assets, and frustrate and impede your recovery.

You have a judgment and you have made no recovery. My suggestion is to keep the judgment current and make a really lame effort at recovering assets, then go silent for a few years. Keep sub-rosa tabs on the subject and when the time is right, go after the subject with all of the new information you have.

There is also the option of selling the claim. Many people buy claims, admittedly for pennies on the dollar. But you get some recovery, and the person who purchased the claim has a fresh vested interest in recovery.

Forgive the debt – explore with your legal counsel and tax professional which IRS form 1099 applies.

Whatever you threaten to do, legally, follow through.

Be mindful of the implications of the Fair Debt Collection Practices Act and any third party you may hire. It is a labyrinthine act with even less clear interpretations. You can run afoul of it easily – so be forewarned. This is where I mention yet again, seek out only those professionals who understand asset recovery, not those who think they can do asset recovery.

Odd Things and Suggestions

For future debt agreement or contracts. The default interest rate in most states is 10 percent, unless your agreement provides for a higher rate. If the rate is too high, judges like to play Solomon and change the agreement. A clever construction I have seen is:

> *"If the agreement goes into default the default interest rate on the defaulted agreement is N% (10% to18% I have seen) plus the annual rate of inflation as expressed by the Consumer Price Index."*

This is a clever idea that deals with impact of inflation on the deflated dollars recovered.

Another clever approach to include in an agreement is ...

> *"The debtor is responsible for all of the actual costs of enforcing this agreement, including actual attorneys fees, court costs, investigative costs and expert costs, and internal allocated overhead associated with enforcing this agreement."*

I think this went a bit far with the "allocated overhead," but it serves to make a point both to the debtor and the creditor that the costs of collection are not confined to just what is owed, it is the cost of dealing with an exception and the subsequent enforcement of the agreement.

What Happened?

Review the path taken to get to this asset recovery position. Determine where the errors were made and what warning signs were available, seen and unseen. THIS IS NOT A MAKE-WRONG SESSION. This is a professional meeting of the minds to study what happened and to prevent it within the boundaries of intelligent business practices. If we begin assessing blame on innocent parties, we'll never get the information we need. An innocent party is anyone who did not get the missing money.

You can never have zero losses, unless it is a theory in academia for modeling. The hint is that only exists in a hypothetical world, not the one in which we live, breathe and create commerce.

Chapter 22

The Impact of the Future and What We Should Watch

"Where a calculator on the ENIAC is equipped with 18,000 vacuum tubes and weighs 30 tons, computers in the future may have only 1,000 vacuum tubes and perhaps weigh 1.5 tons."

Popular Mechanics, March 1949

"The future, according to some scientists, will be exactly like the past, only far more expensive."

John Sladek

We are good at managing those risks we know. Experts in risk management and due diligence have encountered more of life's learning experiences through their work with clients – so they know a bit more. What we are encountering today is such a rapid pace of technological evolution we feel as though as soon as we are comfortable with the risk parameters of a given business situation – that situation is obsolete. We feel this precisely because it is correct. As new payment systems are invented and then evolve, and more distributed computing and processing and storing of information is occurring, only a colossal failure of the imagination will lead one to think we have all of the answers to risk. One has to imagine beyond the possibilities of today to the opportunities and corollary risks of the future. Remember checklists only cover those items we have seen fail in the past.

Agents of Change

Who are the agents of change, and what do they represent? The concurrent emergence of computing power and connectivity are key forces of change. Computing power allows managers to process more complex forecasts, with better information, than any of us could have even contemplated while learning our trade. The mathematical models available to quantify, sift, sort and organize data to enable us to predict future outcomes are generally far ahead of our ability to comprehend their meaning.

> *Only a few short years ago I spent some time with a friend who was a programmer and mathematician by trade. He was hired by a global trading firm to improve the company's ability to calculate yields of many different investments, in response to many different market variables, and overlay the information with both risk scenarios and probabilities of occurrence. The program he inherited had a minimum two- to three-week run time, and had to be interrupted after five days to harvest approximations for the trading desk. As a programmer, he understood the power of distributed computing. He modified the software running these simulations to use all available computers during overnight and weekend hours in all of the company's offices around the world. This change in the use of technology allowed him to run full simulations in less than 30 hours. A report that was once run monthly was now being generated weekly on a global net of re-tasked computers. These same simulations can now be run daily on your desktop computer. As control of data has evolved, these and newer more complex simulations can now be run in real time, incorporating many more variables and delivering more information, with every variable weighted. An astonishing evolution – if we know how to make sense of it.*

The Internet is compelling because of its speed, low cost of experimentation, low cost of adaptation, and immediacy of results. Failure of an idea is inexpensive. The model of research and development is no longer a well-funded central laboratory – it is an adaptation of both closed and open source technologies developed by tens of thousands, if not millions of developers – inexpensive to prototype and test.

Governments are changing too. The legal sandboxes we call countries are regulating their markets toward a conversion in rules in some instances, and yet others continue to emphasize their legal and regulatory jurisdictional differences. Much of what we do and what we call assets, especially with Intellectual Property and Critical Information, can only be created and used within certain concepts of law with reliable enforcement. As the laws and regulations change so does the value of what we hold under those laws. If International Financial Reporting Standards (IFRS) and Generally Accepted Accounting Principles (GAAP) became the same, would the assets of your company change, or just how you can book and value them? Exactly. Now, think of these differences being changed, eliminated or expanded between 195 different countries. As author Thomas Friedman has pointed out, the world may be flat and the ease of doing business in this country or that is but a mouse click away, but sameness is not at hand. There are Smithian advantages between different countries

These innovations and evolutions are changing finance as well as the financial professional. Computing has revolutionized all industries, and they will continue to evolve along with computing power and global connectivity and opportunity. Yet, in the near future, even today's awesome technology will look like a rotary phone.

The evolution in finance is going to be dramatic. Financial professionals will change what they manage, where they manage, how they manage it, and how they interact with the various divisions within a company. There will be new, and sometimes passive, interfaces between vendors, customers and suppliers. In many cases, the transformation will be so dramatic that there may be no need for the financial department's involvement. Relationships will be transformed into data streams. The financial professional may be relegated to a role of interpreting data in the same way as the people they are currently reporting to.

Innovation will impact …

Money

What is more basic to finance than money? But what is money? Puka shells were a hot item at one time. Money is nothing more than a store of value contained in a recognized medium of exchange recognized by a social contract. The society agrees that X is a store of value, and X becomes currency. Hawaiians had a social agreement that the puka shells were their currency, and they could be traded for food or goods at negotiated puka price points. I am fairly sure that puka shells in modern Hawaii have no exchange rate. The social contract has expired. The Mayans had a currency in the form of cacao beans, the Chinese in cowrie shells, and the Mangbetu in the Democratic Republic of Congo used knives. All of these social contracts have expired, concurrently with the value of these items as currency.

The social contract we recognize today is fiat money, represented by paper. The social contract that values this paper is real and (for the present time) robust. The evolution of our fiat currency includes actual notes, numbers on bank statements, slips of signed paper, and finally – binary representations of those instruments. These items, both real and virtual, are recognized and accepted between cooperating institutions worldwide. You can even use sheets of plastic with bumps and a magnetic strip to transfer funds for goods and services. All of these international mediums are aligned – convertible by agreed upon exchange rates to the colorful paper we recognize as money. The social contract is strong.

Currency is a medium to monetize and store labor in an exchangeable form. It's easy to trade colorful paper or binary data for food, rent and gasoline. Can you imagine a lettuce grower trying to swap produce for gasoline or depending upon their goods during a trip to Portugal to negotiate for room and board or fizzy drinks on the beach? Currency is an efficient means of storing and transporting labor, despite the cost of converting goods and services to currency – and back. There is friction.

The social contract that allows us to equate goods and services with currency creates economic friction. Friction is the cost of each step in swapping goods and services for currency, and trading currency for goods and services. Each and every time you add a middleman to a transaction the costs add up. The more intermediaries you eliminate, the more efficient the transaction becomes. Common sense would suggest that the direct swapping of goods and services is as close as we can get to a frictionless transaction. But common sense is often at odds with the real world.

416

Middlemen generally add knowledge and utility to transactions. The question we ask is, how much? They have pricing information from suppliers and understand demands for the goods and services they deal in. They may have added value through transportation or economies of scale. As an example, sweet corn is typically sold by the pallet; about 20 bushels. The average family has no need for a pallet of corn, probably not even a bushel or a peck. In the case of marketing corn, the middleman does provide some value. Now let's change our marketing instincts to laptop computers. Is there a need for a distributor? The nonperishable product is likely to be delivered in a custom format. The consumer can buy a laptop directly from the manufacturer. You can specify what you want delivered to your doorstep. What is the difference in friction? The percentage of the transaction, that's what. The friction, as a percentage, of buying a computer is negligible. The cost of the transaction is small. The cost of delivering individual bushels or pecks of corn will likely exceed the price of the corn. The principle I'm focusing on is that the friction between the producer and consumer decreases the closer the two can navigate toward each other. Time is a determining factor – and in today's world, time is friction. Worldwide computing capability and connectivity are reducing the friction – a cost that was, in the not-too-recent past, recognized as indispensable knowledge.

Payment Innovations

As recently as the 1800s, cash was the accepted form of payment for most of the world. Specie, or paper that could be converted to specie, was the final resolution of debt. Large businesses and wealthy people understood drafts, but use of these instruments was rare and not readily accepted. There was a big business in securing the delivery of business payrolls in the form of pay envelopes – making sure the wagon with the payroll was not robbed. In time, drafts morphed into checks and became more widely accepted once security features, such as magnetic ink character encoding (MICR), were added. Credit cards were the first widely accepted form of money being transferred by electronic bits. It was as recently as 1981 that the first B2B online transaction took place, and a short three years later in 1984 that the first online retail transaction occurred. In 1994, Netscape introduced Secure Sockets Layer (SSL) to protect online transactions, and we were off to the races. By 2009 Forrester Research estimated U.S. retail sales online to be $156 billion! Concurrent with the public's acceptance of electronic transactions, the Automated Clearing House (ACH) system has been quietly revolutionizing the payment process. The physical check is slowly vanishing, and I expect its future is as secure as the payroll wagon. Our grandchildren will not recognize them.

Along with innovations in traditional payment systems there have been innovations in alternative systems. Merchants and shoppers on the Internet have widely adopted what are currently accepted as traditional means of payment – credit cards, debit cards and electronic checks. The new players in this field are structuring payment mechanisms that allow consumers a wide range of flexibility in settlement options, consolidating and streamlining traditional methods, such as PayPal, and alternate storage options, such as e-Gold. More exotic currencies and payment methods are emerging through operations called MMORPGs (massively multiplayer online role-playing games), such as Linden dollars in the virtual world Second Life. Players in these virtual worlds are actively exchanging their virtual dollars for real dollars. Not on your radar screen? It's on the radar screen of Interpol, the FBI and most national crime organizations. These emerging "currencies" which have recognized value and allow near-frictionless, under-the-radar transactions provide a haven to money launderers. I mention this not because I expect you to Google the exchange rate for Linden dollars, but as a harbinger of money's future. Remember, it was only a few years ago that the mainstream media considered bloggers just an annoyance, the "Pajamas Media" typing out their frustrations. The Linden dollar may not be the currency of the future, but the fact that it has a recognized value indicates that spontaneous cooperation is taking place in arenas that may seem foreign to us.

Barter

Barter is a form of exchange with a wide range of transactional friction and opportunity. The opportunities expand with information. Saudi Arabia once purchased 40 Rolls Royce engines in exchange for oil. General Electric won a $150 million turbine project in Romania because it agreed to accept Romanian goods of agreed value in trade. These examples are from the 1980s, before we had the world's information at our fingertips. Barter will, in the near future, have an increasing role in the progressive enterprise. Barter can be more efficient than converting goods to currency and back to goods. The financial professional needs to be in a position to anticipate and facilitate barter opportunities for the enterprise. To do this, the financial professional will require both basic and strategic knowledge of where opportunities exist.

Denationalization of Currency

The general acceptance and adaptation to alternative payment systems and virtual currencies shows a trend toward the denationalization of currencies. Currencies are backed by the faith of those who use it, not by those who issue it. I believe that emerging currencies will not be backed by any sovereign government. As we move forward, I believe currencies will be valued more by a real-time market of interconnected users than by the issuer. The conversion of goods and services into a specific currency represents a risk not often appreciated.

Some examples include: the Euro, which is a multinational currency; gold, which is the oldest denationalized currency, and others such as frequent flyer miles that can be bartered; virtual currencies such as Linden dollars, and barter, which eliminated the use of currency. Denationalized currencies will face less political risk, but greater market risk.

Money Supply

The denationalization of currencies may also have an odd side effect. Central banks, by definition, will not be able to regulate these currencies nor control the amount of these currencies in circulation. How the public values currencies will immediately influence exchange rates. Some argue that denationalized currencies will lead to inflation because none of the states' actors will be responsible to control how much currency is issued, or to deflation because there will be less currency in circulation. For a while, no new currencies will be completely delinked from national currencies – the market will persist.

Exchange Valuation of Exotic Assets

In our recent memory we have witnessed the trading of credit default swaps, collateralized deposit obligations, and other esoteric financial instruments bringing world financial markets to near collapse. It was not the fault of the agreements, the buyers, the sellers, or even the designers of the agreements. It was a market without structure – a market that had no feedback mechanism. Agreements in which neither party has an active participation in the outcome, or lack an exchange of goods or services, have traditionally been unenforceable. A purely speculative contract was traditionally considered a legally unenforceable wager, a bet. According to the 1884 U.S. Supreme Court case of Irwin v. Williar, the "rule against difference contracts" allowed you to wager on anything you liked, from sporting outcomes to prices on commodities. But, the rule required that in order to have a court enforce your agreement, you had to show that one of the parties to the agreement had an interest independent of the wager.

These centuries old traditions were abandoned in the Futures Trading Practices Act of 1992 (FTPA), and legally reversed in the Commodity Futures Modernization Act (CFMA) of 2000. Gambling was made legal – with no market structure.

Consider the following three scenarios.

> 1.) I have an itch about Blue Chip Dan in the 8th race at Arlington Park. I go to my neighborhood sports bar and meet my pal Fat Tony – the local bookie. I tell him about my hunch, and he suggests I see a doctor. He says there's no way that glue pot's going to finish. He gives me 100-1 odds. I bet $1,000 to win on Blue Chip Dan.

> 2.) I believe that gold is going up, so I open an account with a futures commission merchant, Anthony, deposit funds into the account, and buy 10 contracts for December

delivery of 100 ounces of gold. If it goes up, I make money – if it goes down, I lose money.

3.) I am certain that I have problems with my sovereign debt portfolio. I can't figure out what numbskull bought Transnistria National Bonds. I go to the marketplace and find a few firms that are offering what I need. Through the market representative, Antonio, I enter into a credit default swap agreement on the bonds.

Three different wagers. The college exam question is: Which two of these investments are the most similar?

    A. [1+2]
    B. [2+3]
    C. [1+3]
    D. [All the Same]
    E. [All Different]

Answer C. One and three are almost identical in every aspect. Risk, lack of transparency and prospect of being paid.

Outcome 1

Blue Chip Dan wins! I'm holding a $100,000 ticket. I can't wait to see Fat Tony. In reality, Fat Tony is never going to come back to that pub. He will toss his cell phone in a dumpster, and I will never see Fat Tony again.

I could have gone down to the track, or the OTB, but a pari-mutuel wager on Blue Chip Dan would have moved the line. The odds would have been adjusted to reflect the market sentiment on Blue Chip Dan. The feedback from my wager would have dropped the odds to 10-1. On the other hand, the track would have assured me that I get paid for a win.

Outcome 2

Transnistria has just been absorbed by Moldova as a result
of the merging of two soccer clubs. The Moldovan soccer
team played the Transnistrian soccer team in a winner-take-
all claiming match. End score, Transnistria 1, Moldova 4.
Moldova is not going to pay the debts of Transnistria, and
Transnistria's bonds are worthless. You were one smart
financial professional to have entered into the credit default
agreement. But – bad news – the counterparty to your
agreement has no money. Good news! Your government is
going to step in and save your counterparty. What was the
problem here?

Like the bet with Fat Tony, you made your deal with
another private party. There was no true and open exchange
representing the sentiment of the marketplace. Bypassing
the betting windows and market exchanges, in both wagers
the participants were betting against each other without any
market feedback.

Outcome 3

In your bet on gold – win or lose – this wager was unique.
It was a wager made in an open marketplace where the
sentiments of both the buyers and sellers were expressed.
While individual trade information is private to any specific
trader, the composite information is available to the public.
There is a guarantee of payment upon settlement. Anthony
took money from me to ensure that I could honor my end
of the agreement, and Anthony's firm is liable for my losses
whether the firm collects from me or not – so it's going to
make sure the wager is covered. Further, if Anthony were
to default, all of the members of the exchange are jointly
and severally liable for honoring each and every agreement
traded on the exchange.

The Transnistrian wager with Antonio had all of the same failings
as the wager with Fat Tony. In the end Antonio was just as scarce as

Fat Tony. There was no market, there was no market feedback, and there was nobody in place to enforce the agreements. The only real difference is that Antonio's screw-up was charged to the taxpayers. The loss was socialized. The local pub didn't have the option of rescuing Fat Tony and making good on the bet, nor would they. That is the only real difference.

Without a market, exchange or pari-mutuel pool providing information, how can anyone know prices or odds? How would you like to be purchasing ACME stock for $100 only to later find out that the sellers valued it at $5? Without an enforceable mechanism to settle wagers, what restrains the speculator from wagering money he doesn't have? Without a transparent market, what prevents the speculator from selling assets he doesn't own?

These problems with transparency of transactions and pricing information are currently defining legislative agendas. It is unlikely that the Public Company Accounting Oversight Board (PCAOB) will permit the booking of tradable assets whose settlement cannot be backed by a bona fide independent exchange. Credit default swaps, collateralized debt obligations and other exotic agreements will become nearly worthless unless they can be traded on an exchange. The world has shown it has no ability to accurately and reliably determine counterparty risk to these agreements. These are valuable tools, but only if the terms of the contracts can be enforced and the counterparties are solvent. Pricing information will be transparent and settlement will be warranted by a third party called an exchange. These exotics will be mainstreamed and exchange-traded in short time.

Tax Collection

Governments that have traditionally relied upon sales tax for revenue are becoming painfully aware that they have little authority to collect taxes on interstate commerce unless the seller has a footprint in their jurisdiction.

Witness what has come to be known as the "Amazon Tax." New York has determined that if an Internet retailer derives sales through an affiliate that does have a footprint in their state that is a sufficient presence to require them to collect sales tax for the state. New York brick-and-mortar retailers loved the ruling. In the wake of this ruling, Amazon axed every one of its affiliates in New York and the other states that adopted this stance. It was estimated that this program could have generated $50 million in sales tax revenue for New York. In actuality, assuming a 6 percent tax rate, it cost the residents of New York $834 million in income. Legal battles are continuing.

The Supreme Court was very clear in its ruling on Quill Corp. v. North Dakota. It said a retailer had to have a "physical presence" within the state in order to be responsible for collecting sales tax. While this strategy may not have been a brilliant strategic move by the state of New York, it is indicative of the problems states face and the poor choices that are made in an environment they do not understand. While we have always been liable for the sales tax on goods purchased from out-of-state, it's a law that is unenforceable. I see three possible resolutions.

A national corporation, chartered under national law will be required to transact business on the Internet and pay sales tax on a pro-rata basis, similar to how truckers pay fuel and highway taxes. Requiring a license to transact business over the Internet would have the same effect. There is a movement called the Streamlined Sales Tax Project (SSTP) that has degrees of cooperation in most states, but to date has not assembled the enforcement options needed to get serious traction.

A second option is to tax Internet hosts based upon the bandwidth they consume. I think this highly unlikely seeing that bandwidth use has little correlation with commercial transactions or revenue.

The last option and most likely outcome in my opinion, will be a national sales tax with some opaque scheme to distribute revenue among the states.

Tax collections are going to become more aggressive and obtrusive. The efficiencies and changes we are discussing that are being introduced into the marketplace are likely to reduce the total number of businesses. As middlemen begin to disappear, so will their businesses. A wrench made in China used to go from a manufacturer's rep in China, to wholesalers in the United States, and then shipped to regional warehouses for distribution to a retailer's shelf. Today retail locations pass orders directly to the factory in China. This type of efficiency is one of the reasons why we pay less for goods, and why there will be fewer businesses to tax in the future. With fewer taxable opportunities and leaner margins, the tax authorities will be more aggressive in their collection efforts.

Financial professionals will need access to highly specialized knowledge on tax law, tax collection and tax compliance in multiple jurisdictions, in several languages under many different bodies of law and regulation. Tax avoidance is now being characterized as a money laundering offense. Statutes that were originally aimed at multinational criminal organizations are now being focused on those who, even unknowingly, avoid taxes. If someone is prosecuted under the anti–money–laundering statutes, the defendant is subject to greater criminal penalties, heavier fines, and being professionally branded. Tax administration will be outsourced to specialty enterprises for efficacy as well as for corporate and professional liability reasons.

Product Cycles

Product cycles will shorten for those products that possess little liability, and lengthen for those with significant liability. Products with little liability will have more intense competition, be required to innovate faster, and be quickest to market and out of the market. Witness items such as fashion and electronics. For products with greater liability, the product cycles will be longer and innovation will be slower, as all of the risks are sorted out and studied by manufacturers. Witness the speed of innovation in automobiles and medicine. As a result of liability issues, these products are evolving slowly. The last three years of any car model generally all look the same – and the last 10 years all have basically the same engine and transmission. Once a product with great liability is understood to be safe and reliable, the incentive to innovate in any substantial way is greatly diminished.

Both trends contain risks for the financial professional. The rapid life cycle requires careful planning for introduction to the market and a well-coordinated allocation of resources. Knowing when to get out is as important as knowing when to get in. With a longer life cycle you run the risk of encountering a disruptive upstart with less "legacy" risk, allowing the upstart entity to aggressively gain position in the market. This ability will become one of the key focuses of a financial professional's future competencies.

Trade Wars

Competition among nations to be evermore productive and profitable will erupt into trade wars. Once another nation shoots a hole in their boat, there is great political pressure for us to shoot a hole in ours. These wars are cyclical and inevitable. Future trade wars will not look like the trade wars of the last century, focusing on goods and subsidies. They will focus on what is perceived to be unfair advantages in law among jurisdictions. These advantages will be identified in areas such as taxation, regulation, permissiveness, environmental law, and any number of other perceived sleights. You will hear more comments referring to "unfair tax competition," which will spread to "unfair environmental regulation" or "unfair working conditions."

As a financial professional, you need to be ahead of these claims and prepare your response. You may need to realign manufacturing or alter the jurisdiction of the greatest value-added functions so that products can be flagged under a jurisdiction not currently being targeted. Financial professionals will require an awareness of non-sequitur risks. Recently Brazil, after winning several World Trade Organization's arbitration decisions dealing with U.S. subsidies for cotton farming, threatened to retaliate, under WTO rules, by taking for its use private U.S. companies' medicine patents and manufacture the privately patented medicines in their state-run pharmaceutical facilities. This is an example of the interconnected world and the value of Intellectual Property and Critical Information in one event.

Decentralization, Efficiencies and Workspace

Functions that at one time had to be performed at a company location, such as reservations, support services and sales – can often be accomplished in a decentralized fashion through the use of technology. One company cut 75 percent of its stenography pool by sending the work to the Philippines. The dictation was done during the day, the files typed in the Philippines, and documents returned by e-mail the same or next day. Several airlines and cruise companies employ reservations operators who work from their homes. Few businesses require workspace at a central location for every employee. The modern computer, with broadband access and minor modifications can emulate every piece of equipment in the modern office.

We also continue to see impressive gains in manufacturing. What do you do with excess office and manufacturing space? As the custodian of value, the financial professional is going to need to be able to put these assets to work or eliminate their costs.

Intellectual Property and Critical Information

The most valuable asset of most companies is their Intellectual Property and Critical Information (IPCI). Of the businessmen I have worked with in China during the last 15 years, not one of them did so without significant or total loss of IPCI. Moving manufacturing to a foreign location to take advantage of lower wages or regulatory advantages often offered no significant competitive advantage because there was no system of laws in place to protect their IPCI. After all, IPCI is a total and complete creation of Western law. If there is no comparable set of laws where you move your IPCI, it will no longer remain an exclusive asset – which is its only value. The opportunity to lower manufacturing costs was more than offset in the loss of IPCI. These losses have significant impact on companies, and are one of the reasons that we are seeing an increase of "insourcing" – a polite management-speak term reflecting that the company lost control of its IPCI and is now attempting to protect a) what it may have left and b) what it develops in the future and c) dealing with the cost of F^3 (Fiddle Fart Factor an important term of art).

The financial professional is in a key position to evaluate the impact of the loss of IPCI. Any decision to expose IPCI to third parties has to be weighted against the impacts of a potential loss – a loss which frequently represents 75 percent or more of the value in a modern commercial enterprise, as well as the F^3 of outsourcing.

Mini-Multinationals

Offshore Financial Centers are locations outside your base of operation that have a financial advantage crafted into law. We think of a Smithian advantage in things such as skilled labor, and an advantage from division of labor that can also exist in the application of law. Some jurisdictions have significant advantages in key areas of commerce. Most of these advantages are found in areas such as processing, banking, insurance, mutual funds, trusts and intellectual property.

The firm of the future will use these advantages to effectively do what it chooses with a minimum of legal interference with an effective judiciary. The firms of the future will arbitrage the advantages of law between various jurisdictions. Financial professionals will be part of the lead in teams that will make these assessments of advantage.

Increased Volatility

Business cycles and natural forces like to stress and break things that humans create. In the recent past, when large banks had problems, they were merged into even larger banks. The shortcomings were not addressed, just the capital positions. After time, several damaged banks can evolve into fewer, but larger and still damaged banks. One way to address the shortcomings of institutions is to allow them to fail while they are still small. If we don't, all of the combined shortcomings continue to lurk within the larger institutions and can erupt at any given moment.

How many times have we heard mantras about diversity? There is strength in diversity, and it is wise to diversify your portfolio – it is good advice. Diversity in nature represents strength. In genetics this is referred to as biodiversity, and the more diverse the genome of a species, the more robust it is – the less diverse, the more fragile it is. Yet, we continue to regulate our financial institutions out of diversity and push them toward homogeneity with the ideal of standardization and harmonization in their operation. This is occurring both within nations and across international boundaries. In an effort to create a robust financial infrastructure we are making our institutions much more fragile. Thus the financial world of the future will be much more susceptible to disruptive events.

Group-think and group action can spontaneously occur within minutes over the Internet. A dress that is a big hit in Milan during fashion week is in demand all over the world on the same day. Every fashion retailer will want that dress immediately. A retailer may work all of their contacts in order to get 75 dresses for their upscale couture boutique, and just as the order arrives, Anna Wintour is overheard saying that anyone who wears that dress looks like a "molting gamecock." That's the end of that dress, unless looking like a molting gamecock is somehow fashionable at that moment.

A book is no longer a success in just one country, it is a success in many countries. How many people around the world were reading J.K. Rowling's latest release all at the same time – in several different languages? This ability to virally share information increases the volatility of consumer preferences, and of financial markets. Everyone in the world will hear of the same oil-rig disaster in Equatorial Guinea at the same time, and will react at the same time, increasing the size of the market perturbations. The impact of disruptive events, political, sociological, financial or technological will be bigger, faster, closer to simultaneous, and thus add to volatility.

The increased regulation of the central financial institutions we have grown comfortable with will make them more fragile. They will become devoid of any significant innovation and will slowly be again disintermediated out of lending, payment processing, foreign exchange and even holding deposits. Regulations will require increased capital holdings and lower and lower risk profiles for both investing and operations. So how does a large fragile financial institution respond to volatility and risk spikes? It looks to legislators to pass a law against those risks from occurring.

Innovative solutions are already coming online to replace services that financial institutions used to provide. The financial professional will need to seek those that provide the services and flexibility necessary for their enterprise to retain or gain competitive advantages. Most of these services provided by a bank today will be supplied by or through new vendors of the future.

Crime

In the future, your exposure to crime will be greater. With so many ports of access to the value within the enterprise, controlling access to information will become increasingly difficult. I envision expanding theft of Intellectual Property and Critical Information as well as persistent attempts, and successes, at micro-theft. The real value of the company today is IPCI, and the financial professional, as the custodian of value for the company, will manage the asset elements registry as the people in this position once managed the balance sheets. IPCI will be the prime target of criminals.

Micro-theft is the persistent theft of small amounts from many locations. It is the equivalent of losing blood from a thousand cuts. As we use more automated payment systems, and are less familiar with our suppliers, opportunities continue to expand. Battling any single source of fraud becomes a cost, not a recovery – and the sum of these small frauds adds up quickly.

Risk Management

The financial professional will become the penultimate risk manager. All risks are weighted by their financial impact on the company. The financial professional is the manager of the company's finances, under the CFO – responsible for managing risk. It is clear that many people do not understand risk, and this is especially true among the experts. Many times rating agencies have maintained AAA ratings on firms right up to the date of bankruptcy or insolvency. Quants are cute, but they're like Oldsmobiles – on their way to the museum. Quants mine data and design algorithms to fit the data of events that have already occurred. This is the equivalent of driving a car using only information from the rearview mirror. It's better than nothing – but how much better?

Risk management will become an important discipline for the financial professional, and will become an additional area in which the financial professional will need to have both experience and credentials as both a generalist and a narrow-field expert.

Change

The pace of change will favor smaller and more nimble firms over larger firms. Larger firms will continue to use increased regulation and other market protection strategies to hold onto its turf – but eventually the titanopolies will have to find new ways of doing business, and it better look a lot like small business. Large firms will be slain if they are unable to quickly maneuver. They will be slain by the great Zeus of commerce – the marketplace.

Outsourcing – End of Financial Professionals

Innovation will come from outside the major financial institutions, because most simply don't have a structure that promotes innovation or is friendly toward it. Firms that have agility, speed and a willingness to take calculated risks are where innovation is occurring. The Titanopolies will watch innovation pass them by. The solutions provided would no doubt be faster, more elegant and more efficient than what can be provided by an in-house financial professionals department. After all, most of treasury's traditional functions are automated now. Most traditional financial professionals' functions will be outsourced to specialists in the narrow disciplines that currently comprise the financial professional's function.

The financial professional will become a custodian of value for the enterprise only if the financial professional takes custody of the IPCI. This is what financial professionals should do – and those departments that fail to make this shift will close.

iFinancial Professionals Emerge

The iFinancial Professional's function will become a financial discipline focused on management of the IPCI. Challenging and supporting the different operational divisions, this professional will be the penultimate controller of risks inherent in their business, and will focus on delivering long-term shareholder value.

Outsourced, along with some of the liability, will go tax planning, accounts payable, payroll, cash management and consolidation. The iFinancial Professional will focus on planning, choice support and analysis, investor relations and support. What was traditionally a sole area of responsibility for the finance department will be shared with many other departments. The iFinancial Professional will look more like an internal consultant than a bean counter. The iFinancial Professional will rely upon specialized vendors to provide the day-to-day information they were once charged with assembling, and they will spend more time dealing with strategic issues and forward looking activities. The iFinancial Professional will use outside vendors who are focused on their core competencies, allowing the iFinancial Professional to focus on the core competencies of their specific enterprise.

The iFinancial Professional's strategy will be clearly linked to the strategy and objectives of the enterprise.

iFinancial Professionals will be part of the central management, integrated throughout the enterprise, and will distinguish between accountability and responsibility for the enterprise's financial activity.

iFinancial Professionals will have a strong knowledge of the enterprise's goods and services, and how to deploy them. They will have well-honed analytical skills, and act as an internal consultant throughout the enterprise.

iFinancial Professionals will be focused on continuing to be the custodian of value for the enterprise and efficacy on all choices and actions.

iFinancial Professionals' systems will be flexible, able to both withstand and adapt to rapidly changing technological innovations, market pressures, and commercial landscapes – wherever they may be.

iFinancial Professionals will be forward-looking, focused on value – not cost – and constantly challenging its best practices.

The iFinancial Professional's skills will not be limited to finance, they will include risk management, interpersonal communication and a background in business. They will possess credentials in specific disciplines of financial management, risk management and possibly IT.

The future of finance is here and now. Prepare to adapt or risk obsolescence.

Chapter 24

Endnotes

"Virtue has no greater ally than a lack of opportunity."

Anonymous

"The value of an imponderable is always negative."

L. Burke Files

What do I add about due diligence at the end of this book? Thankfully, it is only a few notes. I'm not going to pretend that this book is an exhaustive tome on the subject, but as an author and practitioner of due diligence I feel compelled to complete my thoughts.

Viewpoint

I like to understand the basic structure, or architecture, of the topics I study. I continue to pull on the loose threads of a scheme or idea until I'm comfortable that I understand all of the basic elements. If there is a philosophy I can relate with, it is pragmatism.

I have worked frauds that challenge the GDP of small countries in size. I have also met the victims these fraudsters leave in their wake, and witnessed the hell the fraudsters have brought to pass.

I have seen the overreaction people have to the risk of fraud – investors ceasing to take chances and removing themselves from the marketplace, withdrawing into their shells. I have seen businesses erect well-thought-out barriers to their continued success – well thought out, yet irrational. Governments try to assume the role of a nanny in the marketplace, hobbling the actors who are the lifeblood of those markets.

In summary, if we cannot tolerate failure, we cannot experience innovation, competition or success. There is no right to succeed in the absence of a right to fail.

People Lie

As an investigator who has covered more cases in more countries than I can remember, I have become a connoisseur of the absurd. I have witnessed many outrageous attempts at fraud, and equally outrageous methods to get away with it. The best summary I can offer is, nothing is new.

Why do people lie? Because they can. "They do it to cover their own frailties, to gain money or prestige, or to gain their superior's favor." Ibn Khaldun (1332-1406) in *The Muqaddimah, An Introduction to History*, spent several pages on this very subject. Clearly, it's not a new problem.

Several years ago I was wandering around Mayan territory and learned that the Mayans used cacao beans as a form of currency. I was told that it was common for a family to place cacao beans with the dead as currency for the hereafter. Guess what the undertakers were here after? Many of the cacao pods were filled with dirt as opposed to beans. Almost a perfect counterfeit, as long as you were certain there was no hereafter and you weren't going to be facing thousands of souls awaiting repayment.

So is it a LIE or a lie? Is it an exaggeration that got out of control? Was it useful puffery, used as a catalyst to get a transaction rolling? Is it just another person's perspective and representation? I am sure I don't know.

We are, in spite of nobler expectations, all people.

What does a Good Due Diligence Report look like?

Begin by identifying the parties to a transaction, and gather from all of the parties what they feel is important in the representations made, and what understandings they think have been implied by the other parties. Describe what information needs to be assembled, and what discussions led you to your conclusions. Include a description of the process, your findings, and what additional information was required to complete the process.

The final report should answer all of the questions asked, and satisfactorily address any questions that are not definitively answered. Some questions do not have good answers – state why. The report should contain no opinions. A good due diligence report is neither pro nor con. It is fact based.

If your intent is to paper a clerk's file, remember that you can buy canned reports on the Internet inexpensively. You can get ratings, appraisals, background checks, valuations, and any number of other reports. They will cost you next to nothing, and that is exactly what they are worth. If your intent is to do real due diligence – there are no short cuts.

Large and Small Companies

Large firms exist to extract rent from the government, and erect barriers to competitors. Barriers include Intellectual Property (IP) protection, and regulations that increase capital requirements. Large firms feel invincible, a malady that is untreatable. They generally have excellent margins in their core business activity, and do not realize that this is a result of their size and market position – not their abilities. These common traits are the root of the NIH problem – Not Invented Here – and is exactly what makes large firms vulnerable to disruptive innovations.

Small companies generally operate in a very entrepreneurial manner. Decisions are made on the fly, and outside of committee. Awareness of Intellectual Property and Critical Information (IPCI) in a small company, if given any thought at all, is an afterthought.

Acquisition of a small business presents problems to its ossified counterparts. Due diligence is generally easier in a small firm, but – when acquired, the formal management and structure of a large firm is likely to drive off the talent that made the small firm work. They are completely different structures, and unlikely to function well together under common management. From a due-diligence perspective, looking at it as a beauty contest, you will find that a lot of pimples and warts are tolerated in a small firm that are intolerable in a large firm.

Knowledge and Risk

We live in a world of intelligent beings making decisions with imperfect knowledge. The best we can do is to assemble as much relevant information as is available. Attempts to identify, master and measure risk – especially the risk of rare and consequential events – without sufficient knowledge and history will guarantee a flawed and haphazard model. There is risk in the use of any model, no matter how well prepared, as the tools we use generally assume linearity and normal distributions. These are generally *incorrect* assumptions – but they are often relatively good first approximations. Even information derived from a good model needs to be interpreted against the unknown and the dimension of time. Information from a flawed model should not be interpreted at all – as it will generate pure static. Learning to separate information from noise is an endeavor that has consumed many lifetimes – and all we can do is try to get better at it.

A market whose risk is measured and reported by rating agencies is a very fragile market, because conclusions become homogenized. The more information you are given, the less you may know. It's easy to believe that multiple ratings present confirmation of opinion, when in fact they are simply the reiteration of an opinion based upon a common model. Increased regulation of ratings and due diligence will force increased harmonization and increase the likelihood of systemic failures. The affect of this herd mentality is exacerbated by mark-to-market rules and regulated funds whose portfolios have rating restrictions. The belief that you can have minimal risk *and* that you will be able to sell on the way down is a fool's plan. Use your own due diligence to determine the underlying value of what you are buying – do not depend upon information from a rating agency or appraiser. We have many recent examples that will serve as a testament to how accurate the professionals are. If you use their services – use it to confirm your own conclusions.

We need to go back to what in the common law is known as the "Prudent Man Rule," and be allowed to fail occasionally as individuals. If we substitute institutional regulatory due diligence, we will get harmony – but we will all fail collectively when ratings and regulatory systems founder. Sound familiar!

As a final comment on risk, I'll leave you with the following thought. The further you are from the actual risk, the more imperfect your knowledge.

Regulations

The world is becoming increasingly paternalistic. In a regulatory nannyland nobody ever grows up. It's a handholding society where there are only two hands to hold – the regulators and those they choose to trust. In recent history, both have failed.

In the U.S. we do not have free markets; we have heavily regulated markets. The idea that more regulation is good belies the fact that more regulation removes the feedback mechanisms that help us prevent mistakes. Heavily regulated markets give the false impression that markets are safe, and lulls investors into these supposedly safe harbors. It is sometimes as important to learn what not to do as much as what to do. Our elected officials and regulators would have you think differently. They see rules as a way to ensure that what happened yesterday will not occur tomorrow – it's a bit like driving a car while using information from the rearview mirror only, and being surprised when you hit a tree. What we need to develop is more open markets with more information, not regulations that kill innovation. Markets should be a place where trades are settled and the positions of speculators and hedgers is known to all – not the names, just the positions. It's done openly and transparently at every sports parlor and racetrack in the world – is it really too much to ask for in our financial markets?

Make Wrong

It's hard to say, "I don't know." It's much easier to have an opinion, even if we have no foundation for that opinion. We need to learn to embrace the fact that we don't know when, in fact, we don't know. Having an opinion will make your investigation a search to confirm your belief. Recognize what you don't know.

The central problem I have faced with due diligence and regulatory failures is the regulators' reliance on hindsight. This is a huge make-wrong exercise foisted on risk-takers by theorists. There is no balance in this relationship; there is no safe harbor for honest error – no matter how well-documented.

It is extremely difficult to swim against the tide. As a practitioner of the art of due diligence you will find uncomfortable places where bad choices have been made, irrational checklists are relied upon, people have exceeded the scope of their task, and cheap and cheerful reports have been used to paper a file. A good due diligence practitioner will challenge all of this, using a blend of facts, subjective observations, and the entire sets of life skills assembled on their due diligence team.

Always be ready to revise your assessment. I once thought I had met a complete fool, but I later found that some parts were missing. Remember that nothing is foolproof, because newer and more creative fools are minted every day. You will meet some interesting characters in this line of work, and I look forward to sharing stories with you in the future.

May you in your efforts find a state of grace, or may it find you.

Sincerely,
L. Burke Files

Appendix

Financial Equations

The Time Value of Money Equations

Name	Equation	Information	Example
Calculating Present Value and Future Value	$FV = PV(1+i)^N$	FV=Future Value PV=Present Value i=the interest rate per period N=the number of compounding periods	What is the future value of $40 in 5 yrs @ 5% interest? FV=$40(1+.05)^5 FV=$40(1.2762815) FV=$51.05
Present Value of a future cash flow, annual compounding	$PV = \dfrac{CF^t}{(1+r)^t}$	PV=Present Value CFt=Future Cash Flow which occurs t years from now r=the interest or discount rate t=the number of years	Present Value of $100 to be received 4 years from today @ 10% $PV = \dfrac{100}{(1+.10)^4} = \$68.30$
Future Value of a cash flow, annual compounding	$FV_t = CF_0(1+r)^t$	FVt=the Future Value at the end of year t CFo=the initial investment r=the annual compounded interest rate t=the number of years	FV at the end of 3 years of $100 invested today @ 10% $FV_3 = 100(1+.10)^3 = \$133.10$
Present Value of a cash flow stream, annual compounding	$PV = \displaystyle\sum_{t=0}^{n} \dfrac{CF_t}{(1+r)^t}$	PV=Present Value of the cash flow stream CFt=the cash flow which occurs at the end of year t r=the discount rate t=the year, 0 to n n=the last year a cash flow occurs	PV of cash flow yr1=$100, yr2=$100, yr3=$100, yr4=$100 @10 $PV = \dfrac{100}{(1+.10)^1} + \dfrac{100}{(1+.10)^2} + \dfrac{100}{(1+.10)^3} + \dfrac{100}{(1+.10)^4} = \$316.99$

	Formula	Variables	Example
Future Value of a Cash Flow stream, annual compounding	$FV_t = \sum_{t=0}^{n} CF_t(1+r)^{n-t}$	FVt=the Future Value of the Cash Flow stream at the end of year t; CFt=the Cash Flow which occurs at the end of year t; r=the discount rate; t=the year 0 to n; n=the last year a cash flow occurs	FV of cash flow yr1=$100, yr2=$100, yr3=$100, yr4=$100 @10% $$FV_4 = 100(1+.10)^3 + 100(1+.10)^2 + 100(1+.10)^1 + 100 = \$464.10$$
Present Value of an Annuity, annual compounding	$PVA = PMT\left[1 - \dfrac{(1+r)^{-t}}{r}\right]$	PVA=the Present Value of the Annuity; PMT=the Annuity payment; r=the interest or discount rate; t=the number of years (the number of payments)	Annuity of $100 for 3 years with a discount rate of 10% $$PVA = 100\left[1 - \frac{(1+.10)^{-3}}{.10}\right] = \$248.69$$
Future Value of an Annuity, annual compounding	$FVA_t = PMT\left[\dfrac{(1+r)^t - 1}{r}\right]$	FVA=the Future Value of the Annuity; PMT=the annuity payment; r=the interest or discount rate; t=the number of years (the number of payments)	Annuity of $100 for 3 years with a discount rate of 10% $$FVA_3 = 100\left[\frac{(1+.10)^3 - 1}{.10}\right] = \$331.00$$
Interest rate quoted annually compounded more than once a year	$r = \dfrac{r_{nom}}{m}$	r=the rate per period; r nom=the nominal rate; m=the number of compounding periods per year	A 12% nominal rate compounded monthly is equivalent to a periodic rate of 1% per month.

EAR Equivalent Annual Rate (same as using nominal rate)	$$EAR = \left[1 + \dfrac{r_{nom}}{m}\right]^{m} - 1$$	EAR=the Equivalent Annual Rate r nom=the nominal rate m=the number of compounding periods per year (comparing interest rates with a certain frequency rate with those that have a different frequency rate)	EAR for 10% compounded semiannually $$EAR = \left[1 + \dfrac{.10}{2}\right]^{2} - 1 = 0.1025 = 10.25\%$$ EAR for 10% compounded quarterly $$EAR = \left[1 + \dfrac{.10}{4}\right]^{4} - 1 = 0.1038 = 10.38\%$$
Present Value of a future Cash Flow when the interest rate is compounded m times per year	$$PV = \dfrac{CF_t}{\left[1 + \dfrac{r_{nom}}{m}\right]^{mt}}$$	PV=Present Value CFt=the Cash Flow which occurs at the end of year t r nom=the nominal interest rate m=the number of compounding periods per year t=the number of years mt=the number of compounding periods in t years	Present Value of $100 to be received 3 years from today if the interest rate is 10% compounded quarterly $$PV = \dfrac{100}{\left[1 + \dfrac{.10}{4}\right]^{4(3)}} = \$74.14$$

445

| Future Value of an Annuity when payments occur m times per year and the interest rate is compounded m times a year | $FVA_t = PMT \left[\dfrac{(1 + r_{nom})^{mt} - 1}{\dfrac{r_{nom}}{m}} \right]$ | FVAt=the Future Value of the Annuity at the end of year t
PMT=the Annuity payment which occurs m times a year
r nom=the nominal interest rate
m=the number of compounding periods per year
t=the number of years
mt=the number of compounding periods in t years | Future Value at the end of 3 years of an annuity of \$100 per quarter for 3 years if the interest rate is 8% compounded quarterly

$FVA_3 = 100 \left[\dfrac{(1 + \dfrac{.08}{4})^{4(3)} - 1}{\dfrac{.08}{4}} \right] = \$1341.21$ |

Stock Valuation Equations

Name	Equation	Information	Example
Constant Growth Stock Valuation	$$P_0 = \frac{D_0(1+g)}{r-g} = \frac{D_1}{r-g}$$	Po=the Stock price at time 0 Do=the current dividend D1=the next dividend (at time 1) g=the growth rate in dividends r=the required return on the Stock and g<r	The Stock price given that the current dividend is $3 per share, dividends are expected to grow at a rate of 5% in the foreseeable future, and the required return is 10%. $$P_0 = \frac{3(1+.05)}{.10-.05} = \$63.00$$
Non-Constant Growth Stock Valuation	$$P_0 = \sum_{t=1}^{T} \frac{D_T}{(1+r)^t} + \left(\frac{D_T+1}{r-g_c}\right)(1+r)^{-T}$$	Po=the Stock price at time 0 Dt=the expected dividend at time t T=the number of years of non-constant growth gc=the long term constant growth rate in dividends r=the required return on the Stock and gc<r	The Stock price given that the current dividend is $3 per share, dividends are expected to grow at a rate of 20% per year for 2 yrs and then at a rate of 5% per year from that point on, and the required return is 10%. There are 2 yrs of non-constant growth, so T=2. It is necessary to calculate expected dividends for year 1 thru 3 using provided growth rates. $D_1 = 3(1+.20) = \$3.60$ $D_2 = 3.60(1+.20) = \$4.32$ $D_3 = 4.32(1+.05) = \$4.536$ $$P_0 = \frac{3.60}{(1+.10)^1} + \frac{4.32}{(1+.10)^2} + \frac{4.536}{(.10-.05)}(1+.10)^{-2} = \$81.82$$
Preferred Stock Valuation	$$P_p = \frac{D_p}{r}$$	Pp=the Preferred Stock Dp=the preferred dividend r=the required return on the Stock	The Stock price of a Preferred Stock given that the par value is $100 per share, the preferred dividend rate is 5%, and the required return is 10%. $$P_p = \frac{.05(100)}{.10} = \frac{5}{.10} = \$50$$

447

Bond Valuation Equations

Name	Equation	Information	Example
Bond Price	$$B_0 = \frac{C}{2}\left[\frac{1-\left(1+\frac{r}{2}\right)^{-2t}}{\frac{r}{2}}\right] + \frac{F}{\left(1+\frac{r}{2}\right)^{2t}}$$	Bo=the Bond Value C=the annual coupon payment F=the face value of the Bond r=the required return of the Bond t=the number of years remaining until maturity	Face value of semiannual coupon Bond with face value of $1,000, a 5% coupon rate, and 10 years remaining until maturity given that the required return is 10%. $$B_0 = \frac{50}{2}\left[\frac{1-\left(1+\frac{.10}{2}\right)^{-2(10)}}{\frac{.10}{2}}\right] + \frac{\$1,000}{\left(1+\frac{.10}{2}\right)^{2(10)}} = \$688.44$$
Bond Yield to Maturity	$$B_0 = \frac{C}{2}\left[\frac{1-\left(1+\frac{YTM}{2}\right)^{-2t}}{\frac{YTM}{2}}\right] + \frac{F}{\left(1+\frac{YTM}{2}\right)^{2t}}$$	Bo=the Bond price C=the annual coupon payment F=the face value of the Bond YTM=the Yield to Maturity on the Bond t=the number of years remaining until maturity	Yield to maturity on a semiannual coupon bond with a face value of $1,000, a 5% coupon rate, and 10 years remaining until maturity given the bond price of $688.44. $$\$688.44 = \frac{50}{2}\left[\frac{1-\left(1+\frac{YTM}{2}\right)^{-2(10)}}{\frac{YTM}{2}}\right] + \frac{\$1,000}{\left(1+\frac{YTM}{2}\right)^{2(10)}} \therefore YTM = 10\%$$
Bond Yield to Call	$$B_0 = \frac{C}{2}\left[\frac{1-\left(1+\frac{YTC}{2}\right)^{-2d}}{\frac{YTC}{2}}\right] + \frac{CP}{\left(1+\frac{YTC}{2}\right)^{2d}}$$	Bo=the Bond price C=the annual coupon price CP=the Call price YTC=the Yield to Call on the bond d=the number of years remaining until the Call date	Yield to Call on a semiannual Bond with a face value of $1,000, a 10% coupon rate, 10 years remaining until maturity given that the Bond price is $1,100 and it can be called 5 years from now at a call price of $1,000. $$\$1,100 = \frac{100}{2}\left[\frac{1-\left(1+\frac{YTC}{2}\right)^{-2(5)}}{\frac{YTC}{2}}\right] + \frac{\$1,000}{\left(1+\frac{YTC}{2}\right)^{2(5)}} \therefore YTM = 7.56\%$$

Capital Budgeting Equations

Name	Equation	Information	Example
Net Present Value (NPV)	$$NPV = \sum_{t=0}^{T} \frac{CFt}{(1+r)^t} = CF_0 + \frac{CF_1}{(1+r)^1} + \cdots + \frac{CF_T}{(1+r)^T}$$	NPV=Net Present Value CFt=the Cash Flow at time t r=the Cost of Capital	**Project A** Cash Flow--yr 0= -$500, yr 1=$300, yr 2=$200, yr 3=$200 **Project B** Cash Flow--yr 0= -$500, yr 1=$200, yr 2=$200, yr 3=$300 The calculation of NPV using Project A and B—Cost of Capital is 10%. **Project A** $$NPV = -500 + \frac{300}{(1+.10)^1} + \frac{200}{(1+.10)^2} + \frac{200}{(1+.10)^3} = \$88.28$$ **Project B** $$NPV = -500 + \frac{200}{(1+.10)^1} + \frac{200}{(1+.10)^2} + \frac{300}{(1+.10)^3} = \$72.50$$
Internal Rate of Return (IRR)	$$NPV = 0 = \sum_{t=0}^{T} \frac{CF_t}{(1+IRR)^t} = CF_0 + \frac{CF_1}{(1+IRR)^1} + \cdots + \frac{CF_T}{(1+IRR)^T}$$	NPV=Net Present Value CFt=the Cash Flow at time t IRR=Internal Rate of Return	The calculation of IRR using **Project A and B** from above. **Project A** $$0 = -500 + \frac{300}{(1+IRR)^1} + \frac{200}{(1+IRR)^2} + \frac{200}{(1+IRR)^3} \therefore IRR = 20.64\%$$ **Project B** $$0 = -500 + \frac{200}{(1+IRR)^1} + \frac{200}{(1+IRR)^2} + \frac{300}{(1+IRR)^3} \therefore IRR = 17.5\%$$
Pay-Back Period	*Payback Period=[Last year with a negative NCF]+* $$\frac{[Absolute\ Value\ of\ NCF\ in\ that\ year}{Total\ Cash\ Flow\ in\ the\ following\ year]}$$	NCF=Net Cash Flow **Project A** Yr 1= -200 Yr 2= 0 **Project B** Yr 1= -300 Yr 2= -100	The Payback Period of **Project A and B** from above. **Project A** *Payback Period=1+$\frac{200}{200}$=2 years* **Project B** *Payback Period=2+$\frac{100}{300}$=2.33 years*

Financial Cash Flow

Name	Equation	Information	Example ($ in Millions)
Operating Cash Flow	$OCF = EBIT + D - T$	OCF=Operating Cash Flow EBIT=Earnings Before Interest & Taxes D=Depreciation T=Taxes	$423 + $77 - $30 = $470
Capital Spending	$CS = ENFA - BNFA + D$	CS=Capital Spending ENFA =Ending Net Fixed Assets BNFA =Beginning Net Fixed Assets D=Depreciation	$853 - $920 + 77 = $10
Additions To Net Working Capital	$ANWC = ENWC - BNWC$	ANWC=Additions to Net Working Capital ENWC=Ending Net Fixed Assets BNWC=Beginning Net Working Capital	$380 - 300 = $80
Net Working Capital	$NWC = CA - CL$	NWC=Net Working Capital CA=Current Assets CL=Current Liabilities	$1,150 - $770 = $380
Cash Flow From Assets	$CFA = OCF - CS + ANWC$	CFA =Cash Flow from Assets OCF=Operating Cash Flow CS=Capital Spending ANWC=Additions to Net Working Capital	$470 - $10 + $80 = $540

Cash Flow to Debtholders	$CFD = IE - ELTD + BLTD$	CFD=Cash Flow to Debtholders IE=Interest Expense ELTD=Ending Long-Term Debt BLTD=Beginning Long-Term Debt	$50 - $571 + $710 = $189
Cash Flow to Common Stockholders	$CFCS = DP - (ECS - BCS) - (ECaS - BCaS) - (ETS - BTS)$	CFCS=Cash Flow to Common Stockholders DP=Dividends Paid ECS = Ending Common Stocks BCS=Beginning Common Stocks ECaS=Ending Capital Surplus BCaS=Beginning Capital Surplus ETS=Ending Treasury Stock BTS=Beginning Treasury stock	$201 - ($122 - $120) - ($218 - $210) + ($0 - $0) =$191
Cash Flow To Preferred Stockholders	$CFPS = PDP - (EPS - BPS)$	CFPS=Cash Flow to Preferred Stockholders PDP=Preferred Dividends Paid EPS=Ending Preferred Stock BPS=Beginning Preferred Stock	$C (this company has no Preferred Stock)

| Cash Flow To Investors | $CFI = CFD + CFCS + CFPS$ | CFI=Cash Flow to Investors
CFD=Cash Flow to Debtholders
CFCS=Cash Flow to Common Stockholders
CFPS=Cash Flow to Preferred Stockholders | $189 + $191 + $0 = $380 |

452

Ratio Equations

Name	Equation	Information	Example ($ in Millions)
Short-term Solvency Ratios	Current Ratio: $CR = \dfrac{TCA}{TCL}$	CR=Current Ratio TCA=Total Current Assets TCL=Total Current Liabilities	$1.5 = \dfrac{\$1{,}500}{\$1{,}000}$
	Quick Ratio: $QR = \dfrac{(TCA - I)}{TCL}$	QR=Quick Ratio TCA=Total Current Assets I=Inventory TCL=Total Current Liabilities	$1 = \dfrac{(\$1{,}500 - \$500)}{\$1000}$
Asset Management Ratios	Receivables Turnover: $RT = \dfrac{S}{AR}$	RT=Receivables Turnover S=Sales AR=Account Receivables	$10 = \dfrac{\$1{,}500}{\$150}$
	Days' Receivables: $DR = \dfrac{365}{RT}$	DR=Days' Receivables RT=Receivables Turnover	$36.5 = \dfrac{365}{10}$
	Inventory Turnover: $IT = \dfrac{COGS}{I}$	IT=Inventory Turnover COGS=Cost of Goods Sold I=Inventory	$3 = \dfrac{\$1{,}500}{\$500}$
	Days' Inventory: $DI = \dfrac{365}{IT}$	DI=Days' Inventory IT=Inventory Turnover	$121.67 = \dfrac{365}{3}$
	Fixed Assets Turnover: $FAT = \dfrac{S}{NFA}$	FAT=Fixed Asset Turnover S=Sales NFA=Net Fixed Assets	$1.5 = \dfrac{\$1{,}500}{\$1{,}000}$
	Total Assets Turnover: $\dfrac{S}{TA}$	S=Sales TA=Total assets	$1 = \dfrac{\$1{,}500}{\$1{,}500}$

Debt Management Ratios	Times Interest Earned: $TIE = \dfrac{EBIT}{IE}$	TIE=Times interest Earned EBIT=Earnings Before Interest and Taxes IE=Interest Expense	$43.2 = \dfrac{\$432}{\$10}$
	Debt Ratio: $DR = \dfrac{TD}{TA} = \dfrac{TA - TOE}{TA}$	DR=Debt Ratio TD=Total Debt TA=Total Assets TOE=Total Owners Equity	$50\% = \dfrac{\$2,000 - \$1,000}{\$2,000}$
	Debt to Equity Ratio: $DER = \dfrac{TD}{TOD} = \dfrac{TA - TOE}{TOE}$	DER=Debt to Equity Ratio TD=Total Debt TOD=Total Owners' Debt TA=Total Assets TOE=Total Owners' Equity	$1 = \dfrac{\$2,000 - \$1,000}{\$1,000}$
	Equity Multiplier: $EM = \dfrac{TA}{TOE}$	EM=Equity Multiplier TA=Total Assets TOE=Total Owners' Equity	$2 = \dfrac{\$2,000}{\$1,000}$
Profitability Ratio	Profit Margin: $PM = \dfrac{NI}{S}$	PM=Profit Margin NI=Net Income S=Sales	$25\% = \dfrac{\$500}{\$2,000}$
	Return on Assets: $ROA = \dfrac{NI}{TA}$	ROA=Return On Assets NI=Net Income TA=Total Assets	$33.33\% = \dfrac{\$500}{\$1,500}$
	Return on Equity: $ROE = \dfrac{NI}{TOE}$	ROE=Return On Equity NI=Net income TOE= Total Owners Equity	$50\% = \dfrac{\$500}{\$1,000}$

Category	Formula	Definitions	Calculation
Market Value Ratios	Price/ Earning Ratio: $PER = \dfrac{PPS}{EPS}$	PER=Price/Earning Ratio PPS=Price Per Share EPS=Earnings Per Share	$12.5 = \dfrac{\$25}{\$2}$
	Market-to-Book Ratio: $MTB = \dfrac{PPS}{BVPS}$	MTB=Market-to-Book Ratio PPS=Price Per Share BVPS=Book Value Per Share	$5 = \dfrac{\$25}{\$5}$
Dividend Ratios	Payout Ratio: $PR = \dfrac{DP}{NI}$	PR=Payout Ratio DP=Dividends Paid NI=Net Income	$4.93\% = \dfrac{\$11}{\$223}$
	Retention Ratio: $RR = \dfrac{ARE}{NI}$	RR=Retention Ratio ARE=Addition to Retained Earnings NI=Net Income	$95.07\% = \dfrac{\$212}{\$223}$
Other Ratio Equations	Earnings Per Share: $EPS = \dfrac{NI}{NSO}$	EPS=Earnings Per Share NI=Net Income NSO=Number of Shares Outstanding	$\$0.74 = \dfrac{\$223}{\$300}$
	Book Value Per Share: $BVPS = \dfrac{TOE}{NSO}$	BVPS=Book Value Per Share TOE=Total Owners' Equity NSO=Number of Shares Outstanding	$\$2 = \dfrac{\$600}{\$300}$

Employment And Management Ratios	Payroll Cost % = $\dfrac{P + B}{TS}$	P=Payroll B=Benefits TS=Total Sales	$24.8\% = \dfrac{\$300 + \$72}{\$1,500}$
	Benefit Cost % = $\dfrac{TB}{TP}$	TB=Total Benefits TP=Total Payroll	$24\% = \dfrac{\$72}{\$300}$
	Employee Turnover = $\dfrac{E_1}{TE}$	E1=Employees who left in 1 year TE=Total Employees	$1\% = \dfrac{50}{5,000}$
	Management Weight = $\dfrac{M}{E}$	M=Management E=Employees	$10\% = \dfrac{500}{5,000}$
	Productivity per employee = $\dfrac{TS}{E}$	TS=Total Sales E=Average number of Employees	$\$.30 = \dfrac{\$1,500}{5,000}$
Marketing Ratios	Impression Cost = $\dfrac{I}{MB}$	I = Impressions MB = Marketing Budget	$\$20 = \dfrac{3,000}{\$150}$
	Lead Cost = $\dfrac{SL}{MB}$	SL = Sales Leads MB = Marketing Budget	$\$10 = \dfrac{1,500}{\$150}$

456

Risk & Return Equations

Table 1 – Possible States – One Period into the Future

State	1	2	3	4
Probability (must = 100%)	20%	30%	30%	20%
Return on **Stock A**	5%	10%	15%	20%
Return on **Stock B**	50%	30%	10%	-10%

Name	Equation	Information	Example
Expected Return	$E(R) = \sum_{i=1}^{N} p_i R_i$	E(R)=the Expected Return on the Stock N = the number of states Pi = the probability of state i Ri = the Return on the Stock in state i	Using information from **Table 1, Stock A and Stock B** **Stock A** $E(R_A) = .20(5\%) + .30(30\%) + .30(15\%) + .20(20\%) = 12.5\%$ **Stock B** $E(R_B) = .20(50\%) + .30(30\%) + .30(10\%) + .20(-10\%) = 20\%$

Measure of Risk – Variance and Standard Deviation

Variance	N = the number of states P_i = the probability of state i R_i = the Return on the Stock in state i $E[R]$ = the Expected Return on the Stock $$Var(R) = \sigma^2 = \sum_{i=1}^{N} p_i (R_i - E[R])^2$$	Using **Table 1** and the given **Expected Return** from the previous page, its **Variance** can now be calculated. **Stock A** $\sigma^2_A = .20(.05 - .125)^2 + .30(.10 - .125)^2 + .30(.15 - .125)^2 + .20(.20 - .125)^2 = .00263$ **Stock B** $\sigma^2_B = .20(.05 - .20)^2 + .30(.10 - .20)^2 + .30(.30 - .20)^2 + .20(-.10 - .20)^2 = .04200$
Standard Deviation	Standard Deviation is calculated as the positive square root of the Variance $$SD(R) = \sigma = \sqrt{\sigma^2} = (\sigma^2)^{\frac{1}{2}}$$	Using the **Variance** from above, its **Standard Deviation** can now be calculated **Stock A** $\sigma_A = \sqrt{.00263} = .0512 = 5.12\%$ **Stock B** $\sigma_B = \sqrt{.04200} = .2049 = 20.49\%$

Portfolio Risk and Return

Portfolio Expected Return	$E[Rp]$ =the Expected Return on the Portfolio N=the number of Stocks in the Portfolio w_i=the proportion of the Portfolio invested in Stock i $E[Ri]$=the Expected Return on Stock i $$E[R_p] = \sum_{i=1}^{N} w_i E[R_i]$$ A portfolio with two assets, Stock A and Stock B from Table 1, the equation above can be expressed as $$E[R_p] = w_1 E[R_1] + (1 - w_1)E[R_2]$$	Note: $E[R_A] = 12.5\%$ and $E[R_B] = 20\%$ **Portfolio consisting of 50% Stock A and 50% Stock B** $E[R_p] = .50(12.5\%) + (1 - .50)(20\%) = 16.25\%$ **Portfolio consisting of 75% Stock A and 25% Stock B** $E[R_p] = .75(12.5\%) + (1 - .75)(20\%) = 14.38\%$

Portfolio Variance and Standard Deviations

Name	Equation	Information
Covariance Equation	$COV(R_1, R_2) = \sigma_{12} = \sum_{i=1}^{N} P_i(R_{1i} - E[R_1])(R_{2i} - E[R_2])$	σ_{12} = the Covariance between the Returns on Stocks 1 and 2 N = the number of states Pi = the probability of state i R1i = the Return on Stock 1 in state i E[R1] = the Expected Return on Stock 1 R2i = the Return on Stock 2 in state i E[R2] = the Expected Return on Stock 2
Correlation Coefficient Equation	$Corr(R_1, R_2) = \rho_{12} = \dfrac{\sigma_{12}}{\sigma_1 \sigma_2} = \dfrac{Cov(R_1, R_2)}{SD(R_1)SD(R_2)}$	ρ_{12} = the Correlation between the returns on Stocks 1 and 2 σ_{12} = the Covariance between the returns on Stocks 1 and 2 σ_1 = the Standard Deviation on stock 1 σ_2 = the Standard Deviation on Stock 2

Examples

Example of Covariance and Correlation Coefficient between the Returns on Stock A and B in Figure 1

Note: $E[R_A] = 12.5\%$ $E[R_B] = 20\%$ $\sigma_A = 5.12\%$ $\sigma_B = 20.49\%$

$$\sigma_{AB} = .2(.05 - .125)(.5 - .2) + .3(.1 - .125)(.3 - .2) + .2(.15 - .125)(.1 - .2) + .2(.2 - .125)(-.1 - .2)$$

$$\sigma_{AB} = -.0105$$

$$\rho_{AB} = \frac{-.0105}{(.0512)(.2049)} = -1$$

Either the Correlation Coefficient or the Covariance can be used to calculate the Variance on a Two-Asset Portfolio

$$\sigma_p^2 = (w_1)^2 \sigma_1^2 + (1 - w_1)^2 \sigma_2^2 + 2w_1(1 - w_1)\rho_{12}\sigma_1\sigma_2$$

$$= (w_1)^2 \sigma_1^2 + (1 - w_1)^2 \sigma_2^2 + 2w_1(1 - w_1)\sigma_{12}$$

Example of Variance and Standard Deviation on Portfolio of Stocks A and B in Figure 1

Note: $E[R_A] = 12.5\%$ $E[R_B] = 20\%$ $\sigma_A = 5.12\%$ $\sigma_B = 20.49\%$ $\rho_{AB} = -1$

Portfolio consisting of 50% Stock A and 50% Stock B

$$\sigma_p^2 = (.5)^2(.0512)^2 + (1-.5)^2(.2049)^2 + 2(.5)(1-.5)(-1)(.0512)(.2049) = .00591$$

$$\sigma_p = \sqrt{.00591} = .0768 = 7.68\%$$

Portfolio consisting of 75% Stock A and 25% Stock B

$$\sigma_p^2 = (.75)^2(.0512)^2 + (1-.75)^2(.2049)^2 + 2(.75)(1-.75)(-1)(.0512)(.2049) = .00016$$

$$\sigma_p = \sqrt{.00016} = .0128 = 1.28\%$$

WACC & Gordon Growth Model

Name	Equation	Information	Example
Weighted Average Cost of Capital (WACC)	$$\frac{d}{TF(cd)(1-t)} + \frac{e}{TF(ce)} = WACC$$	d=Debt TF=Total Financing (debt + equity) cd=Cost of Debt t=tax ce=Cost of Equity	The Market Value of Debt = $300 million The Market Value of Equity = $400 million The Cost of Debt = 8% The Corporate Tax rate = 35% The Cost of Equity = 18% $$\frac{300}{700(.08)(1-.35)} + \frac{400}{700(.18)} = 12.5\%$$
Gordon Growth Model	$$P = \frac{D}{K-G}$$	P= Price D=Dividend per Share 1 year from now K=Required Rate of Return for Equity investor G=Growth Rate in dividends	Last year's divided = $1.00, Growth Rate = 5%, Rate of Return = 10%. First figure out D — Next, use the formula $$D = D_0(1+G) \qquad P = \frac{\$1.05}{10\% - 5\%}$$ $$D = \$1.00(1.05) \qquad P = \frac{\$1.05}{5\%} = \frac{105}{5}$$ $$D = \$1.05 \qquad P = \$21.00$$

Risk & Return Equations

Name	Equation	Information	Example
Arbitrage Pricing Theory (APT)	$E(r_i) = \lambda_0 + \lambda_1 b_i$	$E(r_i)$ Expected Return λ_0 =the proportion of the Portfolio consisting of the Risk-free Security λ_1 =represents the Risk Premium for the Macroeconomic Factor b_i =the sensitivity of the Return compared to the Market Return $\lambda_1 b_i$ =represents the proportion of the Risky Asset	Company A Factor Forecast for Market Return 2% 2.5% -1.5% 0.0% Standardized Exposures (factor loading or factor betas) Growth Bond Size ROE Beta -.16 .74 1.47 -0.59 .84 APT 5.33% = (-.16X.02) + (.74x.025) + (1.47X-.015) + (-0.59X0)
Capital Asset Pricing Model (CAPM)	$E[R_i] = R_f + (E[R_m] - R_f)\beta_i$	E[Ri]=the Expected Return on Asset i Rf=the Risk-free Rate E[Rm] = the Expected Return on the Market Portfolio Bi = the Beta on asset i E[Rm]-Rf = the market risk premium	Finding the Expected Return on Stock where the Risk-free Rate is 6%, the Expected Return on the Market Portfolio is 12% and the Beta of the stock is 2. $E[R_i] = 6\% + (12\% - 6\%)\,2 = 18\%$
The Beta for a Stock	$\beta_i = \dfrac{\sigma_{im}}{\sigma^2_m}$	σ_{im} =the Covariance between the Returns on Asset i and the Market Portfolio σ^2_m =the Variance of the Market Portfolio	Finding the Beta of a Stock when its Expected Return is 16%, the Risk-free Rate is 4%, and the Expected Return on the Market Portfolio is 12%. 16% = 4% + (12% - 4%) β_i $\therefore \beta_i = \dfrac{16\% - 4\%}{12\% - 4\%} = \dfrac{12\%}{8\%} = 1.5$

DuPont Ratio Analysis for Evaluating Return on Equity (ROE)

Name	Equation	Information	Example ($ in millions)
Net Profit Margin	$NPM = \dfrac{NI}{R}$	Component 1 NPM=Net Profit Margin NI=Net Income R=Revenue	Revenue = $30,000 Net Income = $4,000 Assets = $30,000 Shareholders' Equity = $14,000. $0.1333 = \dfrac{\$4,000}{\$30,000}$
Asset Turnover	$AT = \dfrac{R}{A}$	Component 2 AT=Asset Turnover R=Revenue A=Assets	$1.00 = \dfrac{\$30,000}{\$30,000}$
Equity Multiplier	$EM = \dfrac{A}{SE}$	Component 3 EM=Equity Multiplier A=Assets SE=Shareholder Equity	$2.1429 = \dfrac{\$30,000}{\$14,000}$ Finally, multiply the three components to calculate the Return on Equity.
Return on Equity	$ROE = (NPM)(AT)(EM)$ ROE is one of the most important indicators of a company's profitability and potential growth.	ROE=Return on Equity NPM=Net Profit Margin AT=Asset Turnover EM=Equity Multiplier	$(0.1333)x(1.00)x(2.1429) = 0.2865 = 28.65\%$ When looking at the components of the Return on Equity over time, the analyst gains insight into what were the causes for improvements of similar companies, even when their ROE is equal.

Fama French Risk and Return Equations

Name	Equation	Information	Example
Fama French Three Factor Model	$E(R_i) = R_f + \beta_i(R_m - R_f) + \beta_2(SMB) + \beta_3(HML)$	E(Ri)=Expected Return for Asset i Rm=Expected Return for the Market Rf=the Return for a Risk-free Asset Rm-Rf=the Market Risk Premium SMB=Expected Return difference of Small and Big Stocks (Small Minus Big) HML=the Expected Return difference of Stocks with High and Low Book-to-Market Equity Ratio (High Minus Low) Bi=Beta of Stock i B2=percentage of Small and Big Caps in Portfolio B3= percentage of Small and Large Cap Stock in Portfolio	Finding the Expected Return on Stock i where the Risk-free Rate is 6%, the Expected Return on the Market Portfolio is 12% and the Beta of Stock i = 2. B2 has 50% Small Cap and 50% Large Caps in this Portfolio. B3 also has 50% Small Caps and 50% Large Caps in this Portfolio. SMB = -.1 and HML = .1. $E(R_i) = 6\% + 2(12\% - 6\%) + .5(-.1) + .5(.1)$ $E(R_i) = .06 + 2(.12 - .06) + .5(-.1) + .5(.1)$ $E(R_i) = .06 + .12 + -.05 + .05$ $E(R_i) = .18 = 18\%$

Information Productivity Assessment

Name	Equation	Information	Example
Information Productivity Formula	$$IP = \frac{EVA}{CIM}$$	IP=Information Productivity EVA=Economic Value Added CIM=Cost of Information Management	Company A $$IP = \frac{\$101,300}{\$1,128,122} = 8.98\%$$

465

Treasury Management Equations

Name	Equation	Information	Example ($ in millions)
Gross Profit Margin	$GPM = \dfrac{GP}{R}$	GPM=Gross Profit Margin GP=Gross Profit R=Revenue	Note: Sales – Cost of Good Sold = Gross Profit $35.7\% = \dfrac{\$610}{\$1,710}$
Operating Profit Margin	$OPM = \dfrac{EBITDA}{R}$	OPM=Operating Profit Margin EBITDA=Earnings before Interest, Taxes, Depreciation, and Amortization R=Revenues	$31\% = \dfrac{\$530}{\$1,710}$
Net Profit Margin	$NPM = \dfrac{NI}{S}$	NPM=Net Profit Margin NI=Net Income S=Sales	$20\% = \dfrac{\$343}{\$1,710}$
Cash Flow to Total Debt Ratio	$CFTDR = \dfrac{CF}{TD}$	CFTDR=Cash Flow to Total Debt Ratio CF=Cash Flow TD=Total Debt	Note: Cash Flow is Net Income plus Depreciation $73.5\% = \dfrac{\$420}{\$571}$
Working Capital	$WC = CA - CL$	WC=Working Capital CA=Current Assets CL=Current Liabilities	$\$380 = \$1,150 - \$770$
Cash Conversion Efficiency	$CCE = \dfrac{CFO}{S}$	CCE=Cash Conversion Efficiency CFO=Cash Flow from Operations S=Sales	Note: Cash Flow from Operations = EBIT+Depreciation-Taxes $27.5\% = \dfrac{470}{\$1,710}$
Taxable Equivalent Yield	$TEY = \dfrac{TY}{(1 - MTR)}$	TEY=Taxable Equivalent Yield TY=Tax-exempt Yield MTR = Marginal Tax Rate	$6.25\% = \dfrac{4.5\%}{(1 - .28)}$
Holding Period Yield	$HPY = \dfrac{(CRM - I)}{I}$	HPY=Holding Period Yield CRM=Cash Received at Maturity I=Amount Invested	$20\% = \dfrac{\$1,200 - \$1,000}{\$1,000}$

	Formula	Definitions	Example
Annual Yield	$AY = HPY\left(\dfrac{DY}{DM}\right)$	AY=Annual Yield HPY=Holding Period Yield DY=Days in Year DM=Days to Maturity	$20\% = .20\left(\dfrac{365}{365}\right)$
Purchase Price	$PP = P - DD$	PP=Purchase Price P=Par Value DD=Dollar Discount	$\$90 = \$100 - \$10$
Dollar Discount	$DD = (DR)(P)\left(\dfrac{DM}{360}\right)\left(\dfrac{360}{360}\right)$	DD=Dollar Discount DR=Discount Rate P=Par Value DM=Days to Maturity	$\$10 = (.10)(100)\left(\dfrac{360}{360}\right)$
Discount Rate	$DR = \left(\dfrac{DD}{P}\right)\left(\dfrac{DM}{360}\right)$	DR=Discount Rate DD=Dollar Discount P=Par Value DM=Days to Maturity	$10\% = \left(\dfrac{\$10}{\$100}\right)\left(\dfrac{360}{360}\right)$
Money Market Yield	$MMY = HPY\left(\dfrac{360}{DM}\right)$	MMY=Money Market Yield HPY=Holding Period Yield DM=Days to Maturity	$20\% = .20\left(\dfrac{360}{360}\right)$
Bond Equivalent Yield	$BEY = HPY\left(\dfrac{365}{DM}\right)$	BEY=Bond Equivalent Yield HPY=Holding Period Yield DM=Days to Maturity	$20.3\% = .20\left(\dfrac{365}{360}\right)$

Bibliography

ADKISSON, JAY D. Adkisson's Captive Insurance Companies: an Introduction to Captives, Closely-held Insurance Companies, and Risk Retention Groups. New York: iUniverse, 2006.

ADKISSON, JAY D. and RISER, CHRISTOPHER M. Asset Protection: Concepts and Strategies for Protecting Your Wealth. New York: McGraw-Hill, 2004.

BENNINGA, SIMON and CZACZKES, BENJAMIN. Financial Modeling. Cambridge, Mass. MIT Press, 1997.

BERRY, ALBERT and INDART, GUSTAVO, eds. Critical Issues in International Financial Reform. New Brunswick (U.S.A.): Transaction Publishers, 2003.

BOLOGNA, G. JACK, LINDQUIST, ROBERT L., and WELLS, JOSEPH T. The Accountant's Handbook of Fraud and Commercial Crime. New York: Wiley, 1993.

BRITTAIN-CATLIN, WILLIAM. Offshore: The Dark Side of the Global Economy. New York: Picador, 2006.

BURNETT, JOHN S. Dangerous Waters: Modern Piracy and Terror on the High Seas. New York, N.Y. Dutton, 2002.

CANTOR, BERT. The Bernie Cornfeld Story. New York: Lyle Stuart, Inc, 1970.

DAMODARAN, ASWATH. Investment Fables: Exposing the Myths of "Can't Miss" Investment Strategies. London; New York: Financial Times Prentice Hall, 2004.

EPSTEIN, RICHARD A. Simple Rules for a Complex World. Cambridge: Harvard University Press, 1995.

FEETHAM, NIGEL and JONES, GRANT. Protected Cell Companies: a Guide to Their Implementation and Use. London: Spiramus Press, Ltd, 2008.

FELDMAN, FRANKLIN, WEIL, STEPHEN E., and BIEDERMAN, SUSAN DUKE. Art Law: Rights and Liabilities of Creators and Collectors. Vol. 1. Boston – Toronto: Little, Brown & Company, 1986.

FELDMAN, FRANKLIN, WEIL, STEPHEN E., and BIEDERMAN, SUSAN DUKE. Art Law: Rights and Liabilities of Creators and Collectors. Vol. 2. Boston – Toronto: Little, Brown & Company, 1986.

FIORENTINI, GIANLUCA and PELTZMAN, SAM, eds. The Economics of Organised Crime. Cambridge: University Press, 1995.

GANTZ, JOHN and ROCHESTER, JACK B. Pirates of the Digital Millennium: How the Intellectual Property Wars Damage Our Personal Freedoms, Our Jobs, and the World Economy. New Jersey: Financial Times Prentice Hall, 2005.

GRADY, MARK and PARISI, FRANCESCO, eds. The Law and Economics of Cybersecurity. Cambridge: Cambridge University Press, 2006.

GREENBERG, THEODORE S., SAMUEL, LINDA M., GRANT, WINGATE, GRAY, LARISSA. Stolen Asset Recovery: A Good Practices Guide for Non-conviction Based Asset Forfeiture. Washington, DC: The World Bank, 2009.

HARCLERODE, PETER and PITTAWAY, BRENDAN. The Lost Masters : WWII and the Looting of Europe's Treasurehouses. New York: Welcome Rain Publishers, 1999.

HEBBORN, ERIC. The Art Forger's Handbook. Woodstock & New York: The Overlook Press, 2004.

HEBBORN, ERIC. Drawn to Trouble : Confessions of a Master Forger: a Memoir. New York: Random House, 1991.
HOUPT, SIMON. Museum of the Missing: A History of Art Theft. New York: Sterling, 2006.

HOVING, THOMAS. False Impressions: the Hunt for Big-time Art Fakes. New York: Simon & Schuster, 1997.

KIELY, TERRENCE. Science and Litigation : Products Liability in Theory and Practice. Boca Raton [etc.]: CRC Press, 2002.

KOLB, ROBERT W. Financial Derivatives. Florida: Kolb Publishing Company, 1993.

LEDENEVA, ALENA V. Russia's Economy of Favours: Blat, Networking and Informal Exchanges. Cambridge: Cambridge University Press, 1998.

MACINTYRE, BEN. The Napoleon of Crime: The Life and Times of Adam Worth, Master Thief. New York: Farrar, Straus, and Giroux, 1997.

NASHERI, HEDIEH. Economic Espionage and Industrial Spying. New York: Cambridge University Press, 2005.

MATHERS, CHRIS. Crime School: Money Laundering: True Crime Meets the World of Business and Finance. New York: Firefly Books (USA) Inc., 2004.

PERKINS, JOHN. Confessions of an Economic Hit Man. San Francisco: Berrett-Koehler Publishers, 2004.

PIETH, MARK, ed. Recovering Stolen Assets. Germany: Peter Lang, 2008.

REILLY, CFA, ASA, CPA, ROBERT F. and SCHWEIHS, ASA, ROBERT P. Valuing Intangible Assets. New York: McGraw-Hill, 1999.

ROSENBLUM, JOSEPH. Prince of Forgers: The Incredible Story of Vrain Lucas, Who Created over 27,000 Literary Forgeries and Sold Them for Millions and the Glory of France! New Castle, Del. Oak Knoll Press, 1998.

SHIM, PHD, JAE K. and SIEGEL, PHD, CPA, JOEL G. Handbook of Financial Analysis, Forecasting, and Modeling. Paramus, N.J. Prentice Hall Press, 2001.

SIMMONS, CHAD. Business Valuation Bluebook: How Successful Entrepreneurs Price, Buy, Sell and Trade Businesses. Prairie Village, KS: Facts on Demand Press, 2009.

STESSENS, GUY. Money Laundering: a New International Law Enforcement Model. Cambridge [England]; New York: Cambridge University Press, 2000.

STEWART, JAMES B. Blind Eye: How the Medical Establishment Let a Doctor Get Away with Murder. New York, Simon and Schuster, 1999

SOX, DAVID. Unmasking the Forger: The Dossena Deception. New York: Universe Books, 1988.

TALEB, NASSIM NICHOLAS. The Black Swan: The Impact of the Highly Improbable. New York: Random House, 2007.

WATSON, PETER. Sotheby's: the Inside Story. New York: Random House, 1997.

WEINBERG, SAMANTHA. Last of the Pirates: The Search for Bob Denard. New York: Pantheon Books, 1994.

WYNNE, FRANK. I Was Vermeer: The Rise and Fall of the Twentieth Century's Greatest Forger. New York: Bloomsbury, 2006.

L. Burke Files, Author

Mr. Files is the head of an international investigative firm specializing in asset recovery, due diligence, anti money laundering and intellectual property matters. Prior to this Mr. Files was a partner in a regional consulting firm specializing in business, financial and securities consulting and served as the Director of Corporate Finance for an investment banking company.

Mr. Files is the Practice Section leader on due diligence, asset recovery and intellectual property investigations. As a financial industry insider he is keenly aware of the type, and accuracy of the information required to make informed and timely decisions. Mr. Files has been the case manager on fraud investigations ranging from ten of thousands of dollars to over 3 billion. Mr. Files is an international expert on due diligence and is regularly sought out for those cases that bedevil the desktop practioners. Using both conventional and unconventional techniques he works with counsel and clients unraveling the money trail finding assets for recovery. The practice section for all companies understanding the future is Intellectual Property and Critical Information or IPCI. Mr. Files has been at the forefront of both understanding the new currency of IPCI and investigating and dealing with infringers.

Mr. Files is a published author of five books, in particular "Due Diligence for the Financial Professional, 1996, 2nd edition 2010" and "Money and Budgets". He is also the author of several studies and white papers, and numerous articles. He has been quoted in many publications both domestic and international. A reasonably complete collection of these quotes, appearances and articles written can be found at: https://www.feeinc.com/media.php. Mr. Files is highly sought out international speaker on these subject matters.

For information on interviewing or arranging for speaking engagement please call Emily Casarona at (571) 213-9894 or email emily@trisideconsulting.com